AF600126

Leo Strauss
and Contemporary Thought

SUNY series in the Thought and Legacy of Leo Strauss

Kenneth Hart Green, editor

Leo Strauss and Contemporary Thought

Reading Strauss Outside the Lines

Edited by

Jeffrey A. Bernstein and Jade L. Schiff

Published by State University of New York Press, Albany

Printed in the United States of America

For information, contact State University of New York Press, Albany, NY
www.sunypress.edu

Library of Congress Cataloging-in-Publication Data

Names: Bernstein, Jeffrey A., editor. | Schiff, Jade L., editor.
Title: Leo Strauss and contemporary thought : reading Strauss outside the lines / edited by Jeffrey A. Bernstein and Jade L. Schiff.
Description: Albany : State University of New York Press, [2021] | Series: SUNY series in the Thought and Legacy of Leo Strauss | Includes bibliographical references and index.
Identifiers: ISBN 9781438483955 (hardcover : alk. paper) | ISBN 9781438483962 (ebook)
Further information is available at the Library of Congress.
Library of Congress Control Number: 2020937135

10 9 8 7 6 5 4 3 2 1

Jeffrey dedicates this volume to
Ingrid Rasmussen, Zachary Bernstein, and Nathaniel Bernstein.

Jade dedicates this volume to
the memory of her father, Bernard Baruch Schiff,
and to the memory of her mother, Gissa Schiff.

Contents

Acknowledgments ix

Introduction 1
Jeffrey A. Bernstein

I. ARTS OF READING AND SEEING

1 Liberalism and the Question: Strauss and Derrida on Politics and Philosophy 11
Jade Larissa Schiff

2 Purloined Letters—Lacan *avec* Strauss 29
Matthew J. Sharpe

3 Seeing through Law: Phenomenological Thought in Soloveitchik and Strauss 51
Jeffrey A. Bernstein

4 Claude Lefort and Leo Strauss: On A Philosophical Discourse 75
Isabel Rollandi

II. HISTORY AND POLITICS

5 A Civil Encounter: Leo Strauss and Charles Taylor on Religious Pluralism 111
Jessica L. Radin

6 Care of the Self and the Invention of Legitimate Government: Foucault and Strauss on Platonic Political Philosophy 135
Miguel Vatter

7 A Fruitful Disagreement: The Philosophical Encounter between George P. Grant and Leo Strauss 161
Waller R. Newell

8 Strauss and Blumenberg on the Caves of the Moderns 187
Danilo Manca

9 Writing the *Querelle des Anciens et Modernes:* Leo Strauss and Ferdinand Tönnies on Hobbes and the Sociology of Philosophy 209
Peter Gostmann

III. CULTURE AND CRITIQUE

10 Leo Strauss and Jürgen Habermas: The Quest for Reason in Twentieth-Century Lifeworlds 237
Rodrigo Chacón

11 Heidegger's Challenge to the Renaissance of Socratic Political Rationalism 259
Alexander S. Duff

12 The Wheel of History: Nihilism as Moral Protest and Destruction of the Present in Leo Strauss and Albert Camus 281
Ingrid L. Anderson

13 Who's Laughing? Leo Strauss on Comedy and Mockery 295
Menachem Feuer

14 Leo Strauss and Walter Benjamin: Thinking "In a Moment of Danger" 333
Philipp von Wussow

About the Contributors 353

Index 357

Acknowledgments

An earlier version of Jade Schiff's essay "Liberalism and the Question: Strauss and Derrida on Politics and Philosophy" appeared in Telos 166 (Spring 2014): 143–160.

Isabel Rollandi's essay "Claude Lefort and Leo Strauss: On a Philosophical Discourse" was written during a semester in Munich with assistance from a scholarship from the Carl Friedrich von Siemens Foundation.

Introduction

Jeffrey A. Bernstein

In *The Enduring Importance of Leo Strauss*,[1] Laurence Lampert tells a compelling story of Strauss's engagement with the esotericism of Maimonides as exemplified in the former's correspondence with Jacob Klein between the years 1937 and 1939. In these letters, and in Lampert's engagement of them, one sees clearly the captivating excitement that held the young Strauss as he discovered both Maimonides's writing between the lines as well as the influences and analogous instances of esoteric writers that preceded him. Before Strauss's eyes, a philosophical world was opening up—one that included Homer, Hesiod, Xenophon, Plato, Aristophanes, Farabi, and Averroes.[2] As the Second World War raged on, and in the midst of professional and financial insecurities, Strauss lived in the urgent wonder of the philosophical life.

This excitement and wonder is doubtless present to all readers who try to engage seriously and thoughtfully with Strauss's own work. Perhaps one of Strauss's many virtues is to have conveyed precisely the excitement that he felt during his formative period to his readers during their/our own. To have shown, for example, that the quarrel between the ancients and the moderns, the relation of the philosopher to the city, and the distinction between Jerusalem and Athens were living topics for reflection is no mean feat. From his early writings on Spinoza and on Medieval Jewish and Islamic thought, through the great lectures on natural right, Machiavelli, and the relation of the city to man in the 1950s and 1960s, up to the intensely difficult later works on Plato and

Xenophon, Strauss successfully re-originates such excitement for all parties interested in the history of philosophy. Recent scholarly endeavors have continued this excitement as concerns the thought of Strauss himself. The inauguration of the *Gesammelte Schriften*—with its inclusion of Strauss's correspondence, unpublished drafts, and marginalia—has so far given readers a clear view of Strauss's intellectual trajectory from Weimar Germany, through Great Britain, and into the beginning of his time in the United States. Similarly, the publication of Strauss's University of Chicago course transcripts by the Leo Strauss Center (both online and in book form) have given readers a good sense of Strauss the teacher, who engaged students' questions and worked closely through texts of thinkers familiar (Plato, Aristotle, Hobbes) and less-familiar (Grotius, Vico) to readers of Strauss's publications. This has, in turn, created vital thematic and historical avenues for scholarly monographs and articles on Strauss. Be it the early Weimar Strauss, the Strauss of the re-orienting 1930s, the Strauss of political philosophy, or Strauss as close reader of philosophical texts, the quality and quantity of secondary literature has decisively established Strauss as a fixed star in the realm of philosophical research. Put differently, the original excitement over the history of philosophy has continued into Strauss's own thoughts about that history and has led to several divergent lines of interest within Strauss studies—one such line being, not surprisingly, Strauss's relation to the very practice of writing between the lines that he discovered in premodern thought. Moreover, this continuous transmission of excitement surrounding the lines of Strauss's work and thought shows no signs of abating any time soon.

If the present volume makes a contribution to the excitement of Strauss studies, we hope it will be by paradoxically continuing to transmit the excitement of Strauss's thought by reading him (to a certain extent) outside the lines already established by the current receptions of Strauss's oeuvre. In placing Strauss's thought in conversation with other contemporary[3] thinkers and topics, we hope that this volume extends Strauss's thought to hitherto unexplored areas of research. This extension seems a natural one to us insofar as many of the other thinkers (e.g., Foucault, Lefort, Tönnies, Derrida, Lacan, and Blumenberg) have been in conversation with similar thinkers in the history of philosophy. Similarly, many thinkers have a thematic affinity with Strauss (e.g., the question of religion in public life, the concern over law). Finally, certain topics (comedy) have been underexplored in Strauss circles. We believe that inaugurating a conversation between Strauss and these thinkers/ topics can only highlight the excitement and reach of Strauss's thought going forward.

~

That Strauss's oeuvre amounts to a sustained argument favoring (in Hans Jonas's Aristotelian coinage) "the nobility of sight" hardly comes as a surprise, and the contributors to part 1 ("Arts of Seeing and Reading") all address this aspect of Strauss's thought. Jade Schiff argues in favor of an affinity between Strauss's and Derrida's practices of reading—their "shared awareness of the perpetually problematic character of politico-philosophical and deconstructive inquiry points to their shared affinity for the Socratic style of investigation that calls into question what we think we know—about ourselves, our political commitments, our world." Matthew Sharpe similarly highlights the readerly qualities that Straussian and Lacanian inquiry share: "there is the near-psychoanalytic attention Strauss asks his readers to pay to 'ambiguous words' like 'rank,' 'virtue,' 'secret,' 'tyranny,' 'the wise,' 'wisdom,' or 'moderation' and 'courage' in revered thinkers. Are these not precisely what Freud calls *condensations:* words in whose double address Lacan espies the 'poetic spark' of metaphor?" In my own treatment of Strauss and Soloveitchik on law, I attempt to show how both thinkers make use of Husserlian phenomenological categories in order to "understand law as an *optic* through which certain fundamental phenomena come to light." Finally, in her treatment of Strauss and Lefort, Isabel Rollandi explores the question of how both thinkers read Machiavelli in order to accentuate the distinction "between *teaching* and *thought*" and the philosopher's "giv[ing] to think in pieces and, following his intention . . . reconstruct[ing] his thought" in the service of "contribut[ing] towards the recovery of the permanent problems."

In the recovery of the political horizon for philosophy, Strauss continuously does battle with historicism without denigrating history. Differently stated, in thinking about the differing perceptions of politics contained in ancient and modern philosophy, Strauss attempts to inoculate readers against viewing philosophy as under the aegis of history by consistently viewing history under the aegis of philosophy. In so doing, Strauss allows readers to appreciate the primacy of the political without giving short shrift to history. The contributors to part 2 ("History and

Politics") evince a notable awareness of this aspect of Strauss's thought. Jessica Radin's comparative study of Strauss and Charles Taylor on religious pluralism shows how both thinkers appreciated the political character of modern society's relation to particular religions: "For neither thinker is the accommodation of religion without limits—we must strive for moderation, for 'reasonable accommodation' that may sometimes mean excluding practices (in a given time and circumstance) as being intolerable. Yet there is both the risk and the hope that those circumstances can change." Miguel Vatter's contribution on Strauss's relation to Foucault on Platonic political philosophy discloses that "[u]ltimately, both Foucault and Strauss agree that 'political philosophy' or 'normative political thought' is not what the western tradition has made of it: it is neither a discourse that seeks to understand the nature of political things, nor does it delineate a theory of justice for the sake of moralizing politics . . . 'political philosophy' is a practice that seeks to replace a democratic political life by the legitimate government of some over others." The difference between the two is that where Foucault views natural right only as "the discourse that makes it possible to implant a pre- or supra-political government of others in a democracy," for Strauss natural right refers to "a discourse for which the government of others is 'by nature' right or in accordance with the needs of the philosophical life." Waller Newell showcases George Grant's prolonged engagement with Leo Strauss in order to better show the former's "deeply interesting contribution to contemporary political philosophy. Like Strauss, within the boundaries of political philosophy, Grant preferred the classical approach over the modern approach . . . like Strauss, Grant accepted the notion that the modern project for the conquest of nature embodied a paradigm shift from the classical search for the eternal order of the whole . . . Unlike Strauss and like Heidegger, however, Grant did accept the proposition that global technology summed up the essence of the modern project . . . And fundamentally, of course, Grant departed from Strauss in his central pre-occupation with Christian revelation in both its positive and its baleful effects." Danilo Manca brings together Strauss and Hans Blumenberg concerning their respective renditions of the Moderns: Strauss and Blumenberg "share the idea that the radicalization of Descartes's rhetoric of a new beginning can in no way work," thus necessitating "pav[ing] the way for retrieving another way of living and thinking." Finally, Peter Gostmann shows the benefits of studying Strauss and Ferdinand Tönnies from the standpoint of the sociology of philosophy by focusing "on the various social actors and groups that Tönnies and Strauss introduce [in their elaborations of the thought of Hobbes]" and considering "the qualities attributed to these actors and groups, as well as the figures of argumentation and figures of speech that [they] apply to explain the interrelations of them." In so doing, he shows that—for all his sensitivity to the distinction between natural right and natural law in Hobbes—Tönnies's approach remains tied to historicism, while Strauss's reading is positioned on the side of ancient philosophy against modern philosophy in its concern over "the problem of the best possible regime."

As with his approach to history, Strauss's approach was never simply to denigrate the very category of "culture" but, instead, to view it from a philosophical standpoint. It is in this vein that the contributors to part 3 ("Culture and Critique") approach the constellation of dialogic reason, comedy and mockery, nihilism, and one's relation to society and its traditions. In his conversation between Strauss and Habermas, Rodrigo Chacón argues that "[i]n their own self-understanding, Strauss and Habermas are critical thinkers . . . the work of critique consists in the dialectical overcoming of fixed oppositions into an expanded conception of reason . . . insofar as [Strauss and Habermas] were guided by problems which, in Strauss's words, are 'coeval with human thought,' they also advanced the work of reason in its movement towards self-consciousness." Alexander Duff treats a facet of Strauss's critique of Heidegger that has (to my knowledge) gone underappreciated in the still small literature on the two thinkers: "namely, his criticism of Heidegger for being inattentive to the comic or the laughable in human experience." For Duff "Heidegger's Socrates takes no account of Socratic irony, his noble dissimulation. He misses the status that opinion has in Socratic philosophy, where opinion is the matrix of thought because it contains a distortion of the truth." Ingrid Anderson explores the convergence concerning nihilism between the thought of Strauss and that of Albert Camus: "Both formulate . . . nihilism as a resounding "No!" directed toward a justifiably disappointing liberal democracy . . . Perhaps most revealing is their shared assertion that resistance to German nihilism and its successors requires a re-discovery of and renewed adherence to some semblance of absolute universal values, values that are not created by the forces of history, but identified *in* history as enduring and therefore fundamental." Menachem Feuer (in like manner to Duff's considerations) wonders about Strauss's conception of comedy: "Attention to Strauss's observations on the differing uses and divergent meanings of humor and comedy may prompt us to think differently about the meaning and place of comedy in his work." By means of a thoughtful journey through his readings of Aristophanes, Maimonides, Spinoza, and Nietzsche, Feuer's Strauss shows readers that "the main thing for both the Socratic/Platonic approach to philosophy and the Jewish approach to Prophesy is that chance and comedy displace fate and tragedy." Finally, Philipp von Wussow explores the relation between Strauss and Walter Benjamin, showing that "the two figures of interwar German-Jewish thought represent two different ways of conceptualizing the dialectics of modernity and premodernity, two models of viewing society and culture from the outside, and two different foundations for the understanding of the political in its relation to culture." Whereas "Strauss took his bearings from Socrates to avoid the political battleground of culture," Benjamin worked through "'documents of culture'—modern literature, art, and everyday culture" in order to achieve a standpoint not simply entrenched in the ideologies of modern life.

We hope that we have conveyed something of the excitement with which these contributions were composed to the readers who read them. We believe that each essay opens the door to potentially important avenues of research and thought. From our perspective, the depth of Strauss's thought is measured not only by how he engages with earlier philosophers, but also by how he converses with—and allows himself to be conversed with by—contemporary figures and ideas as well. That Strauss is, himself, a contemporary thinker in no way obscures his importance in retrieving and re-originating earlier thought (the former may, in fact, even be a precondition for the latter). Our claim is, rather, that the transhistorical philosophical life remains alive today and is visible to readers in these conversations. In reading Strauss outside the lines, we seek to continue and deepen the line that leads back to the philosophical life in the thought and work of Leo Strauss.

Notes

1. Laurence Lampert, *The Enduring Importance of Leo Strauss* (Chicago: University of Chicago Press, 2013).

2. Ibid., 7–31.

3. We interpret "contemporary" capaciously enough to include a figure such as Ferdinand Tönnies. Given the historical reach of Strauss's own studies, however, the nineteenth century is not so far distant from today as to prohibit such an interpretation.

I. ARTS OF READING AND SEEING

1

Liberalism and the Question

Strauss and Derrida on Politics and Philosophy

Jade Larissa Schiff

The end of the Cold War was heralded by many observers as the triumph of liberal democracy, a triumph captured by Francis Fukuyama's infamous declaration of "the end of history."[1] The supposed triumph of liberal democracy was both political and philosophical. Politically, liberal democracy had outlasted its only serious rival, Soviet Communism, which had unceremoniously disintegrated.[2] Philosophically, the triumph of liberal democracy suggested to some that the West had hit upon a fundamental piece of knowledge about the best political order for human beings. Whatever the value of Fukuyama's thesis at the time, the terrorist attacks on September 11, 2001, and the wars in Iraq and Afghanistan put the lie to such confident proclamations. These events, among many others, made clear that the political and philosophical superiority of liberal democracy is not obvious to all. And while popular revolts in the Middle East and North Africa have been revolts against autocracy, it is far too early to say what will come of them.

Renewed questioning of the philosophical foundations and political aims of liberal democracy should bring the relationship between politics and philosophy to the forefront of critical discussion among political theorists and philosophers. How does philosophical activity support and challenge the terms by which we live together? How do our politics enable and constrain philosophy? In this chapter, I compare answers to those questions offered by Leo Strauss and Jacques Derrida, two of the most controversial figures in twentieth- and twenty-first-century political thought, in order to highlight their points of convergence and divergence. In the intense post-9/11 revival of interest in Strauss, no one has put him into systematic conversation with Derrida. On one hand, this is an expected consequence of the politics of political theory. Catherine Zuckert espouses a prominent, though not universally shared, view that "Strauss was politically conservative; Derrida's sympathies are explicitly with the left."[3] Moreover, these thinkers deploy very different conceptual vocabularies. On the other hand, the lack of conversation is surprising. Strauss and Derrida represent two distinct and influential approaches to reading texts, and to understanding what constitutes a "text": esotericism and deconstruction. Moreover, Derrida was clearly aware of Strauss—he refers to him fleetingly in "Force of Law"—and the two had much in common. Both were critical of the self-confidence of liberal democracy, and for both the relationship between politics and philosophy was a central theme of their work. Finally, both turned to the ancient Greeks in pursuing that theme. In light of that, this chapter is partly an effort in translation, in getting Strauss and Derrida to speak to one another despite the mutual disdain of some of their contemporary acolytes.

That conversation is not a simple one. While rightly attuned to some of the above-mentioned similarities, previous scholars have seriously downplayed important differences in ways that threaten to distort the work of both thinkers, while simultaneously overlooking some more surprising points of convergence. Zuckert has suggested that for both Strauss and Derrida, what goes unsaid or unwritten in texts may be more significant than what *is* said or written, and she rightly connects the question of the unsaid or unwritten to the tension between politics and philosophy. Politico-philosophical texts obscure those questions and conclusions whose revelation would disturb extant political orthodoxies that are largely taken for granted. The liberal orthodoxy that has reigned since the Cold War is but one example. But—and here my view differs from Zuckert's—Strauss and Derrida treat far differently the questions of *how* and *why* something goes unsaid or unwritten. This difference is a consequence of their very different understandings of the relationship between philosophy and politics. The articulation of this difference, moreover, reveals some other unexpected and subtle points of agreement between them on the tense relationship between politics and philosophy.

Politics and Philosophy: Concealment or Repression?

Strauss's and Derrida's perspectives on the relationships between philosophy and politics crystallize in their textual approaches. For both thinkers, philosophical texts are more complicated than they may first appear. As Zuckert has noted, "both Strauss and Derrida argue that a careful reading of classic texts shows that they have multiple meanings. . . . According to both . . . what an author does not say can be more important than what is said."[4] She connects this distinction between the said and the unsaid to Strauss's and Derrida's shared sense of a conflict between philosophy and society. Both thinkers explored this conflict by returning to the ancient Greeks. "Like Strauss," Zuckert notes, Derrida "thinks Plato restrained his 'speech' to conceal the more radical challenges philosophy poses to the foundations of morality. But the ways in which the two twentieth-century commentators suggest that Plato exercised self-censorship differ considerably."[5]

Strauss and Derrida do share an interest in what goes unsaid, and for both it does have something to with a conflict between philosophy and society. But I interpret their views on the unsaid, and the conflict, differently. First, if we emphasize the "unsaid" we overlook the specificity of *writing* for both thinkers. While Strauss himself referred to an author's "statement," he insisted that it be understood in the context of "the *literary* character of the whole work,"[6] and refers to such works as "writings."[7] Indeed it is of paramount importance to Strauss that philosophers *wrote* esoteric texts because such recording preserved them, enabling "the truly exact historian" to understand "the thought of the great writers of the past."[8] Without such writing, the teachings of past political philosophers could be lost. Written philosophy, moreover, did not only serve the aims of historians. In "The Three Waves of Modernity"—a lecture at Cornell University—and in the essays contained in *Liberalism: Ancient and Modern*, Strauss turned to ancient political philosophy ("the premodern thought of our Western tradition") as a source of critical philosophical *and* political inspiration for modern liberalism in the face of Soviet Communism.[9] The writing of political philosophy, its material and preserved character, was thus politically significant as well.

Writing was also significant for Derrida, though in a way different from Strauss. Part of the movement[10] of deconstruction is to disturb (however provisionally and unstably) the logocentrism—the priority of *logos*, of the Word, of speech—that had characterized a Western metaphysical tradition in which writing had been repressed in *favor* of speech.[11] To Derrida this was most immediately apparent in "the manifest phonocentrism of structuralism," especially the linguistic structuralism of Saussure.[12] By drawing attention to the repression of writing Derrida simultaneously drew attention to the trace—the "disappearance of origin"[13]—of what was repressed: writing itself. Gayatri Spivak puts it aptly: "The structure of the sign"—in this case, the sign of writing—"is determined by the trace or track of that other which is *forever* absent."[14] As Spivak notes—and this example is perfect here—"the text of philosophy is always written . . . yet that text is always designated by philosophy" as speech "(Plato says . . .)."[15] The written-ness of philosophy is thus present but absent, present *in* its absence. While Strauss emphasized the written because it preserved a tradition of thought, Derrida recovered writing from its erasure in speech.[16] This should not lead us to conclude that Derrida, like Strauss, accorded any straightforward priority to the written, that he sought to restore "the priority of writing over speech in the study of language." Instead, writes Spivak, Derrida showed that "speech too . . . is structured as writing," that "there is no structural distinction between writing and speech."[17] For Derrida we *cannot* give priority to one over the other because writing and speech are not ours to use; language is always woven into a chain of unstable significations in which we always find ourselves already caught. When Derrida identifies arche-writing as "writing before the letter," a kind of original and originary writing *before* writing in the narrow sense, a writing that conditions our writing, he alludes to such a chain. For example, in *The Other Heading*,[18] Derrida suggests a chain involving *cap*, capital, and capitalism. Or, as we will see later, his discussion of "the right to philosophy" shows how the phrase plays on the meaning of "right," so that "the right to philosophy" is likewise caught up in a chain of meaning over whose play we are not sovereign.[19]

The Derridean sense of being caught in language challenges the assimilation of his and Strauss's views in a second way. It highlights the difference between concealment and repression as the dynamic of the relationship between politics and philosophy. For Strauss, Plato and other philosophers had to *conceal* their true views from society. These views were not unwritten, only buried "between the lines" of their texts. For Derrida, what is at issue is not concealed *in* the text, but absent from it, *repressed* by it—what is, indeed, unwritten, to preserve illusions of presence, coherence and wholeness that are forever haunted by what would disturb them. In *Persecution and the Art of Writing*, Strauss articulated the beginnings of a "sociology of philosophy,"[20] an account of the social and political conditions of (especially ancient and medieval) philosophy's production, and so of the relationship between philosophy and society. The phenomenon of persecution is central to that sociology. Strauss points to Farabi's contention that "the philosophers were 'in grave danger' " because "society did not recognize philosophy or the right of philosophizing. There was," Strauss observes, "no harmony between philosophy and society."[21] This gave rise to a need for two philosophical teachings in any text: the exoteric, apparent teaching that would pose no evident challenge to society, and so would preserve its conventions while sparing the philosopher society's disapproval, even wrath; and the esoteric, hidden teaching that would reflect the pursuit of genuine knowledge for the few, and disturb the conventional pieties of social and political life. "The exoteric teaching was needed for protecting philosophy. It was the armor in which philosophy has to appear. . . . It was the political aspect of philosophy. It was 'political' philosophy."[22] The esoteric teaching, in contrast, appeared literally "between the lines," that is, in a middle passage unlikely to attract the attention of censors.[23] The task for "thoughtful men" who are "careful readers" is to "detect the meaning of" the work by recognizing the esoteric message as the true one.[24] This is precisely Strauss's approach to Platonic dialogues. As his commentary on the *Laws* suggests, he distinguishes the "argument" of the dialogues from their "action"—or what is written explicitly from what emerges implicitly in their unfolding, and only appears upon close reading.[25]

For Strauss, interpreting a text is about discerning the author's intent. The conflict between philosophy and politics forced ancient philosophers to conceal their intent from the careless multitudes who were content with conventional pieties. The author's intent can be understood only by the thoughtful reader if he or she reads "between the lines" in order to ascertain the esoteric, and true, meaning of the work. In "Plato's Pharmacy," Derrida makes clear that he thinks very differently about the conflict between philosophy and society. On his reading, Plato did not restrain his speech in order to conceal philosophy's challenges to society. Such voluntary concealment is impossible, since a text always already conceals itself. "Plato's Pharmacy" begins with the following warning: "A text is not a text unless it hides from the first comer, from the first glance, the law of its composition and the rules of its game." This could still be Strauss writing: "The law of its composition and the rules of its game" *could* refer to those techniques of which Strauss availed himself in interpreting Farabi, Maimonides, Plato, and others. And if the first comer's first glance fails to reveal the text, Strauss might suggest that he or she was a careless reader or a careful one who had not completed their task. But Derrida's reference here to "a text"—not the *meaning* of a text but the text itself—opens up a seemingly unbridgeable divide between them. Derrida cannot distinguish the argument of a text from its action (or the exoteric text from its esoteric meaning) in the way that Strauss does, because for him neither is simply present. Indeed, "a text remains, moreover, *forever* imperceptible. Its law and its rules are not, however, harbored in the inaccessibility of a secret"—a text does not contain hidden teachings to be deciphered, as it does for Strauss—"it is simply that they can never be booked, in the *present*, into anything that could rigorously be called a perception."[26] It is not a matter of hidden meaning; the text itself—as an immediate presence, subject (for Strauss) to penetrating interpretation—is *imperceptible*.

Later in the "Pharmacy," Derrida rejects much of what Strauss's esoteric reading entails in more detail: "The word *pharmakon*"—which Derrida translates as both remedy *and* poison—"is caught in a chain of significations."[27] That "is caught" is again revealing: there is no subject here, no catcher, no *author* who has done the catching in the way that, for Strauss, the author conceals his esoteric teaching. "The play of that chain," Derrida notes, "*seems* systematic"; unlike Strauss he does not assume a system to be uncovered. Indeed, he insists that "the system here is not, simply, that of the intentions of an author who goes by the name of Plato. The system is not primarily that of what someone *meant-to say*," and so the point of reading cannot be simply to figure out what an author is trying to tell us under the cover of secret teachings. Within that system, "finely regulated communications are established," as they are for Strauss, but again not primarily through the author's intent. Rather, they are established "through the play of language, among diverse functions of the word and, within it, among diverse strata or regions of culture."[28] We have seen this play at work before, in the examples of capital and the right to philosophy. What, then, accounts for appearance of "a text" in the face of this play and diversity, this *différance*, the "text" always haunted by what is outside, what is absent? The most similar question for Strauss would be: what accounts for the appearance that a text should be taken at face value? His answer: the skill of the author in intentionally concealing the meaning of the text, and the carelessness of the careless reader who will not or cannot uncover it. For Derrida, such an answer is not possible. What, for Strauss, is an instance of concealment is, for Derrida, an instance of repression enacted in the very act of writing, which, by always struggling against what is excluded, maintains a semblance of coherence and wholeness:

> Writing is unthinkable without repression. Its condition is that there be neither a permanent contact nor an absolute break between strata: the vigilance and failure of censorship. It is no accident that the metaphor of censorship should come from the area of politics concerned with writing in its deletions, blanks, and disguises, even if Freud, at the beginning of the *Traumdeutung*, seems to make only a conventional, didactic reference to it. The apparent exteriority of political censorship gives way to an essential censorship which binds the writer to his own writing.[29]

In distinguishing "the apparent exteriority of political censorship" from "essential censorship," Derrida warns against Strauss's notion of an exterior censor actively imposing its will, erasing or forcing us to delete what is undesirable or unacceptable on pain of punishment. The repression of *essential* censorship happens without a censor, *before* external censorship, as a condition of its possibility. The essential censorship that binds a writer to his writing attempts to overcome the virtual disappearance of the writer *in* writing as he is overtaken by the play of language over which he exercises only the illusory authority of an author. The repression involved in writing attempts—but always fails—to secure that authority and to present "the text" as the settled accomplishment of an author.[30]

Derrida's emphasis on essential rather than external censorship (without, to be sure, abandoning the latter notion) suggests that for him the relationship between politics and philosophy is different from what it is for Strauss. Unsurprisingly, in his explicitly political writings—such as *The Other Heading, Spectres of Marx, Politics of Friendship, On Cosmopolitanism and Forgiveness*, and *Rogues*[31]—he diagnoses the same logocentrism as that which underwrites the repression of writing. The repression that constitutes essential censorship—expressed politically in our clinging to conventional illusions of coherent political gestures and ideas that are always inevitably unstable, even aporetic[32]—is the site of a conflict, but not one between the conventions of a society and its rulers on the one hand, and the searching inquiry of philosophers on the other, as it is for Strauss. It is, rather, between a mutually supportive politics and philosophy (specifically, metaphysics) aimed at closure, coherence, and presence; and the disruptive politico-philosophical movement of deconstruction that erupts in the face of essential censorship to trouble such illusions. Derrida does not, as many have suggested, have trouble with political commitments as such—nor is he politically irresponsible.[33] He is committed to the notion that any such commitments are necessarily unstable, haunted by disturbance and disruption by the trace of what is repressed in them. Derrida could never conclude, as Strauss does, that the superiority of liberal democracy arises because "liberal democracy, in contradistinction to communism and fascism, derives powerful support from a way of thinking which cannot be called modern at all: the premodern thought of our western tradition."[34] For Derrida there is too much repressed in those claims: about a liberal democracy whose liberalism and democracy are in question; about a modernity that has not necessarily broken so clearly with the past; and about a Western tradition whose roots are not so settled. Bringing to light such instabilities would call into question the superiority of liberal democracy that Strauss asserts. Not, to be sure, because Derrida prefers communism or fascism—see, for instance, *Spectres of Marx*[35] and *Of Spirit*[36]—or because he sees no appreciable difference between them and liberalism; but, rather, because to take the superiority of liberal democracy for granted is to succumb to the repressions enacted in a logocentric metaphysics. It is to adhere to a philosophy and a politics that affirms, rather than disturbs, the conventional pieties that both Strauss and Derrida regarded with deep suspicion.

Convergences: The Activity of Philosophy and the Trace of the Author

Strauss and Derrida thus offer very different accounts of how and why something is concealed or repressed in a text. For Strauss political philosophers like Plato, fearing for their lives and for the unphilosophic masses, concealed their heretical, esoteric teachings "between the lines" of an exoteric, conventional one. For Derrida Plato, like all writers, is caught in a chain of signification that always involves repression to preserve the illusion of coherence, authority and authorship. The conflict he dramatizes is one between a politics and philosophy aimed at closure and coherence, and the disruptive politico-philosophical movement of deconstruction. In light of this stark difference, it is surprising to see some intriguing points of convergence emerge between Derrida and Strauss. Indeed, it is only when we articulate those differences that these similarities become apparent. In this section I will highlight some of these surprising convergences around logocentrism, authorship and authority, the activity of philosophy, and philosophical humility.

The first surprise is that Strauss, like Derrida, confronts the issue of logocentrism (though he does so implicitly), but he seems to resolve it in a very different way. While Derrida sought to recover writing, whose presence is repressed and effaced by speech, Strauss's confrontation with logocentrism inverts this relationship: he excavates an unexpected lesson in the superiority of *oral* teachings. This becomes apparent in his reading of Maimonides's *Guide to the Perplexed*, which, interestingly, immediately follows the chapter in *Persecution* in which Strauss articulates the distinction between exoteric and esoteric teachings, and where his distance from Derrida initially seems greatest. Strauss asks: "If a book devoted to the explanation of the secrets of the Bible"—as Maimonides's *Guide* purports to be—"is prohibited by law, how then can the *Guide*, being the work of an observant Jew, be a book?" He notes that Maimonides never calls the guide a book but a "*maqâla* (*ma'amar*)," which can mean a treatise or, "and this is its original connotation," a speech.[37] Strauss's strategy here of pointing to dual meanings recalls Derrida's approach to the *pharmakon*. Maimonides, Strauss suggests, "by refraining from calling the *Guide* a book . . . hints at the essentially oral character of its teaching." And "since, in a book such as the *Guide*, hints are more important than explicit statements, Maimonides' contentions concerning the superiority of oral teaching very probably have to be taken quite literally."[38] The "secrets of the Bible" that concern Maimonides were originally transmitted orally. Accordingly, the lesson Strauss draws from Maimonides is that part of the Bible's greatness is that it contains oral teachings. However, it transmits them in written form. The written form of the Bible effaces the superiority of the spoken word, the *logos*, which Maimonides's teaching reasserts.[39]

This is precisely the opposite of Derrida's claim about Plato's dialogues: that the dialogue form conceals and is always haunted by repressed writing. And thus the dual meaning of *maqâla*—as speech *and* as treatise—in this context indicates the fraught nature of their relationship and also parallels the double meaning of *pharmakon* as remedy and as poison. As with Derrida's *pharmakon*, Strauss's *maqâla*-as-treatise threatens to poison its more original meaning as speech. Strauss certainly differs significantly from Derrida in positing one meaning as "more original." Derrida's insistence on the instabilities of our conceptual vocabularies prevents such a move. Nonetheless, their common concern with logocentrism is a surprising and overlooked point of convergence. For both, the tension between politics and philosophy is in part a question of its form of transmission.

Strauss's identification of the dual meaning of *maqâla*, and his analysis of how one of its meanings supersedes the other, contains a second surprising convergence between him and Derrida, this one on the question of authorial intent. Given Strauss's conception of exoteric and esoteric teachings that allow readers to discover what an author intended as his true teaching, it is surprising to find moments at which he seems implicitly to concede something to the view that an author is not necessarily master of his text—that he is indeed caught in a chain of significations in the way that Derrida describes. Thus, the relationship between politics and philosophy for Strauss comes closer to the repressive one outlined by Derrida, and departs from the concealing one that Strauss explicitly describes. Meanwhile, Derrida makes intriguing concessions to authorial intent that appear to bring him closer to Strauss than he initially seemed to be.

While Strauss argues that Maimonides gives priority to oral teachings, neither Strauss's *nor* Maimonides' intentions are necessarily decisive. After suggesting that "the *Guide* as a whole is . . . devoted to the revelation of the secrets of the Bible," Strauss—in a move that Derrida himself might make—points out that "*Secret*, however, has manifold meanings." It can mean "the secret hidden by a parable or word, but it also may mean the parable or word itself which hides a secret."[40] At first, Strauss seems to back away from the manifold character of the word, for he says: "With reference to the second meaning, the *Guide* may more conveniently be said to be devoted to the explanation of the secrets of the Bible."[41] Those secrets are "*ma'aseh bereshit* (the account of creation), *ma'aseh merkabah* (the account of the chariot, Ezekiel 1 and 10), prophecy and the knowledge of God."[42] These are, indeed, parables held to hide secrets. Yet we have already seen that, according to Strauss, Maimonides treats the secrets of the Bible in the first sense as well.

When Maimonides refuses to call the Bible a book but instead uses words that refer to oral teachings, he reveals a secret hidden by a word: namely, that oral teachings are superior to written ones. This example challenges Strauss's strong claims about authorial intent at two levels. First, if Strauss is right about Maimonides's claims, then Maimonides's *Guide* unravels his own intentions by playing on both meanings of "secret" in a manner over which he was apparently not sovereign. Second, since Strauss is silent on the first sense of "secret" in Maimonides but draws on it anyway, *his* text, too, appears to outstrip his intent as an interpreter of Maimonides. At work here is not, or not only, Strauss's and Maimonides's intentions, but the system of language in which they are at play and the semantic instabilities of the sort to which Derrida drew our attention.

If Strauss's treatment of Maimonides appears to bring him a bit closer to Derrida, the latter's treatment of Plato brings him a bit closer to Strauss, albeit ambiguously so. While Strauss implicitly concedes that authorial intent is not all that matters, at some points Derrida appears to concede something to authorial intent—to the idea that we are not *entirely* caught up in chains of signification, but can master them in limited ways.

As we saw earlier, Derrida suggests that "the play of that chain [of signification] *seems* systematic," that "the system here is not, simply, that of the intentions of an author who goes by the name of Plato. The system is not primarily that of what someone *meant-to say*."[43] In my first reading, these claims appeared to distinguish Derrida quite sharply from Strauss. But they can also be read in a way that softens the distinction: the system is not "simply" that of an author's intentions, it is not "primarily" what someone meant to say—so it is not simply or primarily *not* those things either. The system of significations outreaches authorial intent without thereby effacing it altogether.[44] A trace of the author remains:[45] "These communications or corridors of meaning can sometimes be declared or clarified by Plato when he plays upon them 'voluntarily.' "[46] So "Plato," the author caught in this system of significations, can have *some* effect upon them. On one hand, such "voluntary" play ought not to be confused with the stratagems of a persecuted philosopher. Derrida places this word in quotation marks "because what it designates, to content ourselves with remaining within the closure of these oppositions, is only a mode of 'submission' to the necessities of a given 'language.' "[47] He is unwilling to content himself with closure and opposition, insisting that "none of these concepts can translate the relation we are aiming at here."[48] Derrida sees in such "voluntary" declarations and clarifications a misrecognition of one's situation. That is, when we declare and clarify what we "mean," we do so under an illusion. We are always still caught in a play of meaning over which we cannot, finally, be sovereign. That is why, Derrida insists, we cannot "[reconstitute] the entire chain of significations of the *pharmakon*. No absolute privilege allows us absolutely to master its textual system."[49] On the other hand, Derrida places "submission" in quotation marks as well, suggesting a submission that is not quite a submission, or at any rate not a complete one. If Derrida concedes something to the author of texts, he concedes something to the reader as well. For if we cannot reconstitute the *entire* chain of significations, if no *absolute* privilege grants us *absolute* mastery, Derrida allows that we might partially reconstitute the chain, with perhaps only relative privilege affording us limited mastery. This is precisely what Derrida is doing when he reads Plato—or, indeed, anyone else. Derrida's granting of certain limited privileges, not only to the writer but also the reader, closes some of the distance between him and Strauss, for whom both the writer and the *thoughtful* reader enjoy more privileged access to a text.

But access to what exactly? What are we seeking when we read philosophical texts; or, what is the activity of philosophy, especially in relation to politics? Here, too, Strauss and Derrida converge more than first meets the eye. As we saw earlier, for Strauss philosophy is the love of wisdom and truth. A philosophical text properly understood contains the teachings of philosophers about important human truths—about the good, about religion, about justice, and so on. In his "Notes on *The Concept of the Political*," a response to Carl Schmitt written in 1932, Strauss referred to philosophy as the pursuit of "pure and whole knowledge." Later, in *Persecution*, Strauss describes esoteric writing as a "literary technique" for authors to present "their views on all the then crucial questions,"[50] and describes a work's esoteric content as a "philosophic teaching" and the presentation of "basic truths."[51] This stands in stark contrast to Derrida, for whom the movement of deconstruction is always disruptive, unsettling, raising political and philosophical questions that were otherwise repressed in and by the system of a given text. But Strauss is more ambiguous about what is concealed in texts than first appears; and in his ambiguity he draws nearer to Derrida. Elsewhere Strauss stressed that "philosophy as such is nothing but the genuine awareness of the *problems*, i.e., of the fundamental and comprehensive problems." While it "is impossible to think about these problems without becoming inclined toward a solution . . . the philosopher ceases to be a philosopher at the moment at which the 'subjective certainty' of a solution [not unlike those conventional pieties to which societies cling, which are a form of subjective *and* intersubjective certainty] becomes stronger than his awareness of the problematic character of that solution."[52]

Strauss's and Derrida's shared awareness of the perpetually problematic character of politico-philosophical and deconstructive inquiry points to their shared affinity for the Socratic style of investigation that calls into question what we think we know—about ourselves, our political commitments, our world.[53] For both of them, this entails a posture of humility. In Derrida's case, that humility manifests itself as an acknowledgment that texts are forever unstable, "imperceptible," out of reach. For Strauss, it manifests as an acknowledgment of the limits of philosophical knowledge, and of necessity of faith in philosophy.[54] Yet Derrida goes further than Strauss by calling into question the very meaning of philosophy as such. While Strauss may have vacillated between conceptions of philosophy as questioning and as the discovery of basic truths, it was not in the course of questioning philosophy. Derrida, in contrast, devoted considerable attention to the problematic character of "philosophy." While illustrating the ambiguous meaning of the "right to philosophy," Derrida considered three possibilities. The first is that "the right to philosophy already belongs to philosophy completely and by right; it would presuppose . . . an answer to the question 'What is philosophy?'" The second is "that this belonging by right implies no identification of philosophy, no stabilizable answer to the question 'What is philosophy?' . . . but only the participation in the 'community of the question.'" The third is that "we can, finally, . . . admit the thinking, practice and experience of a 'right to philosophy' without presuppositional recourse to either a given essence of philosophy . . . or even the supposedly originary possibility of the question 'What is philosophy?'"[55] If we took this third route, we would thus not give ourselves or demand the right to presuppose either the answer to, or the formulation of, the question "What is philosophy?" nor even the possibility of a question in general, even the question as the ultimate form and final entrenchment of a community, here of a community of *thinking*.[56]

Such thinking "*can*, one can even think that it *must*, lead precisely to philosophy. . . . But it traces a form of strange limit between all the determinations of the philosophical and a deconstructive thinking that, while undertaken *by* philosophy, does not belong to it. . . . Deconstruction . . . is involved in this third possibility."[57] Strauss stands as among those for whom "the right to philosophy" belongs to itself and presupposes an understanding of philosophy, as a path to basic truths and fundamental questions. But here, Derrida presents philosophy as an end, not a means—an end pursued but perhaps never reached through a deconstructive thinking that is not itself philosophical. He thus goes further than Strauss down a road that they travel together.

Conclusion

Strauss and Derrida, and their many students and acolytes, speak very different languages. Perhaps for this reason scholars have made few efforts at translation. This chapter represents such an effort. Despite significant differences between esoteric and deconstructive approaches to philosophical texts, Strauss and Derrida come closer to another than one might think on questions of the relationship between politics and philosophy. Moreover, that relationship is crucial for understanding both approaches. Their divergences, and especially their convergences, are of more than scholarly interest. With "the end of history" very much in question today, Strauss and Derrida offer different but complementary philosophical resources for confronting our unsettled political presents and possible futures.

Notes

1. Francis Fukuyama, *The End of History and The Last Man* (New York: Free Press, 1993).

2. China's aggressive rise to challenge the United States as a global power was not yet underway.

3. Catherine Zuckert, *Postmodern Platos: Nietzsche, Heidegger, Gadamer, Strauss, Derrida* (Chicago: University of Chicago Press, 1996), 201.

4. Ibid., 201–202.

5. Ibid., 223–224. In my view, Zuckert overstates some of these similarities and exaggerates some differences. First, she claims that "whereas Strauss sought to revive the Western tradition in the face of the radical critique leveled by Nietzsche and Heidegger, Derrida wants to carry that critique even further" (201). It is true that Derrida pushes beyond Nietzsche's and Heidegger's critiques of the

Western tradition. But the "con" in de*con*struction, a term of Derrida's inspired by Heidegger's *Destruktion*, signifies a similar recuperative dimension in Derrida's critique. See Jacques Derrida, *Of Hospitality* (Stanford, CA: Stanford University Press, 2000). Second, Zuckert suggests that "unlike Strauss . . . Derrida does not pay much attention to the differences among the philosophical spokesmen, interlocutors, and settings of the dialogues" (Zuckert, *Postmodern Platos*, 224). But Derrida notes in his "Pharmacy" that "a spoken speech—whether by Lysias or by Phaedrus in person . . . would not have had the same effect . . . only hidden [written] letters can thus get Socrates moving"; and later, invites us to "return to the text of Plato, assuming we have ever really left it" (Derrida, *Dissemination*, 71, 95). This points to several ways in which Derrida attends to the sorts of differences that Zuckert says he ignores. First, "a spoken speech—whether by Lysias or by Phaedrus" suggests Derrida's awareness that speeches by Lysias and Phaedrus might indeed be different, even if that difference makes no difference for him. Second, "Let us return to the text of Plato, assuming we have ever really left it" suggests Derrida's acute awareness of the importance of considering Plato's voice in distinction from those of the dialogue's characters.

6. Leo Strauss, *Persecution and The Art of Writing* (Chicago: University of Chicago Press, 1988), 30; see also Paul Cantor, "Leo Strauss and Contemporary Hermeneutics," in *Leo Strauss's Thought: Toward a Critical Engagement*, Alan Udoff, ed. (Boulder, CO: Lynne Rienner, 1991), 279. In a footnote to one of Strauss's early essays on Spinoza, Michael Zank alludes to the connection between *Kritik* as a philosophical critique and as literary criticism. See Leo Strauss, *The Early Writings, 1921–1932*, ed., Michael Zank (Albany, NY: SUNY Press, 2002), 197.

7. Strauss, *Persecution*, 35. Like Derrida—and like Paul de Man, another representative of deconstructive thinking—Strauss thus complicates a distinction between political-philosophical and literary works. On Strauss and de Man, see Cantor, "Leo Strauss and Contemporary Hermeneutics."

8. Strauss, *Persecution*, 30.

9. Leo Strauss, "Three Waves of Modernity," in Leo Strauss, *An Introduction to Political Philosophy: Ten Essays*, ed., Hilail Gildin (Chicago: University of Chicago Press), 98. Strauss's relationship to liberalism has been a flashpoint in the last decade; see, e.g., my "From Anti-Liberal to Untimely Liberal: Leo Strauss's Two Critiques of Liberalism," *Philosophy and Social Criticism*, 36 (2010): 157–181; Nicholas Xenos, *Cloaked in Virtue: Unveiling Leo Strauss and The Rhetoric of American Foreign Policy* (New York: Routledge, 2008); Peter Minowitz, *Straussophobia: Defending Leo Strauss and Straussians against Shadia Drury and Other Accusers* (Lanham, MD: Lexington Books, 2008); Stephen B. Smith, *Reading Leo Strauss: Politics, Philosophy, Judaism* (Chicago: University of Chicago Press, 2006); Steven B. Smith, "Leo Strauss's Platonic Liberalism," *Political Theory* 28 (2000): 787–809; Catherine H. Zuckert and Michael Zuckert, *The Truth about Leo Strauss: Political Philosophy and American Democracy* (Chicago: University of Chicago Press, 2006); Shadia B. Drury, *The Political Ideas of Leo Strauss* (London:

Palgrave-MacMillan, 2005); and Anne Norton, *Leo Strauss and the Politics of American Empire* (New Haven, CT: Yale University Press, 2004).

10. I use the ambiguous term "movement" deliberately: In his "Letter to a Japanese Friend," Derrida insists that deconstruction is not a "method," "act," or "operation." It is, in short, not something that one *does* but rather something that unfolds when one examines, say, a philosophical text. Jacques Derrida, "Letter to a Japanese Friend," in *Derrida and Différance*, eds., David Wood and Robert Bernasconi (Evanston, IL: Northwestern University Press, 1988). On the other hand, to the extent that "deconstruction" is identifiable as both a school of literary criticism—involving figures like de Man, J. Hills Miller, and others—and a constellation of politico-philosophical gestures that excavate the repressed, "the movement of deconstruction" also refers to this interpretive approach.

11. Jacques Derrida, *Of Grammatology*, trans., Gayatri Chakravorty Spivak (Baltimore: Johns Hopkins University Press, 1967).

12. Spivak, "Translator's Preface," in Derrida's *Of Grammatology*, lxix; on Derrida and Saussure, see, e.g., Geoffrey Bennington, "Saussure and Derrida," in Carol Sanders, ed., *The Cambridge Companion to Saussure* (Cambridge, UK: Cambridge University Press, 2004).

13. Derrida, *Of Grammatology*, 61.

14. Spivak, "Preface," xvii.

15. Ibid., lxx.

16. See also Jacques Derrida, "Freud and the Scene of Writing," trans., Jeffrey Mehlman, *Yale French Studies* 48 (1972), 74–117.

17. Spivak, "Preface," lxx.

18. Jacques Derrida, *The Other Heading: Reflections on Today's Europe* (Bloomington: Indiana University Press, 1992).

19. Jacques Derrida, *Who's Afraid of Philosophy? Right to Philosophy I* (Stanford, CA: Stanford University Press, 2002).

20. Strauss, *Persecution*, 7.

21. Ibid., 17.

22. Ibid., 18.

23. Ibid., 24.

24. Ibid., 25.

25. Leo Strauss, *The Argument and Action of Plato's Laws* (Chicago: University of Chicago Press, 1975). For discussions of esoteric writing in Strauss and beyond, see, e.g., Paul J. Bagely, "On the Practice of Esotericism," *Journal of the History of Ideas* 53 (1992): 231–247; Arthur M. Melzer, "Esotericism and the Critique of Historicism," *American Political Science Review* 100 (2006): 279–295; and Michael Frazer, "Esotericism Ancient and Modern: Strauss Contra Straussianism on the Art of Political-Philosophical Writing," *Political Theory* 34 (2006): 31–61.

26. Jacques Derrida, *Dissemination*, trans., Barbara Johnson (Chicago: University of Chicago Press, 1983), 63.

27. Ibid., 95. On the *pharmakon* in Derrida, see Walter Brogan, "Plato's *Pharmakon:* Between Two Repititions," in *Derrida and Deconstruction*, ed., Hugh J. Silverman (London: Routledge Press, 1989).

28. Ibid., 95; on systems in Derrida, see Christopher Johnson, *System and Writing in the Philosophy of Jacques Derrida* (Cambridge, UK: Cambridge University Press, 1993).

29. Jacques Derrida, *Writing and Difference*, trans., Alan Bass (London: Routledge and Keegan Paul, 1980), 285.

30. On authorship and "the death of the author" in Derrida, see, e.g., Séan Burke, *The Death and Return of the Author: Criticism and Subjectivity in Barthes, Foucault, and Derrida* (Edinburgh, UK: Edinburgh University Press, 1998).

31. Jacques Derrida, *The Other Heading*; Jacques Derrida, *Spectres of Marx: The State of Debt, The Work of Mourning, and The New International*, trans., Gregory Collins (London: Verso Press, 1997); Jacques Derrida, *On Cosmopolitanism and Forgiveness* (London: Routledge, 2003); Jacques Derrida, *Rogues: Two Essays on Reason*, trans., Pascale-Anne Brault and Michael Naas (Stanford, CA: Stanford University Press, 2005).

32. On Derrida's aporetic politics, see Richard Beardsworth, *Derrida and the Political* (New York: Routledge, 1996).

33. For a well-known example of this charge, see Mark Lilla, *The Reckless Mind: Intellectuals in Politics* (New York: *New York Review of Books*, 2001).

34. Strauss, "Three Waves," 98.

35. Derrida, *Spectres of Marx*.

36. Jacques Derrida, *Of Spirit: Heidegger and the Question*, trans., Geoffrey Bennington and Rachel Bowlby (Chicago: University of Chicago Press, 1991).

37. Strauss, *Persecution*, 47.

38. Ibid.

39. On Strauss and Maimonides, see Kenneth Hart Green, *Jew and Philosopher: The Return to Maimonides in the Jewish Thought of Leo Strauss* (Albany, NY: SUNY Press, 1993).

40. Strauss, *Persecution*, 41.

41. Ibid.

42. Ibid.

43. Derrida, *Dissemination*, 95.

44. Thus scholars like Paul Cantor are wrong to claim that deconstruction "attempts to sever the text from the author's intention and to give it, as it were, a life of its own." See Paul Cantor, "Leo Strauss and Contemporary Hermeneutics," 279. This is wrong, first, because as I just showed Derrida does *not* sever intention and text entirely; and second, because a text, just like its interpreters, is caught in the play of language.

45. This is hardly surprising given Derrida's own analyses of the trace in *Writing and Difference* and *Of Grammatology*. Derrida uses that notion to resist what he has called a metaphysics of presence. See Derrida, *Of Grammatology*, and Derrida, *Writing and Difference*.

46. Derrida, *Dissemination*, 95.

47. Ibid., 96.

48. Ibid.

49. Ibid.

50. Strauss, *Persecution*, 26, my emphasis. That he emphasized the presentation of views suggests that he thought the questions themselves were left mainly intact.

51. Ibid.

52. Strauss, quoted in Zuckert, *Postmodern Platos*, 123.

53. On Derrida's Socratic inclinations, see, e.g., McCormick, "Derrida on Law."

54. On philosophical humility in Strauss, see Schiff, "From Antiliberal to Untimely Liberal."

55. Derrida, *Who's Afraid of Philosophy?*, 12–13.

56. Ibid., 13.

57. Ibid., 14.

2

Purloined Letters—Lacan *avec* Strauss

Matthew J. Sharpe

> A similar difficulty confronts the political writer who has disagreeable truths to tell to those in authority. If he presents them undisguised, the authorities will suppress his words. . . . A writer must beware of the censorship, and on its account he must soften and distort the expression of his opinion . . . he finds himself compelled either merely to refrain from certain forms of attack, or to speak in allusions in place of direct references, or he must conceal his objectionable pronouncement beneath some apparently innocent disguise: for instance, he may describe a dispute between two Mandarins in the Middle Kingdom, when the people he really has in mind are officials in his own country.
>
> —Sigmund Freud, *Interpretation of Dreams*[1]

Perry Mason and Poe: The Effects of Truth on Desire

After his emigration to the United States, Leo Strauss is said to have warmed to only a few of the artefacts of that nation's profuse culture industries. One of these was the popular television program *Perry Mason*. *Perry Mason*'s eponymous hero was a detective and defense attorney who specialized in defending accused murderers. Strauss's sympathy with Perry Mason reflects his wider love of the detective genre. And, as his friend Alexandre Kojêve was the first to venture,[2] this literary, filmic, and televisual genre could stand as an incisive metaphor for what Strauss remains most famous for, certainly in the academic world. We mean

Strauss's famous claim to have discovered that all great philosophers up to Machiavelli, if not beyond, wrote esoteric texts.[3] On their surface, there is a salutary message, tailored to edify and appease the moral, political, and metaphysical opinions of the authors' day. However, if we read these texts carefully, as a sleuth might, a hidden set of meanings opens up before our suspicious eyes. Strauss himself did not dissuade this comparison of his mode of reading and what it uncovers with the interpretive arts of a detective. Near the heart of Strauss's programmatic "What is Political Philosophy?," Strauss indeed directly compares Hobbes and Machiavelli, the two figures he at different periods believed founded "modernity," to characters from a famous modern detective story. "If you wish, you may compare Hobbes to Sherlock Holmes and Machiavelli to Professor Moriarty," Strauss opines. "For certainly Hobbes took justice much more seriously than Machiavelli had done."[4]

In 1966, when Jacques Lacan was persuaded to publish a collection of his writings from the previous three decades, the renowned French psychoanalyst chose to open his *Écrits* with an adapted transcript from his 1952–1953 seminar (*Seminar II: The Ego in Freud's Theory*). The subject, again, was a famous detective story, Edgar Allan Poe's *The Purloined Letter*. In Poe's story Lacan claims to see represented, as in a "fable," the truth of the enigmatic notion of the compulsion to repeat (*Wiederholung*), central to the post-war Freud's uncanny notion of the death drive.[5] "The Purloined Letter," Lacan claims, "demonstrates in a story the major determination the subject receives from the itinerary of a signifier."[6] Hence, it points to the heart of Lacan's reclaiming of "the meaning of Freud" by way of Saussurian and Jacobsonian linguistics, and the anthropology of Claude Lévi-Strauss.[7]

In fact, Poe's unusual story has more resonances with Lacan's thought, and Leo Strauss's, than this. First, Poe's story indeed turns around a letter, albeit one whose content is never disclosed. However, the situation in which it is "purloined" promises that this letter must express the Queen's hidden, subversive desire. And it is a Minister or royal advisor, D[8], who in the first narrated scene has the presence of mind to filch the letter. The drama is hence one of the highest political rank, to evoke Straussian language. Its stake is *Basileia*, the authority of or behind the throne.[9] Poe's purloined letter is therefore like the esoteric claims of the premodern philosophers, as Strauss proposes that we read them, and whose *Eros* for the truth meant that they had to partly conceal or "play down" their most subversive claims.

In light of Jacques Lacan's and Leo Strauss's shared willingness to identify their interpretive endeavors with those of a detective, it is perhaps surprising that no one to date has systematically compared their teachings. For these sleuthing vignettes point to a series of more substantial and far-reaching intellectual comparisons. Leo Strauss, for his part, writes twice on Freud and Judaism, once near the beginning of his career (with some sympathy) and once near toward the end of his career (more openly critically).[10] In the sole reference either thinker makes directly to the other, Lacan directs his students to Strauss's 1948 work *Persecution and the Art of Writing* in his programmatic piece on the Freudian unconscious, "The Instance of the Letter in the Unconscious":

> It's worth taking the time to read a book in which Leo Strauss . . . reflects on the relations between the art of writing and persecution. By honing in on the sort of co-naturality that this art has to this condition, he allows us to glimpse something that imposes its form here, in the effect of truth on desire.[11]

The reader of Strauss with Lacan, certainly, cannot but be struck by the resonances between the primary processes Freud attributed to the unconscious and many of the techniques Strauss attributes to the "forgotten kind of writing" of Maimonides, Farabi and Halevi, then the ancients and certain moderns.[12] Freud had explicitly predicated his understanding of the psyche upon political metaphors. The unconscious consists of wishes and beliefs that have been repressed as by a political "censor," since they oppose the ego's conscious self-image. To understand the mechanisms of the dream work, one should envisage a political author or cartoonist who strives to publicize officially contraband opinions.[13] Just so, Strauss first presents the necessity for esoteric writing on the basis of the need of philosophers in closed societies to avoid persecution.[14] The esoteric techniques these great writers have used are there to avoid such censorship, and to indicate their true beliefs to careful readers able to read between the lines: by dropping "hints," making "blunders," cultivating "contradictions," leaving "slight omissions or additions," and proffering "insignificant variations" upon repeated claims.[15] Freud had taught that the truth is only ever half said, as Lacan would put it: half-said in "flashes,"[16] exceptional slips, symptomatic actions, dreams, the ravings of the mad; wishes and fears projected onto others, or in the plays of wit.[17] Just so,

Strauss comments that his hypothesis "would then be good reason for our finding in the greatest literature of the past so many interesting devils, madmen, beggars, sophists, drunkards, epicureans and buffoons."[18]

Then there is the near-psychoanalytic attention Strauss asks his readers to pay to "ambiguous words" such as "rank," "virtue," "secret,"[19] "tyranny,"[20] "the wise,"[21] "wisdom"[22] or "moderation," and "courage" in revered thinkers. Are these not precisely what Freud calls *condensations*—words in whose double address Lacan espies the "poetic spark" of metaphor?[23] And when Strauss insists that an author may conceal his true opinion by placing it in inconspicuous places, like in the middle of a list, work or chapter,[24] or in "interruptions"[25] and "digressions," not to say in the mouths of "disreputable characters" such as Plato's Thrasymachus,[26] is Strauss not pointing to the same mechanisms Freud had approached under the heading of *displacement*, the principal means of distortion in the dream?

Mutatis mutandis, does not Freud's (and then Lacan's) unlikely insistence that nothing in the psyche is without reason—down to the most seemingly incidental slip—remind the reader of Strauss's postulation of a "logographic necessity" in philosophical texts—a supposition that "every word," title, chapter heading, example, and ordering of examples in careful writers is necessarily placed exactly where it is?[27] Lacan suggests directly that the formations of the unconscious represent nothing so much as the rhetorical devices of the classical and premodern authors of interest to Strauss:

> Periphrasis, hyperbaton, ellipsis, suspension, anticipation, retraction, negation, digression, and irony (Quintilian's *figurae sententiarum*), just as catechresis, litotes, antonomasia, and hypertosis are the tropes whose names strike me as the most appropriate ones with which to label these mechanisms.[28]

If we look beyond this shared interest of Lacan's and Strauss's in rhetoric and esotericism—and beyond the parallels in their equally divided receptions[29]—however, we find striking biographical and intellectual comparisons between Strauss and Lacan. Both thinkers came to prominence relatively late, and at around the same time, in the early 1950s. Strauss came from an Orthodox Jewish background; Lacan was educated by the Jesuits. Both appear to have lost their faiths by adolescence. Both were young admirers of Spinoza,[30] and were profoundly shaped by the thought of Martin Heidegger.[31] Both Lacan and Strauss attended Alexandre

Kojève's famous lectures on Hegel's *Phenomenology of Geist* in Paris in the 1930s. Both men maintained a lifelong friendship with the eccentric, self-professing Sage—in Strauss's case, despite his forced emigration to the New World.[32] Unusually in twentieth century thought, both Lacan and Strauss elevated a concern for the Law, and its relationship with human desire, to the center of their respective intellectual itineraries.[33] As the crowning apex of these parallel trajectories, Strauss and Lacan gave nearly contemporary seminars on Plato's *Symposium* in 1959–1960 and 1960–1961, respectively in Paris and Chicago—seminars in which each looked to this ancient text on *Eros* to stake out fundamental orientations for their respective endeavors[34]; and in which each concurrently sought out a "primitive Plato" allegedly hidden under layers of Christian reinterpretations of the pagan philosopher.[35]

Contemporary authors such as Jonathan Lear have noted the putative similarities between psychoanalysis and the classical philosophy to which Strauss advocated we should return.[36] Freud himself was keen to emphasize a Platonic heritage, in the *Symposium*, for his own expanded notion of *Eros* in *The Three Essays on Sexuality* of 1905.[37] Plato's Socrates and many of his admirers repeat that, as medicine is for the body, so philosophy should be for the soul: a "therapy of desire" or psycho-therapy that operates by means of thought and speech.[38] Its goal, like Freud's, was precisely that *Eros* should *not* "live like a tyrant" within the enlightened individual, enslaving their reason—rather, where the untamed "id" of the passions was, *logos* should come to be.[39] Of equal importance, psychoanalysis as a *praxis* of "talking cure" also recalls the Socratic aspiration—one that recognizes that the truth at issue here is one that does not abstract from, but *expresses*, the *erotes* of the analysand.[40] Throughout his career, in fact, Lacan would distinguish between "reality," the object of positive knowledge, and the *truth* of concern to psychoanalysis, which by contrast implicates the subjectivity of the knower, her "position of enunciation."[41] Jürgen Braungardt, in an important article, notes that what is most decisive for Lacan, epistemically, is accordingly the opposition of *truth versus lie*, rather than the concern for true versus untrue reportage of states of affairs.[42]

So, here again, a close proximity to Strauss and his reception presents itself. Lacan indeed suggests that analysts must learn how to modulate the traditional definition of truth, *adequatio intellectus et rei*, by hearing the genitive *reus*, "meaning the party in a lawsuit, specifically the accused, and metaphorically he who has incurred a debt . . ."[43]

The Arts of Writing and Their Vicissitudes

It will go without saying that Lacan and Strauss were both immensely cultured men. Strauss's *oeuvre* involves a series of readings of Hesiod, Thucydides, Plato, Aristotle, Farabi, Averroes and Avicenna, Halevi, Maimonides, Machiavelli, Hobbes, Spinoza, and Lessing—and this list is not comprehensive. Lacan for his part reminds prospective analysts that Freud had prescribed "the history of civilisation, mythology, the psychology of religions, literary history, and literary criticism" for the curriculum of his ideal psychoanalyst.[44] To this list, Lacan in his programmatic "Rome discourse" adds "rhetoric, dialectics (in the classical sense . . .), grammar and poetics"[45] as well as linguistics, anthropology, philosophy, game theory and related species of mathematics.[46] Some of the anxiety Lacan's and Strauss's works provokes surely comes from the fact that, to adequately judge their claims, a reader would seemingly need to be somewhere *near* so encyclopedically erudite. Indeed, it is one undeniable merit of their works to have inspired students to read great old books for themselves that might otherwise have remained for them dead letters.

But let me also now address briefly the specifically polemical difficulty of entering into the debates surrounding the legacies of Lacan and Strauss. Following the advent of the "war on terror" led by George W. Bush's neoconservative administration, debates concerning the teaching of Leo Strauss have become the unlikely stuff of mainstream media and political discussion, particularly in the United States.[47] Responding to the influence Strauss had on several political figures associated with neoconservatism, critics have accused Strauss and his students of sponsoring a secret teaching of tyrannical rule by self-professed "wise" leaders; of being metaphysical nihilists who "cloak" themselves in the virtuous rhetoric of "natural right"[48]; of teaching an intellectually irresponsible elitism to the young, and a "black reaction" against liberalism and modernity; and more.[49] In short, we are asked to consider that Strauss's bold thoughts on Machiavelli were not written in criticism of the Florentine patriot, but from an esoteric identification with the Florentine's metapolitical daring:

> If he is an unarmed prophet, or a captain without an army who must recruit his army by means of his books, he must first recruit the highest officers directly responsible to him and commissioned by him. Owing to "the envious nature of men" he cannot expect to find his first adherents among the men of his own generation. He can come to his own only

> after the natural death of his generation, the generation of the desert, as it were. He must appeal to the elite among the coming generations.[50]

Central to Strauss's critics' charges, and to the comparable charges facing Lacan of corrupting the youth, is the claim that Lacan and Strauss were not only discovers of the esoteric arts of writing or the formations of the unconscious. They are arraigned for having themselves practiced or mimicked these indirect, "parabolic or enigmatic"[51] modes of communication. Lacan has a well-earned reputation of being among the most otiose and difficult of authors. When he hired a stenographer in the late 1960s to transcribe his spoken seminars, she was told by well-meaning advisors: "Don't go there, he speaks Chinese!"[52] Lacan's texts, indeed, contain many of the features Strauss teaches that esoteric writers have always used enigmas (e.g., "there is no sexual rapport," "Woman does not exist," "theologians are the only true atheists"); prosopopoeia (most famously, letting first "truth" herself, then a table and a lectern, address the audience in "The Freudian Thing"); ambiguous genitives ("desire is the desire of the other"); long and convoluted sentences; and ambiguous terms that condense multiple chains of inferences inscrutable except to initiates (e.g., "the signifier," "phallus," "the Other," and the famous "mathemes": S1, a, $, I(O) S2, etc.). Lacan casually alludes to classical myths, literature, Freudian case studies, and episodes from the history of philosophy, leaving his audience to guess or chase down the signification.[53]

In "Position of the Unconscious" within the *Écrits*, indeed, Lacan claims a Platonic heritage for his esoteric manner of communicating.[54] His seminars aimed to "bring forth" the "place" where the truth of the unconscious might speak, Lacan explains. It is a matter of "opening more than one ear to hear things that would have been passed over indifferently since they would not have been recognised." He then adds:

> The place in question is the entrance to the cave, towards the exit of which Plato guides us, while one imagines the psychoanalyst entering there. But things are not that easy, as it is an entrance one can only reach just as it closes (the place will never be popular with tourists), and the only way to open it up a bit is by calling from the inside.[55]

As for the "puzzling" effect his discourse creates:

> I have always considered myself accountable for such an effect and, while unequal to the task of guarding against it [*d'y parer*], it was the secret prowess of each of my "seminars." / For the people who came to hear me are not the first communicants Plato exposed to Socrates' questioning. / . . . Of their "philosophy classes," most have retained but a grab-bag of phrases—a catechism gone haywire—which anaesthetises them from being surprised by truth. / They are thus even more easily preyed upon by prestige operations, and by the ideals of high personalism by which civilisation presses them to live beyond their means. / Intellectual means, that is.[56]

The issue of whether Leo Strauss wrote esoterically is less manifestly clear than is the case of Lacan. Reading Strauss's work, indeed, one can sometimes hear the echo of Lacan's Delphic adage that "the signifier represents the subject for another signifier," whereas the subject herself always remains undisclosed. Strauss certainly "avails himself of the immunity of the commentator" or the "historian," devices he ascribes to Farabi, Maimonides and Xenophon.[57] Rarely do we read in Strauss directly his own opinions stated in the first person—and Strauss no less than Lacan, draws our attention to the importance of the use of pronouns, and the first-person singular pronoun in particular.[58] The texts, if not the style, are the man.

As Catherine and Michael Zuckert have pointed out, there is also an apparent contradiction involved in attributing esotericism to Leo Strauss. For Strauss, in *Persecution and the Art of Writing* and elsewhere, is surely the man who outed the secrets of esoteric writing in others. It would be enigmatic indeed if Strauss were then to have practiced the same esoteric means he had publicly broadcast.[59] Yet the paradox here arguably goes somewhat deeper than the Zuckerts present things in their central chapter of *The Truth of Leo Strauss*. On the one hand, one criterion Strauss indicates as to when the historian or philosopher can cautiously assume that an author has written esoterically is when the author, however casually, discusses the possibility and means of writers' concealing their true opinions.[60] Strauss most certainly does this. He also suggests in *Persecution and the Art of Writing* that a person writes as they read, and that careful readers are careful writers.[61] But Leo Strauss, all can agree, was nothing if not an exacting reader.

The careful reader of Leo Strauss cannot help but note that Strauss does not wholly discourage the hypothesis that he applies the techniques he discerns in Maimonides, Farabi, Xenophon, Machiavelli, Plato, Lessing, and Spinoza.[62] Strauss draws attention to his own diversions with a series of tell-tale phrases: "returning once more to the surface,"[63] "however that may be," "certain it is that . . ." He often avails himself of qualifiers ("perhaps," "could it be that . . .") to simultaneously state, while distancing himself from, exceptional propositions.[64] Strauss's paragraphs, more intriguingly, are often as unconventionally long (many run several pages, notably in *Thoughts on Machiavelli*) as Lacan's are often unconventionally short. This observation encourages the notion, duly adopted by some students and commentators, that these paragraphs should be read as artfully devised, significantly numbered sections.[65]

Then there is the role played by the centers of Strauss's texts, which seem to answer Strauss's directives for reading esoteric writings. In Strauss's *On Tyranny*, the central chapter thus exposes "The Teaching concerning Tyranny" and its allegedly theoretical justification or legitimacy, if the leader is wise or advised by wise counsellors—which stands in striking contrast to Strauss's opening declarations concerning the dire state of the modern social sciences, since they are unable to see tyranny for what it is.[66] The central pages of *Natural Right and History* gives voice to Plato's and Aristotle's controversial, putative teachings concerning the right or justice of government by wise leaders, given the limits of positive Law.[67] Strauss's opening, "old fashioned" denunciation of Machiavelli as a "teacher of evil" in *Thoughts on Machiavelli*, meanwhile, is qualified by Strauss's repeated praise for the Florentine's "perverted nobility of a high rank," and his "beautiful" and "very artful" writing.[68] Strauss often tells us that he will present certain ideas only "at their proper place," without further indicating why this place is proper, or where exactly it is.[69]

Many commentators have hence contended that the mature Leo Strauss came to practice esoteric writing at some point after his arrival in the liberal-modern United States. The heated debates concerning this matter are their own eloquent testimony to this possibility. However, in James Rhodes's closing words on Leo Strauss in *Eros, Wisdom, and Silence*, let me add here a disclaimer:

> If I have erred in my interpretation, and if I have been mistaken . . . I greatly regret it. I have two additional things to say. First, considering the vitriolic debates about Strauss's intentions that have raged among his students, I clearly will not be the first to have gone astray. Second, if a brilliant man deliberately writes in order to prevent people from

understanding him, there is an excellent chance that he will succeed in achieving this aim.[70]

The Ancient and the Modern

The greatest, indeed insuperable difference between Lacan and Strauss concerns how they orient themselves with regard to the famous *querelle* between the ancients and the moderns. Strauss, we know, became convinced shortly after the appearance of his first book on *Spinoza's Critique of Religion* that a theoretical, if not practical, return to premodern political philosophy was possible and necessary.[71] One component of his work is therefore a powerful re-narration of modern political thought. It is fair to say that Strauss seeks, in the guise of the historian of ideas, to undermine modern political thought's claims to legitimacy. Choosing a Platonic metaphor Strauss thus talks of "three waves" of modernity, remaining silent in this piece about the meaning of the third wave in the *Republic*.[72] The third wave of modernity, beginning with Nietzsche, culminates in metaphysical nihilism, ethical or political relativism, epistemological historicism, and proclamations of "the end of philosophy."[73] On Strauss's telling, however, modernity or modern thought—for Strauss does not strongly distinguish the two—culminates in this lamentable terminus on the basis of inner necessities operating far above the heads or intentions of its philosophical protagonists. Strauss traces these necessities back to the philosophical revolution he sees inaugurated by Niccolò Machiavelli[74]—all this, just as if he were an historicizing thinker who understands the moderns better than they understood themselves, rather than a categorical anti-historicist.[75]

However that may be, Jacques Lacan's psychoanalytic teachings can only show up in Strauss's narrative as a pre-eminently *modern* position. Machiavelli inaugurated "modernity," according to Strauss, by setting his back against the classical solutions to the questions of political philosophy and ignoring the superior possibility of the contemplative or philosophical *bios*. Near the center of *The Prince*, in his fifteenth chapter, Machiavelli famously renounces ancient political thought for imagining principalities that can exist in speech alone. The task for his new political teaching will be to cease striving after such improbable virtues and achievements. As the modern natural sciences were soon to also teach, we cannot know men's final, highest ends: whether rational contemplation or obedience to the revealed Word of God. Lowering our standards, therefore,[76] we should aim for achievable models of better commonwealths or principalities. *Fortuna* or chance hence replaces providence or the divine rule of the cosmos in modern philosophy. But *fortuna*, who Machiavelli supposes is a woman, can be actively conquered, at least much of the time.[77] In order to secure this conquest, the modern prince should begin with how human beings are, rather than how philosophers or priests have opined that they *ought* to be. The origins of human civilization lie not in divine plenty but in scarcity, fear, or "Terror."[78] Human beings can no longer take their moral standards from nature, and transcendent revelation is increasingly subject to crippling forms of epistemic skepticism: Montaigne's "what do I know?" Given the insufficiency of the original "state of nature," human beings should henceforth take aim at *progress* into the future. The natural sciences, subservient to the end of relieving the human estate, thereby supplant philosophy's premodern, essentially private or contemplative calling. The need to craft ever more total institutions "with teeth in them"[79] replaces education to virtue as the lawmaker's principal preoccupation. What is new and young replaces the old as what is highest or best. History takes on new import as the unfolding testament to the progress of the human spirit, rather than as a compendium of elevated ancient models and commonplaces. The exceptional and demotic *virtu* of courage (and later, forms of "authenticity") supplants the aristocratic virtues of moderation or contemplation.[80] In Machiavelli, the founder or new prince should be unafraid to use lawmaking violence, and is declared to have "the most exalted" status.[81] In Hobbes, society itself is engendered on the basis of pre-political individuals in the state of nature, their natural rights to self-preservation, and their bankable fear of violent death.[82]

With these Machiavellian parameters of Strauss's moderns in mind, it is hard not to see in Lacanian psychoanalysis a particularly pure embodiment of all that Strauss manifestly opposed. This opposition would explain Strauss's lasting silence concerning psychoanalysis as a whole, despite working amidst its twentieth-century heyday in the United States.[83] Psychoanalysis' exceptional founder, Sigmund Freud,[84] famously positioned his claim that man is not the master even over his own psyche as a third modern blow to human beings' prescientific narcissism, following Copernicus in astronomy and Darwin in biology.[85] Science, to whose *Weltanschauung* Freud wished to subordinate "the talking cure," is the most far-reaching triumph possible for human beings over wish-fulfilling fantasy. Preeminent among the things psychoanalysis thereby challenges are religious "illusions" led by the politico-theological claims of the great monotheisms.[86] To live truthfully may not make us happy. But modern science and its "probity" ought for Freud to be sufficient, if only to "transform neurotic misery into common unhappiness."[87]

Lacan in no way challenges these fundamental Freudian orientations. He radicalizes them. In the beginning was the human infant's uniquely long postnatal dependence on its first others: psychoanalysis' state of nature.[88] Next comes the primary narcissism of toddlers, always verging on rivalrous aggressiveness.[89] The child's lasting helplessness means that culture—and what Lacan will call "the discourse of the Other"—marks itself earlier and more deeply in human being and desire than has been previously fathomed. The decisive episode in bringing this desire to order, and repressing its most aberrant predilections, is the Oedipus complex and its resolution through the acceptance of "symbolic castration," with the assumption of the patronym or "name of the father." Henceforth, the subject can no longer demand instant satisfactions from the (m)Other, or more widely. S/he must seek out the echoes of her/his lost fantasmatic unity with this first Other through speech, subject to the social Law governing the relations between the sexes and generations, founded upon the prohibition of incest. The subject's always-transgressive desire will now reveal itself only in exceptional moments—through slips, inhibitions, anxieties, dreams, repetitions, and theatrical symptomatic actings-out. It is difficult to think of a central Lacanian notion—whether the name of the father, the phallus, the subject, the act, *objet petit a* or *sinthome*—that does not direct our attention to what "sticks out" from the symbolic order that ordinarily governs how subjects communicate and see themselves. Each of these notions points to an "*extimité*," as Lacan puns—exceptional instances that nevertheless shape the most intimate core of subjects as speaking beings alienated from their own deepest desires and separated from the Real object of those desires by the order of social Law.

Psychoanalysis for Lacan then should in no way renounce its Freudian adherence to the disillusioned worldview of modern science.[90] The subject of psychoanalysis, the later Lacan will instead insist, is the subject of modern science. The famous mathemes are therefore advertised as belonging to a lineage that Lacan traces back to the Keplerian and Newtonian mathematizations of celestial mechanics. They aim to cut through all imaginary misrecognitions—that the world is fundamentally a harmonious, sphere-like Whole; or that mind and world, or the two sexes, exist in a complementary relationship. It is a matter of codifying with maximal impersonality what Lacan called the Real and its effects on human subjectivity.[91] Lacan never ceded his commitment to unveiling this uncomfortable truth, even though he was also as arguably dour and conservative as his master when it came to assessing the prospect that human beings will ever conquer the *Unbehagen* in civilization, or the human "passion for ignorance."[92] The view Marlowe attributed to Machiavelli that was cited by Strauss—"I hold there to be no sin but ignorance"[93]—also applies very well to Jacques Lacan.

To complete this section, let me underscore here what many readers will have for some time been wanting to interject. Strauss's hypothesis concerning esoteric writing points to a conscious, fully intentional, deployment of the rhetorical devices of esoteric writing by a few great writers.[94] Lacan's own esotericism notwithstanding, Lacanian psychoanalysis, by contrast, accepts in full both the Freudian postulate of the unconscious and its demotic implications[95] when it comes to where we the truth of human desire is to be found:

> It is especially necessary to the scholar, the sage, and even the quack, to be the only one who knows. The idea that deep within the simplest of souls—and what's more, in the sickest—there is something ready to blossom is one thing. But that there may be someone who seems to know as much as them about what we ought to make of it . . . It is not fitting that these country bumpkins should keep us breathless by posing enigmas to us that prove overly clever.[96]

Psychoanalysis, that is, also continues what Strauss located as a modern tendency to view the high—the human excellences, the achievements of poetry, philosophy, politics, and religion—from the perspective of the low, if not the common. Strauss comments that it is "safer" to view things from the perspective of the high because seeing the base from this perspective does not denature the base, whereas the same does not hold for forms of reductionism.[97] In reply to this, on one hand, intellectual probity cannot accept a cautionary argument by itself. No psychoanalyst, and few philosophers, will take a recommendation as to the safety of an opinion as binding upon an assessment of its truth. On the other hand, Lacan himself offers us this characteristically paradoxical riposte concerning Freud's central interest in the ostensibly "vulgar" subject of sexuality:

> The intolerable scandal when Freudian sexuality was not yet holy was that it was so "intellectual." It was in this respect that it showed itself to be the worthy stooge of all those terrorists whose plots were going to ruin society.[98]

Progress or Return?

There would then be little value for any scholar venturing a comparative study of Leo Strauss and Jacques Lacan in underplaying the fundamental differences between the two men. Such a study would also have to be very careful before it attempted, as Lacan did with "Kant avec Sade," to claim that one of these thinkers gives "the truth" of the other, in something like the manner that a symptom bespeaks the repressed truth of a person's subjectivity.[99] Ecumenism is for the "feeble-minded," Lacan once opined, ridiculing liberal Catholicism with a characteristic, anti-dialectical bravura that echoes Strauss's lifelong, arguably post-Nietzschean opposition to all mediating "internalisations" of fundamental alternatives whether of ancient and modern, Athens and Jerusalem, poetry or philosophy, or philosophy and "the city."[100]

Nevertheless, there can be little question that Strauss and Lacan were two of the most influential thinkers of the twentieth century, and that their extraordinary itineraries were in many ways meaningfully convergent. We future generations are still, in some ways, trying to catch up with their untimely provocations. Perhaps most of all, Lacan and Strauss stand out beside myriad other thinkers of the last hundred years, who limited themselves to accounts of one or other particular subject—of language, interpretation, or some text author or texts. More ambitious than this, Lacan and Strauss can be read as presenting two fundamentally alternative accounts of the meaning of the whole, or at least the whole of *ta anthrôpina*. Freudian and Lacanian psychoanalysis are almost unique in the human sciences of the last century in proffering a full-fledged, modern alternative to the visions of the human condition proffered by the ancient philosophers and the monotheistic religions. In how many other twentieth-century thinkers, it can be asked, do we find devoted interrogations into the relationship between literature and philosophy, comedy and tragedy, Athens and Jerusalem, desire and the law, Judaism and Christianity, and the ancients and the moderns? For both Lacan and Strauss, moreover, the stakes of returning to these fundamental issues were *actuel*, as the French say:

> It is not self-forgetting and pain-loving antiquarianism nor self-forgetting and intoxicating romanticism which induces us to turn with passionate interest, with unqualified willingness to learn, toward the political thought of classical antiquity. We are impelled to do by the crisis of our time, the crisis of the West.[101]

Lacan indeed sometimes maintained that the ultimate stake of psychoanalysis involved "nothing less than the recreation of human meaning in an arid era of scientism."[102] This is why, echoing Strauss, after conceding that the subjects (rhetoric, dialectic, poetics, grammar, and *witz*) that he recommends for psychoanalysts in his Rome Discourse "may sound somewhat old-fashioned," Lacan too insists that "I would not hesitate to recommend them as a return to our sources."[103]

If we were to choose, therefore, one image for what a future examination of "Lacan avec Strauss" might aspire to, that image would come from Plato's *Republic*. Socrates has been talking of the relations between the accounts of justice in the individual soul and the city. Because his sight in these matters is so dim, Socrates ironizes, he is unable to espy justice unless he considers it first in the larger thing, the *polis*. So, he proposes a "comparative methodology" to Glaucon that will allow them, for the moment, to proceed. For:

> . . . it may be that, by examining [the two things] side by side and rubbing them against one another, as it were from the fire-stick we may cause the spark of justice to flash forth, and when it is thus revealed confirm it in our own minds.[104]

Notes

1. Sigmund Freud, *The Interpretation of Dreams*, trans. James Strachey (New York: Basic Books, 2010, 167). I dedicate this chapter to Dr. Daniel Townsend,

author of the PhD thesis *Leo Strauss and Islam*, available online at https://core.ac.uk/download/pdf/33199889.pdf.

2. Alexandre Kojève, "Tyranny and Wisdom," *On Tyranny* (Chicago: University of Chicago Press, 2000), 136n.

3. Leo Strauss, *Persecution and the Art of Writing*, 22–37.

4. Leo Strauss, "What Is Political Philosophy?," in *What Is Political Philosophy and Other Studies* (Chicago: University of Chicago Press, 1959), 48. In *Natural Right and History (Chicago: University of Chicago Press, 1965)*, Strauss writes that for Hobbes, "death insofar as man can do something about it, i.e., death insofar as it can be avoided or avenged, supplies the ultimate guidance." To this observation he affixes an enigmatic note (180, n18): "One would have to start from here to understand the role the detective story plays in present-day moral orientation."

5. Jacques Lacan, "Seminar on '*The Purloined Letter*,'" in *Écrits: The First Complete Edition in English*, trans. and ed. Bruce Fink (London: W. W. Norton & Sons, 2007), 6.

6. Ibid., 7.

7. Jacques Lacan, "The Freudian Thing," in *Écrits*, 334.

8. Whose name, as well as action, anticipate the detective Dupin, with whose "genius for solving enigmas" Lacan identifies the psychoanalyst; see Lacan, "Seminar," 10.

9. Lacan, "Seminar," 11; compare Leo Strauss, *Socrates and Aristophanes* (Chicago: University of Chicago Press, 1966), 188–189, with my "Publicising the Essentially Private: Leo Strauss' Platonic Aristophanes," *Symposium* 18, no. 2 (2015): 23. On Strauss's association of forbidden knowledge with a woman, then of Eve with the Greek *Mêtis*, see Leo Strauss, "Jerusalem and Athens," in *Studies in Platonic Political Philosophy* (Chicago: University of Chicago Press, 1983), 164; with Shadia Drury, *The Political Ideas of Leo Strauss* (London: Palgrave, 2005), 44–48, esp. 47.

10. Leo Strauss, "Sigmund Freud, The Future of an Illusion," in Michael Zank ed., *Leo Strauss: The Early Writings* (Albany, NY: SUNY Press, 2002), 202–211; "Freud on Moses and Monotheism," in Kenneth Hart Green, ed., *Jewish Philosophy and the Crisis of Modernity* (Albany, NY: SUNY Press, 1997), 285–310.

11. Jacques Lacan, "Instance of the Letter in the Freudian Unconscious," in *Écrits*, 412.

12. Leo Strauss, "On a Forgotten Kind of Writing," *What is Political Philosophy?*, 221–232.

13. Freud, *Interpretation of Dreams*, 167–168, 354, 532.

14. Strauss, *Persecution*, 22–24.

15. Leo Strauss, "The Literary Character of *The Guide for the Perplexed*," in *Persecution*, 53–54, 56 (on an esoteric interpretation of an esoteric text), 60–64.

16. See Jacques-Alain Miller, "The Symptom: Knowledge, Meaning and the Real," *The Symptom. Online Journal*, online at url: http://www.lacan.com/symptom7_articles/miller.html. Compare Strauss, "Literary Character," 63.

17. Strauss, "Literary Character," 66.

18. Strauss, *Persecution*, 36.

19. Strauss, "Literary Character," 57.

20. Leo Strauss, *Of Tyranny* (Chicago: University of Chicago Press, 2000), 75–77.

21. Strauss, "Literary Character," 72.

22. Strauss, Ibid., 81, 89.

23. Lacan, "Instance of the Letter," 422.

24. See Leo Strauss, *Thoughts on Machiavelli* (Chicago: University of Chicago Press, 1958), 52; *Persecution*, 24; "How to Study Spinoza's *Theologico-Political Treatise*," in *Persecution*, 184; *Studies in Platonic Political Philosophy*, 224; *What is Political Philosophy?*, 166; and *On Tyranny*, 275.

25. Strauss, "Literary Character," 61.

26. See Strauss, *Persecution*, 36.

27. Strauss, "Literary Character," 64, 69; *Thoughts on Machiavelli*, 121. Yet what, *mutatis mutandis*, should we make of Lacan's claim that analysts should learn to hear in "even the rest of a silence the whole lyrical development it stands for," if it is not an echo of Strauss's assertion that even the silences of the wise can be deafeningly important? (Strauss, "Literary Character," 79; See Jacques Lacan, "The Function and Field of Speech and Language in Psychoanalysis," in *Écrits*, 209).

28. Jacques Lacan, "The Direction of the Treatment and the Principles of Its Power," in *Écrits*, 521.

29. Then there are the comparable, unusually polemical receptions of the two figures. Both created schools of students devoted to comprehending their work and carrying forward their interpretive programs. Both Lacan and Strauss knew how to use bold rhetoric to discredit intellectual opponents: for Strauss, the contemporary social sciences and modern thought more widely; for Lacan, the post-Freudian, ego-psychological variants of psychoanalysis. Straussians and Lacanians are both accused by critics of obscurantism and sectarianism. Both Strauss's and Lacan's followers have split on how to interpret the teacher's legacy: there are thus East and West coast Straussians, as there are Millerian and non-Millerian Lacanians. There are in each case disenchanted former "insiders" (Anne Norton for Strauss, or with qualifications, Stanley Rosen and Lawrence Lampert; or, for Lacanians, Marcel Marini and Marie Pierrakos) as well as critics who present their critiques as exercises in "lifting the veils": Shadia Drury, Nicolas Xenos, Alan Gilbert, and William Altman for Straussians, and Alan Sokal and Jean Bricmont for Lacan.

30. For Lacan and Spinoza, see Elisabeth Roudinesco, *Jacques Lacan: Esquisse d'une vie, histoire d'un système de pensée* (Paris: Fayard, 1993), 29–31, 83–84, 93;

on Strauss and Spinoza, see my "*Che Vuoi?* Politico-Philosophical Remarks on Leo Strauss' Spinoza," *Bible and Critical Theory* 3, no. 3 (2007): 1–14.

31. See Stephen Smith, *Reading Leo Strauss: Politics, Philosophy, Judaism* (Chicago: University of Chicago Press, 2006), 328. Lacan translated Heidegger's later essay "Logos" into French, visited him (as did Strauss) in the Black Forest, and drove him around Paris. See William J. Richardson, "Towards the Future of Truth," *Heidegger and the Greeks: Interpretive Essays*, edited by Drew A. Hyland, John Panteleimon Manoussakis (Bloomington & Indianapolis: Indiana University Press, 2006), 95–96.

32. See Stanley Rosen, "Kojève's Paris," in *From Metaphysics in Ordinary Language* (New Haven, CT: Yale University Press, 1999).

33. See Leo Strauss, *Philosophy and Law: Essays Towards an Understanding of Maimonides and His Predecessors*, trans. Fred Baumann (Jewish Publication Society of America: Philadelphia, [1935] 1987).

34. Leo Strauss, "On Plato's *Symposium* (Chicago: University of Chicago Press, 2003); with Jacques Lacan, *Seminar VIII: On transference*, trans. Cormac Gallagher (London: Karnac, 2011), sessions I–XIII. See my "The Poetic Presentation of Philosophy: On Leo Strauss' *Symposium*," *Poetics Today* (2013) 34 (4): 563–603; with "Hunting Plato's Agalmata," *The European Legacy*, 14, no. 5 (2009): 535–547.

35. For Lacan, if Plato "has been understood differently" in the West than in the ways he seeks to recover, this is due to "the fact that Christian desire, which has so little to do with these [Platonic] adventures" has engendered a "complete misunderstanding." Jacques Lacan, *Seminar VIII: On transference*, trans. Cormac Gallagher (London: Karnac, 2011), session VI, 7. Compare Strauss on "primitive Platonism," in "On Plato's *Republic*," *City and Man* (Chicago: University of Chicago Press, 1964), 61.

36. See esp. Jonathan Lear, *Happiness, Death and the Remainder of Life* (London: Harvard University Press, 2002).

37. See Sigmund Freud, *Three Essays on Sexuality*, trans. J. Strachey, with a new foreword by Nancy Chodorow (New York: Basic Books, 2000), xxx. Cf. Plato, *Republic*, 360c, with 359c–360b and 571c–d).

38. See esp. Marcus Tullius Cicero, *Tusculan* Disputations, Proemia of books I & III. Cf. Martha Nussbaum, *The Therapy of Desire* (Princeton, NJ: Princeton University Press, 1994).

39. Plato, *Republic*, 574e.

40. Lacan, "Function and Field," 242.

41. Ibid., 213.

42. See Jürgen Braungardt, "Thinking versus Being: Lacan and Parmenides," at www-site http://braungardt.trialectics.com/projects/my-papers/lacan-parmenides, 6, and my "Killing the father, Parmenides: On Lacan's anti-philosophy," *Continental Philosophy Review* online first (2015), at www-site https://doi.org/10.1007/s11007-015-9330-8.

43. Lacan, "Freudian Thing," 361.

44. Lacan, "Function and Field," 238, 244.

45. Ibid., 238.

46. Ibid., 236–237.

47. Strauss for a brief period taught Paul Wolfowitz and was an avowed inspiration for Irving and then William Kristol. See Ann Norton, *Leo Strauss and the Politics of American Empire* (New Haven, CT: Yale University Press, 2005), 13–18; Shadia Drury *Leo Strauss and the American Right* (London: St Martin's Press, 1999). Then there is Abram Shulsky of the "Office of Special Projects," charged with assembling the questionable "intelligence" concerning Saddam Hussein's weapons of mass destruction. Shulsky, in a widely cited article with Gary Schmitt, claimed that: "Strauss' view . . . suggests that deception is the norm of political life, and the hope—to say nothing of the expectation, of establishing a politics that dispenses with it is the exception." See Abram Shulsky and Gary J. Schmitt, "Leo Strauss and the World of Intelligence (By Which We Do Not Mean Nous)," in *Leo Strauss, the Straussians, and the American Regime*, edited by Kenneth L. Deutsch and John Albert Murley (New York: Rowman & Littlefield, 1999), 410.

48. See Nicholas Xenos, *Cloaked in Virtue: Unveiling Leo Strauss and the Rhetoric of American Foreign Policy* (London: Routledge, 2007).

49. See Drury, *Political ideas*, William H. F. Altman, *The German Stranger: Leo Strauss and National Socialism* (Lanham, MD: Lexington, 2010); Xenos, *Cloaked in Virtue*; Alan Gilbert, "Do Philosophers Council Tyrants?," *Constellations* 16, no. 1 (2009): 106–124.

50. Strauss, *Thoughts on Machiavelli*, 168.

51. Strauss, "Literary Character," 57.

52. Roudinesco, *Jacques Lacan*, 567.

53. Lacan's esotericism is considered, and compared in passing to that of Strauss, in Jean-Claude Milner, *L'Oeuvre Claire: Lacan, la science et la philosophie* (Paris: Éditions du Seuil, 1995), "Chapitre Premier: Considérations sur une œuvre." The "Overture" to Lacan's *Écrits* closes by relating the undeniable difficulty of the author's own style to what "the audience to which they were addressed required." To his new reader, Lacan laconizes: "I want to lead the reader to a consequence in which he must pay the price with elbow grease." At *Écrits* 4–5.

54. Jacques Lacan, "Position of the Unconscious," in *Écrits*, 709–711. Perhaps through the discussions with Kojève, Lacan also was very clear about the esotericism of Plato's writing. As he warns the audience in *Seminar VIII*: "You must not blame me if I do not give you the last word on Plato because Plato was quite determined not to tell us this last word" (Lacan, *Seminar VIII: On Transference* [IV 11]). Lacan has this to say on the *Republic*, although the dates make it impossible that he could have read Strauss's *City and Man*: "What Plato sees on the horizon is a communal city just as revolting to his eyes as to our own. A kind of stud farm, this is what he promises us in a pamphlet which

has always been a bad dream for all those who with their sentiment of the good cannot get over the ever-accentuated discord of the order of the city. In other words, this is the *Republic* and everybody took it seriously. People believe that is really what Plato wanted!" (Lacan, *On Transference*, VI, 7).

55. Lacan, "Position of the Unconscious," 711.

56. Ibid., 709.

57. Strauss, *Persecution*, 14. He is speaking here of Farabi.

58. Cf. Strauss, "Literary Character," 83; Jacques Lacan, "Thou art," in *Seminar III: The Psychoses*, ed. Jacques-Alain Miller, trans. Russell Grigg (New York & London: W. W. Norton, 1993), 295–309.

59. Catherine and Michael Zuckert, *The Truth about Leo Strauss* (Chicago: University of Chicago Press, 2006), 115 ff.

60. Strauss, *Persecution*, 36.

61. Ibid., 25–26.

62. For friendly commentators who yet see Strauss as writing esoterically, see Lawrence Lampert, "Nietzsche's Challenge to Philosophy in the Thought of Leo Strauss," *The Review of Metaphysics* 58, no. 3 (2008); Daniel Tanguay, *Leo Strauss: An Intellectual Biography* (New Haven, CT: Yale University Press, 2007), 69; and Allan Bloom, "Leo Strauss: September 20, 1899–October 18, 1973," *Political Theory* 2, no. 4 (1974): 372–392.

63. Strauss, *Thoughts*, 45.

64. See Strauss, "Literary Character," 78.

65. There are for instance 26 paragraphs in Strauss' chapter on Machiavelli's *Prince*, which has 26 chapters, in a text (*Thoughts on Machiavelli*, 52) that reflects on the numerological significance of multiples of 13. See Zuckert and Zuckert, *The Truth about Leo Strauss* (Chicago: University of Chicago Press, 2006), 138.

66. Strauss, *On Tyranny*, 66 ff. For Strauss's claim that Xenophon's apparent advocacy of benevolent tyranny is a theoretically, not practically, valid thesis, which nevertheless made his readers believe that democracy was not the simply best political order, see 76.

67. Strauss, *Natural Right*, 156–161; see Gilbert, "Do Philosophers"; Matthew Sharpe, "The Philosopher's Courtly Love? Leo Strauss, Eros, and the Law," *Law and Critique* 17, no. 3 (2006): 357–388.

68. Strauss, *Thoughts*, 8 ("beautiful" and "artful" come in the thirteen paragraph of the "Introduction" to *Thoughts on Machiavelli*).

69. See Lawrence Lampert, "Leo Strauss's Recovery of Esotericism," *Cambridge Companion to Leo Strauss*, 63–92; Altman, *German Stranger*, 45, 454–455.

70. James Rhodes, *Eros, Wisdom, and Silence: Plato's Erotic Dialogues* (Columbia: University of Missouri Press, 2003), 95.

71. Leo Strauss, "Preface" [1962] to *Spinoza's Critique of Religion* (Chicago: University of Chicago Press, 1962), 31.

72. That is, Strauss, "The Three Waves of Modernity." The third wave in the *Republic* involves philosophers becoming kings, or kings philosophers.

73. Ibid., 94–98.

74. See Strauss, *Thoughts*, 120; "Three Waves," 89–94.

75. See Altman, *German Stranger*, 150–153.

76. See Leo Strauss, *An Introduction to Political Philosophy*, ed. Hilail Gildin (Detroit: Wayne State University Press, 1989), 41.

77. See Machiavelli, *The Prince*, chapter 26.

78. Strauss, *Thoughts on Machiavelli*, 167–168. This extraordinary passage on the beginnings of political regimes has arguably not been remarked upon sufficiently. Unless I miscount, Strauss begins thirteen sentences with a biblical "in the beginning," and the word "terror" gets nine uses, the last time with a capital T. The term is used eleven times in Machiavelli's entire *Discourses on Livy*, never with particular capitalization and on one only of these occasions in connection with the need for republics, not all regimes, to periodically renew themselves (book III, chapter 1).

79. Strauss, *Introduction*, 43.

80. See Leo Strauss, *The Political Philosophy of Hobbes: Its Basis and Genesis* (Chicago: University of Chicago Press, 1952), "II. The Moral Basis."

81. See Strauss, *Thoughts*, 105.

82. Strauss, *Natural Right*, 181–186, 248, with 1.

83. A silence broken twice; first, in Leo Strauss, "Review of *The Future of an Illusion*, by Sigmund Freud," *Der Judische Student* 25, no. 4 (August 1928) and second, in "Freud on Moses and Monotheism," in *Jewish Philosophy and the Crisis of Modernity*, ed. Kenneth Hart Green (Albany, NY: SUNY Press, 1997).

84. Freud was never himself analyzed.

85. See, on these three blows to human narcissism, Sigmund Freud, *A General Introduction to Psychoanalysis*, trans. G. Stanley Hall, "Eighteenth Lecture," online at www-site https://ebooks.adelaide.edu.au/f/freud/sigmund/general-introduction-to-psychoanalysis/complete.html#chapter18.

86. See Drury, *Political Ideas*, 60–67, for a direct contrast between Freud and Strauss on the theologico-political issue.

87. On "probity," see Leo Strauss, *Philosophy and Law: Contributions to the Understanding of Maimonides and His Predecessors*, trans. Eve Adler (Albany, NY: SUNY Press, 1995), 137–138, n13; *Liberalism, Ancient and Modern* (Chicago: University of Chicago Press, 1968), 252. Compare Altman, *German Stranger*, 109–111, with Robert C. Miner, "Leo Strauss's Adherence to Nietzsche's 'Atheism From Intellectual Probity,'" *Perspectives on Political Science* 41, no. 3 (2012): 155–164.

88. Jacques Lacan, "The Mirror Stage as Formative of the *I* Function as Revealed in Psychoanalytic Experience," in *Ěcrits*, 75–81.

89. Jacques Lacan, "Aggressiveness in Psychoanalysis," 82–101.

90. See esp. Lacan, "Science and Truth," in *Ěcrits*, 726–745. This chapter closes the collection.

91. See Milner, *Oeuvre Claire*, "Chapitre IV: Le deuxième classicisme lacanien."

92. See for example on "the passion of ignorance," a legatee of Freud's observations concerning analysand's resistance to analysis, Alain Vanier, "The Passion of Ignorance," *Cliniques Méditerranéenes* 70: 2 (2004), online at www-site http://www.cairn-int.info/abstract-E_CM_070_0059--the-passion-of-ignorance.htm.

93. Strauss, *Thoughts*, 13.

94. For an express denial of the possibility of the unconscious being operative, see Strauss, "Literary Character," 69.

95. Compare the classic study: Philip Rieff, *Freud: The Mind of the Moralist* (Chicago: University of Chicago Press, 1979).

96. Lacan, "Instance of the Letter," 433–434.

97. Strauss, *Liberalism, Ancient and Modern*, 225.

98. Lacan, "Instance of the Letter," 435.

99. Jacques Lacan, "Kant with Sade," *Écrits*, 645–669.

100. Lacan, "Science and Truth," 742; with Strauss, *Law and Philosophy*, 28–29; on Strauss post-Nietzschean opposition to mediation, see Matthew Sharpe, "*Che Vuoi?* Political-Theological Remarks on Leo Strauss' Spinoza," *Bible & Critical Theory* 3, no. 3 (2008): 41.9–41.10.

101. Strauss, *City and Man*, 1.

102. Lacan, "Function and Field," 239.

103. Ibid., 238.

104. Plato, *Republic*, 434e–435a.

3

Seeing through Law

Phenomenological Thought in Soloveitchik and Strauss

Jeffrey A. Bernstein

The law wishes . . . to be the discovery of what is, but the humans who, in our opinion, do not at all times use the same laws are not at all times capable of discovering what the law wishes—what is.

—Plato, *Minos*, 315b[1]

And another [baraita] taught: "That you may look upon [the precept] and remember . . . and do [the commandments]": looking leads to remembering, and remembering leads to doing.

—Babylonian Talmud, Tractate Menachoth, 43b[2]

Introductory Remarks

Today we seem to have little taste for law. We complain when the strictures are too tough, and we mistrust the authority that legitimates law when it does not work for us. Whereas before we were suspicious of the architects and executors of law, today we seem to be suspicious of the legal machinery or architecture itself. Law becomes something the function of which is simply to exercise a ban over people leading, in turn, to the hope that we might reach a point where law will be rendered obsolete or put out of commission.[3] If the situation is not that extreme, we at least worry that we are at a point in history where the institutions that used to provide legitimation for law are drastically weakened if not altogether undermined. We seem, in other words, to be undergoing a crisis of law—that is, we are unsure of its scope, function, and legitimacy. What is law such that its disappearance becomes either a blessing or a curse? If it is not this crisis of law's legitimacy that motivates two otherwise disparate thinkers—Joseph Soloveitchik and Leo Strauss—to undertake their paradoxically similar projects of discovering and describing what law is, it is at least certain that their investigations into law emerge from perceptions of crisis.

To term this similarity "paradoxical" is to acknowledge the seemingly vast differences between the two. Soloveitchik (in his role as the *Rosh Yeshiva* of Yeshiva University) became one of the foremost philosopher-theologians of American Modern Orthodox Judaism; Strauss (in the Political Science Department of the University of Chicago) became one of the most original thinkers in political philosophy as well as in the history of philosophy. Soloveitchik engaged primarily with conceptual resources from the nineteenth-century Brisker tradition of Talmudic interpretation and, later on, Kierkegaard and Buber; Strauss drew conceptual resources from the premodern (i.e., pre–seventeenth century) philosophies of Socrates, Plato, Xenophon, Aristotle, Thucydides, Farabi, and Maimonides. Soloveitchik was a man of faith; Strauss was an unbeliever.[4] To speak of these very real differences does not exclude the fact that general similarities do exist. First, both Soloveitchik and Strauss received philosophical educations in Germany at a time when Hermann Cohen's form of neo-Kantianism was prominent; this had a decisive effect on both thinkers (Soloveitchik did his dissertation in 1932 on Cohen, while Strauss did his dissertation in 1921 with Ernst Cassirer—one of Cohen's students[5]). That both thinkers came to reject much of Cohen's thought (particularly, but not exclusively, as it concerned Judaism) means only that they were formed and informed by a similar intellectual discussion (involving, e.g., the claim that religion is simply derivative of culture). Second, both thinkers maintained an independent intellectual stance with respect to Judaism. Strauss's *Philosophy and Law* (which we will consider here) was read by Gershom Scholem as promoting "an affirmation of atheism as the most important Jewish watchword."[6] While no one (to my knowledge) ever accused the "Rav" of atheism, his (1) treatment of miracles as natural and (2) acknowledgment that the truth or falsity of a religious view does not depend upon (even strong religious) consensus shows Soloveitchik to have been a thinker who refused to ground Judaism simply in traditionally religious arguments.[7] In short, when their different personae and orientations are viewed alongside the similar background and temperaments, a complex and interesting conversation between Soloveitchik and Strauss emerges as a possibility.[8]

This possibility, I hold, is founded on the concern with law (Soloveitchik expresses this concern in terms of "halakhah"—the body of Jewish law as expressed in the Talmud) in the early work of both thinkers—that is, primarily Soloveitchik's *The Halakhic Mind* (written in 1944, published in 1986)[9] and Strauss's *Philosophy and Law* (published in 1935).[10] Furthermore, I believe that both thinkers approach the problem of law in a manner that illustrates phenomenological motifs as developed in the work of Edmund Husserl. This is to claim *neither* that Husserl is the most important historical figure for either thinker nor that Soloveitchik and Strauss were uncritical of him. In fact, their criticisms of Husserl are rather straightforward. Soloveitchik holds Husserl partly responsible for the irrational move toward emotive intuitionism adopted by some of his students (read: Heidegger) during World War II.[11] Similarly, Strauss faults Husserlian phenomenology for failing to develop a politically edifying philosophy that would allow nonphilosophers to be able to bring phenomenology as a rigorous science together with their own lived experience.[12] Nonetheless, the fact that both thinkers (in the texts under examination) resonate with moments in his work is notable. The Husserlian motifs found in their texts—which, in turn, allow us to approach these texts within a general phenomenological horizon—is useful in helping us understand their respective construals of law. In short, I hold that both Soloveitchik and Strauss understand law as *an optic* through which certain fundamental phenomena come to light. In Soloveitchik's case, these phenomena are the figures of *homo religiosus* and (eventually) Halakhic man; in Strauss's case, these phenomena are religion and politics (as they come to constitute the theological-political problem), and the relation between the philosopher and the city. Finally, I believe that Soloveitchik and Strauss "see through law" in three senses: (1) they use law as a lens/optic through which to see the aforementioned phenomena, (2) they see through the appearance of the law as simply an external yoke that binds humans, and (3) insofar as they both allow readers to see through the appearance of law by construing law as an optic, they allow readers to take law seriously. In so doing, they actualize the figure of law—that is, they see through law in the sense of "seeing law through." Insofar as we need to understand the reasons that prompted Soloveitchik's and Strauss's investigations into law, this study will assume the following structure: (1) the Path to Law, and (2) Law and its Phenomena.

The Path to Law

Husserlian phenomenology, whatever else it may be, is an inquiry centered on *seeing*. As an eidetic science (deriving from the Greek *eidos*—look, shape, form), phenomenology seeks to perceive essence in matters-of-fact.[13] It constitutes a retreat—or *reduction*—from the perspective of lived experience allowing the inquirer to understand and describe how phenomenal objects *emerge* into consciousness; that is, how they become constituted as objects[14]: "It is, therefore, a matter of inquiring . . . into how objective unities of any region and category are 'constituted in the manner peculiar to consciousness.' "[15] Such an inquiry can only be descriptive, insofar as the phenomenologist's job is simply to watch the very constitution of objects *as they occur* in consciousness.[16] In order to accomplish this—in order to assure that the reduction/retreat from lived experience actually takes place—the phenomenologist must examine their own consciousness very carefully in order to put any unwarranted assumptions (that is, prejudices) out of play. In Husserl's succinct formulation, "Prejudices blind[.]"[17] Put differently, in taking a proposition about reality as self-evidently true when its self-evidence is in question, our ability to see the phenomenon for what and how it is becomes limited. The phenomenologist must observe and describe. That an absolute standpoint from which to view phenomenal objects may be impossible is no reason to abandon the rigor of phenomenological analysis as such. This all-too-brief description of Husserlian phenomenology is necessary in order to fix our sights on the constellation of phenomenological moments in Soloveitchik's and Strauss's respective works as they deal with the figure of law. We are, therefore, in a better position to observe both the phenomenological motifs that they use and how the figure of law comes to occupy the center of their analyses. Where Soloveitchik inherits Husserl's concern with eideticism and description, Strauss inherits

Husserl's concern with bracketing prejudice. They both, however, appeal to the emergence of phenomena as a figure leading to the importance of law.

If the debate between philosophical holism and scientific mechanism discloses, for Soloveitchik, a plurality of ontological registers concerning the evaluation of religous cognition, is religion (and its concomitant philosophical inquiry) to be understood as merely derivative of one or the other approach? Or, rather, does it embody a unique realm of inquiry and call for an original analysis all its own? Rejecting the approach of thinkers like Cohen, Soloveitchik holds that religion does in fact have a unique realm. However, its uniqueness requires that it borrow aspects from both science and philosophy in order for one to see clearly how the mindset of *homo religiosus* is constituted and to what it points. To place religion in conversation with philosophy and science is to acknowledge that it amounts to a form of knowing that can be subjected to an analysis of essences: "religion, too has a cognitive approach to reality. Religious experience is not only of emotional or ethical essence, but is also deeply rooted in the noetic sphere. Indeed, the urge for *noesis* is of the very essence of religion . . . The noetic component of the religious experience must be independently examined. If and when an eidetic analysis discerns cognitive components in the religious act, then the theory of cognitive pluralism will substantiate the claim of religion to theoretical interpretation."[18] As it happens, the reason that religious cognition must constitute a unique sphere that borrows from both philosophy and science is that it cognitively intends both the absoluteness of God as well as the plurality of worldly experience: "The religious experience is a composite phenomenon involving not only God but the ego and the sensuous environment of the *homo religiosus*."[19] The essence of religion's "compositeness" lies in the fact that it extends to both the subjective and objective realms of existence: "Religion, which is perhaps more deeply rooted in subjectivity than any other manifestation of the spirit, is also reflected in externalized phenomena which are evolved in the objectification process of the religious consciousness. The aggregate of religious objective constructs is comprised of ethico-religious norms, ritual, dogmas, theoretical postulates, etc."[20] This means that religious consciousness is directed from the interior to the exterior: "[Religious consciousness] objectifies itself in the emergence of a certain order which in turn finds its correlate in space and time extension."[21] Soloveitchik elaborates the two parts of this process (here quoted at length):

> The objectifying process consists of two incongruous parts. The first remains within the world where subjective and objective aspects are rooted in pure qualitative strata, differing only to the degree of distinctness and as to their proximity to the psychophysical border. The second is an act of emergence of "spiritual" reality into outward tangible forms. This concrete physical order, enveloped by time and space, is coordinated with its correlate in the internal world. The internal subjective correlate is, in turn, the objectified expression of some more primitive subjectivity. Religious subjectivity, for example finds its correlate in a certain norm which, though remaining within spiritual bounds, strives towards the mysterious junction of *psyche* and *physis*. This norm is much nearer to the outer fringes of externality than its counterpart, the quasi-non-normative subjectivity. The norm, in such a semi-objectified state, attempts to break through the barrier separating the physical from the spiritual in order to appear in the arena of life. The consummation of the religious act always takes place in a non-personal world.[22]

For Soloveitchik, religious consciousness starts from the sensate realm located at the border between the interior and the exterior, and (as it were) presses outward to achieve formation in the "non-personal world." Put differently, religious experience is not simply inward and personal. In order to be something more than a private language, it must involve community. The only way it can achieve this is by constituting norms in the environing world that correlate to the consciousness that give rise to them. In so doing, religious cognition therefore embraces both the subjective and objective realms of existence. Focusing only on personal religious testimony would be every bit as prejudicial as focusing only on the architectural mathematics determining houses of worship. It must take account of both in order to view the emergence and constitution of religion in the world and to understand its essential character. In sum, philosophers of religion needs to begin from the same realm as the scientist—the realm of worldly plurality—in order to then show how they express (or, are directed to) a relation with the absolute (more characteristic of philosophical holism).

The essential character of religion has both a universal and a particular aspect to it. Soloveitchik elaborates: "The existence of an ethical norm is a common denominator in all religious systems. The unique character of a particular religion, however, appears only in the ritual."[23] The question now becomes how one must coordinate these objective aspects of religious experience with the subjective experiences (e.g., of longing for God). This experience cannot be understood along the straightforward lines of mechanistic causality: "It is impossible to construct a causal bond in objectified spiritual reality without recourse to its subjective correlate."[24] There is nothing about how the synagogue was built that directly expresses its connection with divinity. The same is true with the development of the laws of *kashrut*. What is needed is an account of the subjective experience that accompanies prayer and study in synagogue or maintaining the kosher dietary laws: "The task of the . . . philosopher is not to survey the cognitive act from a causal perspective [read: scientific], but from a normative and descriptive perspective. The genetic problem is the concern of the anthropologist and explanatory psychologist but not of the philosopher . . . In contrast with genetic methodology, a philosophy of religion, following a retrospective procedure—from the objective to the subjective realm—. . . offers a multidimensional religious outlook to the *homo religiosus*."[25] Both realms are real (although they may be so in different senses), but the ways in which one conceptually grasps them are not the same: "while objectivity is constructed by an incomprehensible act of the 'logos' and is methodologically prior to the subjective aspect, subjectivity is reconstructed by an epistemological act. Subjectivity cannot be approached directly; it must first be objectified by the 'logos.'"[26] One might conceive of this along the lines of the Aristotelian dictum stating that what is first in the order of being is last in the order of knowing. Similarly, for Soloveitchik, what is first—that is, subjective perception—can only be reconstructed out of the later objective constructs of religion. It is at this point that Soloveitchik gives precedence to philosophy over science: "the [correlative] principle of reconstruction should be adopted while the causal survey should be rejected. In this respect the metaphysical thesis that the problem of philosophy is not the 'how' but the 'what' is correct."[27] It is at this point that we see Soloveitchik most deeply embrace the Husserlian procedure of description: "The philosopher of religion in his regressive movement from objectivity to subjectivity should not undertake the explanation of religious norms by antecedence, for there is no causal continuity in the passage from one order to another. The subjective correlate does not interpret an objective commandment. The reconstruction method is recommended, but it cannot generate a causal explanation of religion."[28] We can interpretively describe what a commandment means and to what level of consciousness it is supposed to direct its practitioner. We cannot explain the stages of objective composition of a commandment and do it any amount of religious justice. This, in fact, is Soloveitchik's major criticism of Maimonides's accounts of laws as presented in his *Guide of the Perplexed* (as opposed to the presentation contained in his *Mishneh Torah)*: "Maimonides' failure to impress his rationalistic method [in the *Guide*] upon the vivid religious consciousness is to be attributed mainly to the fact that the central theme of the Maimonidean exposition is the causalistic problem. The 'how' question, the explanatory quest, and the genetic attitude determined Maimonides' doctrine of the commandments. Instead of describing, Maimonides explained; instead of reconstructing, he constructed."[29]

Of course, the condition for the possibility of Maimonides's success and/or failure at divining the meaning of the commandments was the fact that, for Soloveitchik, he dared to investigate the laws and present them to the Jewish community. Maimonides, therefore, is the privileged example insofar as he attempted to investigate what, for Soloveitchik, amounts to the pinnacle of religious co-ordination between the subjective and objective realms—Halakhah: "Objectivation reaches its highest expression in the Halakhah. Halakhah is the act of seizing the subjective flow and converting it into enduring and tangible magnitudes. It is the crystallization of the fleeting individual experience into fixed principles and universal norms. In short, Halakhah is the objectifying instrument of our religious consciousness, the form-principle of the transcendental act, the matrix in which the amorphous religious hyle [matter] is cast."[30] As a body of instruction that addresses every aspect of a Jew's life, Halakhah spans the entire realm from private to communal, personal to political, and theoretical to practical. Its all-encompassing character compels Soloveitchik to construe it as the object out of which all Jewish subjective life can and must be reconstructed. He ends *The Halakhic Mind* with the following programmatic statement: "Modern Jewish philosophy must be nurtured on the historical religious consciousness that has been projected onto a fixed objective screen. Out of the sources of Halakhah, a new world vision awaits formulation."[31] Soloveitchik's phenomenological investigations into the stuff of religion in general, and Judaism in particular, lead to law.

Strauss's investigation, in *Philosophy and Law*, involves bracketing the prejudices of modern thought in order to recover a specifically premodern understanding of philosophy in its relation to religion and political life. The twentieth century's emphasis on religious consciousness shows that "the moderns are unequivocally instructed by a modern court, that is, by their own historical research . . . [instead of acknowledging] the Jewish tradition as the judge of modern thought."[32] By presupposing modern categories (such as "religious consciousness" and "philosophy of religion") as the way to approach medieval philosophy, Strauss holds, modern thought exhibits a prejudice favoring its own time rather than attempting to understand medieval philosophy from out of itself: "So long as we do not purposely struggle against our own prejudices through historical reflection . . . we find ourselves fully in the power of the mode of thought produced by the Enlightenment and consolidated by its proponents or opponents."[33] It is impossible, according to Strauss, to understand the fundamental phenomena of human life—as understood by the premoderns—from a modern perspective. In order to return to these phenomena (following the Husserlian imperative "to the things themselves!"), we must return (as best we can) to the quarrel in which the modern Enlightenment rejection of orthodoxy ensued: "The quarrel between orthodoxy and the Enlightenment that is thus possible without further ado must be resumed or rather . . . the quarrel between the Enlightenment and orthodoxy . . . must be understood anew . . . Only by doing this, or more precisely, only by having the full course of that quarrel before one's eyes, may one hope to be able to attain a view of the hidden premises of both parties that is not corrupted by prejudices."[34] By revealing the modern prejudices, we interrupt their authority and can see the situation anew.

There is little question that Strauss would take issue with certain aspects of the content of Soloveitchik's thought as being too beholden to modernity—in particular, the emphasis on religious consciousness. Yet the form of the thought—its Husserlian inheritance—shows that they proceed in an analogous phenomenological manner. This, I hold, is what brings the disparate content of Soloveitchik's and Strauss's thought into conversation. And it is this concern with form, for Strauss, that characterizes the main focus of medieval philosophy. While the medieval Jewish and Islamic thinkers evince a notable preference for Aristotle in terms of the specific tenets to which they hold, the horizon in which their thinking occurs is Platonic: "[the medieval] philosophers are Platonists not because they accept this or that Platonic theorem, however important—in this sense they are Aristotelians rather than Platonists—but because, in the foundation of philosophizing itself, they are guided by Plato to answer a Platonic question within a framework layed out by Plato."[35] Whereas the modern interpreters of medieval philosophy by and large view the latter as a variant of Aristotelianism, Strauss holds that the form of their thought is characterized by Plato—in particular, Platonic politics. For Strauss, this form in which we perceive medieval philosophy (in Husserlian terms, the perceptual horizon) determines how all the moments of content must be grasped: "the *emergence* [Hervorgehen] of this teaching from Platonic philosophy must be conceived in its potentiality."[36] Put differently, it is only an understanding of the correct form of medieval thought that will yield a complete understanding (that is, of the actual occurrence as well as of the conceptual limits) of medieval thought.

Strauss makes a similar claim with respect to the medieval and modern treatments of the Hebrew Bible: "To be sure the *content* of the Bible is better preserved by [Moses] Mendelssohn than by his medieval forerunners; but he can no longer account for its *form*, for its revealed character, as satisfactorily as his predecessors."[37] Strauss holds that the modern approach to the Bible is grounded in the question of religious consciousness, while the medieval approach is grounded in revelation. In denying the efficacy or intelligibility of revelation, the moderns determine the Bible solely according to modern categories: "The Bible [for the moderns] must no longer be understood as revealed, but as the product of the religious consciousness; and the task of 'philosophy of religion' no longer consists in the harmonizing of the doctrines of revelation with the doctrines of reason, but in the analysis of the religious consciousness."[38] The issue of one's technical grasp of particulars in the Bible is, for Strauss, a moot point given the fundamentally modern distortion of the whole of the Bible. It is through an understanding of the status of revelation in medieval philosophy that we can recover the Platonic philosophical horizon of medieval thought.

For Strauss, the medieval philosophers find themselves in a world characterized by an un- or pre-philosophic premise—the context of revelation: "The men whose teachings offer the readiest access to the philosophical and hence unbelieving basis of medieval Jewish (and Islamic) philosophy, the medieval rationalists, developed in greater or lesser detail and coherence a legal foundation of philosophy, that is, a defense of philosophizing before the bar of revelation. This fact . . . is already sufficient proof that the reality of the revelation, of the revealed law, is the decisive pre-philosophic premise of these philosophers . . . *before* all endeavors and convictions of this kind, before *all* philosophizing, the fact of the revelation stands firm.[39] Put differently, irrespective of whether or not the philosophers *believed in* the fact or reality of revelation (and, for Strauss, they were not compelled to do so[40]), the *political* fact or reality of revelation governed the very world in which they found themselves. Unlike in Plato's time, the medieval philosophers encountered a world in which revelation was taken as the self-evident horizon: "Out of the new *situation* of philosophizing, the obligation *by* the revelation, there thus emerges *(hervor)* a new *problem* for the philosophers, their accountability *to* the revelation."[41] The philosophers must, therefore, philosophize with the fact of revelation in mind; they must both relegate their unbelief to secrecy as well as make the case for the justification of philosophy according to revelation; they must "create a space for the pursuit of philosophy"[42] within the horizon of the political fact of revelation. Living in a situation where "the *fact* of the revelation is certain," the medieval Jewish and Islamic philosophers "derive Platonic politics from an un-Platonic first premise."[43] The need to justify philosophical activity before the bar of revelation, as well as hide their unbelief, constitutes the esoteric character of medieval philosophy.

What is the substance of revelation for the Jewish and Islamic philosophers? It is not (as for the medieval Christians) divine *word* (which relates to belief) but divine *law* (which refers to action). The medieval Jewish and Islamic philosophers therefore find themselves (as intimated above) in a world constituted by politics and religion equally—these are (as it were) "the *original* facts" of medieval life.[44] Therefore, philosophers had to create a space for philosophical activity that (following Aristotle) privileged the contemplative life, in a context that compelled practical obedience. In this way, the un-Platonic premise of the reality of revelation is actually analogous to the end of the Platonic cave parable: "The essential difference between Plato and Aristotle is revealed only in the way in which they *conduct* themselves toward theory as the highest perfection of man. Aristotle sets it completely free; or rather, he leaves it in its natural freedom. Plato, on the other hand, *does not permit* the philosophers 'what is now permitted them,' namely the life of philosophizing as an abiding in the contemplation of the truth. He '*compels*' them to care for the others and to guard them, in order that the state may really be a state, a true state . . . The Platonism of [the medieval] philosophers is given with their *situation*, with their standing in fact under the law, they admittedly no longer need, like Plato to *seek* the law, the state, to *inquire* into it . . . they are, as authorized by the law, free to philosophize in Aristotelian freedom: they can *therefore* aristotelize."[45] Just as the philosopher of Plato's *Republic* is compelled to return to the cave and care for the cave-dwellers, the medieval philosopher is compelled to justify his activity before the bar of revealed law: "What Plato *called for*—that philosophy stand under a higher court, under the state, under the *law*—is *fulfilled* in the age of belief in revelation."[46] "Philosophy," in other words, "owes its authorization, its freedom, to the law; *its freedom depends upon its bondage*."[47]

What Strauss finds in his return from the Enlightenment to the medieval Jewish and Islamic context is a horizon obscured by the modern concepts of "philosophy of religion" and "religious consciousness" (as well as the aforementioned concept of "experience"). It is *that* horizon that constitutes the natural situation of philosophizing insofar as it amounts to the situation in which philosophers (uncorrupted by the modern prejudice that all people are willing and able to undergo philosophical education) *always* find themselves. The significance of this situation is not diminished by its having become actualized in a determinate historical period insofar as one can find analogues in any number of historical periods. Because philosophy is "not simply sovereign,"[48] because it always faces the need for self-justification at the bar of an unphilosophical society, the situation of the political fact of revelation—that is, the horizon of law—gains transhistorical significance: "the leading idea of the medieval Enlightenment that has become lost to the modern Enlightenment and its heirs, and through an understanding of which many modern certainties and doubts lose their force [is] the idea of Law."[49] If, for Strauss, Maimonidean rationalism amounts to "the true natural model, the standard to be carefully protected from any distortion,"[50] it is not because he is true to Plato in all of the latter's particulars; rather, it is because Maimonides attempts to Platonically navigate the philosophical life in relation to law.

To sum up, the crisis between contemporary mechanistic natural science and philosophical holism leads Soloveitchik back to the question of religious cognition. Seeing the necessity of an objectifying structure for accessing subjective religious experience, Soloveitchik turns to Halakhah as the privileged "object" of examination. Halakhah allows inquirers to reconstruct religious experience and the cognition of that experience. For Strauss, the crisis of traditional authority—both religious and political—brought about by distorting modern concepts of "religious consciousness," "philosophy of religion," and "experience"—leads back to the actualized natural situation in which philosophers find themselves. That situation is the perceptual horizon of revelation. The political fact of revelation reveals itself substantially through the (idea of) law. While Soloveitchik and Strauss differ greatly in their particularities, the analogous phenomenological character of their inquiries lead them to focus on the importance of law for their respective accounts. The questions we must now ask are: What, for Soloveitchik and Strauss, is law? And what are the phenomena that law lets us see?

Law and Its Phenomena

As I intimated in my introductory remarks, we generally experience law as something (a set of rules, the application of certain principles) imposed on us from without. As such, we find it hard to rid ourselves of the suspicion that the law is, in some sense, arbitrary. Not fully corresponding to our wants, and not having been created by us, we maintain an uneasy relation to it. This view of law may be termed (along Husserlian lines) the "natural" conception of law. I believe that both Soloveitchik and Strauss provide a more nuanced conception of law. I say "conception," in the singular, because I believe that—despite the many differences in their particular construals—the fundamental thrust of their accounts are deeply similar. Both conceive of law as an optic through which we see fundamental phenomena in the world. For Soloveitchik, these phenomena are *homo religiosus* and (its cousin) Halakhic man. For Strauss, they are the fundamental needs of religion and politics in their symbiosis as the theological-political problem. It is through law, therefore, that (for Soloveitchik and Strauss) we learn something important about the make-up of human beings.

Interestingly enough, Soloveitchik does not discuss Halakhah in any great depth in *The Halakhic Mind*—one is left wondering whether his text presupposes knowledge of Halakhah or is the primer for a later inquiry into it. However this may be, we are justified in supplying his account of Halakhah from three other texts (two of which were written around the same time as *The Halakhic Mind*). These texts are *And From There You Shall Seek* (drafted in the 1940s and appearing in print in 1978), *Halakhic Man* (published in 1944), and his September 12, 1952, letter to an unknown correspondent on the nature of the Halakhah.[51]

The first thing to note concerning Soloveitchik's conception of Halakhah is that it traditionally belong to the realm of politics: "The Halakhah deals with the laws of government and political administration, sociological issues such as state, society, family life, and the interaction between individuals, marital status and similar matters."[52] This political emphasis of law (with which Strauss concurs) is in keeping both with the normative Rabbinic tradition as well as the ancient Greeks. Soloveitchik's attribution of "sociological" to some of these issues shows his acceptance, contrary to Strauss, of modern categories. Both Soloveitchik and Strauss, however, agree that law is directed at both the individual and the community. Perhaps the grand divergence from Strauss occurs in Soloveitchik's postulation of Halakhah as having been received from God?[53] To accept that bold proclamation without qualification, however, would be rash. For while Jewish law is given by God, the interpretation of it remains in the hands of humans: "The real Halakhah-noesis realizes itself through pure thought and ideation. The scholar does not have to guess the opinions of others nor even to divine the will of some heavenly court of justice. In the halakhic field man is vested with absolute authority. No one can overrule his judgment."[54] Put differently, while it may indeed be the case that law is of divine origin, all the discussions of the political issues contained therein are interpretively elaborated by humans in pluralistic conversation with one another. Halakhic interpretation and judgment is not only *about politics*, it is *a political activity*. This in no way means that, according to Soloveitchik, *homo religiosus* and Halakhic man are self-consciously political actors. Rather, it means that, in the Aristotelian sense (explicitly adhered to by Strauss), humans are political animals (that is, they are born into, and naturally thrive in, communities). While Strauss (as a philosopher) would take issue with the divine origin of the law, it is neither this nor the political context of legal interpretation that sets the particularity of Soloveitchik's conception apart from Strauss's.

What ultimately sets the two conceptions apart is the fundamental phenomena that (for Soloveitchik) are inquired into by Halakhah. Readers will recall that (in *The Halakhic Mind*) Halakhah amounts to the objectifying structure through which the subjective experience of *homo religiosus* can be reconstructed. Soloveitchik will (in *Halakhic Man)* develop an entire anthropology of Halakhic man as a category related to, but distinct from, the former. While this is not the place to entertain a complete discussion of the distinction between the two (let alone how these terms are understood in Soloveitchik's different texts), this much can be said: While *The Halakhic Mind* presents *homo religiosus* as basically identical to how Soloveitchik will come to refer to Halakhic man, the former term undergoes a widening in his other texts. *Homo religiosus* comes to stand for a universal religious individual, while Halakhic man refers to the individual who rationally cognizes Halakhic wisdom. What both have in common, however, is their desire for proximity to the absolute (God). Whereas the *homo religiosus* of *Halakhic Man* and *And From There You Shall Seek* seeks proximity to the absolute through actions, and beliefs (e.g., in the miracles recounted in the Hebrew Bible), Halakhic man seeks that proximity through interpretative cognition of the law: "Primarily halakhic man cognizes God via His Torah, via the truth of halakhic cognition. There is a halakhic epistemology, there is a halakhic thinking 'the measure thereof is longer than the earth' [Job 11:9]."[55] Halakhic man, like *homo religiosus* in *The Halakhic Mind*, seeks religious cognition in order to gain proximity to the absolute. Whether one's approach is based on actions and beliefs (which, as based on revelation, Soloveitchik sees as an exoteric direction to this proximity)[56] or on intellectual cognition (which Soloveitchik sees as an esoteric direction[57]), Soloveitchik holds that they both express the desire to (in some respect) transcend the finite condition in which humans find themselves. Ultimately, it is both approaches that come to be found in the Halakhah: "The halakhic ideal is embodied in its striving for joint revelational and intellectual activity."[58] Whereas Soloveitchik attempts to show how Jewish law contains both elements of what is commonly referred to as Athens and Jerusalem (i.e., intellectual striving for wisdom and religious striving for wisdom), Strauss maintains the stark separation between the philosopher and the religious person. While the texts of each tradition can be approached by the other one, the philosopher is not a believer, and the believer is not beholden to human wisdom as the one thing needful. It is the encapsulation of both directions *solely within the sphere of religion* that differentiates Soloveitchik's approach from Strauss. The phenomenon of *homo religiosus*/Halakhic man exists in a religious world that, for Strauss, would be (at best) a partial rendition of lived experience.

What does it mean to say that Halakhah shows us the phenomenon of *homo religiosus*/Halakhic man? What is law such that we can *see* this figure in or through it? If *homo religosus*/Halakhic man visibly emerges in the world as a result of our reconstruction of him out of Jewish religious rituals and practices, this can happen only by means of an optic that allows us to see it. Soloveitchik refers to Halakhah as an "*a priori* ideal system"[59] that allows for the cognition of "the relationship between that ideal world [or system] and our concrete environment in all its visible manifestations and underlying structures. There is no phenomenon, entity, or object in this concrete world which the a priori Halakhah does not approach with its ideal standard."[60] Granting the Kantian echoes contained in this phrase, to say that the Halakhah is an a priori ideal is, I maintain, to say that it does not directly participate *as a concrete thing within* the whole, but allows us to see the whole as a whole. Operating at the limit of the observable world, Halakhah first allows us to cognize the concrete "primitive datum, apprehended by our senses"[61] as religious phenomena. In this way, everyday objects and events appear as religiously inflected. Differently stated, in order to *look* at the world in a Jewish way, one needs to look *through* the Halakhah. And this looking is, in part, dependent on the person or persons doing the looking: "Halakhah is not confined to mere commands but is a creative gesture out of which the norm is associated."[62] For this reason, it "does not preclude a diversity and heterogeneity as methods and objectives."[63] To be sure, this diversity is not limitless. The point is that in order for humans to creatively understand their proximity to God, they require a perceptual "organ" that allows them to see things with a religious meaning. Halakhah is that "optical organ."

According to Strauss, the Jewish and Islamic medieval thinkers understood revealed law as "a guideline for inquiry" that is "prior to philosophy."[64] Qua its divine origin, it "serves the highest end, the specific perfection of man . . . [i.e.,] knowledge of God."[65] In this way, the religious context of Strauss's conception of law (as it exists for the medievals) is set. Yet, as Soloveitchik would presumably have seen, the religious context of the law's legitimacy and authority is not the same as the religious context of the law *simpliciter*. The philosophers, compelled as they were to defend philosophy in front of the law, do not simply derive their conception of the law from religion. Beyond the fact that the philosophical view is "unbelieving," Strauss does not tell us much about the philosophical *understanding* of law in *Philosophy and Law*. We can presume (as Platonic and Aristotelian thinkers) that such an understanding would not derive from its revealed character. Strauss is more explicit about what such an understanding of law looks like in a recently published lecture from 1937, "The Origin of Modern Political Thought." In this lecture, Strauss elaborates the classical conception of law rejected both by the moderns as well as by the (Christian) medievals. For our purposes, it can serve as the "unbelieving" account accepted by the medieval Jewish and Islamic philosophers—that is, those who accepted the thought of Plato and Aristotle as their point of departure. Strauss holds that "the conception guiding Plato as well as Aristotle . . . may be summed up in the formula: Law is an order, a distribution and assignation of something; it owes its validity to its having emanated from wisdom and understanding; law is right order, found out by reason, and it is law not because it is consented to by the citizens, but because it is founded on perception of what is good. Law is right order, a rule and measure, not imposed on man, but understood by man."[66] This account of law (while, strictly speaking, coming from a text written after *Philosophy and Law*, when Strauss was rethinking many of his key concepts) is wholly in keeping with the understanding of law occurring in the thought of Farabi, Maimonides, and Averroes. While nonphilosophers understand the law as imposed from without, the philosophical interpretation of law is as a product of the good. Or rather, the law can be understood independently of whether or not it was given by God.

The divine origin of the law[67] thus becomes (in the hands of philosophy) a political imperative rather than a metaphysical truth. Thus, when Strauss states that "[i]f philosophy as authorized by the law leads to a result that conflicts with the literal sense of the law, if the literal sense is *therefore* impossible, then we must interpret the literal sense, that is, treat it as figuratively meant,"[68] he makes explicit the radical difference between the philosopher and the nonphilosopher. As stated earlier, the philosopher is in continual need of (politically) justifying philosophical activity before the bar of the nonphilosophical majority and the political structure in which it emerges. In other words, *philosophy always emerges within the situation of law*. Moreover, the only type of law that can legitimately lay claim to the perfection of human beings is *divine* law. The fact that "the medieval philosophers understand religion . . . as law"[69] makes manifest two fundamental characteristics of humanity: (1) that human beings are confronted by *the theological-political problem*—that is, humans are political beings requiring a lawmaker and laws, the most legitimate kind of which are divine; in this way, politics and religion are the two original facts of human life, and (2) that philosophy will always be in need of justifying its own activity within the theological-political constitution of the *polis*; that is, "the philosopher is dependent on revelation as surely as he is a *human being*, for as a human being he is a political being and thus is in need of a law . . . directed to the perfection proper to man."[70] In other words, it is through the medium of law that (on Strauss's account) we see the theological constitution of society and the philosopher's uneasy role within it. Whereas Soloveitchik construes law ultimately as religious, Strauss articulates a conception in which the political and religious constitute the primal scene in which philosophy uneasily finds itself.

What does it mean to say that, through the medium of law, we encounter the emergence of the theological-political and the relation of the philosopher and the *polis?* As with Soloveitchik's construal of Halakhah, Strauss understands law as an optic that emerges from the fundamental phenomena it wishes to describe. It allows us to view the theological-political problem and the relation between the philosopher and the *polis* (as it were) after the fact. Put differently, it is as a result of the tensions between intellectual freedom (wherever it may lead) and the need for order, security, and peace that (divine) law comes to occupy the place it does in political life: "the law summons to the understanding and to the demonstration of the truths that it imparts. Therewith it implicitly commands knowledge of the world; for God can be known only from His works."[71] This summary restatement of Maimonides's view has phenomenological significance for the present reading of Strauss. In order for the law to summon the truths it imparts (about religion, politics, and philosophy) to the understanding and to demonstration, the truths of the law must present them to consciousness. The law becomes the boundary screen through which such truths come to sight. Like Soloveitchik, Strauss conceives of law as something that guides nonphilosophers and allows philosophers to understand the world and their place in it.

Concluding Remarks

As mentioned in the introduction, there are three senses of "seeing through law" that unfold from our explication of Soloveitchik's and Strauss's respective phenomenological accounts of law. These senses can be counted as their conceptual achievements.

First (as explicated in the preceding section), Soloveitchik and Strauss "see through law" insofar as law is an optic through which phenomena come to sight. If Plato is correct that law wishes to be the discovery of what is, then that-which-is occurs by means of the discourses and institutions of law. Law, in other words, gives us insight and wisdom about our world. Whether such insight refers to a religious context (like

Soloveitchik) or a trans-religious one (like Strauss), law lets us see the phenomena for what they are. Optics/lenses are never perfect—they always distort that which they show. That distortion is (as it were) coeval with human perception; so while it is susceptible to distortion, it is no less susceptible to improvement. *Second*, Soloveitchik and Strauss "see through law" insofar as they call our attention to the essentials of law. Law's "natural" appearance to (and conception by) humans is of a yoke being imposed from without. If this "natural" appearance were true, law's essence would amount to willful arbitrariness. To be sure, *this appearance is never simply false*—laws often enough are arbitrary and willful, being a product of punitive authority. Moreover, even incomplete or distorted appearances bear some relation to the essence in question. By "seeing through" this appearance of law, Soloveitchik and Strauss are able to recover (for a humankind often too exhausted to see it) the essence of law as optic that imparts wisdom and insight. They recover a conception of law as teacher. *Third*, Soloveitchik and Strauss "see through law" in the sense of taking law seriously—that is, of "seeing law through." If law cannot be taken seriously, it loses its capacity to form and inform individuals and societies—it becomes inoperative. In this case, thinkers such as Agamben would be correct in viewing law as a disused object fit for mere play and posthumous study. Soloveitchik and Strauss give us a reason why we might consider not simply succumbing to the aforementioned crisis that accompanies the "natural" appearance of law. Paraphrasing Tractate Menachoth, it is by virtue of our looking at law that we remember the wisdom imparted through it and, in so doing, actively engage law. At the very least, the phenomenological accounts adumbrated here compel us to revisit law as a significant category for the phenomena that inhabit our consciousness and our life.

Notes

1. Plato, "Minos," trans. Thomas L. Pangle, in *The Roots Of Political Philosophy*, ed. Thomas L. Pangle (Ithaca, NY: Cornell University Press, 1987), 56.

2. *Babylonian Talmud*, Soncino edition, Tractate Menachoth, 43b. Translation slightly altered.

3. See Jean-Luc Nancy, "Abandoned Being," trans. Brian Holmes, in Jean-Luc Nancy, *The Birth To Presence*, trans. Brian Holmes et al. (Stanford, CA: Stanford University Press, 1993), 44–46, and Giorgio Agamben, *State Of Exception*, trans. Kevin Attell (Chicago: University of Chicago Press, 2005), 64.

4. Leo Strauss to Gerhard Krüger, December 27, 1932, in Leo Strauss, *The Strauss-Krüger Correspondence: Returning to Plato through Kant*, ed. Susan Mald Shell (New York: Palgrave MacMillan, 2018), 52.

5. See Robert Erlewine, *Judaism and The West: From Hermann Cohen to Joseph Soloveitchik* (Bloomington: Indiana University Press, 2016), 131; Michael Zank's introduction to Leo Strauss, *The Early Writings (1921–1932)*, ed. and trans. Michael Zank (Albany, NY: SUNY Press, 2002), 6. In this context, mention should be made of the fact that both Soloveitchik and Strauss struggled with Cohen's interpretation of Maimonides, finally rejecting aspects of it (see Joseph Soloveitchik, *Maimonides between Philosophy and Halakhah*, ed. Lawrence J. Kaplan [New York: KTAV Publishing/URIM Publications, 2016], 125; Leo Strauss, *Philosophy and Law: Contributions to the Understanding of Maimonides and His Predecessors*, trans. Eve Adler [Albany, NY: SUNY Press, 1995], 129–133; Leo Strauss, "Cohen and Maimonides," trans. Martin D. Yaffe and Ian Alexander Moore, in Leo Strauss, *Leo Strauss on Maimonides: The Complete Writings*, ed. Kenneth Hart Green [Chicago: University of Chicago Press, 2013], 221).

6. Gershom Scholem to Walter Benjamin, March 29, 1935, in *The Correspondence of Walter Benjamin and Gershom Scholem: 1932–1940*, ed. Gershom Scholem, trans. Gary Smith and Andre Lefevre (Cambridge, MA: Harvard University Press, 1989), 156.

7. Joseph Soloveitchik, *The Emergence of Ethical Man*, ed. Michael S. Berger (New York: Ktav Publishing, 2005), 187–188, 6. See also Yoram Hazony, "The Rav's Bombshell," *Commentary*, April 2012, 48–55.

8. This is not to suggest that no attempts have been made at bringing about a conversation between the two. Jonathan Cohen attempts just this from the vantage point of Judaism. The present study, in contrast, is an attempt to initiate a philosophical conversation. See Jonathan Cohen, "Strauss, Soloveitchik and the Genesis Narrative: Conceptions of the Ideal Jew as Derived from Philosophical and Theological Readings of the Bible," *The Journal of Jewish Thought and Philosophy* 5: 99–143.

9. Joseph B. Soloveitchik, *The Halakhic Mind* (New York: The Free Press, 1986).

10. Leo Strauss, *Philosophy and Law: Contributions to the Understanding of Maimonides and His Predecessors*, trans., Eve Adler (Albany: State University of New York Press, 1995).

11. *The Halakhic Mind*, 53.

12. While this is a point that Strauss makes in his published piece "Philosophy As Rigorous Science and Political Philosophy (*Interpretation* 2/1 [Summer 1971]: 1–9), there is perhaps no clearer expression of this criticism—along with the high esteem in which Strauss holds Husserl—than the one given in his 1971–1972 St. John's course on Nietzsche's *Beyond Good and Evil*: "The greatest and most passionate attempt to restore philosophy to its rightful place and to its commanding position was made in our century by Husserl. Husserl claimed

(and that is unique) that by restoring philosophy to its rightful place and to its commanding position, he would actualize for the first time the character of philosophy as a rigorous science. He thought of Plato when he wrote these sentences. Yet Husserl had to admit that for the foreseeable future—in principle, for all future—philosophy as [a] rigorous science which establishes the standards of knowledge and of action has to live in an uneasy companionship with what he called philosophy as *Weltanschauung*, worldview, which is admittedly unscientific. The hybrid, consisting of philosophy as rigorous science and philosophy as worldview, could not possibly give the human race that unitary and unifying guidance which Nietzsche expects from the new philosophers." See Leo Strauss, "Nietzsche's *Beyond Good and Evil*: A Course Offered in 1971–1972, St. John's College, Annapolis, Maryland," ed. Mark Blitz, Estate of Leo Strauss, 2016, 196; https://wslamp70.s3.amazonaws.com/leostrauss/s3fs-public/Nietzsche%27s%20Beyond%20Good%20and%20Evil.pdf.

13. Edmund Husserl, *Ideas Pertaining to a Pure Phenomenology and to Phenomenological Philosophy: First Book*, trans. Fred Kersten (Boston: Kluwer Academic Publishers, 1982), 16–17.

14. See Rodrigo Chacon, "Strauss and Husserl," *Idealistic Studies* 44: 2–3 (2014): 284; Jacob Klein, "Phenomenology and the History of Science," in Jacob Klein, *Lectures and Essays*, eds. Robert B. Williamson and Elliott Zuckerman (Annapolis, MD: St. John's College Press, 1985), 67.

15. *Ideas*, 209; translation slightly modified.

16. Ibid., 137.

17. Edmund Husserl, "Philosophy as Rigorous Science," trans. Quentin Lauer in Edmund Husserl, *Husserl: Shorter Works*, eds. Peter McCormick and Frederick Elliston (South Bend, IN: University of Notre Dame Press & Harvester Press, 1981), 170.

18. *The Halakhic Mind*, 40–41.

19. Ibid., 46.

20. Ibid., 67.

21. Ibid., 68.

22. Ibid.

23. Ibid., 70.

24. Ibid., 71.

25. Ibid., 88.

26. Ibid., 75.

27. Ibid., 86. In using the principle of reconstruction and objectivation through correlation as he does, Soloveitchik is wedding his own Husserlian procedure to moments of Paul Natorp's philosophy of the social sciences. See Erlewine, 145–148, and Dov Schwartz, *Religion or Halakha: The Philosophy of Joseph B. Soloveitchik—Volume One*, trans., Batya Stein (Boston: Brill, 2007), 47. For an intimation of Soloveitchik's relation to the Cohenian conception of objectivation, see Joseph B. Soloveitchik's letter to Leo Jung, September 5,

1939, in Joseph B. Soloveitchik, *Community, Covenant and Commitment: Selected Letters and Communications*, ed. Nathaniel Helfgot (Brooklyn: KTAV Publishing House, 2005), 271–272; and Heshey Zelcer and M. Zelcer, "A Note on the Original Title for 'The Halakhic Mind,'" *Hakirah* 23 (2017): 75.

28. Ibid., 86–87.

29. Ibid., 92. While the distinction between explanation and description is clearly a major aspect of Husserlian phenomenology, it also plays a role in Cohen's thought. For a Cohenian reading of this distinction as it occurs in Soloveitchik, see Schwartz, 67.

30. *The Halakhic Mind*, 86.

31. Ibid., 102.

32. *Philosophy and Law*, 54–55.

33. Ibid., 24.

34. Ibid., 26–29.

35. Ibid., 75.

36. Ibid., 76.

37. Ibid., 44.

38. Ibid., 45.

39. Ibid., 81.

40. See Philipp von Wussow, *The Philosophy of Leo Strauss: Culture, Religion, and the Political*, Habilitationschrift, 2016, 190.

41. *Philosophy and Law*, 59.

42. Benjamin Aldes Wurgaft, "Culture and Law in Weimar Jewish Medievalism: Leo Strauss's Critique of Julius Guttmann, *Modern Intellectual History* 11, no. 1 (2014): 132.

43. *Philosophy and Law*, 128.

44. Ibid., 138n2.

45. Ibid., 132–133. In this context, see Dana Hollander, "'Plato Prophesied the Revelation': The Philosophico-Political Theology of Strauss's *Philosophy and Law* and the Guidance of Hermann Cohen," in *Judaism, Liberalism, and Political Theology*, eds. Randi Rashkover and Martin Kavka (Bloomington: Indiana University Press, 2014), 80.

46. *Philosophy and Law*, 132.

47. Ibid., 88.

48. Ibid., 132.

49. Ibid., 39.

50. Ibid., 21.

51. Joseph B. Soloveitchik, *And From There You Shall Seek*, trans. Naomi Goldblum (Brooklyn: KTAV Publishing House, 2008); Joseph B. Soloveitchik, *Halakhic Man*, trans. Lawrence Kaplan (Philadelphia: The Jewish Publication Society, 1983); Joseph B. Soloveitchik, "On the Nature of the Halakhah," in *Community, Covenant, and Commitment*, 273–277.

52. *And From There You Shall Seek*, 121.
53. *Halakhic Man*, 19.
54. *Community, Covenant, and Commitment*, 275.
55. *Halakhic Man*, 85.
56. *And From There You Shall Seek*, 54–60.
57. Ibid.
58. Ibid., 119.
59. *Community, Covenant, and Commitment*, 273.
60. *Halakhic Man*, 19–20.
61. *Community, Covenant, and Commitment*, 273.
62. Ibid., 274.
63. Ibid., 276.
64. *Philosophy and Law*, 76.
65. Ibid., 90.
66. Leo Strauss, "The Origin of Modern Political Thought (1937)," in Leo Strauss, *Toward* Natural Right and History, eds. J. A. Colen and Svetozar Minkov (Chicago: University of Chicago Press, 2018), 179.
67. *Philosophy and Law*, 100.
68. Ibid., 90.
69. Ibid., 60. In this context, see Dana Hollander, "Understanding Law ('Gesetz' and 'Recht')," in Hermann Cohen, "With Help from the Early Strauss," *Idealistic Studies* 44: 1–2 (2014): 268.
70. *Philosophy and Law*, 71.
71. Ibid., 89.

4

Claude Lefort and Leo Strauss

On a Philosophical Discourse

Isabel Rollandi

It is possible to suggest that a dialogue between Claude Lefort and Leo Strauss revolves around the figure and the work of Machiavelli. Despite the various lines of intersection and possible dialogues between these two authors,[1] Machiavelli's thought can be said to have a special place in their work: For Lefort, it constitutes a starting point for the development of his work;[2] for Strauss, it provides an opportunity to think about and practice philosophy.[3] Furthermore, an analysis of Lefort's Machiavelli in conversation with Strauss' can shed light on the relationship between their work.

We would like to venture a hypothesis: A debate between Lefort and Strauss about "the teachings of Machiavelli" and the definition of political philosophy sheds light on their respective understandings of the relationship between the *work*[4] and the *exercise of philosophy*. To address this relationship, a challenge or question that Strauss poses to readers of Machiavelli, and that Lefort accepts,[5] will help us begin the inquiry: *how should we read Machiavelli?* Strauss presents this question and points toward the proper way in the middle of the first chapter of *Thoughts on Machiavelli*. Lefort does this explicitly at the outset of his interpretation of Strauss's reading. This question as a point of departure will force us to focus on something that exceeds the *logos* of the text; it will force us to consider the literary character of the work and its "effective" potential.

To unfold the implications of this debate, we will first seek to present Lefort's critique of Strauss's interpretation of Machiavelli's work, paying particular attention to the relation Lefort establishes between the author, the reader, and the text. Additionally, we will try to clarify Strauss's view on the topic; that is to say, we shall focus on Strauss's understanding of the "art of reading and writing" in Machiavelli. We shall not embark on a comprehensive reading of the work of both authors—such a reading would extend beyond our aims. Trying to understand the *particular necessity* with which Machiavelli confronts them, namely, a hermeneutical challenge, we shall try to reconstruct the aspects of this possible dialogue regarding the status of the philosophical work and the philosophical activity.

Lefort's Critique of the "Teaching"

In 1972, Claude Lefort[6] published *Le Travail de l'Oeuvre Machiavel*, a study (as he stresses) of the *enigma* that emerges from the reading of Machiavelli's works[7]. On this occasion, he includes an interpretation of Leo Strauss's work on the Florentine, which he defines as "exemplary." Lefort's interpretation of *Thoughts on Machiavelli*, as we mentioned, is guided by the question that places the *work* at the center, that is, how to read Machiavelli. We would be deceived, Lefort claims, if in reading Strauss's approach to this question we tried to separate his own understanding of the hermeneutics from his setting in motion of a comprehensive interpretation of Machiavelli's philosophical project. It is true, according to Lefort, that these two tasks cannot be separated: Strauss's interpretation links the question of *the meaning of the discourse* in Machiavelli to the question of its *reading*. Lefort states that thoughts are born in questioning a discourse's mode of intelligibility. This point of departure enables a legitimate interrogation of the work. Lefort presents this subject as the relation between the interpreter and the work.

There is an assumption, Lefort holds, that underlies Leo Strauss's interpretation: the proper perspective is achieved by the reader only when we discover *the permanence of the problems* confronted by human thought as well as Machiavelli's concern for addressing them.[8] The approach to Machiavelli's work or the starting point for the reader should be, thus, a detachment from contemporary thought and a liberation from the "actual prejudice" toward his work. According to Lefort, Strauss wants to understand not only what is *said* in the discourse but its *productivity* as well.[9] To understand the work, we need to return to the moment in which the discourse emerges, to its origin, and be amazed by what caused amazement.

Lefort tells us that Machiavelli, according to Strauss, must, in the first place, be read as a classical philosopher as Strauss understands it. This statement would accordingly mean that, for Leo Strauss, Machiavelli knows the difference between science and opinion, between the wise reader and the ignorant reader, and makes use of his writing as *art* in the service of this difference. To open up Machiavelli's discourse we must occupy the place of the wise reader who can grasp what the writer gives to understand and master his teachings. Once we adopt this perspective, Lefort states, we shall come to understand how Machiavelli's work (according to Strauss), carefully read, reveals a *deviation* from classical philosophy and, with it, the signs of the decline of the philosophical task.

Beginning an Interpretation

Lefort follows Strauss's advice on how to read a philosophical text. To read Machiavelli as a philosopher, we must pay attention to his warnings and assertions, as well as to his reading norm, that is to say, the way he reads. Therefore, understanding how Machiavelli reads Livy will guide our interpretation of Machiavelli's writing. In doing so, we learn that part of his discourse is contained *between* the lines, that his writing contains *slyness*, and that there is no communication without *discretion*. We learn that Machiavelli's *silences* point directly to the heart of his teaching. The principle of the reading consists of identifying signs that lead us toward the unsaid—what is thought but reserved for the investigator's sagacity. However, attention to the unsaid is not enough; we must understand the *intention*, which Lefort calls the "non-tangible," reserved for the wise reader who "knows that the idea governs the appearance."[10]

Lefort observes that the strategies Strauss finds in Machiavelli's writing serve the need to communicate prudently: a writer must be cautious, for there is *always* a dominant power that restricts expression. Thus "to disseminate some principles that are new," says Lefort, it is required to write "*in an oblique way*."[11] However, the "more particular hypothesis" suggests that the "specific dominant power" in Machiavelli's times—the Christian religion—lends its specific character to the philosophic expression. Moreover, this combat between philosophy and religion is revealed as even more fundamental when we understand that not only Machiavelli but also "entire lineages of thinkers" were opposed to the same power of revealed religion. Hence, Lefort will state, following his reading of the Straussian text: "It is necessary to agree that the rules of reading Machiavelli—like the rules of writing—are only defined when the identity of his enemy is suggested."[12]

Lefort defines the art of writing as presented by Strauss in the first place as a *strategy*: it involves certain operations, secret instructions, and the use of a code. Using the term "strategy," writes Lefort, Strauss wants us to recognize that "the writer symbolically reveals the method which he uses to attack the enemy reader, cantoned in the fortress of the antique *modi ed ordini*."[13] However, the definition of writing as a strategy is insufficient: the *means*, writes Lefort, are subordinated to the objective of *teaching*.[14] "Teaching" involves a particular relationship between a subject that possesses knowledge in a specific domain, and other subjects that supposedly acquire it by virtue of the former's action. The nature of the "art of writing," for Lefort, indicates that the author is a *teacher* who *masters* his *knowledge* completely and *communicates* it by an appropriate *technique*. When the operation of reading coincides with that of writing, the good interpreter is also the good teacher.[15]

Contradictions in the Discourse

Lefort uses the tools Strauss proposes for reading Machiavelli to read Strauss' own interpretation of him. He discovers tensions and contradictions in Strauss' arguments and, as Strauss does with Machiavelli, uses them to identify Strauss' intentions. The issue is *how to understand* the contradictions. Strauss's interpretation is not grasped by solving the contradictions, writes Lefort: its terms cannot be "sublated" or overcome without introducing a fiction. The deviations and references that disconcert the reader and leave him perplexed should be understood as signs of the author's *generosity* and the opening of a way to access its true content. To go through the contradictions means rising above appearances, giving up images contained in a particular proposition, and to progressively dominate the language, in order to reconstruct the thesis behind its apparent negations. Therefore, in order to progress toward the Straussian interpretation of Machiavelli, Lefort states that we must press through the contradictions—that is, we must repeat as it were the progression of philosophy.[16] Lefort thus traverses Strauss's text, highlighting five contradictions in it. Along the same path, he presents his critiques of Strauss's thoughts as well. Each contradiction is linked to the previous one and leads to the next. Arriving at the last contradiction, Lefort will expose his critique to what he takes to be the *fundamental proposition* of Strauss, linked to *his fundamental contradiction*. Seeking to understand this contradiction, Lefort will critically consider, once again, what he believes to be the *premise* that organizes Strauss' thought, and which makes him assume while interpreting Machiavelli the role of a *teacher* mastering his discourse.

Lefort begins by presenting three contradictions: connected to Strauss's presentation of Machiavelli's arguments: how to understand Strauss's depiction of Machiavelli both as a philosopher and a destroyer of philosophy;[17] how to understand Strauss's emphasis on Machiavelli's fundamental attack on religion and his simultaneous emphases on Machiavelli's attacks on religion and classical philosophy alongside his proposal of a new normative philosophy;[18] and his simultaneous concerns with glory and truth.[19] After dealing with these first three contradictions, Lefort arrives at two additional contradictions: one between Strauss' analysis of Machiavelli's disclosures and dissimulations; and between the *new* and the *old*,[21] or the impossibility of surpassing the horizons of classical philosophy. These last two contradictions illuminate, in turn, Strauss's own "art of writing" and his intention in *Thoughts on Machiavelli*, according to Lefort. By focusing on these last two contradictions that Lefort finds in Strauss's text, we shall come to understand how Lefort links what he considers the *core* of Strauss's interpretation of Machiavelli, what we just referred to as his *premise*, with what he understands to constitute the problem of the *statute of the work* and the position of the *interpreter*.

Dissimulating and Disclosing

The tension between dissimulating and disclosing comes to sight, according to Lefort, when we approach two features simultaneously: (1)

Strauss's criticism of Machiavelli's lack of caution to communicate (as he states openly and in his own name) principles known to the ancient philosophers that they communicated with great discretion, and (2) his acknowledgment of the Florentine's effort to communicate his thought with an indirect language, writing as a philosopher, in an oblique way, and thus seeking to mislead the common reader and conceal his statements from a censoring power.

To understand this tension between disclosure and dissimulation in Strauss's reading of Machiavelli as presented by Lefort, we need first to clarify how he understands Strauss's account of the difference between classical philosophy and modern political thought.

Lefort restates Strauss's argument: Machiavelli is a philosopher, different from the sophists and hedonists because he knows the truth of the organization of the city, and he recognized the highest pleasure in the exercise of philosophy.[23] The "truth of the organization of the city" pertains to the "low principles" on which it is founded. According to Lefort's interpretation, for Strauss classical philosophy holds the view that "virtue is subordinated to necessity" or that "moral virtue is only determinable on account of an amoral conception of virtue."[24] Nevertheless, Machiavelli does not appropriately understand the distance between philosophy and the city, the need of "placing the supreme Good beyond the common good"—he does not know how to "supplement the insufficiency of justice." This lack of understanding makes Machiavelli try to found the city on the lowest of the needs: on man's bestiality. "For the first time the relationship between man and God is eliminated and replaced with that between men and beast."[25] However, in a new twist to the argument, we see that this alternative, states Lefort following Strauss, had already been conceived by the Greek philosophers and deliberately discarded. Lefort asks: what leads Machiavelli, then, to this reversal of *high* and *low* according to Strauss?

We have to return, according to Lefort, to Strauss's understanding of Machiavelli's confrontation with religion, and furthermore, discover by ourselves what Strauss only halfway mentions. Machiavelli, throughout his philosophical effort and his critique of Christianity, will suffer "the effects of the enterprise he fights," Lefort interprets, precisely because, according to Strauss, the philosophical tradition he resorts to had already been corrupted by the Christian teaching; it was, according to Lefort, already a *denaturalized* thought. Therefore, Machiavelli's complaint against the "God of the established religion" and his "effort to reconcile himself with Socrates"[26] will fail, because he does not grasp this previous corruption.

Lefort suggests that in identifying himself with the Antichrist Machiavelli *forgets the truth at the heart of philosophy*, "which was his secret and forbade both the belief in the cave and the belief in a *real* world illuminated by a *real* sun."[27] This would mean that Machiavelli, in his attempt to eliminate the Biblical distinction between this world and the afterworld—or the reference to transcendence in the name of truth—consequently prompts the elimination of the distinction between the sensible and the intelligible, between the just and the unjust, between philosophy and politics.[28] The movement that began with Machiavelli cuts the bond with transcendence, Lefort argues, and instead of broadening the horizons of human thinking, opens the path toward the era of obfuscation. Machiavelli's *novelty* is then an *error*.

By exposing "the truth about injustice or necessity," previously accessible only to those who could appreciate the difference between justice and wisdom, Lefort holds that Machiavelli divulges a corrosive truth for the city; he offers the public what was meant only for the wise and pretends to turn the politicians into "the promoters of the truth."[29] Machiavelli, as a result, undoes the distinction between philosophers and nonphilosophers. Therefore, what is new in his teaching is *disclosure*. However, Strauss tells us, according to Lefort, that Machiavelli is also an heir of the ancient "art of writing," and "that what is said in the discourse is what is not said, that the most significant in his teaching is the most secret."[30]

This tension between concealing and revealing, for Lefort, is illuminated when we understand that *the new* offers only a well-developed figure of the *discourse of corruption*,[31] which was already a part of the teaching of the classics. Machiavelli's *new modes and orders* are nothing but *corruption*.[32]

After achieving this understanding, says Lefort, "this thought would only impose the double task of recovering the Machiavellian teaching against the opinions—halfway positivist and halfway religious—of the moderns, and restoring the teaching of the classics against the Machiavellian teaching, which, along its movement of critique, has been trapped in the orbit of the adverse discourse."[33] That is to say, Machiavelli, in his critique of the transcendence of the religious discourse, had reduced his inquiry toward human nature to the dimensions of the cave.

Classical Teaching and Novelty

The return to the classics, thus presented, hastens the last contradiction: the modern discourse, according to Strauss, was known by the Greek philosophers not only in terms of its principles but also in its conditions of success. Therefore, the only thing that stands to oppose the "teaching of the classics" would be, following Lefort's interpretation, "the inability of men for theory."[34]

To clarify Lefort's assertion, we must return to Strauss's text. Lefort follows Strauss's arguments presented at the end of chapter IV of *Thoughts on Machiavelli* (298–299), and reinstates the understanding that, according to Strauss, the classics had of the distance between science and practice: science, as understood by the classics, should remain theoretical because its practical application could lead to a "universal tyranny." Nevertheless, they had to make a crucial exception regarding the art of war, that is, the admission of innovations for the defense of the city. This exception, notes Lefort (following Strauss), paved the way for an expansive usage of science. However, according to Strauss, modern change is not a consequence of the bare fact of these innovations, but of the practical use of science that made them possible. And for the classics, such use of science was excluded by "the nature of science as a theoretical pursuit." Therefore, the only thing that can lead to the modern consequence is a misunderstanding of the premise of the classics. According to Lefort, for Strauss, "only the incapacity [*défaillance*] of men for theory" "could be opposed to the understanding of the classics."[35]

Lefort thus argues that Strauss's judgment concerning the corruption of classical thought imposes a difficulty on the task of restoring the teaching of the classics that destroy its efficacy.

Reaching this final position, we arrive at what is arguably the main point of Lefort's dispute with Strauss: the proper way of understanding *novelty* in history. In this sense, Lefort writes: "Strauss, therefore, calls for the restoration of the teaching of the classics departing from premises which analysis of the modern world destroy its efficacy; or, to say it better, he transforms into *practically utopic* what he thinks has *never had the statute of a utopia*; he reinstates a distance between philosophy and politics that, according to his own argument, Plato would never have accepted."[36]

The impossibility of conceiving, even as a utopia, the idea of the best regime, the confluence between the wise man and the ruler or between the philosopher and the politician, and the recovery of classical thinking in these terms leads Strauss's argument, according to Lefort, to a last and fundamental contradiction.[37]

The problem for Lefort is therefore that either Strauss fails to account for *the new* in Machiavelli's thought, or he does not know the meaning of classical philosophy.

Lefort does not solve this last contradiction. "It is not our intention to take the question further," he states and refers immediately to the relation of interpreter and text. In order to clarify this matter, we must clarify the position of the interpreter (Strauss) in relation to Machiavelli's work. We need to ask again the question regarding *how to read Machiavelli*. We argue that Lefort's movement from the analysis of the argument of the text toward the question concerning the interpretation and the discourse constitutes his way of suggesting a solution to that last contradiction.

The Interpreter and the Discourse of the Work

After studying the development of Strauss's arguments in *Thoughts on Machiavelli*, Lefort introduces his critique of Strauss's exegesis. Strauss's interpretation of Machiavelli depends, for Lefort, on Strauss's premise concerning the art of reading and writing, and the intention he reads (or holds must be read) in Machiavelli when interpreting his writing. He adds: "this postulate of Strauss lacks legitimacy; it is associated with a conception of philosophy as teaching, or the philosopher as a teacher, a conception which has no established foundations."[38]

Lefort claims that Strauss's discourse has a particular referent, designated by a particular figure: philosophy as *teaching*. "The transformation of philosophy into teaching, the emergence of *The Philosophy* within the philosophical discourse, its denomination as classical philosophy, has an inevitable consequence: the writer does not study Machiavelli despite the appearance, that is, he never compromises his principles in the adventure that is inaugurated by the work."[39] Strauss's premise, thus, forces the work to talk *about* philosophy—it gives the work the statute of *teaching*, and to Machiavelli, the place of the *teacher*.

This operation, Lefort indicates, is "in a sense unnecessary."[40] But nevertheless, the positioning of Machiavelli as a teacher also appears to be indispensable for Strauss's argument: Strauss himself (according to Lefort) occupies the position of philosopher/wise reader, and reduces "the discourse of the Other" to "a moment of his own." Therefore, if Strauss points out that nothing in Machiavelli's discourse is without intention, it is because in effect, according to Lefort, no thought may have escaped Leo Strauss. Hence, as a reader of Machiavelli, Strauss makes himself the *author* of this discourse, and the difference between reading and writing is ideally abolished.[41]

We arrive at the answer to our initial question regarding how to read Machiavelli, although it is hidden, according to Lefort, because it does not emerge from the reading. On the contrary, the reading is organized by the answer that results from Strauss's understanding of philosophy as *teaching* and the position of the *teacher* (i.e., master of his discourse). Every analysis of the omissions and transgressions of a discourse will, therefore, operate always within pre-set limits, the limits of a particular intention.[42]

According to Lefort, Strauss thus conceives of an author as a master of his speech. In this sense, we can say that Strauss conceives of the author as a sovereign ruler of his discourse. And in the same vein, he conceives of the interpreter as one who can master that discourse.[43] By doing so, according to Lefort, Strauss cannot conceive of the reach of Machiavelli's interrogation of the political.

Founding and Origin in the Oeuvre

Lefort concludes his interpretation of *Thoughts on Machiavelli* by stating that Strauss's understanding of classical philosophy "and the philosopher's place as a teacher and a master of his speech" ultimately determines all of his analysis. According to Lefort, Strauss fails to see the *novelty* of Machiavelli. "The interpreter forgets to interrogate the incontestably new and unusual proposition, according to which the cause of the greatness of Rome lies in disunity."[44] This proposition is crucial, according to Lefort, because Machiavelli situates the *origin* of the Roman Republic not in a *foundation* but rather in *a conflict*, and reveals a division in the social body, a disunion of the city, which is primeval. This matter, states Lefort, which runs through the work, is erased by Strauss, who is unwilling to recognize the question of the *origin* in Machiavelli's discourse.[45] Strauss's restoration of what he considers to be the classical teaching has this price: the differentiation between philosophy and politics he affirms, according to Lefort, prevents him from *reading the original question* in the development of the political matter, in the order of the events.[46]

With this analysis, Lefort criticizes a conception of interpretation that we have called sovereign. Lefort argues that "it is no accident that the concept of *founder* shall be articulated with that of the *teacher*."[47] According to Lefort, Strauss would position himself, as an interpreter, in the place of a *founder*, and make of Machiavelli also a *founder*. Thus, according to Lefort, a sovereign author meets a sovereign interpreter, and the difference between one's discourse and the discourse of the other seems to dissolve.

CONCLUDING REMARKS

Summarizing our presentation of the arguments, we see that Lefort moves through the contradictions he finds in the text, arriving at his most fundamental point of conflict with Strauss: the question of the interpretation of *novelty* in history. Lefort decides to discuss this point through the tension between the reader, the work, and the author—that is, by studying the interpreter's relation to the work. In this sense, the trajectory of his criticism returns to the beginning, namely, the question regarding the proper reading of Machiavelli.

According to Lefort, Strauss's interpretation finds a guarantee for the truth of the discourse that is "in a place strange to the thought of the author: it is, apparently, the place of classical philosophy."[48] Consequently, Lefort argues that Strauss is unable to go beyond the horizon that he himself has instituted: he interprets and measures Machiavelli's reflections based on a foundation outside the work.[49]

The place of the interpreter is, therefore, that of someone who knows beforehand where his exegesis is leading, who identifies with the *teacher* and understands philosophy as *teaching*. Therefore, an event is only readable as a moment of philosophic interpretation, that is, according to the premises of classical philosophy.

The conclusion of a judgment operating from this vantage point, argues Lefort, cannot be other than that Machiavelli deviates from classical philosophy. Novelty can only be corruption or ignorance, which in both cases, according to Lefort, evinces a lack of understanding of "the nature of philosophy."[50]

However, according to Lefort, it is Strauss who cannot see Machiavelli's "incontestably new and unusual proposition." Strauss avoids explaining the original division of *social discourse* (the conflict of humors), as well as the original division of discourse *in the work* and *in the institution of interpretation* (between reading and writing).

Already from the title of his book, *Thoughts on Machiavelli* Strauss anticipates, according to Lefort, the type of intellection or thought activity that he conceives as the task of interpretation. The work contains *thoughts* that are the result of the reflection of a wise reader, provoked by the object he studies, the work of a philosopher with a teaching that the reader can dominate and communicate as master of the philosopher's speech. Lefort's critique is further enhanced when we reflect upon the title of *his* interpretation of Machiavelli: *Le Travail de l'Oeuvre Machiavel.* With his title, Lefort points toward his particular understanding of the relationship between the work and the reader; it focuses on the *effect* that the author's work does on the reader and on time, removing both interpreter and author from their positions of sovereignty; both are "worked upon." The work appears in the heart of history as an event that provokes a particular movement of institution and dis-institution of tradition and authority.

The Art of Reading and Writing in Leo Strauss's *Thoughts on Machiavelli*

After presenting Claude Lefort's critique, it is appropriate to try to grasp Leo Strauss's understanding regarding these points. If, according to Lefort, Strauss's reading of Machiavelli is governed by the idea of classical philosophy—articulated through the notion of a *teaching* from a philosophical master to a pupil who acquires a particular *knowledge* regarding the truth after reading the masterfully crafted book—we shall try to clarify the notion of *teaching* criticized by Lefort as well as the decisive place of classical political philosophy in Strauss's interpretation.[51]

In order to understand the idea of *teaching* as presented in *Thoughts on Machiavelli*, we first need to become aware of the distinction between the notion of the *teaching* of a philosopher and his *thought*. Teaching, according to Strauss, refers to the twofold presentation: first of what a philosopher desires to communicate, a doctrinal content, revealing a needed reflection or an answer regarding the specific political circumstances in which this thought takes place; and, second, with his teaching, the philosopher must be able, at the same time, to hide the most important from the careless reader and reveal the true meaning of what he wants to communicate to the careful reader.[52] And yet, the *thought* of a philosopher points directly to the philosophic activity, and can be achieved or reached only through a penetrating inquiry into the philosopher's intention.[53] Understanding this distinction will allow us to address Lefort's critique properly.

According to Strauss, *teaching* is not the transference of a corpus of dogmas to a reader by means of artful rhetoric; there is no sovereign position in this sense, neither of the writer nor the reader; on the contrary, when the true teaching finds its suitable addressee, a dialogue between kindred natures takes place.[54]

Moreover, we shall see that Strauss does not refrain from presenting his critique of the classical teaching, rendering impossible the idea of the latter's comprehensive superiority, as Lefort suggested. The motif of the "superiority" of "classical political philosophy," or "the teaching of the ancients," does not point toward the recovery of "a body of true propositions." We could argue that the Straussian emphasis on "the classics" should be properly understood as a means to put into focus a renewal of philosophy through a confrontation, and thus enable a further ascent to the activity of philosophy.

Teaching and Thought

Leo Strauss's *Thoughts on Machiavelli* moves between two terms. The term *teaching* is present twice in the titles of chapters (1—as twofold—and 4); the term *intention* is also present two times, referring to Strauss's reflections on *The Prince* and the *Discourses*.[55] The *teaching* at both ends of the work discloses the *intention* of the philosopher Machiavelli, which we can only reach by reading him carefully and trying to understand him as he understood himself.[56] Further, the title of the book should call the reader's attention, as it encompasses the main activity of the philosopher. The work sets forth a particular progression: a philosophical inquiry.[57] Through a careful reading, we become aware of the movement of the book that leads us from the *surface* of the *teaching* of Machiavelli—and its most superficial problem, its twofold character—to the *core* of the *thought*.[58] The study of the *intention* of Machiavelli allows Strauss to finally move toward a single presentation of the *teaching*—along with a critique—and its historical consequences.[59] Illuminating the meaning of the philosophic activity in *Thoughts on Machiavelli*, the reader comes to understand that the teaching of some philosopher cannot be simply the *truth* of his thought. In the same sense, for Strauss, the point of arrival could not be a restitution of the teaching of "classical political philosophy." But by the end of the Introduction to *Thoughts on Machiavelli*, Strauss writes: the "purpose of the critical study" could not be other than "to contribute toward the recovery of the permanent problems."[60]

THE ART OF READING AND WRITING

To address the meaning of the philosophic activity in *Thoughts on Machiavelli*, we should try to illuminate Machiavelli's art of reading and writing in Machiavelli as presented by Strauss. Moreover, reading chapter 1 will allow us to clarify the meaning of an access to the *thought* through a *teaching* that is twofold.[61] The chapter begins focusing on one of the most familiar problems of Machiavelli's scholarship: the *obscure* relationship between the two books in which he explicitly tells the reader that he presents "everything he knows."[62] No reader, no matter how *superficial*, can overlook this duality. However, the presentation of his teaching in a twofold manner, as we will see, is indeed a *treat* from Machiavelli to the careful reader, according to Strauss. When considering the problem of the surface—that is, the duality of a teaching—we are compelled to raise the question regarding Machiavelli's *intention*, "whether Machiavelli's perspective is identical with that of the *Prince* or with that of the *Discourses* or whether it is different from both perspectives."[63] Therefore, the *thought* of the author is in focus. The first part of the chapter draws attention to the weight of the hermeneutic question.[64] And the paragraph articulating the two halves of the chapter gives us to understand that the level on which we should move in order to reach what the author is intending is that of *the art of careful writing*: "The question which we raised can be answered only by reading Machiavelli's books. But how must we read them? We must read them according to those rules of reading, which he regarded as authoritative. . . . His manner of reading Livy may teach us something about his manner of writing."[65]

The second part of the chapter deals in particular with Machiavelli's art of writing, explaining the way toward the careful reading of a philosophical text. Strauss will present Machiavelli later in the book as a *worthy heir* of this art: the writer is guided with serenity by reason—he knows how to use "the gift of nature," he knows how to persuade, how to talk to future philosophers, and he knows how to hide his thoughts from those who cannot read him with care.[66] Machiavelli knows that the communication of a finding is dangerous, that he must present his *thought* "in an *oblique way*," both revealing and concealing.[67] He therefore expresses with audacity only those opinions that are tolerable and is very careful with those that lack support whatsoever. The intention is not disclosed but "intimated": Machiavelli, pointing toward a reflection that necessarily exceeds the limits of the written speech, seeks intimacy with a reader, writes Strauss. The art of writing relies upon the addressee: "to speak the truth is sensible only when one speaks to wise men."[68]

The ways in which Machiavelli suggests what "he is unable to state" should be ("it is indispensable" that they be) discussed, says Strauss. He moves forward to show ten devices[69] of the art of writing used by Machiavelli to communicate his thought: Silences (paragraphs 18–23); manifest blunders (24); contradictions (26); difference between titles and body of the text (27–28); irony (30); repetitions (31); digressions (32); ambiguous terms (33); curious numbers (34 and 36); and concealed blasphemies (35). In each point of the discussion of a device, we learn how it will appear in Machiavelli's writing; we also learn how to move toward the author's *intention*. The progress through gradual revelations allows the reader to recognize something *beyond* the "substance of his teaching." The careful reader must unveil; he must understand what is intended through a blunder, and he must follow the writer through different propositions and learn that a philosophical discourse cannot be that of mere force, or that Machiavelli could never speak like Thrasymachus. The reader, seeking to understand the intention of the author, begins his own reflections: he thinks *what he is given to understand*. Machiavelli, by offering the reader a half-way reflection or by concealing a statement, implicates him in his thought and makes him his accomplice.[70]

But thinking about the writer's statements and silences does not suffice. To understand the *intention*, we must *analyze the action*, which is different from what is said or silent in the text. Studying *Discourses* III, 18, Strauss notes that Machiavelli calls our attention to a silent contrast that, although not new, "*performs a function*," or "two different, if related functions." It points toward "some aspect of the central problem," while it presents "the general lesson" in a less obvious or an opposite mode to the one he usually used: "the spirit of comedy, not to say levity, is not absent from his two most serious books."[71] The silent contrast that we are given to think is that between gravity and levity. The discourse will *perform*, and its function will be, in part, "to amuse."[72] A careful reader should not refrain from appreciating this feature, and be amused.

The proper understanding of the devices a philosopher uses to communicate through the web of the argument also points toward the identity of the adversary's speech. Analyzing what Strauss calls Machiavelli's "parody of scholastic disputations,"[73] we become aware of his critique of the Bible: Machiavelli seems to infer that "the dogmatic teaching of the Bible" has "the cognitive status of poetic fables."[74] Following Strauss's advice in the footnote, we learn about a "pre-history of this view" and realize that Farabi shared this notion.[75] The parody of scholastic disputations hides a dispute between two fundamental alternatives regarding the status of human knowledge and a philosophical critique of the truth of revealed religion.[76]

The devices of the esoteric writing, in sum, set in motion the thoughts of the reader who seeks to understand the writer's intention—they demand an effort. We can reach an "adequate understanding of his intention," writes Strauss "provided 'we put 2 and 2 together' or do some thinking on our own."[77] Machiavelli's twofold presentation deliberately installs an obscurity in the center of his writing, and it is "essential" to "the presentation of his teaching"[78] because it forces the reader to *think for himself*—from particular propositions—the whole of the former's discourse.[79] In the last paragraph of chapter 1, the relationship between Machiavelli's books is presented again, yet modified: while first identified as *obscure*, it is now described as *enigmatic*.[80] The contrast between the terms is *thought-provoking*: from an obscurity to an enigma, the progress of the thought is displayed; we are offered a *riddle*. Approaching its truth (or, accessing the enigma of the work[81]) requires an *unassisted effort* from the reader.

Nevertheless, not every reader will follow the movement of Machiavelli's thought, according to Strauss. Only the true addressee is *seduced to thinking*: "Concealment as practiced by Machiavelli is an instrument of subtle corruption or seduction.[82] He fascinates his reader by confronting him with riddles. Thereafter the fascination with problem-solving makes the reader oblivious to all higher duties if not all duties."[83] The last sentence of chapter 1 offers us the identity of the primary addressee: the *young* readers.[84] *The young* are fascinated by the task of thinking and the freedom of thought: only a theoretical interest occupies their mind, and they forget authority.[85]

Moving forward from the particular to the general—from the *double teaching* to the unity of the *thought*—we move from the surface to the core of the argument and recognize that there is a discourse revealed to us only when we involve ourselves in the totality of the author's thought and move along with him. The art of writing allows us to share the experience of the philosophical task. We think for ourselves what the author gives us to understand, but we are never under the logic of persuasion, nor do we lay down "our own arms," the power of human thought, *a guidance coeval with man as man*. The idea of a writer that is sovereign and a reader that masters a teaching is dissipated when we consider that the destiny of the discourse is linked to the journey the reader must travel beyond what is written, to initiate a dialogue between philosophical natures.

The Consequences of a Teaching

We are thus led to the second point of our discussion. A philosopher offers a *teaching* in response to his understanding of the historical situation of philosophy.[86] The last chapter of the book, *Machiavelli's Teaching*, serves the purpose of exhibiting what Strauss has come to understand as *the* teaching of Machiavelli, one not initially offered by the author and thus needed to be reconstructed, making an ascent from opinions and discovering his intention. We now grasp the movement from *thought* to *teaching* situated on the other end of his philosophical enterprise.[87]

It is possible to find a critique made by Strauss of Machiavelli's teaching with regard to its world-historical consequences in Strauss's distinction between ancients and moderns, at the end of the last chapter of his book. We nevertheless cannot balance this critique with a simple praise of the "teaching of the classics." Strauss, as we will see, also presents a critique of *this* teaching and recovers Machiavelli's thought *against* the classics on a particular point. This critique is made clear in the last section (84–87) of chapter 4.[88] Machiavelli's novelty, we read, is not to be founded on "a more thoroughgoing or comprehensive analysis of political phenomena as such."[89] Strauss brings Machiavelli very close to the classics before emphasizing his distance from them. A distinctive treatment of Machiavelli's teaching regarding *foreign policy* appears to be the key element for Strauss's critique of the classics.

Following what Strauss calls the treatment of the consequences of "Machiavelli's action," we read: "we must not forget the fact that for Machiavelli himself the domination of necessity remains the indispensable condition of every great achievement and in particular of his own."[90] We must therefore understand what the character of this necessity is that had to be dominated—one that would make an enterprise stand or fall. Yet Strauss places next to it a strong critique pointing to the posthumous consequence: "the transition or the jump from the realm of necessity into the realm of freedom will be the inglorious death of the very possibility of human excellence."[91] If a critique of the "modern world" is in place, we must ask what led to it, or what necessity made it plausible. We "cannot cease wondering," writes Strauss, how the modern enterprise could appear as reasonable, "what essential defect of classical political philosophy could possibly have given rise to the modern venture."[92] This is the place where we can read a critique of classical political philosophy.

The last paragraph of the book begins to inquire into this "necessity," which "spurred on Machiavelli and his great successors" but is no longer in force. If their effort is no longer so evident, writes Strauss, it is because "their adversary" is no longer powerful; we learn that *necessity* thus arose from the encounter of an adversary. Understanding this necessity shall help us illuminate the specificity with the challenge faced by Machiavelli and his specific answer to it, or his philosophic politics. The attitude toward necessity shall entail a novel position regarding *foreign policy*, a distance from and a critique of the classical teaching.

Following Strauss, the classics were "for almost all practical purposes" what we now call conservatives: they were distrustful of political and technological change. Strict moral-political supervision of inventions was demanded. From the point of view of classical political philosophy, the use of science for inventions was excluded by its theoretical nature. Technology liberated from moral and political control would lead to disastrous consequences.[93] But the confrontation with inferior cities forced them to admit the need of innovations with regards to the defense or to resistance; they had to make an exception within the *art of war*. This exception meant that "the good city" had to take its bearings from the practice of "bad cities." The classics neglected *foreign policy*, and foreign policy reveals a philosophical understanding of the self-sufficiency of the city and of the nature of external enemies.[94]

The emergence of a particular necessity, a pressing external power such as the Catholic Church, changed the scope of the challenge:

not only were the classics unable to prevent the Church's victory, but furthermore, they let Christianity profit from their teaching. Despite restricting science to a theoretical pursuit, the crucial exception regarding the art of war paved the way for an expansive usage of science for practical purposes. We read: "The difficulty implied in the admission that inventions pertaining to the art of war must be encouraged is the only one which supplies a basis for Machiavelli's criticism of classical political philosophy."[95] Confronted by the particular challenge of Christianity, Machiavelli had to give an adequate answer. But his teaching regarding foreign policy, we said, has an antecedent or is *not completely novel*: it can be traced back to Farabi, another philosopher who faced a foreign power and who shared the understanding of necessity in this sense.

Machiavelli's teaching, we understand, is not measured against the teaching of classical political philosophers and declared insufficient, corrupted or subversive, as Claude Lefort would have stated. Strauss lets his readers understand that an adequate critique of the incapacity of the classics for giving a proper account of the necessity for a foreign policy can be proposed. Their protection of the philosophical life appears defective in the most important way: if it had been sufficient it would not have been so easily adapted to the requirements of the revealed law.[96]

Nevertheless, it is possible to argue that Strauss understands that even if Machiavelli's enterprise proved to have a huge political success, it eventually weakened the position of philosophy as a distinct way of life.[97] Machiavelli, according to Strauss, was the founder of modern political philosophy.[98] It accordingly means that Machiavelli is a *philosopher*, that a new tradition of philosophy is continued after him, but that his philosophy is no longer Greek.[99]

Final Remarks

However this may be, Strauss's book ends with a sentence that suggests a return to the activity of thinking through "a return to the fundamental experiences."[100] After following Strauss's arguments across the book, we see Strauss meet Machiavelli in philosophical dialogue and give us *his own thoughts* to understand. *Philosophy*, the quest for knowledge, cannot become a doctrine; it must be grasped as a way of life. It can be argued that, according to Strauss, the only way for a philosopher to preserve his *thought* is to be able to prompt some *thoughts* in the mind of the student of philosophy who reads his books. But this would mean that every upcoming philosopher must, in a way, retrieve the perspective of the original thought and begin anew, for he cannot take the *philosophy* from tradition. In this sense, he himself must be a *founder*.[101]

In this regard, the doctrines that the philosopher necessarily needs to present as a part of his teaching are an integral part of his teaching.[102]

The Interpreter and the Work

We are now able to face a proper understanding of the relationship between the interpreter and the philosophical work in the view of Strauss—one that might escape Lefort's critique. Claude Lefort's understanding of a philosophical work guides his critique of Strauss's reading. According to Lefort, as we read in his interpretation of Machiavelli, the work of an author will open up to the reader only once he abandons the idea of securing its meaning: "it would be futile," he writes, "to pretend to remove the oeuvre from the risk on which it is founded, to give it mastery over its domain. It awaits the risk of the other, expecting from him a new putting back into play that testifies to the first one."[103] In this sense, his critique of the idea of the "teaching" becomes clearer when we grasp his understanding of the dimension that a work opens: "once the oeuvre exists, it is its lapse into the past: the word that is proffered there is for everyone, beginning with the author."[104]

Therefore, according to Lefort, the movement of expression of the *oeuvre* can only be followed provided we continuously face the *unknown*.[105] The route that the text describes is discovered by the author in its development, while the reader discovers the writer's stroke following his intention. In this sense, the labor of the interpreter coincides with that of the writer. Embracing the indeterminacy that the philosophical text inaugurates is the path to an understanding of its enigma. "To seek the meaning of the oeuvre," says Lefort, "is necessarily to seek the *being* of the oeuvre; it is to learn to discover the interrogation in the oeuvre and to confront the enigma of instauration, without ever being able to sidestep the risk that the word of the other initially assumed."[106] The philosopher embarks on this task and through interrogative thinking tries to think what the author signifies. Political philosophy does not seek a guide for intellection of the phenomena, nor pretend to be outside or above society and its self-knowledge. The knowledge of the political can never assume a point of exteriority with respect to its own historically situated existence, but it does not thereby fail to produce judgments about the political.[107]

If in Lefort's critique the problem is set in the interpretation of philosophy as teaching, and the art of writing as transmission of knowledge from a teacher to a student, we now see that Strauss's text could not allow this critique.

In Strauss's understanding, the action of the text implicates the reader who knows how to read and binds him to the movement of the philosopher's thought. Moreover, Strauss doesn't impose a referent strange to the discourse; rather, he thinks what the philosopher gives to think *in pieces* and, following his intention, he reconstructs the *thought*. Lefort cannot see this duplicity between *teaching* and *thought*—or, rather, he flattens it.

It is, however, true that Strauss speaks of a "sovereign" author elsewhere. In "On the Interpretation of Genesis" Strauss writes (when interpreting the *book* as *a work of art*) that "[t]he book in this sense is a conscious imitation of living beings. There is no part of it, however small and seemingly insignificant, which is not necessary so that the whole can fulfill well its function. When the artisan or artist is absent or even dead, the book is living in a sense. Its function is to arouse to thinking, to independent thinking, those who are capable of it; the author of the book, in this highest sense, is sovereign. He determines what ought to be the beginning and the end and the center. He refuses admission to every thought, to every image, to every feeling which is not evidently necessary for the purpose or the function of the book. Aptness and graces are nothing except handmaids of wisdom." The author is sovereign as long as he can lay out his book responding solely to the necessity of his reasoning. But this does not mean that he seeks to simply transmit doctrines: the book is meant *to arouse thinking, independent thinking*, writes Strauss. And he continues: "The *perfect book* is an *image* or an *imitation* of that all-comprehensiveness and perfect evidence of knowledge which is aspired to but not reached. The perfect book acts, therefore, as *a countercharm to the charm of despair* which the never satisfied quest for perfect knowledge necessarily engenders. It is for this reason that Greek philosophy is inseparable from Greek poetry."[108] The *perfect* book remains an *imitation* of the whole as perfect knowledge; man is not in possession of an "all comprehensive and perfect evidence of knowledge." Nevertheless, against despair, the image of perfection, both of the book and the mind of its author, some "outstanding" or "exemplary" natures prevent us from falling into despair.[109]

It can safely be said that, in *Thoughts on Machiavelli*, Strauss seeks to *reopen a reflection* and not to *interrupt* it at a point of arrival. As we have come to understand, the purpose of the "critical study of Machiavelli's teaching" cannot be other than a contribution "toward the recovery of the permanent problems."

Notes

1. Authors who have explored the connections between Lefort and Strauss include Pierre Manent, "Toward the World and toward the Work," in *Modern Liberty and Its Discontents* (New York: Rowman & Littlefield, 1998); Bernard Flynn, *The Philosophy of Claude Lefort: Interpreting the Political* (Evanston, IL: Northwestern University Press, 2005); Gilles Labelle, "Can the Problem of the Theologico-Political Be Resolved? Leo Strauss and Claude Lefort," *Thesis Eleven* 87 (November 2006): 63–81; Claudia Hilb, "Claude Lefort as Reader of Leo Strauss," in ed. Martin Plot, *Claude Lefort: Thinker of the Political* (New York: Palgrave Macmillan, 2013); Newton Bignotto, "Lefort and Machiavelli" in ed. Plot, *Claude Lefort: Thinker of the Political* (New York: Palgrave Macmillan, 2013).

2. "I consider Machiavelli a fundamental reference in my work. But I should specify that nowhere in my writings have I erected him as a master and I don't claim we should follow what would be his teaching." Claude Lefort, "Conversación con Claude Lefort," in *Maquiavelo. Lecturas de lo Político* (Madrid: Trotta, 2010), 567. My translation.

3. What Strauss presents in *Thoughts in Machiavelli* is of exceptional relevance for his author: his "observations and reflections" on "the problem of Machiavelli." Strauss, *Thoughts on Machiavelli* (Glencoe, NY: The Free Press, 1958), Preface (1957). Consider also the title of the book as a suggestion concerning the activity of the philosophy.

4. Throughout this text we will refer to the idea of "work" alluding to the writing of a philosopher. This is a reference to Lefort's particular understanding of an *Oeuvre*, that is, a work of thought, a book, that *works*. Consider the title of his book on Machiavelli: Claude Lefort, *Le Travail de L'Oeuvre Machiavel* (Paris: Gallimard, 1972).

5. We believe that Lefort *accepts* Strauss's suggestion regarding the liaison between the hermeneutical and the philosophical tasks that Machiavelli's work compels us to undertake. See Manent's interpretation of this relation: he suggests that both authors *share* this principle of reading. Cf. Pierre Manent, "Toward the Work and Toward the World: Claude Lefort's Machiavelli," 49. Consider Lefort's review of *Thoughts on Machiavelli* published in 1960 with the title "Machiavel jugé par la tradition classique" in *European Journal of Sociology* 1, no. 1, where the author devotes himself at length to studying Strauss's art

of reading and writing (ibid., 162). Also, consider Lefort's comment on the Straussian writing in C. Lefort, "Machiavel et la verità effettuale," in *Écrire. À l'épreuve du politique* (Paris: Calmann-Lévy, 1992).

6. Claude Lefort (1924–2010) was a French philosopher known for his reflection around totalitarianism, political philosophy, and modern democracy. In his youth Lefort was politically engaged: as a Marxist, he remained critical of the Soviet Union and co-founded along with Cornelius Castoriadis the journal *Socialisme et Barbarie* (1948–1958). Lefort was profoundly influenced by Merleau-Ponty and his phenomenological reflection and problematization of the opposition between subject and object. Eventually, Lefort edited Merleau-Ponty's posthumous works *The Visible and the Invisible* and *The Prose of the World*. Lefort's thought, as Bernard Flynn puts it, expresses a "continuation of a philosophical sensibility" of Merleau-Ponty. Bernard Flynn, "Introduction" in *The Political Philosophy of Claude Lefort* (Evanston, IL: Northwestern University Press, 2005, xxii). Lefort wrote his doctoral dissertation on Machiavelli under the supervision of Raymond Aron, published as a book entitled *Le travail de l'oeuvre Machiavel* (1972). His reflection on Machiavelli shifted the way he perceived politics and the "conflict of classes"; he perceived that an inner conflict with no resolution always pulls apart society. Lefort continued working on his political reflections *in Essais Sur La Politique* (1986) and on totalitarian and democratic regimes in *L'invention Démocratique* (1995) and *Les Formes De L'histoire* (2000), among many other works.

7. The *Oeuvre* is a key concept in Lefort's interpretation of Machiavelli. It points simultaneously toward a "work of thought" and the task of the interpreter before that work. *Oeuvre* illuminates the place of Machiavelli as an author, as well as the *ouverture* that his work produces, both on the plane of "thinking" and of the "world." According to Lefort, the interpreter facing that *Oeuvre* and *ouverture*, that "work" and that "opening," will be compelled to inquire into the *enigma* that constitutes a work of thought but remain open to it (Lefort, *Le Travail*, 58–59, 70). Lefort writes: "When we inquire of Machiavelli, we inquire political society: our task is to explore the ties woven between thought in the work and political thought" (ibid., 306). All translated passages from the French are my own.

8. To recover the *permanence of the problems* is for Strauss, according to Lefort, tantamount to recovering the premises of classical philosophy. Only then will we be able to grasp how Strauss understands Machiavelli's *novelty*, argues Lefort.

9. The productivity of the discourse indicates the effect of the work on its readers and in history. In Lefort's words, this means to examine the "representation" of Machiavelli and the "imaginary" that surrounds his name. (Cf. the second section of Lefort's book, with the title "Le nom et la representation de Machiavel," 71–93.)

10. Lefort, *Le Travail*, 269.

11. Ibid., 271. Lefort's reference to "an oblique way" is a direct quotation from Strauss's work. Cf. Strauss, *Thoughts on Machiavelli*, 33. If this sentence is universal, argues Lefort, every philosopher, including Strauss, will express himself in an *oblique way*.

12. Lefort, *Le Travail*, 272. With this remark, Lefort anticipates his critique of Strauss's hermeneutical principles: if we criticize the legitimacy of the identity of the enemy, he argues, we shake the premises of Strauss's exegesis. The critique of christianity, religion in general, and the idea of revelation can be differentiated in Strauss's account of Machiavelli's thought.

13. Ibid., 274.

14. The repetition of the term *teaching*, writes Lefort, articulates in this sense, the composition of the book. From the first chapter, "The Twofold Character of Machiavelli's Teaching" to the last chapter, "Machiavelli's Teaching," Strauss has carefully built the span of his argument. Cf. Lefort, *Le Travail*, 274.

15. This will be a central point of Lefort's critique of Strauss. Lefort argues that Strauss "stages his interpretation like a *teacher* who prepares his audience for a discovery. Leo Strauss knows from the beginning where he wants to conduct his reader; . . . Showing him the signs of his *dominion*, he wants to put him in a good disposition that will allow him to *learn* to read Machiavelli. After this, he [Strauss] will let him know the 'fundamental question' of his work; and even after that, the relation this question holds with the truth" (ibid., 265; my emphasis). Toward the end of our presentation, we shall encounter this critique as a point of arrival of Lefort's argument.

16. Ibid., 290. Consider Strauss's definition of philosophy in *Natural Right and History* (Chicago: University of Chicago Press, 1953): "Philosophy consists, therefore, in the ascent from opinions to knowledge or to the truth, in an ascent that may be said to be guided by opinions" (ibid., 124).

17. Lefort retrieves this contradiction from an analysis of the Introduction of *Thoughts on Machiavelli*, which is known for commencing with the statement that Machiavelli was a "teacher of evil" (Strauss, *Thoughts on Machiavelli*, 9). Lefort notes that Strauss revises his statement throughout the introduction. However, if Machiavelli is indeed a philosopher according to Strauss, Lefort wants to know how is it possible that his work, also according to Strauss, initiates the decline of philosophy. Lefort's conclusion is that, for Strauss, Machiavellian *destruction* must be understood as *corruption*. Cf. Lefort, *Le Travail*, 260–265.

18. Cf. ibid., 281–287. Lefort brings to the surface this contradiction through an analysis, first, of chapter 1 of *Thoughts on Machiavelli* and a reflection on what Strauss considers to be the chief enemy of Machiavelli's writing, that is, the religious authority. Second, through an analysis of chapters 2 and 3 of Strauss's book, devoted to studying Machiavelli's "intention" in *The Prince* and *Discourses* respectively: Lefort examines Strauss's understanding of Machiavelli's "new principles" and their essential opposition to what Strauss calls the "Great Tradition."

19. The treatment of the theme of *glory* in *Thoughts on Machiavelli* reaches a peak in chapter 4 (281–286). Lefort follows Strauss's arguments and finds a chief contradiction between Machiavelli motivation toward the "highest glory" and his motivation toward the truth. Cf. Lefort, *Le Travail*, 287–295. On this point, Heinrich Meier interprets Strauss differently: "That Machiavelli abstracts from *eros* and does not advocate for the turn to philosophy does not imply that he has forgotten the 'true conversion.' It means that the reader of the *Prince* and the *Discourses* who has reached the point at which he sees himself confronted with opposite conclusions and applications of the teaching is compelled to the *periagoge* that remains omitted in Machiavelli's presentation." Heinrich Meier, *Political Philosophy and the Challenge of Revealed Religion* (Chicago: University of Chicago Press, 2017), 100.

20. Lefort, *Le Travail*, 295–298. The question concerning Machiavelli's disclosure of principles that the classics knew how to keep concealed is linked to the point of arrival of the contradiction concerning the motivation for glory: the only appropriate audience for a glorious enterprise must be the *multitude*, he argues, and thus a discourse of *divulgation*. Lefort traces the problem back to the Straussian statements concerning Machiavelli's art of writing.

21. Ibid., 298–299. Lefort explores this tension in the last section of chapter 4 of *Thoughts on Machiavelli*. His critique of what we may call Strauss's fundamental proposition is presented here: Strauss's appeal to a restoration of classical philosophy.

22. Lefort formulates these principles in the following manner: "The Greek philosophers, we understand, didn't ignore the effective conduct of political men nor of its necessity, considering the conditions of its exercise; but the idea of what a society should be according to nature forbade them from confusing fact with right; the prudence with which they spoke of injustice testifies to the *distance* between philosophy and politics, as well as to the certainty that the establishment of the right order, despite its improbability, *was possible*" (ibid., 296). This is the nerve of Lefort's understanding of the Straussian account of Greek philosophy: there is a subordinate relationship between politics and philosophy, and the actualization of the best regime is possible in principle.

23. This argument redirects us to what we called the first contradiction, that is, the contradiction between Machiavelli as a philosopher and destroyer of philosophy (see note 17).

24. Ibid., 265.

25. Ibid.

26. Ibid., 266.

27. Ibid. Original emphasis.

28. Lefort deals with Strauss's understanding of Machiavelli's critique of religion when analyzing the second contradiction we referred to above. According to Strauss, the Florentine seeks to "denounce the lie of tradition" in order to conduct his reader toward "the true principles in their nakedness" (ibid., 180). However, according to Strauss, Machiavelli's critique of Biblical teaching leads

to a critique of classical philosophy and, for Lefort, culminates in the affirmation of Machiavelli as the sole authority. Yet, in Strauss's analysis, writes Lefort, the novelty in Machiavelli is nothing but his *incapacity* of understanding "the nature of philosophy as such" (ibid., 281). As a conclusion to this contradiction, Lefort states that, for Strauss, the new "principles" that constitute the "normative teaching" of Machiavelli, rooted in the twofold principle of glory and necessity (Cf. Strauss, *Thoughts on Machiavelli*, 252–253), are ultimately based on his desire of immortal glory. This statement hastens the consecutive contradiction: that between the desire of truth and the desire of glory.

29. Lefort, *Le Travail*, 296.

30. Ibid., 296. Cf. Strauss, *Thoughts on Machiavelli*, 120.

31. Lefort refers to the third chapter of *Thoughts on Machiavelli*, where Strauss writes: "Admiration for ancient Rome was the only publicly defensible base from which he could attack the Biblical religion. . . . To apply to Machiavelli his own expression, not being able to blame Caesar, he praised Brutus" (Strauss, *Thoughts on Machiavelli*, 144). By the same token, Strauss argues that Machiavelli uses Livy's authority to criticize the Biblical authority. But, Lefort writes, "Titus Livius performs therefore a double function." (Lefort, *Le Travail*, 281): Machiavelli, according to Strauss, progressively undermines Livy's image, so that he can be left alone in the place of the authority.

32. As we already mentioned, the whole tradition Machiavelli opposed had already been corrupted. Lefort states: "In Strauss's eyes, Machiavelli is the prince of modern political thought, but he is admirable like Caesar for his audacity, and if he gives *his name* to the principles of a corrupt politic, he does no other thing than extracting the consequences of the degradation of philosophy" (ibid., 266; my emphasis). Lefort refers to an argument of Strauss in the last chapter of *Thoughts on Machiavelli*: "[people] believe for instance that it was Caesar's *wickedness* that was responsible for the fall of the Roman republic . . . ; they do not see that the Roman republic fell because of its *corruption* which *antedated Caesar* . . ." (Strauss, *Thoughts on Machiavelli*, 245–246). Analogously, it would seem that we should not blame Machiavelli's *wickedness* for the decay of classical philosophy since its corruption was already there.

33. Lefort, *Le Travail*, 298.

34. Ibid., 299.

35. In other words, the only thing we can think about beyond the teaching of the classics (according to Lefort) is insufficiency or incapacity to understand that theory must rule over practical matters. To further grasp this argument, see Strauss's account of Aristotle's understanding of science in *Natural Right and History*, 23. Science is essentially theoretical.

36. Lefort, *Le Travail*, 299. My emphasis.

37. Consider Claudia Hilb's analysis of this question in Hilb, "Claude Lefort as Reader of Leo Strauss." Strauss, in Lefort's understanding, transforms philosophy, in a sense, into a utopia.

38. Lefort, *Le Travail*, 290. According to Lefort, Strauss cannot dispense with the representation of the philosopher, his intention, or the addressee of his writings. The *philosophic work* thus institutes a *philosophic reader*; no criticism can cut the knot that constitutes "the link of his reader with what makes his link with the truth," ibid., 291.

39. Ibid., 299.

40. Lefort refers to Strauss's argument toward the end of chapter 4 of *Thoughts on Machiavelli*, where the author says that Machiavelli fails to grasp "that moral virtue" is not only "a qualified requirement of society" but also "that it is a requirement of philosophy or of the life of the mind. As a consequence, he is unable to give a clear account of his own doing" (Strauss, *Thoughts on Machiavelli*, 294). This judgment, writes Lefort, contrasts the weighted demonstration of Strauss "according to which Machiavelli would have full awareness of the effects that his word is meant to produce on his interlocutors" (Lefort, *Le Travail*, 300).

41. Lefort remarks: "It is not by fortune that he shall say that Machiavelli goes half the way to encounter his reader, leaving him the task of making the other half of the way alone. Through his operation, both halves are united" (ibid.). Strauss would suggest, therefore, according to Lefort, that *everything is readable* (ibid., 301).

42. Cf. ibid., 302. Lefort concludes then that the presentation of an adequate reading of Machiavelli's texts by Strauss must support a tacit thesis: the discourse of Machiavelli is "designed with an objective," that is ruining religion. All the signs of his writings are organized in the service of this intention. Strauss installs a criticism of the Bible at the heart of Machiavellian discourse.

43. Lefort is critical of any conception of an omniscient writer/interpreter. On this point, consider Bignotto's, remark: "Guided by Merleau-Ponty, Lefort states that, upon looking at a philosophy from the past as a 'building of knowledge,' we leave aside the most important issue, namely, that every piece of work contains an 'unthought-of' (impensé), a fringe of indetermination, which is exactly what makes us think" (Bignotto, "Lefort and Machiavelli," 35). As we mentioned, Strauss's understanding of Biblical criticism and the arguments against revelation must be differentiated.

44. Lefort, *Le Travail*, 304.

45. In *Sur une colonne absente*, Lefort writes: "the concept of origin designates not a beginning in itself, but that which is sought in the junction of a past and a future, of an outside and an inside . . ." (Paris: Gallimard, 1978), 28. The relationship between foundation and origin in Strauss might be said to be more intricate. For a treatment of the problem, see Meier, *Political Philosophy and the Challenge of Revealed Religion*, 80, note 106.

46. Following Lefort, even if we agree that the Machiavellian speech seeks the destitution of the traditional form of authority, his critique will necessarily exceed its objective: what is questioned is "the statue of a guarantee that is

alien to the proof of knowledge," says Lefort. And "this discussion," he argues, is in itself the spring of the philosophical discourse." Lefort, *Le Travail*, 294. Lefort seems to point toward the destitution of the place of the interpreter as a sovereign, but furthermore, to any *sovereign discourse*. Cf. Strauss, *Natural Right and History*, 92: "the distinction by which philosophy stands or falls, the distinction between reason and authority."

47. Lefort, *Le Travail*, 260. My emphasis.

48. Ibid., 260. Cf. ibid., 267.

49. This external grounding of the work would be both a specific content (classical philosophy and its *teachings*) and also a particular style (the art of reading and writing in service of the transmission of a *teaching*). This understanding, according to Lefort, would be supported by a hypothesis regarding classical philosophy, according to which a philosophical work should be understood as the transmission of teachings from a sovereign author to its adequate reader.

50. Cf. ibid., 281. The reason for Machiavelli's mistake, or his inability to adequately understand the philosophic task, as we stated, is related to his confrontation with the Bible, according to Lefort.

51. Further, we have noticed that Lefort does not make a distinction between what he calls "classical philosophy" and "classical *political* philosophy." As we know, the Straussian definition of political philosophy, which includes the "Socratic turn," implies the protection of philosophy and the philosophic life but moreover for the justification of its possibility and necessity as the best life. Consider *Natural Right and History*, 120–121; *What is Political Philosophy?* (Chicago: University of Chicago Press, 1959), the philosophical treatment of political issues (ibid., 10) and, more profoundly, the political or popular treatment of philosophy, or the introduction to philosophy (ibid., 94).

52. Consider Strauss, *Persecution and the Art of Writing* (Chicago: University of Chicago Press, 1952), 28, 36, and Strauss, "Restatement on Xenophon's Hiero" in *On Tyranny* (Chicago: University of Chicago Press, 1961), 221.

53. Heinrich Meier explains this tension with great clarity: "As interpreters, we can attempt to do justice to the internal dynamics of political philosophy solely by setting out from the level of the doctrinal presentation and inquiring back to the intention of the author in order to involve ourselves in the movement of thought that took place within that quadrilateral and takes place in it ever anew." Meier, *Leo Strauss and the Theologico Political Problem* (New York: Cambridge University Press, 2006), 107.

54. In another place, the nature of this encounter is made clear: "the 'original' or 'personal' 'contribution' of a philosopher is infinitely less significant than his private, and truly original and individual, understanding of the necessarily anonymous truth." Leo Strauss, "Farabi's Plato," in ed. Louis Ginzberg *Jubilee Volume* (New York: American Academy for Jewish Research, 1945), 337.

55. The book is composed with great care: a typical preface with unusual comments, an introduction with twelve paragraphs as published by *The Free*

Press in 1958, and four chapters that form an arch from the first one to the last one: I. "The Twofold Character of Machiavelli's Teaching"; II. "Machiavelli's intention: *The Prince*"; III. "Machiavelli's intention: *The Discourses*"; IV. "Machiavelli's teaching." The importance of the structure of the book forces us to refer in each quotation not only to its page but also to its chapter. An additional reference to the paragraphs should be made but will be omitted in this article.

56. Machiavelli's books are particular: both his work and the nature of his thought have a philosophical status. To accept the description of Machiavelli as philosopher places him in a particular ground, defined by a particular concern. Cf. Strauss, *Thoughts on Machiavelli*, 17; Cf. Machiavelli, *Discourses on Livy*: i, 56. As we have seen, Lefort notices that Strauss's emphasis on the description of Machiavelli as a philosopher comes into tension with Strauss's simultaneous critique of Machiavelli. However, the direction and articulation of this critique of Strauss will reveal that for him the core of Machiavelli's though remains philosophical.

57. The introduction offers a clear example: starting with "the old-fashioned and simple *opinion*," he moves forward to the consideration of "the intrepidity of his *thought* . . ." Then, the plan: "Not the contempt for the simple *opinion*, nor the disregard of it, but the considerate *ascent* from it leads to the core of Machiavelli's *thought*." Strauss, *Thoughts on Machiavelli*, Intro, 9–13. Our Emphasis. Lefort, as we saw, points toward this understanding as well when he deals with what he identifies as the first contradiction in Strauss's book.

58. "The problem inherent in the surface of things, and only in the surface of things, is the heart of things." Ibid., Intro, 3. This sentence is a token that shall be put into practice throughout the book; it is "the golden sentence." Cf. Benardete, "Leo Strauss's *The City and Man*," *Political Science Reviewer* 8 (1978): 1. It is possible to suggest that this *golden sentence* articulates Strauss's approach to philosophical books and the *art of reading and writing*, as well as a particular definition of philosophy as *political philosophy*, beginning from what is *first for us*, with *opinions*, and ascending to knowledge.

59. We cannot forget that Strauss presents in the last chapter the unity of Machiavelli's teaching, which means that the chapter does not present merely the new political teaching of Machiavelli.

60. Strauss, *Thoughts on Machiavelli*, Intro, 14.

61. In footnote 50 of chapter 1, Strauss refers to his book *Persecution and the Art of Writing*, 13, for the first and only time in this chapter. Cf. Strauss, *Thoughts on Machiavelli*, 41. That this chapter is dedicated to studying Machiavelli's art of writing is nonetheless obvious.

62. Cf. Machiavelli, Epistle Dedicatory of *The Prince*; Epistle Dedicatory of *Discourses*.

63. Strauss, *Thoughts on Machiavelli*, 29.

64. Heinrich Meier notes: "The first chapter, which explicitly deals with the twofold presentation of Machiavelli's teaching and is devoted to Machiavelli's

art of writing, consists of two parts. While the second part provides an answer to the hermeneutic question, . . . the first part shows that the hermeneutic question is the actual philosophic question." Meier, *Political Philosophy and the Challenge of Revealed Religion*, 31.

65. Strauss, *Thoughts on Machiavelli*, 29.

66. Ibid., 120.

67. Ibid., 33. In each case, the rhetorical techniques Strauss describes work under the assumption of a double speech: one popular, which answers to and supports the conventional opinions, and one concealed, hidden between the lines, destined to those who can think for themselves what the author only suggests or veils with his writing. The qualified reader ascends "from 'first statements' which are . . . respectable or publicly defensible, to 'second statements' of a different character." Ibid., 43.

68. Ibid., 34. The addressee is qualified by the end of this chapter, when Strauss writes: "Ultimately, the twofoldness of perspective reflects a twofoldness of 'purpose' which is effective in each book and which corresponds to the difference between the 'young' readers and the 'old.'" Ibid., 53. Cf. Strauss, *Persecution and the Art of Writing*, 36. The definition of the "true" addressee of Machiavelli's books is nonetheless even more complex. Cfr. *Thoughts on Machiavelli*, 77; 81.

69. Strauss shall also use these devices in *Thoughts on Machiavelli*. Cf. Meier, *Political Philosophy*, 31, n16. The author illustrates ten devices presented by Strauss, referring to nine notes of his text. The reference to "manifest blunders" is missing.

70. Strauss, *Thoughts on Machiavelli*, 50.

71. Ibid., 40. Cfr. *Thoughts on Machiavelli*, 292.

72. Ibid., 82. Cfr. *Thoughts on Machiavelli*, 56.

73. The parody takes place in Machiavelli's *Discourses* II, 12.

74. Strauss, *Thoughts on Machiavelli*, 41.

75. Cf. Strauss, *Persecution and the Art of Writing*, 13: "The praise of philosophy is meant to rule out any claims of cognitive value which may be raised on behalf of religion in general and of revealed religion in particular." The advice also highlights a "historical" relationship between Machiavelli and Farabi regarding the challenge of *revealed* religion in particular.

76. Consider Strauss, *Natural Right and History*, 74–75.

77. Strauss, *Thoughts on Machiavelli*, 36.

78. Ibid., 47.

79. Consider the relevance of the Socratic insight presented in *Natural Right and History*: "To understand the whole, therefore, means no longer primarily to discover the roots out of which the completed whole, . . . has grown, . . . but to understand the unity that is revealed in the manifest articulation of the completed whole." *Natural Right and History*, 123. Consider Strauss, *Thoughts on Machiavelli*, 13.

80. See Meier's understanding of this variation in Meier, *Political Philosophy*, 36.

81. Cf. Lefort's understanding of the *enigma* of an *Oeuvre* above and Strauss's interpretation of the enigmatic character of Machiavelli's books.

82. For an adequate understanding of *corruption*, consider: "It goes without saying that the man who, from the point of view of the established order, necessarily appears as a corrupter may in truth be the first discoverer of those modes and orders which are simply in accordance with nature." Strauss, *Thoughts on Machiavelli*, 169.

83. Ibid., 50.

84. Machiavelli's esoteric addressees present a particularity. To understand this *utmost important* distinction, see Meier, *Political Philosophy and the Challenge of Revealed Religion*, 41. It is double: the "philosophers of the future" and the potential "philosopher-prince." Those for whom the theoretical interest is true *simply* and those for whom it is *for the time being*. Cf. Strauss, *Thoughts on Machiavelli*, 77.

85. We cannot, therefore, conceive the young as servants or soldiers. Cf. Strauss, *Thoughts on Machiavelli*, 153–154. If we understand them as "future captains" (ibid., 276), the character of the enterprise needs to be clarified. Machiavelli, as a philosopher, would never seek to be "the head" of a conquest (Cf. Machiavelli, *Discourses* III, 35). Cfr. *Thoughts on Machiavelli*, 19, 28, 29, 34.

86. Machiavelli is "undoubtedly concerned with teaching the truth and the true way." Strauss, *Thoughts on Machiavelli*, Intro, 14.

87. Nevertheless, as we will see, the chapter will end with a new appeal to the *thought* and the *thinking activity* of the philosopher.

88. As we have seen, Lefort devotes himself to analyzing this last section of *Thoughts on Machiavelli* in particular in what we called the fifth and last contradiction. Lefort perceives that Strauss is introducing a critique to classical political philosophy, although he does not pursue the study of what it entails. He grasps what he understands is an unsurpassable contradiction between the praising of this classical teaching and what would be the practical impossibility of its restoration. We can argue now that for Strauss a restoration of a teaching *tout court* would never leave the doctrinal plane; it would never be a restoration of a *philosophical activity*.

89. Ibid., 293.

90. Ibid., 298.

91. Ibid.

92. Ibid.

93. Cf. Strauss, *Natural Right and History*, 23.

94. It is possible to argue that this assertion entails a rhetorical reference to the relationship between philosophers and nonphilosophers. In this sense, foreign policy could be understood alternatively in relation to transcendence. Cf. Strauss, *Thoughts on Machiavelli*, 65, 295. Cfr. Leo Strauss, *The Political Philosophy of Thomas Hobbes: Its Basis and Its Genesis*, 161–163.

95. Strauss states: "Only in this point does Machiavelli's contention that the good cannot be good because there are so many bad ones prove to possess a foundation." Machiavelli's "overstatement" that good arms are "the necessary and sufficient condition of good laws" or "his eventual identification of the most excellent man with the most excellent captain" can be recognized. Ibid., 299. Cfr. Leo Strauss, *Gesammelte Schriften. Band 3. Hobbes' politische Wissenschaft und zugehörige Schriften—Briefe*, 272.

96. The merging of classical philosophy and the Biblical teaching is the state of things in which Machiavelli finds himself when attempting to put into motion his thought. Consider Machiavelli's silence on natural right (ibid., chapter 4, n145). Cf. *Natural Right and History*, 120: "The particular natural right doctrine which was originated by Socrates and developed by Plato, Aristotle, the Stoics, and the *Christian thinkers* (especially Thomas Aquinas) . . ." my emphasis; *What is Political Philosophy?*, 44. Cfr. *Persecution and the Art of Writing*, 163.

97. Svetozar Minkov provides an intelligent analysis of the last six paragraphs of *Thoughts on Machiavelli* in "An Irony beyond Machiavelli's Irony," in *Leo Strauss on Science. Thoughts on the Relation between Natural Science and Political Philosophy* (Albany, NY: SUNY Press, 2016). "What, then, is Machiavelli's innovation (whether based on a new insight or a new mistake)? Strauss can no longer postpone getting to the fundamental issue and to his fundamental concern: the status of philosophy. What is at stake and becomes the theme in the following two paragraphs is not Machiavelli's new way, but the status of philosophy in Machiavelli's thought" (ibid., 136–137).

98. Consider also Socrates's figure as a founder. "Socrates could become the founder of political philosophy." Strauss, "The Origins of Political Science and The Problem of Socrates," 1996, *Interpretation* vol. 12, n2, 163. Also, consider the tension between "founder of political philosophy" and "originator of the whole natural right teachings" in *Natural Right and History*, 120; a similar emphasis in *Socrates and Aristophanes* (New York: Basic Books, 1966), 6; *Xenophon's Socratic Discourse* (Ithaca, NY: Cornell University Press, 1970), 83. The linkage between the "problem of Socrates" and the "problem of Machiavelli" can be said to be one of the greatest homages that Strauss makes to the philosophy of the Florentine. Cf. *Thoughts on Machiavelli*, Preface, 1957, 5; "The Problem of Socrates" in *Interpretation* vol. 22, n3 (1995); "The Origins of Political Science and The Problem of Socrates," ibid.

99. Strauss, "Niccolò Machiavelli" in ed. Strauss and Cropsey, *History of Political Philosophy* (Chicago: Rand McNally, 1972), 297. Cf. Strauss, *Thoughts on Machiavelli*, 294.

100. Ibid., 299.

101. Consider here the contrast with what Lefort understood as Strauss's emphasis on the author and reader as founder. Cf. Strauss, "Farabi's Plato," 361.

102. Strauss, *Thoughts on Machiavelli*, 299.

103. Lefort, *Le Travail*, 60.

104. Ibid., 63.

105. Ibid., 151.

106. Ibid., 66.

107. Explaining this assertion, Lefort writes: "We are always brought back to the question of meaning, or more accurately, we never cease confronting it. But it can only be rightly formulated if we remain within the space of the oeuvre, if we do not cease relating our position to a place, to a time of discourse, and continue to undergo the experience of its origin." Lefort, *Le Travail*, 66.

108. Strauss, "On the Interpretation of Genesis" in *L'Homme. Revue française d'anthropologie 21*, no. 1 (January–March 1981): 19–20. My emphasis.

109. Concerning the notion of "exemplary nature," see Alberto Ghibellini, "Leo Strauss, Carl Schmitt and The Search for the 'Order of Human Things'" in *History of Political Thought* XL, no. 1 (Spring 2019): 138–157. The author interprets that, according to Strauss, nature must be understood as exemplary order (ibid., 157). We would suggest that it is rather the evidence of the philosophical thought of certain outstanding natures that reveals an exemplary order.

II. HISTORY AND POLITICS

5

A Civil Encounter

Leo Strauss and Charles Taylor on Religious Pluralism

Jessica L. Radin

> To be sure that something of a certain general kind will happen is quite compatible with being unsure, and indeed with its being uncertain, exactly what will happen.
>
> —Neil MacCormick, *Rhetoric and the Rule of Law*

Like all the contributions to this volume (whether they concern thinkers or topics), this chapter puts Leo Strauss in new company—in this case, Charles Taylor. Other than the novelty value of introducing an imagined conversation between two objectively interesting thinkers, what can we learn from such a pairing? I want to argue that from an imagined conversation between Taylor and Strauss a new way of considering the relationship between religion, politics, and society emerges. Yet these two thinkers, who wrote about politics in the same language and on the same continent at the same time, have no record of responding to one another's thought. There is one intellectual degree of separation between them—that of Isaiah Berlin—but our topic here is the back and forth between Strauss and Taylor, who received his PhD under Berlin's supervision in 1961 in the midst of a flurry of writing.[1] As Strauss published *What Is Political Philosophy?* (1959), Taylor was publishing articles as a graduate student and then newly minted PhD on the arms race, Cold War neutrality, and the relationship between the state and secularism—articles that even then demonstrated his awareness of the importance of a shared moral center, and his doubts that human beings could, in the absence of a transcendent principle, create such a moral center for themselves. Similarly, Strauss recognizes the particular challenges that religion poses to a modern and pluralistic democracy—Strauss sees both the positive resistance that religious belief offers from social and communal homogeneity (the descent into mass culture) and the fact that religious traditions in power inevitably end up rendering all other groups outliers or outsiders.

In some ways the intent of this chapter, and the desire to write it, come from the whisper I hear when I read Taylor or Strauss: perhaps, maybe, a better and more civil/civilian community comes from having more and not less religion. Is it possible that having more religion and religions in a community simultaneously results in citizens who have both stable principles (Strauss) and greater sensitivity toward people who are different from themselves (Taylor)?

The methodology of this chapter takes its cue from the particular melody of Strauss and Taylor's work: that political philosophy, and particularly political philosophy concerned with the role and impact of religion on the world, cannot be divorced from the real, material, and human world in which religious practice(s) and conflict(s) arise. For that reason the chapter takes into account more than the place of Strauss and Taylor in the history of philosophy and seeks to show how their awareness of their own thought as a part of the philosophical continuum is coupled with an awareness of the particular context—both time and place—in which each of them wrote. Both Strauss and Taylor identified themselves with what could accurately be called a philosophy of investment, often contrasted with the thought of Nietzsche and certainly in contrast to any form of philosophical and political contemplation that does not address the past, and the traditions of its texts and praxis, respectfully and with seriousness.

Material Histories

Strauss, raised in the aftermath of World War I and educated in Germany, eventually fled the rising Nazi tide in Germany and eventually found a home at the University of Chicago, where he was a teacher for many years. He never took a government post or in any way participated in the formulation of government policies—although there are those who say that he did so behind the scenes or through his students.[2] Some of the undergraduates who heard Strauss lecture have followed his own career path, becoming professors in universities and colleges across North America, Canada, and Europe, while some opted for more public and occasionally notorious careers in (primarily the United States) government. Strauss is widely read, and his readers can be found in academic departments ranging from political science to the study of religion, from history to education, and from Jewish to Islamic Studies. Whether simply reading Strauss and thinking that his thought is eloquent and important is enough to make one a "Straussian," or whether that descriptor requires an ideological affinity, is a different question.[3]

Biographically, Charles Taylor is unlike Leo Strauss in almost every possible way (though they are both white men who held tenured positions at world-class universities). Taylor is both a lawyer and an academic; a public intellectual, his writing can be found in Canadian and, on occasion, international newspapers: and he has worked directly for the Canadian government, most famously as one of the two eponymous co-chairs of the Bouchard-Taylor Report (2008).[4] Canada, and specifically Quebec, is one of Michael Walzer's "mixed regimes" of toleration. It has a significant immigrant and first-generation community, combined with the descendants of those who arrived in the region as colonists, and Indigenous Peoples whose residence pre-dates all other groups.[5] The Bouchard-Taylor Report was commissioned by the government after a spate of incidents (and an absolute explosion of press) regarding situations in which "religious accommodation" had taken place. The goal of the Report was to clarify and make recommendations about the state of multiculturalism in Quebec and how legal and social issues could be more clearly and productively addressed. The fact that the stumbling block to multiculturalism in Quebec was around questions of religious canons and state civility is no coincidence; as Strauss noted, religious faith and even more so religious practice make it difficult to homogenize people, or to unify them, if one is concerned about "nationhood." In the Report, Bouchard and Taylor describe the specifics of known incidents, legal precedents and possibilities, and concrete attempts to define—for both legal and rhetorical purposes—a vocabulary of toleration. And most fascinatingly for an examination of secularization and toleration, it was a report delivered to a government that already had a legal framework for dealing with potentially borderline issues of state duty/individual rights:

reasonable accommodation. In other words, Canada has already been operating under the presumption that the state has a duty to accommodate, within specific limits, the disturbance and potential pressure on resources generated by Canadians who believe that their faith requires them to do a certain thing, perform a certain prayer, or wear certain clothes.[6]

Taylor's works, from the early leftist essays of the late 1950s and '60s through the substantial and deep tomes of 1989 (*Sources of the Self*) and 2007 (*A Secular Age*), presuppose that secularism—as both a government position and a social concept—involves figuring out how actual political and social institutions can balance a commitment to freedom of religion with the need for adherents of all religions to interact nonviolently and on equal footing before the state. Strauss, further removed from politics explicitly, was more worried about the ability of states to find that real balance, and took very seriously the possibility that in fact genuine political equality among religions might be impossible, and that some degree of "otherness" would have to be accepted by minorities in the nation-state.[7]

Political Scientist, Philosophers of Politics, Historians of Political Philosophy

Despite the fact that Strauss never participated in politics directly, one of the reasons for his fame and infamy is the pertinence of his work to the challenges of democracy. However timely his insights into the issues of democracy might be, Strauss himself maintained that there was a fundamental distinction between the philosopher and the politician, or to phrase it differently, between the virtue of the philosopher and the virtue of the politician. The virtue of the philosopher is a never-ending, critical, careful search for the truth. The virtue of the politician is his ability to direct the community of people that make up a polity toward peace and prosperity, and therefore stability.[8] Obviously, these goals of the philosopher and the politician are not always the same, and in fact are often opposed to one another. The politician promotes ideas and practices, and in fact promulgates laws, that ensure the survival of the community. That (relatively) peaceful stability is the virtue for which he strives. The philosopher, on the other hand, promotes debate about the truth, about the morality of a given law, about the foundations of an uncritical belief. In short, the philosopher provokes discord not for its own sake, but *makhloket l'shem shamayim*—for the sake of a higher power that demands the truth, regardless of whether that truth may have negative consequences for an individual, a group, or the legitimacy of a political regime itself.[9] Philosophy therefore appears in much of Strauss's work as fundamentally in conflict with politics and different games whose players keep tripping over one another because they are on the same field.[10]

Political philosophy is a particular problem because for Strauss the attempt to conduct political philosophy in the modern world can only be a third- or fourth-stage imitation of Classical political philosophy that, as we will see below, was anchored in its time and place to physical, material, even "natural" occurrences in a way that no succeeding generation of political philosophers (doomed to speculate about and view everything through their understanding of the classics) ever was. What is notable about the political philosophy that developed at the time of Nietzsche was that it ceased to even make such an attempt, casting off the requirement that one understand the past or search for any kernels of truth within it. This is disastrous, according to Strauss, on a number of levels: while a critique of our predecessors may be both the prerogative of and a necessity for the new generation, Nietzschean political thought would have us throw the baby out with the political bathwater. Acknowledging the need for our predecessors—as teachers, as resources, as examples of what is good and what can go wrong—is one of the things that Strauss and Taylor share.[11] For Taylor, the attempt to create a better and more virtuous society cannot involve a radical break from the prior systems that we now regard as oppressive or patriarchal, unless that break somehow involves the deep understanding of oppression and patriarchy that makes us at least somewhat less likely to repeat the same exclusions and aggressions in a different form. For Strauss, it is only by understanding the thinkers of the past as they understood themselves that we can begin to seriously critique and analyze our own world. Strauss's command that we "understand the thinker of the past as he understood himself" has been the subject of a great deal of controversy. At the most basic (or exoteric, if you like) level, Strauss acknowledges the potential impossibility of such a venture (though this does not undermine the importance of the attempt).[12] On a deeper level, Strauss's insistence points us to his own work on the thinkers of the past; and, in the case of the Classical and to a certain extent Medieval political philosophers, to the fact that their political philosophy, unlike our own, owed its legitimacy to its direct confrontation with the circumstances in which they developed it rather than to its knowledge of prior thinkers.[13]

For Taylor, the relationship between political science and philosophy is more evenly divided, between the science that analyzes political movements and provides information about them, via public news sources or government policy recommendations; and the investigation of concepts and ideas deployed (often uncritically) in those contexts. The easiest way to identify this distinction in Taylor is by looking at the Bouchard-Taylor Report of 2008, which gave more than thirty-five explicit recommendations to the Quebec government about its limits and responsibilities of the government to reasonably accommodate their religiously plural citizens (both as groups and as individuals). The Report contained practical and pragmatic suggestions—for example, that the crucifix currently hanging in the National Assembly be removed to another location in the building where its cultural significance to Quebec would be acknowledged without imposing Christian symbolism upon Muslim, Jewish, and Sikh representatives of the Québécois. While as a whole the Report seemed to show a path toward greater accommodation and tolerance, it also articulated specific limits, such as the recommendations that people who visibly wield the power and potential violence of the state (specifically police and judges) should not wear religious symbols.[14] The Bouchard-Taylor Report was a work of public policy—and two years later, along with Jocelyn Maclure (an expert analyst in the final editing of the Report), Taylor published *Laïcité et la Liberté de Conscience*, plainly stating in the Forward that "clearly a public report is not a philosophical treatise. The report of a government commission must be clear, accessible, concise, and above all, wholly devoted to understanding the social and political issues that it must clarify and the identification of concrete courses of action." The later text is devoted to investigating philosophically the questions that arose from the chapter in the Report devoted to secularism.[15]

The Report investigated the definition of secularism and the variety of ways that it might be expressed in both state and civil society. Its authors concluded that since secularism is related to the rights and freedoms of individuals, both religious and nonreligious, Quebec would be best served by pursuing an open and inclusive version of secularism that does not confine religion solely to the private sphere but that respects visible and religiously based differences in the public sphere.[16] *Laïcité et la Liberté de Conscience* is a philosophical follow-up to the principles underlying this determination. As a political scientist, Taylor provides his considered opinion regarding political activity, both state and social; as a philosopher, or even philosopher of politics, he is concerned not with clearing the way for a course of action but with how the terms, principles, and values of politics are formulated. Rather than simply providing a list of four characteristics displayed by secular governments, the philosophical plunge distinguishes between the operations of secularism and the moral principles (equality and liberty of conscience) that those operations uphold.[17] He even asks whether those values—or virtues—are true virtues capable of creating the kind of stable and shared national identity necessary for a democracy to function.

Strauss's constant referral to medieval Arabic sources in his work is not simply the result of his identification of the medieval authors with the development of esoteric writing. It is because the medieval political philosophers, one step removed from the Classical thinkers, understand that in order to cohere in the face of pressure (internal or external) a community must have not only shared values but shared practices. Farabi acknowledges the importance of religion in providing shared practices, but also the threat that it can pose to political thought when the religious leader is more persuasive than the legislator. Ibn Rushd expresses the same concerns in his analysis of the Aristotelian concept of rhetoric, recognizing the power of persuasion both to mislead the naïve and to stimulate the thoughtful.[18] For Maimonides the apple of Eden marks the moment when, sent out of the Garden and equipped with social morality (and labor pangs) for the first time, Adam and Eve become part of a political and not metaphysical community. For these thinkers, political cohesion is not abstract, but based upon the stability of a political system within which all other endeavors, including philosophy, can take place. For Strauss the ability to live in political harmony with one another is a precondition of leading a philosophical life, and in "Political Philosophy and History" Strauss writes that Classical and Medieval philosophers

> distinguished as a matter of course between the philosophic question of the best political order, and the practical question as to whether that order could or should be established in

> a given country at a given time. They took it for granted that political action guided by the belief that what is most desirable in itself must be put into practice in all circumstances, regardless of the circumstance, befits harmless doves, ignorant of the wisdom of the serpent but not sensible and good men.[19]

In other words, the great value of Classical political philosophy was that it was pragmatically inspired by the political conditions that existed, and which were primarily logical rather than theoretical. Classical political thought was philosophical because it shared with philosophy a concern with the question of "What is virtue?"[20] Classical philosophers writing about politics were not "mediated by a tradition of political philosophy which acted like a screen between the philosopher and political things regardless of whether the individual philosopher cherished or rejected that tradition."[21] The Classical thinkers believed that politics was ideally the regime of living-togetherness that guided the greatest possible number of people toward virtue, often that virtue was determined with reference to inherited and/or religious sources.

Strauss distinguishes Classical political philosophy from that of Nietzsche, the political philosophy of the third wave of modernity that Strauss believes rejected the viability of "sources" and therefore was incapable of creating the necessary bond between political and moral regimes.[22] Both Strauss and Taylor disagree with Nietzsche on this point, as philosophers and political thinkers for whom the resources of the past and the history of philosophy and political thought must be grounded in an understanding of the very real effects that ideas end up having on actual human beings. For Strauss, a political regime must be grounded in a virtue whose pursuit will lead to the increasing virtue of the citizens. The need for this virtue makes for a shared meal between Strauss and Taylor. What is interesting, however, about their simultaneous emphasis on virtue is that their approach to its pursuit is strikingly different in important ways.

For all their differences, Strauss and Taylor agree that political philosophy done right is an examination of the specific in light of the universal and vice versa. That is the point when the rubber hits the road in terms of theory, and when the political philosopher must be ready to change his opinions and theoretical deductions in the face of circumstance.

On Democracy—the Educated, the Bad, and the Ugly

Much has been made of Strauss's purported disregard for democracy, or at least his lack of warmth toward it. In point of fact, Strauss appreciated liberal democracy because of the freedom it granted the philosopher to advance whatever conclusions they might reach and the freedom of religious observance that it granted to its citizens, whether in the direction of more or less. Strauss approved of liberal democracy because he saw in it at least an attempt at what Michael Walzer identifies as the steps that might make possible different overlapping regimes of toleration: local autonomy, including individual autonomy of speech and action; engaged and discursive legal debate; and a move toward unity in education, and specifically in the inculcation of shared virtues.[23] Liberal democracy, in the sense that Strauss most frequently uses the term, is not neutral in terms of minority/religious rights. It is either more liberal or more democratic, and both can tend toward unpleasant consequences. If a regime is more liberal in the Classical sense, then it will acknowledge the existence, and to some extent the right, of the minority to be protected (as a minority) within the system. However, the price of such protection is high; modern liberalism demands of minorities that they accept individualism, and that things change—and Strauss's critique of modern liberalism is that it ultimately values such personal and individual expressions of beliefs to a degree that it forms a barrier to unity among those individuals. Democracy of course, comes with even more obvious baggage, or at least an Achilles heel; mobs are vulnerable to emotional appeals that influence their direction, and legitimizing that emotional decision-making in a democracy facilitates the slow destruction of the intellect in politics.[24]

Self-proclaimed secular democracies are not neutral—that claim to secularity masks its foundation by some majority that then permits "others" to be a part of "their" nation. Liberal democracies can commit gut-wrenching acts of violence in the name of a final peace, and liberal democracies that claim to be secular have marginalized, assimilated, and erased groups toward which they claim to be neutral.[25] Yet famously, secular democracy in the United States was one that Strauss praised, and not merely tolerated, for the freedom that it granted—*de facto*—to philosophers, albeit by marginalizing the relationship between philosophy and politics to a certain degree.[26] He made no bones about the extent to which a secular and pluralistic democracy requires sacrifice from minority communities; he crafted no mirages of a nation-state genuinely neutral toward all of its citizens.

It is in the impossibility of neutrality on the part of a political regime that we first begin to see what Michael Walzer might have called a consociation between Strauss and Taylor.[27] Writing in 1962 (three years after Strauss first published *What is Political Philosophy?*), Taylor faced a very particular historical moment: the nuclear and geopolitical arms race between the United States and the Soviet Union and the peculiar status of certain countries, including his own Canada, as "neutrals."[28] Taylor rejected the idea that "neutrality" in general and Canadian neutrality in particular was actually the nonopinionated, uninvolved, stance that it claimed to be, and he did so for at least two reasons. First, because such a claim was fundamentally at odds with the fact that Canada's so-called neutrality was protected by its intimate relationship with the United States. Taylor appears to have had little doubt, very reasonably, that while Canada might have advocated an end to the nuclear arms race, in the event of actual action it would stand with the United States.[29] In fact, the ability of any state to be neutral in a conflict is predicated on the existence of stronger and more forceful states with which "neutral" states can *de facto* affiliate, and in whose general well-being the main contenders in the fight are invested. Second, there was a moral and existential reason for states to be "neutral": Regardless of the fact that the center of the nuclear arms race was in Europe and the fact that no one was really taking aim at Canada, Taylor wrote that "if the nuclearization of Europe does not affect our military security, it does impact our political security."[30] For Taylor, it was necessary to investigate Canada's affiliation with the engaged nations of North America and Western Europe in order "to know if that first reflex is well founded and justified by events, as a [political] policy; or if, from the opposite side, all politics is nothing but a form of treason to the goal it pretends to serve."[31] Taylor's argument was that it should be seriously considered whether Canada's first inclination—to be *de jure* neutral and *de facto* U.S.-leaning in the Cold War—was morally and situationally justified, or whether it was justifiable only because neither side was actually committed to their stated goals, making principled neutrality with an inclination to the proximate the only pragmatic response.

For Taylor the stance of neutrality, while not in fact neutral at all in the way that it is used in common parlance, did do something essential, opening up a sort of third space for peace; even if occupied only occasionally and always imperfectly, the neutral states serve as examples of an alternative to a traditional binary conflict and as a potential interlocutor for both sides, a facilitator of sorts. One might say that, for Taylor, commitment to a neutral stance was important, even if actual neutrality was not possible. What is true of the political neutrality of states during the Cold War is also true of religious neutrality, and possibly even secularism, in a democratic and pluralist society. Or as Taylor noted in the same period: "The state which is civil-in-principle is not necessarily neutral. The opposite might be true."

I choose here to translate Taylor's *laïcité* as civil or civilian for several reasons. It is accepted practice to translate *laïcité* in Taylor as either secularization or political secularization.[32] But there is already a French word, *sécularisme*, that is a cognate for the English "secularism." *Laïcité*, on the other hand, evokes the English "lay" or "layman," a term referring originally to anyone or anything outside the purview of church or canon law. In English, "civil" is a more apt antonym to "canon." By making this choice, I allow the nonreligious character of the phrase to remain. Jane Marie Todd's decision to translate *laïcité* as "political secularisation" (and *sécularisme* as "secularism") is functional, but in a sense emphasizes too greatly the distinction between the political and the social, and the role that civil governments play in creating (more or less) secular societies.[33] For Taylor, we should never forget the fact that a commitment to a political identity involves social investment in the instantiation of that identity; in other words, something like toleration cannot be simply emphasized in government-run schools—it must also be evidenced in the world. The people or group that students are taught to tolerate should also have a voice—festivals, restaurants, social programs—such that both mind and body are disciplined into toleration. Once we think of *laïcité* as "civility," then the mannered nature of that form of politics becomes emphasized. At the current moment everyone may not know that the term "civil" was derived in order to distinguish something from "canonical," but they will identify being uncivil with a lack of manners and respect for the other person, with violating the standards by which we think we ought to treat one another. For example, an observant Jew might be visiting the house of a Christian friend, who asks him if he would like something to eat; if the Jew keeps to strict standards of *kosher* eating, his answer will have to be negative. Yet there is both a civil and uncivil way for him to refuse the food.[34] Civility indicates a nonmilitary, noninstitutional class of citizens (civilians), the nongovernmental sphere of community organizations (civil society), and an attitude of interaction between both individuals and groups (civility.) A *gouvernement laïque* is a civil government, and *laïcisation* is the civilizing of society. This civility, these manners and niceties, are in fact essential, according to both Taylor and Strauss, for maintaining a genuinely pluralistic society. There is something genuinely positive about a (politely) heterogeneous nation.

Strauss is a defender of pluralism and of difference not only because of the positive effect such a culture has for both Jews and philosophers, but because he held that homogeneity and conformity lead to the creation of a "mass culture," which is then particularly vulnerable to the linked illnesses of mass culture, political indifference, and messianic expectations.[35] One danger of democracy for Strauss is that it purports to be rule by the masses, but the mass as such cannot rule—democracy therefore requires the mass to deputize people to rule in their name. But here's the rub: the aristocracy necessary in a democracy that explicitly rejects aristocratic rule governs most effectively (maintains the smooth flow of governance) when it governs a mass culture characterized by homogeneity and apathy. Strauss writes:

> One of the most important virtues required for the smooth working of democracy, as far as the mass is concerned, is said to be electoral apathy, viz., lack of public spirit; not indeed the salt of the earth, but the salt of modern democracy are those citizens who read nothing except the sports page and the comic section. Democracy is then not indeed mass rule, but mass culture. A mass culture is a culture which can be appropriated by the meanest capacities without any intellectual and moral effort whatsoever and at a very low monetary price.[36]

This is the dark side of a democracy that hides its inability to provide what it promises, the Janus-face of democracy in which the democratic regime requires and teaches a level of political indifference in order to ensure the power of the elite and smooth flow of governance. Becoming a mass culture, as Strauss defines it, is just a part of the slippery slope by which democracy degenerates.[37]

The art defined by Aristotle as the political art par excellence is the art by which disparate individuals are united in the pursuit of a particular project or virtue—it is called rhetoric, the art of persuasion, and it is the only one of the Classical arts judged solely by whether it is successful, not by whether the conviction generated is in line with the truth or some other virtue.[38] This is the art that both Strauss and Taylor are wary of, a dangerous art that can lead to disaster, but it is also a necessary skill if an individual is required to represent—or at least appear to represent—a plurality of citizens.

The problem with rhetoric, particularly powerful rhetoric, is that it motivates people by means of the imagination and arouses their passion rather than their reason. So the representative democracy whose election is the result of rhetoric will elect people with whom they feel they have common feeling. This conviction that one shares beliefs and feelings with another is impervious to rational analysis concerning what that shared feeling is based on, as well as to any criticism of the representative who now is an extension of one's own heart and soul. Rhetoric creates affinity, and can link the elected and elector by means of a passionate emotional connection. And the more that a society is homogenous, the more a greater and greater majority will respond to the same cues and pressures, the easier it is for a rhetorician to convince the people through those emotional pressure points and shared references rather than through logic, reason, or an argument that might not be heart-rending but could unify a people.

Personal and historical reasons aside, one important feature of Jews and Judaism for Strauss was that "the belief in religious faith—in dedication to what simply transcends humanity—is the obstacle par excellence to conformism."[39] A good democracy, one in which the citizens are engaged and moderate and thoughtful, must provide people of many faiths the stability required for moderate and thoughtful reflection, as well as provide them with an education that inclines them toward engaged rather than indifferent tolerance.[40] If we expect high school students to value tolerance as a virtue in itself to the extent that they police one another's tolerance, then there must be a civil regime that aims to create a civil society and that promulgates a curriculum in aid of that civility. Insofar as that curriculum must be capable of being used by a deeply heterogeneous system and population, it must inculcate the value of toleration in a way that does not threaten or countermand the religious faiths of the population to the extent that they end up rejecting the curriculum. Michael Walzer suggests that "the best educational program might well involve nothing more than a graphic description of religious or ethnic warfare."[41] The implication of this is that students continually exposed to the bloody and inevitably varied results of religious and ethnic warfare (no religious or ethnic group has not suffered defeat at some point) will understand the results of intolerance in their gut. They will value tolerance not simply as a moral virtue but as an existential necessity.

Rather than inculcating tolerance by exposing students to the bloody results of intolerance, Strauss's Great Books curriculum is designed to lead students to moderate and critical thinking. Strauss himself admits that the figures who inspired some of the bloodiest regimes have been liberally educated (as were both Marx and Nietzsche.) Strauss's case is that a liberal education is necessary but not sufficient for the development of moderate, critical, and engaged citizens; Taylor also emphasizes the role of education as both an experience and the acquisition of knowledge in creating community.[42] In order for those who are liberally educated not to follow the path of that "stepfather of fascism," Nietzsche, the student must also have an inclination toward moderation, a tendency to question any regime that seems to be veering toward the extreme.[43] To be moderate and to be tolerant require the same quality of character, the same unwillingness to allow what is shocking or alien to invoke an emotional and unthinking response, the same tendency to neither dismiss nor wholeheartedly endorse any program out of hand.

The virtue that Strauss was seeking is prominently present in Taylor's work: tolerance, the virtue without which it is impossible to live peacefully in a pluralistic society—and not being a pluralistic and specifically multi-faith society is increasingly unlikely, certainly in the "immigrant societies" of North America. Now tolerance, of course, takes many different forms. Taylor's recent definition of the version of tolerance that he wishes to see adopted is the tolerance of the immigrant nation-state, the active validation of tolerance as a positive virtue and inculcation by both institutional and social means.[44]

The virtue of tolerance alleviates what Taylor believes to be the danger of modern democracy based on individual freedom expressed via a majority system. If each individual is as well-equipped as another to rule, a numerical majority deputizing an individual has moral (and legal) force. Our technological moment may be making absolute direct democracy more theoretically possible than ever.[45] But such a democracy has yet to make an appearance—instead democracies remain representative. Each citizen may cast their vote for the candidate that they believe best represents them, and if that person receives a majority of the votes cast, he has both legal and moral authority. The stability of the democracy depends upon the recognition of that authority by those who did not vote for that candidate, fundamentally indicating a belief that the opposing candidate does not constitute an existential threat to their existence.[46] As Taylor notes, "free societies require a high level of mutual trust."[47] I must be able to trust that a man I did not vote for and I may not trust is still (however much I may regret it) my legitimate representative.[48] A person may not like the elected representative, may in fact loathe them, but the strength of the democracy is evidenced by the trust of citizens in the process and corrective powers of the democratic system.

Religion and Tolerance

What, then, if a democratic representative does not believe that tolerance is a virtue? What if the majority elects a representative who wants to curtail the rights of specific religious groups? It could be argued that such a regime is at least theoretically secular, if it has no affiliation with or provides specific favors to another religious group. As early as 1963, Taylor advanced a definition of secularism that addressed this particular problem, a definition of a civil society that he recognized was unusual. In his first work to explicitly address the relationship between the state and religion, he wrote: "I conceive of *laïcité* as a never-ending effort to establish true freedom of options, and therefore equality between options, beyond any global formula. If some respond that this is not *laïcité* but something else, I'm ready for them to tell me what that word is. It is the reality, above all else, that is the most important."[49]

This is his conclusion to a piece that addresses the particularly partisan nature of the Quebec government when it comes to institutions like schools. The schools are Taylor's primary example not only because they fit the narrative but because education is so critical to a pluralistic society. In 1963, the government had public schools open to all, subsidized Catholic schools, and provided no money for students to attend schools with other confessional leanings. According to Taylor this demonstrates that the government is not secular, and not just because it privileges Catholic schools. A government that provides no funding for confessional schools of any kind would be one kind of secular, but still a secular that attempts to assimilate all pupils into a homogenizing system. In fact, true secularism means that a citizen of Quebec can send their child, without financial consequence, to a public school, a Catholic school, a Jewish school, or a Chinese school. Secularism that supports educational homogeneity always supports the homogeneity of the masses because education is the means by which students are socialized. Forcing or encouraging parents to send their children to a public rather than a confessional school because of the economic burden of the confessional school is not in the least neutral, and therefore not really secular. It prescribes the options available to its citizens and encourages them to choose the option that is a version of a Christian scholastic education.[50] Both the government that rejects all religion and the government that chooses an affiliation with a religion relegate some portion of its citizenry to second-class status. In the first case those who are religious will feel alienated from the state, and in the second all those who are not members of the state's confession will be aware that they are fundamentally separated from the state.

In pluralistic societies religious people and religious groups promote inclusivity on a formal level during events intended to reinforce the virtue of tolerance, but these official inclusions of different groups are themselves subject to criticism for allowing one or another religion into the public sphere. The yearly lighting of a Jewish Hanukkah menorah at the White House has become an unremarkable practice—however much it once contributed to the rhetoric of a war on Christmas. But the tradition of a White House Iftar (break-fast) during Ramadan lasted for only two decades (1996–2016). That the White House Iftar was cancelled in 2017 is no doubt due to the Islamophobic political rhetoric of the period—the Chief Executive could not be seen to celebrate with Muslims while enacting policies to prevent their entry into the country. But the accommodation of Muslim practices dates back as far as Thomas Jefferson, who, while he may not have held a celebration, altered the timing of a formal dinner to accommodate the Ramadan observance of a guest in 1805. This is relevant not because it says anything about the prejudices and proclivities of those in office at a given moment, but because it demonstrates that formal and informal expressions of toleration are not always on the same page.

In other words, interaction between people with different traditions and different relationships to those traditions happens on the individual level.[51] Toleration in a society cannot be judged purely by its institutionalization in government policies regarding schoolchildren's attire or bank holidays, to name just two examples. Toleration takes place on buses, in line for the bathroom, in the waiting room of the Department for Motor Vehicles. It is when an Amish family knows that they are welcome to use their Muslim neighbor's telephone if the need arises (but that they should perhaps keep visits short on afternoons during the month of Ramadan), and when the Jewish farmer next door knows that he has a market for his lamb every Eid al-Adha. For toleration to become a unifying virtue, it must be taught and encouraged through state education and example—but the toleration that holds and remains, even when democracy shows its shadow side and the majority incline toward exclusion and marginalization (if not deportation and execution), is the toleration of people for one another.

The Stability of the Rule and the Flexibility of the Ruled

I'd like to end this chapter with a consideration of change, and of the dangers and possibilities that Strauss and Taylor identified in both legal/institutional and social change. Taylor is, in some ways, the exemplar of the thinker who is willing to change his mind depending on the circumstances; in late 2017 he reversed the controversial recommendation from 2008 that some state actors should not display symbols of belief. In an opinion piece published in the Quebec daily *La Presse*, Taylor said he could no longer endorse the recommendations of the Report for a number of reasons. They boil down to the fact that in the almost-decade since the Report was published, Taylor saw an enormous rise in Islamophobia and anti-Semitism at both social and governmental levels. The practical result in Quebec was that the small subsection of state actors whose religious displays were discouraged by the Report was enlarged from (primarily) the police and judges to public transit workers, nurses, university teachers, and so on. In other words, the intention of that recommendation was to increase tolerance by taking away barriers between people already in a fraught situation (as most interactions with the police are). Instead he saw his recommendation being used to erect barriers between citizens of non-Christian confessions and the public sphere, and, unwilling to have his recommendation mutilated in that way, he very publicly withdrew his support. [52]

Although he never committed quite as confidently public an about-face, Strauss also believed that change was good—as long as it was restrained. He may have longed for the intellectual probity of the medieval and Classical thinkers, but he did not wish to be a philosopher and a Jew in Andalusia. He wanted to be who he was, and perhaps could only be everything that he was, in a modern nation-state that explicitly divorced its government institutions from religious affiliation. But change, Strauss argued, must be gradual and careful—constant change in both legal and social orders means that the population can never develop the "high level of mutual trust" necessary for existing in a de facto political and social alliance with those who are different.[53]

Neither Strauss nor Taylor approves of the exclusivist version of secularism that banishes religion from the public sphere. What unites them is their rejection of homogeneity as the source of political entropy (Strauss) and as the marginalization if not erasure of the multiple identities that make individuals, groups, and nations what they are (Taylor).

If we combine Strauss's insight that religious belief is resistant to the decline into homogeneity with Taylor's recommendation that various religious practices should be welcomed as much as possible into shared spaces, we are left with a surprising version of what a richly civil society might look like: a society governed by the civility of its citizens toward one another, that values that civility and its practice, and in which civility can only be cultivated by the multiplication and diversification of religious practices and differences in our everyday lives. For neither thinker is the accommodation of religion without limits—we must strive for moderation, for "reasonable accommodation" that may sometimes mean excluding practices (in a given time and circumstance) as being intolerable. Yet there is both the risk and the hope that those circumstances can change—what we find foreign and alien can become dear, or it may be something that we resolutely refuse to accommodate. That refusal is an exclusion—it may cause individuals to feel that they cannot live in our society comfortably—and we must accept the responsibility for making those exclusions.

But we also continue to argue about them, passionately debating and justifying why we are not willing to accommodate certain things.

We may or may not change our opinions. Such an argument requires proponents of at least two sides who genuinely disagree and who sincerely believe in their position. That kind of disagreement is about more than one side winning—it is about the sides trying to arrive at a mutual understanding of the best course of action to pursue.[54] An inclusive secular society, one that holds difference and tolerance as at least provisional virtues, is one in which there is more religion, more tradition, and more systems of belief. The political unity that both Leo Strauss and Charles Taylor seek is to be found in the ability of such different citizens to be civil—and more than civil—to one another.

Notes

1. There is a gap in scholarship on the mediated relationship between Leo Strauss and Isaiah Berlin that remains to be filled.

2. This is not the place to argue about Strauss's responsibility for the policies promulgated by his students. The point is simply that Strauss declined any government role. For his life and intellectual biography, see among others Thomas L. Pangle, *Leo Strauss: An Introduction to His Thought and Intellectual Legacy* (2006); Daniel Tanguay, *Leo Strauss: An Intellectual Biography*, trans. Christopher Nadon (2007); Steven B. Smith, *Reading Leo Strauss: Politics, Philosophy, Judaism* (2006).

3. It has never been clear what the term "Straussian" means. It is commonly deployed in reference to those who agree with Strauss's division of communication into the esoteric and exoteric, but there is more to Strauss than that insight.

4. Gérard Bouchard and Charles Taylor, "Building the Future: A Time for Reconciliation (Report)," *Government of Quebec* 2008. www.mce.gouv.qc.ca/publications/CCPARDC/rapport-final-integral-en.pdf

5. Michael Walzer, *On Toleration: The Castle Lectures in Ethics, Politics, and Economics* (New Haven, CT: Yale University Press, 1997), 44–47.

6. The legal standard that calls for "reasonable accommodation" is "sincere belief." This is the Canadian legal doctrine that the relevance of observances should be judged based on the conviction of the believer that the observance is necessary—certified and ordained religious authorities are not experts in civil law courts concerning whether or not a practice is important to the religion or not (see Syndicat Northcrest v Amselem (2004) 2 SCR 551, 2004 SCC 47: paragraph 43 and supra). Canada is an example of Walzer's mixed regime (Walzer, *On Toleration*, 37–51), where the nation-state takes over the legislation of activities once covered by canon law, opening up spaces "unconventional," individual, or queering interpretations of a tradition.

7. Ibid., 22–24.

8. See Leo Strauss, *Philosophy and Law: Contributions to the Understanding of Maimonides and His Predecessors* (1935), trans. Eve Adler (Albany: SUNY Press, 1995), 1–39; "On Classical Political Philosophy" (1945) in *What is Political Philosophy? And Other Studies* (Chicago: University of Chicago Press, 1988), 83–87.

9. This is a traditional Rabbinic principle evoked throughout the Talmud and that translates literally as "arguments for the sake of heaven": it generally refers to debates in which the shared goal is the improvement of knowledge or the world rather than some type of victory for one side in the debate. It may be a passionate argument, but if it is truly "for the sake of heaven," the vehemence of the debaters is no indication of discord or acrimony.

10. Leo Strauss, "On Plato's Republic," in *The City and Man* (1964) (Chicago: University of Chicago Press, 1978), 125–131; "Liberal Education and Responsibility" (1968), in *Liberalism Ancient and Modern* (Chicago: University of Chicago Press, 1995), 14–15.

11. Charles Taylor, "Alienation and Community," *Universities & New Left Review*, no. 5 (1958): 16; Leo Strauss. "Political Philosophy and History," in *What is Political Philosophy?* 56–77. Note that the imperative to learn from one's predecessors is obvious to the medieval philosophers that Strauss analyzes; Farabi, Ibn Rushd, and Maimonides all reference Aristotle, often Plato, and one another insofar as chronology allows. For Taylor, as a legal expert, a system of law that does not recognize precedent or the history of law itself would be ludicrous. For both Strauss and Taylor, the past is at the very least something we must grapple with—not ignore, regard as artifacts, or submit to auto-da-fé.

12. Strauss, "Political Philosophy and History," 70–77.

13. Leo Strauss, "An Epilogue," in *Liberalism Ancient and Modern*, 203–223. It would be horrifying, in this schema, for a person to be legitimized as a "political philosopher" or even political thinker simply because he has read and seems to have understood some points made by political thinkers of the past. To receive a PhD solely because one is skilled at intellectual and textual reproduction would be repugnant to Strauss. The true end of working to "understand the thinkers of the past as they understood themselves" is to develop the trained critical eye that can be directed toward thinkers of the present.

14. We will return to this later in the chapter. For now it is simply useful to note that one reason for this restriction was that, given the often contentious and unpleasant relationship of the citizen to the state actor, citizens who feel that they have been unjustly punished might attribute that injustice to the religious group of the punisher, and/or would not be willing to interact with officers of the law who they perceived to have an already-prejudiced opinion of them by virtue of an often assumedly strained relationship between two religious groups (Jews and Muslims, for example).

15. Charles Taylor, *Laïcité et la liberté de conscience* (Quebec: Editions du Boreal, 2010). All translations from the French are my own unless otherwise noted.

16. Concerned primarily with the ability of the law in Quebec to negotiate a rapidly diversifying group of people, the Report notes that a closed secularism of the state—the one that forbids all public demonstration of religion—cannot help but exclude those who are religiously devout or orthodox. The Report states, specifically concerning students displaying religious signifiers, that they also "obviously display a desire to integrate into society. They will mix with young people from all milieus, learn French if they do not already speak the language . . . Do we want a society in which only one relationship to the religious is tolerated?" (Bouchard-Taylor Report, 146); see also Strauss, *Philosophy and Law*, 24–25.

17. Taylor, *Laïcité*, 30–33.

18. For the medieval Arabic thinkers, Aristotle's *Rhetoric* was classed in the *Organon* as a logical work. *Rhetoric* was not considered a logical work in the Latinate world.

19. Strauss, "Political Philosophy and History," 61; "Jerusalem and Athens" (1967), in *Jewish Philosophy and the Crisis of Modernity: Essays and Lectures in Modern Jewish Thought*, ed. Kenneth Hart Green (Albany, NY: SUNY Press, 1997), 386–387.

20. Strauss, "On Classical Political Philosophy," 90–91.

21. Strauss, "What is Political Philosophy?" 27.

22. Strauss's first invocation of Nietzsche in "What is Political Philosophy?" is an unmarked usage of the phrase "human, all too human" (27) to describe the type of political thought that at the end of his essay Strauss castigates as leaving people with "no choice except that between irresponsible indifference to politics, and irresponsible political opinions" (55). This is in contrast to Strauss's description of the student whose liberal education also trains them in the principle of moderation "that will protect us from the twin dangers of visionary politics and unmanly contempt for politics" (Strauss, "Liberal Education and Responsibility," 24).

23. See Strauss, "On Plato's Republic," 131–132; Walzer, *On Toleration*, 71–76.

24. Strauss, "An Epilogue," 222–223; "What is Liberal Education," 4–7; this chapter, note 36 and accompanying text.

25. See Walzer, *On Toleration*, 24–36; Charles Taylor, "L'État et la laïcité," in *Cité Libre* 14, No. 50 (1963): 3–7. Strauss, "Liberal Education and Responsibility," 16–24, "Political Philosophy and History," 58–61, "Jerusalem and Athens," 378–380.

26. Strauss, "On Classical Political Philosophy," 90–94.

27. Walzer, *On Toleration*, 22–24.

28. Charles Taylor, "La bombe et la neutralism," *Cité Libre* 13, no. 42 (May 1962): 11–15.

29. Ibid.

30. Ibid., 15.

31. Ibid., 11.

32. The published English translation of *Laïcité et liberté de conscience* is Jocelyn Maclure and Charles Taylor, *Secularism and Freedom of Conscience*, trans. Marie Todd (Cambridge, MA: Harvard University Press, 2011).

33. Maclure and Taylor, *Secularism and Freedom of Conscience*, 15.

34. What distinguishes the civil from the uncivil in common usage is whether the rejection (in word or affect) displays a negative judgment of the one who made or rejected the offer. For an excellent text that discusses the nature of civil and legal discourse, see Neil MacCormick, *Rhetoric and the Rule of Law: A Theory of Legal Reasoning* (2005) (Chicago: University of Chicago Press, 2010.

35. Strauss, "Perspectives on the Good Society" in *Jewish Philosophy and the Crisis of Modernity: Essays and Lectures in Jewish Thought*, ed. Kenneth Hart Green (Albany, NY: SUNY Press, 1997), 431–445, see 433–435; "What is Liberal Education?" 5; "On Plato's Republic," 113.

36. Strauss, "What is Liberal Education?" 5.

37. Strauss's understanding of the ways that democracy can degenerate is no doubt influenced by his reading of Farabi, particular Farabi's *Ideal City*. See Abu Nasr Farabi, *Mabadi' ara' ahl al-madinat al-fadilah (On the Perfect State)*. Revised Arabic text, translation, and commentary by Richard Walzer (Oxford University Press, 1985; reprinted by Great Books of the Islamic World, Inc., 1998, chapters 16–18). There Farabi notes that while democracy is in theory one of the best kinds of political regime, it is also unstable and prone to engaging in truly horrific activities if the passions of the *demos* are wholly determinative of the political regime.

38. Strauss, "On Plato's Republic," 53–59, 80; "On Classical Political Philosophy," 83.

39. Strauss, "Perspectives on the Good Society," 263 cf. 442. A number of books have examined the pivotal role of Judaism for Strauss, in particular by professor Kenneth Hart Green of the University of Toronto—see his "Editor's Introduction: Leo Strauss as a Modern Jewish Thinker," in *Leo Strauss, Jewish Philosophy and the Crisis of Modernity: Essays and Lectures in Modern Jewish Thought* (Albany, NY: SUNY Press, 1997), 1–84; and *Jew and Philosopher: The Return to Maimonides in the Jewish Thought of Leo Strauss* (Albany, NY: SUNY Press, 1993).

40. Walzer, *On Toleration*, 32.

41. Ibid. 12.

42. For the theoretical importance of education for Taylor, see Charles Taylor, *Modern Social Imaginaries* (Durham, NC: Duke University Press, 2004), 15–20; for the practical importance of education see the recommendation of the Bouchard-Taylor Report regarding a standardized curriculum encouraging toleration and multiculturalism (Bouchard-Taylor Report, 80–84).

43. Strauss, "Liberal Education and Responsibility," 12–13, 24–25; "What is Political Philosophy?" 36–37.

44. For Taylor's early definition, see Taylor, "L'État," 6 and infra note 49 and accompanying text. See also Walzer, *On Toleration*, 3.

45. Genuinely absolute democracy still lives where so many not-yets have made their debut—science fiction. A first-season episode of the FOX television show *The Orville* (season 1, episode 7, "Majority Rule") demonstrates the potential consequences of majority morality in an absolute democracy, along with the variety of ways that such a system can either go to dark places on its own or be hacked from the outside. See also Charles Taylor, *A Secular Age* (Cambridge, MA: Harvard University Press, 2004) and Charles Taylor, "The Poverty of the Poverty of Historicism," *Universities & New Left Review*, no. 4 (1958): 77–78.

46. Instability is introduced not by the election of a candidate who many or a majority of people actually dislike, but when those people become disillusioned and contemptuous of the system that put him in power.

47. Charles Taylor, "Identity and Democracy," *Iyyun: The Jerusalem Philosophical Quarterly* 59 (July–October 2010): 16.

48. Once the United States of America elects a female president I will consider using gender-neutral pronouns in discussing the representative nature of the U.S. presidency.

49. Taylor, "L'état et la laïcité," 6.

50. Ibid., 4–5.

51. Leo Strauss, "On Aristotle's Politics," in *The City and Man* (1964) (Chicago: University of Chicago Press, 1978), 48–49.

52. Charles Taylor, "Neutralité de l'état: Le temps de la réconciliation." *La Presse du Montréal*, February 14, 2017, http://plus.lapresse.ca/screens/36c5c72e-28b9-49df-ba29-514fc56d647a__7C__pUtyV30bPPsb.html; "Can Political Philosophy Be Neutral?" *Universities and Left Review* 1, no. 1 (1957): 59–60.

53. Charles Taylor, "Identity and Democracy," 16; see also supra note 47 and accompanying text.

54. See supra note 9 and accompanying text.

6

Care of the Self and the Invention of Legitimate Government

Foucault and Strauss on Platonic Political Philosophy

Miguel Vatter

On Reading Foucault with Strauss: Some Preliminary Remarks

This chapter[1] offers an interpretation of Michel Foucault's last lectures at the Collège de France, *The Courage of Truth: The Government of Self and Others II*, by reading them against the backdrop of Leo Strauss's conception of classical natural right formulated in such works as *On Tyranny*, *Natural Right and History* and *What is Political Philosophy?* The justification for what appears, at first blush, an unseemly and even shocking comparative exercise is that in these last lectures Foucault's chosen theme is the one preferred by Strauss—namely, the opposition between Platonic political philosophy and democratic political life. His analysis coincides with the genealogy offered by Leo Strauss on several key points. Ultimately, Foucault and Strauss agree that "political philosophy" or "normative political thought" is not what the Western tradition has made of it: it is neither a discourse that seeks to understand the nature of political things, nor does it delineate a theory of justice for the sake of moralizing politics. For these two authors, "political philosophy" is a practice that seeks to replace the pre-philosophical practice of political life in democracies with a new practice of politics: the philosophically justified "legitimate government" of some over others.

Foucault and Strauss both seek to determine the origins and meaning of "political philosophy" in the Socratic tradition. They both start out by analyzing the *agon* between (democratic) political life and the "philosophical life." Both understand philosophy as a "way of life," rather than a doctrine or corpus that is in competition with the political way of life. Both reject two traditional ways to understand the opposition between philosophy and politics: the first of these, which I call the "spiritual" reading of their *agon*, sees philosophy, and then theology, as discourses that are opposed to politics because they seek to direct human beings toward a form of salvation that depends on following the guidance of a political representative of the divine.[2] The other traditional approach to the conflict between philosophy and politics, which I call the "liberal" reading, sees in philosophy's fight with democratic politics the expression of the principle of individual freedom (of speech, of conscience, etc.) against the will of the community or state.[3] In sharp contrast to these spiritual and liberal interpretations of the conflict between philosophy and politics, Strauss and Foucault agree that the philosophical life is itself "political" through and through and yet is also entirely anti-political, if by politics we mean the kind of life that is made possible by the *polis* or by the *res publica*. The main goal of this chapter is to make sense of this paradoxical anti-political philosophical politics. It argues that philosophical politics is "anti-political" in two senses: for those (the many) who are subject to it, philosophical politics is experienced as "government" and not as a political life that engages the best part of their lives. For those (the few) who subject others to their government, philosophical politics is "anti-political" either because it gives rise to a doctrine of being that is no longer "relative" to humanity (Strauss) or because it gives rise to a doctrine of self or psychology that is radically unencumbered by the social relation to others (Foucault).

Recent scholarship on Strauss agrees that the identification and defense of something called "political philosophy" is perhaps the guiding aim of his work.[4] Curiously, Strauss is never mentioned in Foucault's last lectures on classical political philosophy. Likewise, to date there has been no sustained comparative study of Foucault's and Strauss's interpretations of Platonic political philosophy.[5] My general thesis is that both Strauss and Foucault see in Platonic political philosophy the birth of a governmental (as opposed to political) discourse. Foucault defines governmentality by a reflexive formula: "the conduct of conduct." In this formula, the term "conduct" has a double sense "since the word 'conduct' refers to two things. Conduct is the activity of conducting (*conduire*), of conduction (*la conduction*) if you like, but it is equally the way in which one conducts oneself (*se conduit*), lets oneself be conducted (*se laisse conduire*), is conducted (*est conduit*) and finally in which one behaves (*se comporter*) as an effect of a form of conduct (*une conduite*) as the action of conducting or of conduction."[6] Governmentality refers to the "technology of self" that produces a certain *ethos* or self-conduct, such that this self is then enabled to conduct or govern others, in the sense of leading them. But whereas for Foucault the Platonic conception of governmentality is centered on ethical autonomy, for Strauss it is centered on ontology. The conclusion of the chapter spells out what is at stake in this difference.

A proper comparison of Strauss's and Foucault's readings of Platonic political philosophy is much too vast and complex an enterprise to be adequately addressed in the space of a single chapter. I have focused my efforts on a drastically reduced selection of texts from both authors, drawing mainly from Foucault's last lectures and from Strauss's essays "On Classical Political Philosophy" and "Restatement on Xenophon's *Hiero*," both found in *What is Political Philosophy?* A consideration of Foucault's lectures in the context of these essays by Strauss sheds new light on the question of the relation between Platonic political philosophy and the history of governmentality that was important for Foucault already in his first series of lectures on governmentality, *Security, Territory, Population* (1977–1978). It is generally acknowledged that one of Foucault's most significant theoretical innovations was to introduce a fundamental distinction between sovereign power and another form of power that he called biopower and to which he linked the term "biopolitics." The project of a "history of governmentality" was intended to clarify the distinction between sovereign and bio-power.[7] In the *Homo Sacer* series, Giorgio Agamben made a "correction" to Foucault's conception of governmentality by arguing that sovereignty and biopower are in reality two sides of one practice of governmental power.[8] The difference between Agamben and Foucault on sovereignty has since become a topic of great discussion and controversy, one that even Derrida's last lectures on sovereignty takes up.[9]

In *Security, Territory, Population*, Foucault sought to determine the genealogy of governmentality by linking it to the history of the pastorate or pastoral power. By "pastoral power," Foucault means the practice of the "government of souls": "pastoral power . . . is only concerned with individual souls insofar as this direction (*conduite*) of souls also involves a permanent intervention in everyday conduct (*conduite*), in the management of lives, as well as in goods, wealth and things."[10] In the same lecture, commenting on Gregory Nazianzen's use of *oikonomia psuchon* (management of the soul) to designate the pastorate, Foucault explains: "this Greek notion of economy . . . [that] designated the typical management of the family, of its goods and wealth, the management and direction of slaves, of the wife, of the children and possibly the management of clients, takes on a completely different dimension and a completely different field of references with the pastorate."[11] This discussion of Gregory is one of the places in Foucault's lectures on governmentality where Agamben intervenes by introducing the idea of an "economic theology" as the crucial discourse linking together liberal governmentality and modern political economy.[12] Indeed, Foucault's discussion of pastoral power as the power of salvation of the flock is very close to Carl Schmitt's politico-theological discussion of the roots of *nomos* in the practice of shepherding.[13] The problem for Foucault is that Schmitt argued that sovereignty was a concept that depended on political theology. Additionally, Schmitt tried to find Greek roots for his conception of political theology and sovereignty. In this endeavor he was followed by Agamben. Foucault, at least in these first lectures of 1978, seems to reject the connection between political theology and sovereignty, and is willing to link political theology (in the form of pastoral power) only to governmentality. "I think pastoral power, its form, type of functioning, and internal technology, remains absolutely specific and different from political power, at least until the eighteenth century."[14] For Foucault, pastoral power in general is "not a Greek idea"; its origin is Egyptian, Assyrian, and especially Hebrew.[15]

Even at this early stage of his investigations, Foucault was conscious of the fact that his entire construction of pastoral power as an alternative to sovereignty is brought into question by the case of Plato. Plato's texts are full of references to the political king or leader as a shepherd: "to be a good shepherd is to be not only the good magistrate, but quite simply the true, ideal magistrate. You find this in *Critias* 109b–c, *The Republic* I, 343a–345e, III 416a–b, 440d, *The Laws* V 735b–e, and the *Statesman* 267c–277d."[16] In order to maintain his distinction between sovereign and pastoral power intact, Foucault offers a reading of *The Statesman* in which he claims to show that Plato, so to speak, deconstructs the model of the statesman as shepherd in order to propose another model of statesman as weaver.[17] There is no space here to engage this reading in any detail.[18] I mention it here because when he returns to discuss Platonic texts in his last cycle of lectures dedicated to *parrhesia*, Foucault appears to have changed his mind with regard to his thesis on Plato. Or, perhaps more precisely, Foucault's last division between Platonic and Cynic understandings of philosophy as ways of self-conduct seems to indicate that whereas the Platonic route may indeed lead to or be complicit with pastoral power, the Cynic route is the one he thought most likely to undermine it.[19] Be that as it may, in what follows I will show that Foucault's new way of reading Plato is strikingly similar to the hypotheses that Strauss developed with regard to Platonic political philosophy; and, further, they lend weight to the hypothesis that Platonic political philosophy may lie at the origin of Western governmentality. In the final section I discuss where the two thinkers diverge with respect to the content of Platonic anti-political "politics" and what is normatively at stake in this divergence.

The First Platonic Reversal: Good Politics as Critique of Democracy

Both Strauss and Foucault approach Platonic political philosophy by hypothesizing the existence not of one, but of two Platonic "reversals" of traditional Greek political thought. They agree, roughly, about the content of the first reversal, but they disagree with respect to the second and more crucial one. Generally speaking, the content of the first reversal takes the *agon* between philosophy and democracy as proof that a good politics cannot be a democratic politics. If the good of the city is paramount, then its government ought not to be democratic. The content and meaning of the second Platonic reversal is much harder to pin down in Foucault and Strauss. Again, in general terms, this second reversal refers to the way in which philosophy, which begins by struggling against politics, comes to reconcile itself with politics in the form of a paradoxical "politics" of and for philosophy. For both Foucault and Strauss, it is this "philosophical" politics, found in the city but not of the city, that constitutes the real legacy of Socrates and Plato.

Foucault presents and explains the first Platonic reversal of accepted political opinion by introducing a distinction between what he calls "political" truth-telling or *parrhesia*, which has a long tradition in Greek and Athenian political life, duly reconstructed in the first volume of

The Government of Self and Others; and something that he identifies as "philosophical" truth-telling. The latter is a new form of truth-telling introduced into Athenian political life only by Socrates and Plato. The conflict between democracy and philosophy exists, according to Foucault, because these two forms of truth-telling exclude each other. Political truth-telling is defined in terms of "the right to have one's say in the city affairs."[20] This right or freedom is inherent to all the citizens of the city by virtue of "birth" not by "knowledge." Political truth-telling, in this sense, is the *sine qua non* of a democratic political life.

Political truth-telling is a standpoint open to all citizens; that is, it is inherently democratic because it is a question of expressing one's opinion about what is best for the city, not the truth about this question. Opinions can be true or false, good or bad. Strauss adds that Greek political life was characterized "by conflicts between men asserting opposite claims. . . . In practically all cases claims are raised . . . in the name of justice."[21] However, neither Foucault nor Strauss leaps to the conclusion that what is most needful, for political philosophy, is a "theory of justice" that would somehow resolve the political conflict of opinions about or interpretations of justice, in the way that Rawls does.[22] On the contrary, for both Foucault and Strauss, questions of "justice" are merely an intermediary step on the way to the true content of Platonic political philosophy.

The figure of Solon stands at the beginning of both Foucault's and Strauss's presentations of the uniqueness of Platonic political philosophy. Solon was the prototype of the pre-Socratic lawgiver who established political life through the ideal of *eunomia*, which later transmuted into the democratic ideal of *isonomia*.[23] In the *Athenian Constitution* there is a discussion of a strange law made by Solon that seems to enjoin citizens to take up arms in a situation of civil conflict or *stasis* on pain of being excluded from their rights as citizens, which has given rise to much discussion because of its apparent contrast with the spirit of Solon's ideal of *eunomia*.[24] Valerij Gouschin has recently and convincingly argued that Solon intended the law on *stasis* to counteract the rise of Pisistratus's tyranny, an event that Solon conceived as putting an end to political life itself and its inherent clash of opinions. Both Strauss and Foucault refer obliquely to Solon's law in order to distinguish the actions of Socrates. For Strauss, Socratic political philosophy is one possible response to the danger of *stasis*: "the conflict calls for arbitration, for an intelligent decision that will give each party what it truly deserves. . . . The umpire par excellence is the political philosopher." But it is not simply that Socratic political philosophy offers an alternative way to that proposed by Solon in order to put an end to *stasis*. Rather, Strauss means to say that Socratic political philosophy seeks to counteract Solon's law on *stasis* because it proposes that the Socratic political philosopher deal with the danger of tyranny otherwise than by calling for all citizens to take up arms in defending their common political freedom, whether they be democrats or aristocrats. This other path requires a certain *phronesis* ("intelligent decision") that takes the form of a just law ("give each party what it truly deserves"): it requires the new "legislation" of a Socratic "political philosopher." It is interesting to notice that the supposed "duty" of the philosopher to act as umpire in the case of *stasis* is, for Strauss, a "political" duty because it is derived from the citizen's duty to bring about the cessation of "civil strife . . . and to create, by persuasion, agreement among citizens."[25] In other words, and the suggestion is brimming with irony, by bringing an end to Athenian political life through this new "just" legislation, Socrates would nevertheless still be acting in the spirit of a "true" citizen, perhaps as the only real "citizen," as Plato reports in *Gorgias* 521d.

Like Strauss, Foucault also refer to Solon in order to distinguish the different kind of activity of Socrates as a political philosopher. For Foucault, Solon's law on *stasis* is still a reflection of political truth-telling (although it is grounded on a supra-political "wisdom") in enjoining the struggle against the tyrant. This is no longer the case with Socrates's form of philosophical truth-telling: Socratic truth-telling remains constantly active at a "political" level (to be better specified below), while it never directly takes a stand against either tyranny or democracy. Like Strauss, Foucault perceives an ironical component to Socrates's deviation from Solon: Socrates's apparent "neutrality"—in contravening Solon's law on *stasis*—mimics Solon's earlier preaching of *eunomia* as a kind of neutral standpoint that balances both sides (the poor and the rich, the many and the few) involved in the political conflict. For both Strauss and Foucault, the comparison with Solon serves to show that from a democratic perspective Socratic truth-telling is not "political" at all. Socrates defended his apparent neutrality in the *Apology* on the grounds that any active—that is, political—opposition would have brought him a premature death, making it impossible for him to be "useful" to and do "good" for the city.[26] I shall return below to the danger of persecution for the philosophical life, and what is needed in order to avoid it, since it is crucial to both Strauss's and Foucault's reading of Socratic political philosophizing and its peculiar "courage of truth."

The distinction between Solon and Socrates serves to underscore the important point that for Platonic political philosophy, or philosophical truth-telling, *parrhesia* is not restricted by conditions of citizenship (which Solon appears to have thought includes the duty to fight the tyrants). To the contrary, the philosophical truth-teller can be, or perhaps must be, a "stranger" to the city.[27] This theme is central to Strauss's interpretation: the Platonic political philosopher can play the part of the umpire, standing above and over the civil strife of opinions because he speaks from the standpoint of the true knowledge of politics, which is not bound by any territorial frontiers. According to Strauss, the conflict arising from differing opinions as to what is good or fitting for the city is not brought to an end by Platonic political philosophy by appealing to a standpoint that is transcendent to political life itself (the standpoint of pre-Socratic "wisdom"), but by elevating the given knowledge of politics found in the city to the level of a "science": Platonic political philosophers are the true founders of (empirical) "political science."

Strauss argues that Socrates acknowledges that there already exists a knowledge of political things prior to political philosophy. In the first instance, "political science" means the "skill possessed by the excellent statesman or politician."[28] But Strauss points out that even this political skill is "transferable" from one city to another. The elevation of political knowledge beyond the borders of the city is evident when one considers what is the first variant of political science, namely, the skill in public speaking taught by rhetoricians or sophists who travelled from city to city selling their art to those aristocrats who could afford it. Rhetoric is an even more "universal" type of political science than the political skill of politicians because it can be taught to everybody. However, Socratic political philosophy is the highest elevation of political knowledge beyond the city, and it rejects the claim that rhetoric is a truly political science.[29] Instead, the true Platonic political science raises the "most universal political questions" that are needed in order to fashion political constitutions: "the political philosopher who has reached this goal is the teacher of legislators. The knowledge of the political philosopher is 'transferable' in the highest degree. Plato demonstrated this . . . by presenting *in the guise of a stranger* the philosopher who is *a teacher of legislators*."[30] Platonic political philosophy is therefore at the furthest possible remove from what Foucault calls political truth-telling because it undermines entirely the autochthonous right of citizens to legislate in the name of a new form of legislation that is given by individuals who are "strangers" to the city that they govern. I shall first discuss the nature of this philosophical legislation, and then turn to why "true political science" is, paradoxically, entirely "foreign" to the political life that it sets out to govern.

Foucault and Strauss agree that the new form of legislation made possible by Platonic political philosophy is best understood as a "constitution" or *politeia*.[31] It is common to define a "constitution" as a "form of government," not realizing that this very way of thinking about legislation is a Platonic invention. Prior to the Platonic reversal, Greek political life did not know of "constitutions" as "forms of government." Rather, as a legislating power, the body of citizens was best described as form-less and an-archic rather than a "form of government."[32] In a democracy, laws were made not in order to "govern" a people, but in order "not to be governed," to employ Foucauldian terms.[33] Foucault and Strauss both see Platonic constitutionalism as a form of governmentality: constitutions are conceived as a way to conduct a people or population, rather than as a reflection of the "sovereign will" of a democratic people.

The originality of Foucault's thesis is that a Platonic constitution establishes what he calls the "ethical differentiation" of a body of citizens, separating those citizens who are "good" from those who are "bad" and giving the power to make laws only to those who will do good for the city because they are "ethically" good individuals. The salient point here is that the pursuit of the well-ordered city by way of a doctrine of constitutionalism in reality turns on an ethical distinction between "good" and "bad" citizens (as opposed to, say, a political distinction between rich and poor); and this ethical distinction, in turn, rests on what Foucault calls the Socratic practice of "care of the self." The ethical distinction and the care of the self are the discursive presuppositions that lie at the basis of the Platonic idea of *politeia* or, to employ the Straussian term, of "regime."

Foucault reconstructs the Platonic argument for ethical differentiation as follows: since democracy gives everyone the right to say what they please, democracy is dangerous to the city because political truth-telling allows "true and false discourse, useful as well as bad or harmful opinions, [to] become mixed up and intermingled in the game of democracy."[34] In the Platonic dialogues this problem is designated as that of "flattery"; contemporary political science speaks of it as the problem of "populism." Additionally, in a democracy those who do speak the (philosophical) truth to the citizenry run the risk of losing their lives: democracy is also dangerous to philosophical truth. This second point illuminates the sense of Foucault's subtitle of the lectures: "the courage of truth" refers to the fact that only speaking the philosophical truth to and against democracy calls for true "courage."

Since "there cannot be any division between true and false discourse in democracy," democracy and philosophy are antithetical to each other: "when there is *parrhesia* as freedom for everyone, there cannot be *parrhesia* as courage to speak the truth."[35] This lapidary formula actually puts into crisis the idea of "public reason" as an instrument of governmentality.[36] Thus, for Foucault the first Platonic reversal rejects the belief that (political) truth-telling is constitutive of democracy and substitutes for it the belief that (philosophical) truth-telling is antithetical to democracy. From the Platonic perspective, the democratic city is not a city where the best people, the true aristocrats, are free to speak. In such an aristocratic city, the best people look after their own interests by looking after the best interest of the city; that is, by seeking the common interest. In a democracy, instead, decisions are made by the many (not the few). The interest of the many is essentially that of not being slaves; that is, not serving the interests of the best and of the city, but in ruling themselves. Foucault makes the point with a play on words: the many seek what is good for those who are "worst" off (the poor), and this ultimately justifies in a democracy giving the right to speak freely even to those who are the "worst" sorts of people (the bad). The inevitable result is that the many will legislate what is the worst for the city as a whole.[37]

Foucault explains that the contradiction between philosophy and democracy follows from two linked principles found in Plato's discourse: the difference between the few and the many, and the difference between the best and the worst. The ethical distinction between the best and the worst people corresponds to a political distinction: the best will do what is best for city; the worst will do what is worst for the city. It follows that what is good for the city cannot actually be said in a democratic city. Conversely, "the [philosophical] truth can be told in a city and political structure only when an essential quantitative division between the good and the bad is marked, maintained and institutionalized."[38] The institutionalization of the ethical distinction between the good and the bad citizens takes the form of a constitution, *politeia*, that is related to the idea of philosophical *nomoi* (laws established for the sake of leading a philosophical life). Philosophical truth-telling (the difference between true and false) entails an ethical differentiation (the difference between good and bad individuals) that is realized in the form of a *constitutional* government. Platonic political philosophy is therefore a constitutional discourse. Through a constitutional order what Foucault calls the (first) "Platonic reversal" is effected: "If indeed it is true that one cannot find *parrhesia* in democracy . . . then . . . true discourse, when it is established through philosophy and in the form of philosophy as the foundation of the *politeia*, can only eliminate and banish democracy."[39]

The risks of democracy for the city, the danger in democratic law-making, and the risk of persecution of philosophy in a democracy are, of course, well-known themes in Strauss's works such as *Persecution and the Art of Writing* and *Natural Right and History*. For reasons of space, here I wish to emphasize only that Foucault's position comes very close to Strauss's thesis that the antithesis of philosophy and democracy is both realized and resolved by the idea of "constitutional" government. As mentioned above, Strauss also says that the Platonic political philosopher seeks to eliminate the political strife (*stasis*) characteristic of political life by resolving "the question of the best political order."[40] In Platonic political philosophy, the political constitution is intended to decide the controversy "as to what type of men should rule the community."[41] In this sense, constitutionalism is inherently aristocratic because it seeks to give access to government only to those who are deemed good citizens: "Aristocracy (the rule of the best) presented itself as the natural answer of all good men to the natural question of the best political order."[42] For Strauss, it is a piece of "natural right" that what is best for the city can be achieved only when good men are in charge of government because it is only they who have the city's interest as a whole in mind.

Just like Foucault, Strauss thinks that the insight that political constitutions effect the "ethical differentiation" of a population of citizens is only a preliminary result. Foucault will argue, as I discuss below, that such distinction between good and bad citizens is possible only by introducing a new practice of government tied to the Socratic idea of "care of the self." Strauss also says that the aristocratism of Platonic political philosophy is merely a "pre-philosophic political knowledge;" it is not the authentic or original content of Platonic political philosophy. Platonic political philosophy moves beyond this pre-philosophical political knowledge "by trying to understand fully the implications of these pre-philosophic insights" in order to "defend" from the opposite opinion, namely, that "bad men" can be even more useful to the city because "the just" and the "useful" are not the same.[43] The latter is the point of the struggle between Socrates and Thrasymachus or Callicles staged in some of Plato's dialogues.

However, in one of the most obscure passages of his essay, Strauss diverges from Foucault because he argues that the "implications of these pre-philosophic insights" are not themselves of an ethical character. The "good men" who are to govern others are not "good" in the common sense of the term, nor do they engage in what Foucault calls "care of the self" (a term that is absent, as far as I can tell, in Strauss). It is true that Platonic political philosophy takes as its starting point "the moral distinctions as they are made in everyday life," the common sense ideas of "goodness" and "justice."[44] But, according to Strauss, Socrates and Plato do not believe that one can "demonstrate" the truth of these ethical ideas to those who are not already good. For Strauss, Socrates knows that he cannot "convert" Thrasymachus or Callicles by the force of argument alone. For that reason, Platonic political philosophy addresses only "men who . . . took those distinctions for granted," namely, the "natural" aristocrats, those who know that they are the "good" ones. The basic idea is that "the political community cannot tolerate a political science which is morally 'neutral' and which therefore tends to loosen the hold of moral principles on the minds of those who are exposed to it."[45] Strauss means that political life itself depends on justice, irrespective of whether there exists a "fact of the matter" about what is justice or not—so Platonic political philosophy must address the fundamental question of "what is justice," but this does not necessarily mean that it believes "justice" exists by nature or is a "fact" of reality. These considerations prepare Strauss's interpretation of the second Platonic reversal discussed below.

The Second Platonic Reversal: Ethics and Ontology as Governmental Apparatus

To recapitulate the argument so far: the first Platonic reversal consists in turning the practice of truth-telling against democracy by demonstrating that there is no space to speak the truth for those who are good in a democratic city: or that democracy depends on allowing bad people to speak freely. The consequence of this first reversal is that a city where those who are good can speak the truth will not be a democratic city but one governed by a constitution given by philosophers. This Platonic doctrine begs the question: how does one transition from a democratic city to a constitutional government? Plato's answer, as is well known, is that the philosopher will need the help of a beneficent tyrant in order to establish a constitutional government.

The alliance between Platonic philosophy and tyranny is what Strauss's *On Tyranny* famously designates as the "tyrannical teaching" of Platonic political philosophy.[46] The main point of that analysis is that Platonic political philosophy contains a "tyrannical teaching" according to which the "best government" need not take the form of a "rule of law": "as a matter of principle, rule of law is not essential for good government."[47] Good government depends on the "extent to which the tyrant or the 'constitutional' rulers will listen to the counsels of him who 'speaks well' because he 'thinks well.'"[48] The beneficent tyrant is "the tyrant who listens to the counsels of the wise."[49] This "tyrannical teaching" presupposes, as Strauss shows, that the direct rule by philosophers in a democratic city is impractical or impossible. The best solution, in ideal theory, needs to be substituted by a "second best" solution, namely, a constitutional form of government: "Where the law is despot over the rulers and the rulers are slaves of the law, there I foresee safety and all good things which the gods have given to cities" (*Laws* 715D), as long as one can "give the name of 'law' to the distribution ordained by intelligence" (*Laws* 714A).

In the essay dedicated to "Classical Political Philosophy," Strauss does not discuss in any detail this tyrannical teaching, but the next essay in the volume, "Restatement on Xenophon's *Hiero*" takes up this topic. It would take me too far afield here to discuss the changes that Strauss puts in place with respect to his original book *On Tyranny* or his critique of Kojève's own interpretation of Platonism as the need for the wise man to rule directly over the many.[50] For purposes of my argument here, the important point is that in the "Restatement" Strauss does assert that "in a situation that is favorable to radical change, the citizen body will for once follow the advice of a wise man or a founding father by adopting a code of laws which he has elaborated" and that this code of laws ought to be administered by an aristocratic class of "equitable men" (*epieikis*).[51] In other words, Platonic political philosophy favors constitutional government as a second-best solution to what Strauss calls the "utopia of the best tyranny," which remains for him the regulative ideal.[52]

I mention this Xenophontic background of Strauss's reading of Platonic political philosophy because it happens to be of concern to Foucault as well. Citing from Xenophon's corpus, he makes the point that if political truth-telling is necessarily democratic, then philosophical truth-telling is necessarily associated with a tyrannical form of government.[53] The new relation between (philosophical) truth-telling and government is exemplified by the government of the Prince (or tyrant) and his counselors.[54] Foucault's second thesis about Platonic political philosophy starts from the question, why is the individual tyrant a better subject to hear philosophical truth-telling than the many? Foucault's answer is that "the chief's soul as such, and precisely to the extent that it is an individual soul (the *psyche* of the individual), is capable of ethical differentiation which is introduced, enhanced, formed and made effective through a moral training and development which both makes him capable of grasping the truth and following from this, teaches him to limit his power."[55] Foucault's hypothesis is that the passage to a constitutional (i.e., moderate or limited) regime is premised on the philosophical education of the tyrant because philosophical truth-telling is itself focused on the nature of the souls of individuals.

Foucault therefore gives a new interpretation of the Platonic thesis that the best regime can be had only when the philosopher and an appropriate tyrant join forces: "the way in which he [the prince] governs the city depends on his *ethos* . . . and that this *ethos* is formed and defined through the influence of the true discourse addressed to him. . . . This *ethos* is the principle and matrix of his way of governing, then this *ethos* is the element which enables veridiction, *parrhesia* to articulate its effects in the field of politics, in the field of the government of men, in how men are governed."[56] This claim constitutes Foucault's second major thesis about Platonic political philosophy: philosophy becomes properly "political" not in its rejection of democracy (that was the first reversal), but in effecting a turn toward the "care of the self" that operates through the invention of *ethos*, understood as a governmental apparatus designed to "conduct" the way in which the leader conducts or leads others.[57]

It now becomes clear that Platonic political philosophy is the prototypical form of governmentality: Plato's "ethical differentiation" is the first laboratory for the "conduct of conduct" that Foucault traced forward into Christian pastoral power and eventually into modern liberal governmentality. The reflexive structure of governmentality ("the conduct of conduct") sheds light on the title of Foucault's lectures: "the government of self and others." As far as I know, this title has not been explained in the relevant literature. On my interpretation, the disjunction between "self" and "others" corresponds to the distinction between the philosophical government of self (through the *ethos-psyche* complex) and the "constitutional" government of others (the many) by this philosophically educated self. Out of the democratic belief that everyone, indiscriminately, has a justified claim to rule (because no one is a slave by nature), Platonic political philosophy works out an entirely different conception of politics: only those individuals who are constituted as "selves" through philosophical veridiction and the implantation of an *ethos* are capable of governing, and their government will be constitutional or legitimate by definition. Those who do not constitute themselves into "selves," the others, exist for the sake of being governed by those whose "self" is true and good.

The subtitle of Foucault's last lectures, the "courage of truth," refers to the equally Straussian *topos* that philosophers, in their truth-telling to democracy, face the risk of persecution and violent death. In his critique of Kojève, Strauss argued that the philosophers could not desire to rule in first person because their main activity was that of questioning, or illuminating the (unanswerable) basic problems or "ideas."[58] By sticking to this "zetetic" activity of questioning, philosophers avoid the struggle for power that would inevitably lead to their demise and can continue the philosophical activity that is most useful to the city. Foucault, instead, has a slightly different interpretation of the reason for zetetic activity than the one mentioned by Strauss: Socratic truth-telling starts from a divination or prophecy (namely, that Socrates is the wisest man), which Socrates tries to put to a "test" by questioning those who claim to have wisdom or be wise. For Foucault, this zetetic search is motivated by the goal of achieving a true science of government, for it is intended to make Socrates's soul "the touchstone (*basanos*) of the souls of others."[59] In other words, Socratic zetetic activity is not an attempt to leave politics to its own devices; it is not simply an admission that the philosopher ought not to be a king. Quite to the contrary, zetetic activity is the fundamental practice for the division between the "government of self" and the "government of others," where the soul or self that is truest (Socrates's soul) becomes the model to be imitated by the souls or selves of others (his philosophical friends), forming them into potential *condottieri* of the many. Foucault agrees with Strauss that what makes someone embark on the quest of "taking care of one's self" is the attempt to answer the question of what is justice. But for Foucault, Socrates's answer consists in the zetetic mission to teach everyone how to take care of their own soul: "This other aim is in fact to see to it that people take care of themselves, that each individual attends to himself [as] a rational being having a relation to truth founded on the very being of his soul. And in this we now have a *parrhesia* on the axis of ethics."[60]

Strauss offers a very different idea of the point of Socrates's zetetic activity. Strauss, as far as I can ascertain, never mentions the idea of the "care of the self" in his best-known discussions of Platonic political philosophy. Rather, his genealogy of Platonic political philosophy traces the crucial move away from political truth-telling and toward philosophical truth-telling back to the need to confront the many opinions about justice by raising the question of "what is justice?" or "what is virtue?" in an ontological sense. In order to settle the basic conflict about justice in political life, the political philosopher "had to raise an ulterior question which is never raised in the political arena." Although the pre-philosophical knowledge of politics assumes that the "good man" is the best ruler for all concerned, only Platonic political philosophy poses the "what is" question about goodness itself: "What is that virtue whose possession—as everyone admits spontaneously or is reduced to silence by unanswerable arguments—gives a man the highest right to rule?"[61]

In order to answer the "what is" question, Strauss argues that the philosopher "is ultimately compelled to transcend not merely the dimension of common opinion . . . but the dimension of political life as such; for he is led to realize that the ultimate aim of political life cannot be reached by political life, but only by a life devoted to contemplation, to philosophy."[62] For the Platonic political philosopher, the answer to "what is justice?" is nothing political as such, but a distinct "way of life"; "the highest subject of political philosophy is the philosophic life: philosophy—not as a teaching or as a body of knowledge, but as a way of life—offers, as it were, the solution to the problem [of justice/moral virtue] that keeps political life in motion."[63]

When he has to explain why the philosophical life can approach an answer to the question of what is virtue, Strauss argues as follows: "the philosopher's dominating passion is the desire for truth, that is, for knowledge of the eternal order, or the eternal cause or causes of the whole. As he looks up in search for the eternal order, all human things and all human concerns reveal themselves to him in all clarity as paltry and ephemeral."[64] Thus, whereas in Foucault the second Platonic reversal consisted in a shift from care of the city toward care of the soul or self, for Strauss the second Platonic reversal consists in a shift from care of the city to a state of what we could call carelessness; that is, the contemplation of the eternity of Being from the perspective of which all human matters become a matter of indifference.

This is an Aristotelian answer to the Socratic question, what is justice? But why does Strauss offer such an Aristotelian answer to the problem of justice? The important point for the purposes of my argument here is that the Aristotelian flight from political life into the heights of ontology and metaphysics is part of the paradoxical "politics" of and for philosophy. For Strauss it is clear that ontology is merely an apparatus of ethical differentiation:

> the philosopher who as such has had a glimpse of the eternal order is therefore *particularly sensitive to the difference among human souls*. In the first place, *he alone knows what a healthy or well-ordered soul is*. And secondly, precisely because he has had a glimpse of the eternal order, he cannot help being intensely pleased by the aspect of a healthy or well-ordered soul. . . . Hence *he cannot help being attached to men of well-ordered souls: he desires "to be together" with such men all the time*. . . . Hence he cannot help desiring, without any regard to his own needs or benefits, that those among the young whose souls are by nature fitted for it, acquire good order of their souls. But the good order of the soul is philosophizing. The philosopher therefore has the urge to educate potential philosophers simply because he cannot help loving well-ordered souls.[65]

Aristotelian ontology, for Strauss, becomes the discourse through which Platonic philosophical veridiction makes the ethical differentiation between good ("well-ordered") and bad ("ill-ordered") souls. The good souls that are ethically differentiated from the many lead a kind of "political" life that is, strictly speaking, extra-political: it is a form of common life based on philosophical not political *philia*.

For Strauss, and contra Kojève, the ethical differentiation achieved by the philosophical life—that is, the pursuit of the zetetic activity of achieving "genuine awareness of the problems"—is not motivated by the political desire for recognition (to be "loved" by the many) and, thus, by the pursuit of direct political rule on the part of the philosophers.[66] But this does not mean that the philosophical life does not need a "politics" of its own: the philosopher needs to descend into the marketplace and face the conflict with politics "in order to fish there for potential philosophers."[67] The way in which this "fishing" occurs is by putting forth the Aristotelian division between philosophical and political lives. In reality, this division is merely the "rhetorical" or "popular" presentation of philosophy to democracy in order to avoid the persecution that would lead to the demise of philosophizing *tout court*. After all, living in cities and depending on the social division of labor,[68] the Platonic political philosopher needs to justify himself before "the tribunal of the political community." Political philosophy must be able to answer the question that political life poses back to the philosophical life: "Why does political life need philosophy?" "From this point of view the adjective 'political' in the expression 'political philosophy' designates not so much a subject matter as a manner of treatment; from this point of view, I say, 'political philosophy' means primarily not the philosophic treatment of politics, but the political, or popular, treatment of philosophy, or the political introduction to philosophy, the attempt to lead the qualified citizen, or rather their qualified sons, from the political life to the philosophical life."[69] This political justification, given by Plato, is that "the well-being of the political community depends decisively on the study of philosophy."[70] What is meant here is not simply the utility of having philosophical constitutions for the city. The ultimate justification of philosophy before the tribunal of political life takes the form of Aristotelian philosophy, which turns out to be the true "politics" of Platonic philosophy. Philosophy's political self-presentation to democracy takes the form of Aristotle's ranking between dianoetic or intellectual virtue and political or practical virtues; Aristotle's division of the two ways of life also gives insight into the "limits of the moral-political sphere."[71] Lastly, "the question [of what is virtue] functions as an entering wedge for others whose purpose is no longer to guide action but simply to understand things as they are."[72] Aristotelianism reconciles philosophical truth-telling with political truth-telling by transforming the latter from a political and rhetorical practice into an (empirical) "political science"—that is, into a social science. Only Aristotle's "political science" provides the philosopher with an understanding of the nature of political life "exactly as they are understood in political life" in order to be able to justify philosophical life to political life. By introducing the Aristotelian division of philosophical and political lives, the danger of persecution is potentially thwarted, at least for a time. The philosopher protects himself by saying that what he does is only ontology, and that his utility to political life consists in providing a scientific study of what people do in cities, namely, social scientific policy studies.

Conclusion

Foucault and Strauss both show that Platonic political philosophy seeks to replace democracy with the idea of a legitimate or good government as the key characteristic of political life by pursuing the question, "what is justice?" Legitimate government, in turn, depends on the self-conduct of leaders whose *ethos* is formed by a nondemocratic way of life, designated as a "philosophical life" and characterized by a sui generis "politics" in regard to democracy. The characteristic activity of this life, for Foucault, is the "care of the self" whereas for Strauss it is the study of ontology.

The second Platonic reversal, for Foucault, consists in shifting the meaning of politics from the question of who is best fitted to care for the city, to the problem of how best to take care of the self or soul. Foucault concludes that for Platonism "the objective of [philosophical] truth-telling is therefore less the city's salvation than the individual's soul."[73] Platonic political philosophy fashions for itself an idea of *psyche* or self or soul in order to produce a "non-political *parrhesia*" (i.e., philosophical truth-telling), which claims to be most useful to the city and its political life because it essentially invents the idea of the legitimacy of power. Conversely, Foucault's analysis of Platonic political philosophy shows that democracy, if it is going to exist, must retain an essential relation to an-archy or the desire "not to be governed," and should resist being reduced to a constitutional form of government.

The second Platonic reversal, for Strauss, consists in employing the question of what is justice to break free from the priority of justice found in political life. What this means is a point of extreme controversy in the Straussian literature. Two general positions can be discerned within the Straussian literature, sometimes referred to as "East Coast" and "West Coast" Straussianism.[74] The first position holds that Strauss shows that the philosophical life dedicated to the pursuit of the "idea of the good" is actually amoral or unethical. "What is justice?" does not receive an answer that can be given a constitutional expression because it is not ultimately a political question, but a matter of ontology. The expression "natural right," in this sense, designates an empty set. The second position holds that those engaged in the philosophical life do so in order to find out what is by nature, that is, ontologically, good (where "good" has its traditional, ethical meaning of the term). The purpose of the philosophical life is to discern what is by nature "right" or "just," which in itself is often in contrast with positive right.

In light of Foucault's own discourse, it is possible to put forward a third possibility for what Strauss takes to be the true teaching of Platonic political philosophy: philosophers govern themselves through ontology, but govern others by making them ethically good through constitutional laws. The meaning of "ontology" is not supra-political but radically political. First, ontology offers a cover for the true governmental activity of philosophers; and, second, ontology shows that the very order of the world, of nature, is about the government of selves over others, of superior over inferior souls, and thus such government of others is right by nature or in accordance with the nature of things. The ultimate difference between Foucault and Strauss on natural right is as follows: for Foucault, "natural right" only designates the discourse that makes it possible to implant a pre- or supra-political government of others in a democracy. For Strauss, instead, "natural right" designates a discourse for which the government of others is "by nature" right or in accordance with the needs of the philosophical life.

Notes

1. An early version of this chapter was presented at the Foucault Circle meeting, UNSW, Sydney, June 2016.

2. For one example among many, see Francis Oakley, *Empty Bottles of Gentilism: Kingship and the Divine in late Antiquity and the Early Middle Ages* (New Haven, CT: Yale University Press, 2010).

3. This reading is found, for instance, in Hegel's claim that with Socrates the beginnings of an idea of individual or subjective freedom sees the light of day.

4. See Thomas Meyer, "The Origins of Leo Strauss's Political Philosophy," *Idealistic Studies* 44, no. 2–3 (2014); Michael Zuckert and Catherine Zuckert, *Leo Strauss and the Problem of Political Philosophy* (Chicago: University of Chicago Press, 2014); Jeffrey Alan Bernstein, *Leo Strauss on the Borders of Judaism, Philosophy, and History* (Albany, NY: SUNY Press, 2015); Rafael Major, ed. *Leo Strauss's Defense of the Philosophical Life: Reading What Is Political Philosophy?* (Chicago: University of Chicago Press, 2013). Foucault's plurennial lectures on Platonic political philosophy are not discussed in any of these works. In Major's edited volume explicitly dedicated to *What Is Political Philosophy?* Foucault's name does not appear in the index.

5. Steven B. Smith, ed. *The Cambridge Companion to Leo Strauss* (New York: Cambridge University Press, 2009) does not mention Foucault in the index. Catherine H. Zuckert, *Postmodern Platos* (Chicago: University of Chicago Press, 1996) was written before Foucault's lectures on Plato were published. For an earlier statement on the question of Foucault and the ancients, see Frédéric Gros and Carlos Lévy, ed. *Foucault Et La Philosophie Antique* (Paris: Éditions Kimé, 2003), which also does not discuss Strauss at any length. Some of the early attempts to read Foucault's themes of *parrhesia* and care of the self in connection with Plato, such as Alexander Nehamas, *The Art of Living: Socratic Reflections from Plato to Foucault* (Berkeley: University of California Press, 2000), and Sara Monoson, *Plato's Democratic Entanglements: Athenian Politics and Practice* (Princeton, NJ: Princeton University Press, 2000) do not discuss Strauss. These two works also seek to portray a "liberal democratic" Plato while missing the fact that the discussions of *parrhesia* in the late Foucault are entirely determined by the project of writing a "history of governmentality," which diminishes the value of their analyses for the comprehension of Foucault's reading of Plato.

6. Michel Foucault, *Security, Territory, Population: Lectures at the Collège De France 1977–1978* (New York: Picador, 2009), 193. For the debate on governmentality in Foucault and after, see Ottavio Marzocca, *Il Governo Dell'ethos. La Produzione Politica Dell'agire Economico* (Milan: Mimesis, 2011); Mitchell Dean, *The Signature of Power: Sovereignty, Governmentality and Biopolitics* (London: Sage, 2013); Vanessa Lemm and Miguel Vatter, ed. *The Government of Life: Foucault, Biopolitics, and Neoliberalism* (New York: Fordham University Press, 2014).

7. On all this, see Thomas Lemke, *Gouvernementalität und Biopolitik* (Wiesbaden: VS Verlag fuer Sozialwissenchaften, 2007), and *Biopolitics: An Advanced Introduction* (New York: New York University, 2011).

8. In *Homo Sacer*, Agamben identifies sovereign and biopower, among other things through a reference to the archaic Greek formula of *nomos basileus*. Giorgio Agamben, *Homo Sacer: Sovereign Power and Bare Life*, trans. Daniel Heller-Roazen (Stanford, CA: Stanford University Press, 1998), 30–38. In *The Kingdom and the Glory*, sovereign power is revealed to be a cover for governmental power. *The Kingdom and the Glory: For a Theological Genealogy of Economy and Government* (Stanford, CA: Stanford University Press, 2011). For an influential discussion of sovereignty and biopolitics in Foucault, see Roberto Esposito, *Bios: Biopolitics and Philosophy* (Minneapolis: University of Minnesota Press, 2008). For discussions of these shifts in Agamben's thought, see Daniel McLoughlin, "The Fiction of Sovereignty and the Real State of Exception: Giorgio Agamben's Critique of Carl Schmitt," *Law, Culture and the Humanities* (2013); Jessica Whyte, "'The King Reigns but He Doesn't Govern': Thinking Sovereignty and Government with Agamben, Foucault and Rousseau," in *Giorgio Agamben: Legal, Political and Philosophical Perspectives*, ed. Tom Forst (London: Routledge, 2013); and Daniel McLoughlin, ed. *Agamben and Radical Politics* (Edinburgh: Edinburgh University Press, 2016).

9. See Jacques Derrida, *The Beast and the Sovereign, Volume I* (Chicago: University of Chicago Press, 2011), and Amy Swiffen, "Derrida Contra Agamben: Sovereignty, Biopower, History," *Societies* 2, no. 4 (2012).

10. Foucault, *Security, Territory, Population: Lectures at the Collège de France 1977–1978*, 154.

11. Ibid., 192.

12. Agamben, *The Kingdom and the Glory: For a Theological Genealogy of Economy and Government*, 23–27, 126–127. On economic theology, see Nicholas Heron, *Liturgical Power: Between Economic and Political Theology* (New York: Fordham University Press, 2018).

13. See Foucault, *Security, Territory, Population: Lectures at the Collège De France 1977–1978*, 126ff, and on *nomos* and pastoral power in Schmitt, Carl Schmitt, *Verfassungsrechtliche Aufsätze aus den Jahren 1924–1954* (Berlin: Duncker & Humblot, 2003), 489–504 and *Der Nomos der Erde im Völkerrecht des Jus Publicum Europaeum* (Berlin: Duncker & Humblot, 2011), 36–48. On all this, see Mika Ojakangas, "Carl Schmitt and the Sacred Origins of Law," *Telos*, no. 147 (2009).

14. Foucault, *Security, Territory, Population: Lectures at the Collège De France 1977–1978*, 154.

15. Ibid., 123–124.

16. Ibid., 138.

17. "The royal art is not at all that of the shepherd, but the art of the weaver." Ibid., 146.

18. For a different approach to the significance of *The Statesman* I refer to Miguel Vatter, "Machiavelli, "Ancient Theology," and the Problem of Civil Religion," in *Machiavelli on Liberty and Conflict*, ed. Nadia Urbinati, David Johnston, and Camila Vergara (Chicago: University of Chicago Press, 2017). For an argument that sees biopower originating in Plato and Aristotle, see Mika Ojakangas, *On the Greek Origin of Biopolitics: A Reinterpretation of the History of Biopower* (London: Routledge, 2016).

19. See Vanessa Lemm, "The Embodiment of Truth and the Politics of Community: Foucault and the Cynics," in *The Government of Life: Foucault, Biopolitics, and Neoliberalism*, ed. Miguel Vatter and Vanessa Lemm (New York: Fordham University Press, 2014), for a reading of Foucault and the Cynics that goes in this direction. See Simona Forti, *New Demons: Rethinking Evil and Power Today* (Stanford, CA: Stanford University Press, 2014) for an argument that develops an affirmative reading of Plato in Foucault, one in which Platonic political philosophy is not only governmental in character. For an affirmative reading of care of self in Foucault and the politics of human rights, see Alexandre Lefebvre, *Human Rights and the Care of the Self* (Durham, NC: Duke University Press, 2018).

20. Michel Foucault, *The Courage of Truth: The Government of Self and Others II: Lectures at the Collège de France 1983–1984* (New York: Palgrave Macmillan, 2011), 34.

21. Leo Strauss, *What Is Political Philosophy? and Other Studies* (Chicago: University of Chicago Press, 1988), 80.

22. For recent attempts to capture Foucault's understanding of normativity in connection with Rawlsian theory of justice and public reason, see Paul Patton, "Government, Rights and Legitimacy: Foucault and Liberal Political Normativity," *European Journal of Political Theory* 15, no. 2 (2016); "Foucault and Normative Political Philosophy," in ed. Timothy O'Leary and Christopher Falzon, *Foucault and Philosophy* (London: Wiley-Blackwell, 2010); Mark Redhead, "Complimenting Rivals: Foucault, Rawls and the Problem of Public Reasoning" *Philosophy and Social Criticism* 42, no. 6 (2016).

23. See the classic account in Martin Ostwald, *From Popular Sovereignty to the Sovereignty of Law* (Berkeley: University of California Press, 1986).

24. For the discussion by classics scholars, see P. E. Van 'T Wout, "Solon's Law on *Stasis*: Promoting Active Neutrality," *Classical Quarterly* 60, no. 2 (2010) and Valerij Gouschin, "Solon's Law on *Stasis* and the Rise of Pisistratus in 561/60 Bc," *Acta Classica* 109 (2016). For a discussion of *stasis* in contemporary political theory, see Dimitris Vardoulakis, "Stasis: Beyond Political Theology?," *Cultural Critique* 73 (2009), and Giorgio Agamben, *Stasis: Civil War as Political Paradigm* (Stanford, CA: Stanford University Press, 2015). Interestingly, as noted by Schmitt and then Agamben, the concept of *stasis* is an important concept also in Gregory Nazianzen's Christology. See here Stathis Gourgouris, "Political Theology as Monarchical Thought," *Constellations* 23, no. 2 (2016). But I have no space to discuss the role of this concept in connecting Nazianzen's role in Foucault's idea of governmentality to Nazianzen's role in Schmitt's and Agamben's idea of political theology.

25. Strauss, *What Is Political Philosophy? and Other Studies*, 81.

26. Foucault, *The Courage of Truth: The Government of Self and Others II: Lectures at the Collège de France 1983–1984*, 74.

27. For a critical reading of the function of the stranger in Strauss and in Plato, see William Altman, *The German Stranger: Leo Strauss and National Socialism* (Boulder, CO: Lexington Books, 2011).

28. Strauss, *What Is Political Philosophy? and Other Studies*, 82.

29. Ibid., 83.

30. Ibid., 84; emphasis mine.

31. As such, this thesis is not new: C. H. McIlwain, *Constitutionalism: Ancient and Modern* (Ithaca: Cornell University Press, 1947) already identified Plato's late dialogues like *The Statesman* and *Laws* as the cradle of Western constitutionalism. Foucault and Strauss are interested in the discursive preconditions for constitutionalism to take root in a democracy.

32. On this point, see the essays collected in Sheldon S. Wolin, *Fugitive Democracy and Other Essays*, ed. Nicholas Xenos (Princeton, NJ: Princeton University Press, 2016).

33. For a recent argument to this effect, see Jacques Rancière, *Hatred of Democracy* (London: Verso, 2009) and compare with Melissa Lane, "Popular Sovereignty as Control of Office-Holders," in *Popular Sovereignty in Historical Perspective*, ed. Richard Bourke and Quentin Skinner (Cambridge: Cambridge University Press, 2016).

34. Foucault, *The Courage of Truth: The Government of Self and Others II: Lectures at the Collège de France 1983–1984*, 36.

35. Ibid., 40; ibid., 39.

36. Recent studies on Foucault's *parrhesia* such as Henrik P. Bang, "Foucault's Political Challenge: Where There Is Obedience There Cannot Be Parrhesia," *Administrative Theory and Praxis* 36, no. 2 (2014), and Torben Bech Dyrberg, "Foucault on *Parrhesia*: The Autonomy of Politics and Democracy," *Political Theory* 44, no. 2 (2016), do not register the radical opposition between political and philosophical *parrhesia*. Instead, they try to use the motif of *parrhesia* as a sort of bridge between democracy and governmentality. However, Foucault is quite clear about the fact that philosophical *parrhesia* makes possible government, but at the cost of democracy. Conversely, a democracy based on political *parrhesia* is literally ungovernable.

37. Foucault, *The Courage of Truth: The Government of Self and Others II: Lectures at the Collège de France 1983–1984*, 42.

38. Ibid., 44.

39. Ibid., 45.

40. Strauss, *What Is Political Philosophy? and Other Studies*, 79.

41. Ibid., 84.

42. Ibid., 86. Interestingly, in *What Is Political Philosophy?* Strauss refers to Jefferson's claim that the best government is the government of the "natural aristocracy." Jefferson was the author of more than one constitution.

43. Ibid., 86.

44. Ibid., 89.

45. Ibid., 90.

46. *On Tyranny* (New York: Free Press, 1963), 75; *Thoughts on Machiavelli* (Chicago: University of Chicago Press, 1995), 291.

47. *On Tyranny*, 76.

48. Ibid., 75.

49. Ibid., 75, and *What Is Political Philosophy? and Other Studies*, 86. I refer the reader to my analysis in Miguel Vatter, "Natural Right and State of Exception in Strauss's Teaching on Tyranny," in *Crediting God: Sovereignty and Religion in the Age of Global Capitalism*, ed. Miguel Vatter (New York: Fordham University Press, 2010). Long contested (see Catherine and Michael Zuckert, *The Truth About Leo Strauss: Political Philosophy and American Democracy* [Chicago: University of Chicago Press, 2006], 158–166), this point has been recently acknowledged even by Straussian commentators: "Moreover, Strauss indicates that Socrates and Xenophon both accept the 'tyrannical' teaching as a true

teaching." Eric Buzzetti, "A Guide to the Study of Leo Strauss' *On Tyranny*," in *Brill's Companion to Leo Strauss' Writings on Classical Political Thought*, ed. Timothy W. Burns (New York: Brill, 2014), 238. "Tyranny at its best is the rule of the philosopher-tyrant. Xenophon's highest political standard is identical to Plato's insofar as the philosopher-tyrant is, in the highest sense, indistinguishable from the philosopher-king: both are beneficent rulers guided by knowledge alone." Ibid., 251. "Strauss has led us to a noble vision of harmony and cooperation between the tyrant and the wise man, where they work together to benefit the city without recourse to laws." Ibid., 252.

50. For a subtle and comprehensive treatment of the Strauss-Kojève debate, see Alessandra Fussi, *La Città nell'anima. Leo Strauss lettore di Platone e Senofonte* (Pisa: Edizioni ETS, 2011).

51. Strauss, *What Is Political Philosophy? and Other Studies*, 113.

52. Ibid., 106.

53. Foucault, *The Courage of Truth: The Government of Self and Others II: Lectures at the Collège de France 1983–1984*, 58–60.

54. Ibid., 57.

55. Ibid., 61.

56. Ibid., 63.

57. On the concept of apparatus, see Giorgio Agamben, *What Is an Apparatus? And Other Essays* (Stanford, CA: Stanford University Press, 2009).

58. Strauss, *What Is Political Philosophy? and Other Studies*, 116ff.

59. Foucault, *The Courage of Truth: The Government of Self and Others II: Lectures at the Collège de France 1983–1984*, 84.

60. Ibid., 86.

61. Strauss, *What Is Political Philosophy? and Other Studies*, 90.

62. Ibid., 91.

63. Ibid., 91.

64. Ibid., 118.

65. Ibid., 121; emphasis mine.

66. Ibid., 116; ibid., 117.

67. Ibid., 125.

68. "The philosopher needs the services of other human beings and has to pay for them with services of his own if he does not want to be reproved as a thief or fraud." Ibid., 119.

69. Ibid., 94.

70. Ibid., 93.

71. Ibid., 94.

72. Ibid., 94.

73. Foucault, *The Courage of Truth: The Government of Self and Others II: Lectures at the Collège de France 1983–1984*, 65.

74. See Zuckert and Zuckert, *The Truth about Leo Strauss: Political Philosophy and American Democracy*, for a cartography of these Straussian camps.

7

A Fruitful Disagreement

The Philosophical Encounter between George P. Grant and Leo Strauss

Waller R. Newell

George Grant began his philosophical career as a believer in Hegelian progress. However, an exposure to the thought of Leo Strauss contributed to making him less optimistic about the progress of history and its fulfillment in the present. In particular, Strauss's focus on the ancients and their superiority to the moderns appealed to him. But Grant's doubts about the progress of history, while stimulated in part by Strauss, took on a different and more radical form. This was due to his exposure to Heidegger and his teaching about global technology, a variation of which was Kojève's notion of the Universal Homogenous State (UHS). It was also due to the guiding concern of Grant's life, Christian revelation. Moreover, while Strauss always maintained a sharp divergence between classical philosophy and revelation, Grant was a Christian Platonist who believed the two were not irreconcilable.[1]

Grant's interest in Heidegger's view that history had culminated in global technology, together with his belief in Christian revelation, made it difficult for him to accept either Strauss's exclusive orientation by classical natural right or his apparent preference for philosophy over revelation. (This preference is, in my view, far from self-evident or straightforward; but since Grant believed it to be the case, for the purposes of this discussion we will assume so too.) That difficulty was compounded by what

Grant took to be Strauss's indifference to Christianity, which for Grant remained both our mainstay for alleviating to the degree possible the baleful effects of modernity; and at the same time, especially in its Calvinist form, responsible in some ways for technological modernity itself.

Concomitant with this philosophical parting of the ways with Strauss was the difference between two over assessing modern politics. Grant, in my view reflecting the influence of Heidegger, tended to view distinctions among better and worse political systems as trivial in comparison with the titanic sway of technology, whose global juggernaut assimilated all such proximal distinctions among better and worse forms of authority. This difference in perspective came to a head over their comparative assessments of modern liberal democracy. Strauss, while making it clear that he found both classical political philosophy and revelation to be deeper sources of human illumination than any version of the modern project, maintained a prudent regard for liberalism's positive achievements: the extent to which it had maintained at least an attenuated foothold in classical rationalism and natural right—unlike the radical historicism of Nietzsche and Heidegger—and for the fact that, among all available contemporary political alternatives, it was self-evidently preferable to totalitarianism.

This conditional endorsement of American liberal democracy took Strauss's legacy down the road, in the view of some, to neoconservative foreign policy. The contrast with Grant could not be more dramatic. For in the American way of life, culminating in the Vietnam War, Grant saw the nadir of the working-out of global technology and the de-humanization of modernity as a whole, and his voice was definitely heard on the left. Whereas Allan Bloom—who I think can be taken as representative of Strauss's approach here—found John Rawls's *A Theory of Justice* to be psychologically impoverished and a vulgarization of Aristotle and Kant, pedestrian but not particularly destructive, for Grant the Harvard professor's liberal contractarian teaching justified, if only by omission, the worst horrors of America's imperial adventure in Vietnam.[2]

Although Grant's published reflections on Strauss were not extensive—mainly confined to his essay *Tyranny and Wisdom*—an unspoken debate with Strauss along the lines sketched above runs, as we will see, throughout a number of his works. It was, I hope to show, a fruitful disagreement.

Kojève's Hegel and Grant's Strauss

In Grant's presentation in *Tyranny and Wisdom* of Strauss's debate with Kojève, Strauss concedes that while modern tyranny differs from ancient tyranny due to its project of the conquest of nature, ancient tyranny is the only basis for thinking that difference through. The ancients rejected the conquest of nature as "preposterous," according to Strauss, but understood the assumptions behind it, and therefore modern tyranny cannot be said to have outmoded the ancient understanding. For Kojève, by contrast, philosophers going back to Plato have posited an ideal society, and the contradiction between that ideal and existing historical conditions were progressively negated by conquerors and statesman like Alexander the Great. The Church prefigured an ideal society premised upon human equality; modern philosophers like Hobbes and Spinoza secularized that ideal by negating Christian theism, thus making human equality a "realisable political order," as Grant puts it, in the here and now. This is why Kojève interprets Hegel as an "atheistic" thinker. During the period stretching from Napoleon until 1945, the conditions for the UHS have been actualized. The end of history is tantamount to the end of philosophy, because wisdom has been actualized for all.[3]

According to Grant, Strauss's main riposte to Kojève was that Kojève's arguments that the UHS is "the best social order" and "will be built by man" are both highly questionable.[4] Orienting himself by classical political philosophy, Strauss argues that the best social order is eternally knowable and transcends historical action. Plato's *Republic* is not, as Kojève would have it, a rational blueprint to be imposed on nature by the assertion of human freedom to negate nature. Strauss assumes that the Socratic/Platonic account of the whole is permanently true, whereas for Kojève, the full truth about the whole does not emerge and cannot be known until a certain epoch, that of Hegel. For Kojève, therefore, political philosophy does not transcend history, but comprehends it. Hence the debate between Strauss and Kojève about tyranny is not merely political—it is grounded in diametrically opposed assumptions about the whole.

Why then, Grant asks, doesn't Strauss address this cosmological and ontological debate head on, instead of approaching it through the debate about the proper relationship between tyranny and wisdom?[5] The answer, in Grant's view, is that Strauss is not concerned merely with refuting Hegelian and historicist philosophy as it bears on the assessment of tyranny, but with showing that the classical account of tyranny is consistent with its account of philosophy and political philosophy altogether, consistent with its account of the whole. If doubt can be cast on the validity of the UHS by establishing the superiority of the classical account of tyranny, that would imply that classical political philosophy as a whole is still viable and has not been outmoded by the progress of history. A belief in the progress of history makes even thoughtful and well-educated people believe that the classics are outmoded and can't be taken seriously, let alone as superior to modern thought. But if the enduring validity of the classics can be demonstrated proximally through the superiority of their account of tyranny—something everyone in our dangerous times can relate to—that will help to demonstrate their superior worth altogether.

So for Grant, Strauss's claim that the UHS will not turn out to be the best social order but, according to the classical understanding, a tyranny is merely a "secondary claim" to his larger and primary purpose of demonstrating the superiority of the classical understanding on every level—although surely, I would add, the secondary claim would follow from and be entailed by the first. However, Grant dutifully refuses to translate the passage from the original French edition of *On Tyranny* in which Strauss, revealing late in the proceedings his interest in that primary aim, concedes that he and Kojève have all along been debating the meaning of Being, not merely ancient and modern tyranny. Grant confines himself to including the French text in his essay, presumably out of respect for Strauss's wish to exclude it from the English version.[6] Strauss's apparent reticence about including this passage in the English version may be evidence that Grant is correct that he wished to keep that primary purpose somewhat occluded by the "secondary claim," perhaps believing that English-speaking readers in 1955 would not be ready for it, especially with its allusion to a then largely unknown (in the Anglosphere) Heidegger. Better to stick to the more concrete issue of tyranny.

Kojève's UHS, Grant relates, is a synthesis of the master and slave—classical and Christian—moralities. But because that synthesis will be universal when fully actualized, there will be no more wars and revolutions in which those earlier clashing moralities were major actors. Whereas it was centuries of such struggle and work that "raised man above the brutes," at the end of history there will be nothing left to do.

Hence, paradoxically, the satisfaction we achieve at the end of history is tantamount to the withering away of our most admirable or at least our most distinctive human traits.[7] For Strauss, by contrast—and Grant appears to agree with him—according to the classics, universal happiness is not possible. The best regime of Plato's *Republic* embodies the highest degree of happiness of which human nature is capable—philosophy and (in my view) civic virtue. Moreover, the best regime cannot be brought about by the negation of nature in the progressive pursuit of freedom, as in Kojève's Hegelianism, but "depends on chance" for its actualization—not an impossibility, but so remote as to not be worth anticipating or fighting for. By contrast, modern political philosophy as represented by Kojève tries to guarantee the actualization of the best regime by lowering the standard from moral virtue to universal recognition. Therefore, as Grant sums it up, while the classical best regime is highly improbable, the modern solution is entirely impossible. Why? Because the classical best regime provides us with an immutable standard by which to judge any form of authority. By contrast, the modern solution destroys any standard independent of the historical situation.

For Strauss, according to Grant, the "universal and final tyrant" of the UHS will not be a wise man, but will have to suppress philosophy because it would cast doubt on the adequacy of the "recognition" provided by the UHS for all. More specifically, I would add, for Strauss the philosopher is not dependent on universal recognition for his own justified self-admiration, so his capacity for an entirely independent satisfaction calls into radical question the claims of the UHS to universality.[8] Unlike past tyrants, who were content with glory, the Final Tyrant poses as a Wise Man. His is the only permissible philosophy and there will be no escape from his tyranny, as it had been possible to flee from tyrannies in the past, because it will be worldwide.

Having to my mind impressively summarized the debate between Strauss and Kojève, Grant now digs deeper and sets forth his own approach. As Grant interprets Strauss's position, for excellence of soul to exist there must be, as the classics maintained, an eternal and unchangeable order to the cosmos. If, on the other hand, as the moderns hold, man can master nature and necessity, meaning that no such truth transcends historical action, then there is no possibility of human excellence.[9] According to Grant, the Kantian account of freedom as an "archimedean point" beyond space and time, which identifies freedom with the mastery of nature, is foreign to the classics, for whom happiness and virtue unfold within the order of nature. I would add that for Kant to identify freedom with the purity of intention to rise above the natural inclinations puts him diametrically at odds with the Platonic view that certain passions such as eros can, properly educated, lead the soul to virtue and happiness. Similarly, whereas for Kant the pure intentionality of a free will to transcend the inclinations cannot be tainted by a natural desire for material goods, for Aristotle certain virtues such as liberality cannot be practiced without the acquisition of material wealth.

Grant wonders whether Strauss may be reading into the classics a clarity about their rejection of the conquest of nature that is not clearly present in any of their writings because he wants to highlight a massive alternative to the modern project. It is a valid question, although for me the priority of eros as a natural passion that, properly educated, can lead the soul on a continuous ascent toward virtue and wisdom (as in Plato's *Symposium*) surely implies this rejection. Whereas the modern conception of freedom is self-assertive, eros is self-forgetting as it is drawn "on up" toward the Idea of the Good. For the ancients, freedom is a harmonious ordering of the mind and the affects within the order of nature; for the moderns, freedom is our ability to strive to stand outside of nature and reshape it to our purposes. I have argued elsewhere that, strictly speaking, there is no concept of the will in classical philosophy in the sense of an ability or aspiration to stand outside of nature.[10] In my view, Machiavelli's summons to the conquest of Fortuna is a post-Christian concept—the City of Man minus the City of God—in which the Abrahamic God's capacity to reshape nature is transferred at least speculatively or prospectively to the human agency of the prince. Hegel, in my interpretation, also held this view, which is why *Moralität*, the sphere of the freedom to oppose nature (including one's own nature) emerging with the Reformation and culminating in Kant, must be distinguished from *Sittlichkeit*, the realm of communal and customary being that began with the Greek polis and character formation (paideia). For Hegel, in other words, freedom of will is a distinctively modern faculty.

Alluding to the untranslated French paragraph, Grant observes that for Strauss, one must not react to one's revulsion for the modern project by "escaping into anti-social dreams," and mentions Heidegger in the accompanying footnote, a likely allusion to his commitment to Nazism.[11] Although it would take us too far afield to dwell on this, for me the entire Strauss/Kojève debate has a deep Heideggerian undercurrent because Kojève's UHS is essentially what Heidegger means by global technology, but without regrets. Although Strauss tries to link arms with Kojève as a fellow student of the real-world political phenomenon of tyranny in contrast with Heidegger, whose obsession with Being led him to overlook or even endorse it, I'm not sure that Kojève was really much of an ally in Strauss's quest to restore political philosophy. At least Heidegger entertained some revulsion for technology, especially during his Nazi phase when he hoped "the revolution" could make a stand against it (likely an example of the "anti-social dreams" of which Strauss writes). Later, when Heidegger's hopes for the Nazi revolution failed, he embraced technology as ushering in a global either/or between the annihilation of humanity and the millenarian advent of man as "the Shepherd of Being." But in both Heidegger's and Kojève's assimilation of the entire meaning of the modern project to global technology, anything resembling a concern for a just or legitimate modern political order or for civic virtue vanishes. Heidegger's remark in 1935 that America and Russia were "metaphysically the same" as avatars of global technology was reportedly one of Kojève's favorite sayings.

Now we reach the core of Grant's difference with Strauss.[12] Technological progress, Grant observes, is often and understandably justified by claims that it helps "the poor, the diseased, the hungry and tired"—the use of technological power for, to recall Bacon's phrase, "the relief of man's estate." The suffering many cannot contemplate limiting technology's power to help them with "the equanimity of the philosopher." The historical materialist and atheist Feuerbach's maxim that "compassion is before thought" is ultimately "Biblical in origin." According to Grant, Strauss is aware of this Biblically grounded justification for modernity but does not confront it. In Grant's view, however, any argument for the superiority of classical political philosophy must come to terms with the challenge of revelation, a deeper source of the claim that "compassion is more important than thought" than Kojève's or other versions of the modern secularization of it.

According to Grant, for Kojève Hegel's synthesis of the Greek and Biblical, or master and slave, moralities is superior to the classics because the slave morality is higher than the master morality (inasmuch as it advocates equality), yet because it is the secularization of that religious insight it is also philosophic. Strauss, "on the other hand" according to Grant, argues that Hegel's doctrine of historical progress was not Biblically grounded even to a degree, but was founded on Machiavelli and Hobbes: Hegel's teaching about the master-slave dialectic is grounded in Hobbes's account of the state of nature.[13] Therefore Hegel's theory, like that of Hobbes, is based on the assumption that (as Strauss writes) "man as man is thinkable as a being that lacks awareness of sacred restraints or is guided by nothing but a desire for recognition." But whereas Grant depicts Strauss's interpretation of Hegel's political doctrine as being "on the other hand" from that of Kojève, I think that when Strauss equates Hegel with Hobbes, this is his characterization of what Kojève and Hegel share in common. More than this: it is clear from his other works that Strauss does not elsewhere equate Hegel's teaching entirely with that of Hobbes—or with that of Kojève. I believe that Strauss assumes this equation solely for the sake of the debate at hand in *On Tyranny*, and even then he qualifies the equation of Kojève's interpretation of Hegel with Hegel's own teaching through his use of the phrase "Kojève's Hegel."

It is clear from his other writings that Strauss does not, for instance, endorse Kojève's interpretation of Hegel with respect to Hegel's philosophy of nature, which Kojève jettisons: he takes Kojève to task for failing to see that for Hegel, if there is no teleology of nature, man's transformation of it through historical progress must be hopelessly solipsistic. To this I would add that in *The Phenomenology of Spirit*, Hegel does not identify nature with mere biological life, as material fodder for man's negation in the pursuit of freedom, as does Kojève. Instead, Hegel identifies "life" as at bottom the source of the family and the pre-Olympian Greek religion of ancestral custom; in other words, of the *Sittlichkeit* of the Greek polis, a communal dimension to history's unfolding of no less importance than "the labour of the negative" that transforms nature, a communality that re-emerges through "the Beautiful Soul" and the "re-appearance of God in history" after the French Revolution. Above all, Strauss praises Hegel for restoring the importance of the study of religion to philosophy and for ranking revealed religion higher than the "art-religion" of the ancients as exemplified by the plays of Aristophanes.[14]

So in Strauss's overall assessment of Hegel there is no evidence that Hegel views man as a being "that lacks awareness of sacred restraints," and a great deal of evidence to the contrary. Grant appears to overlook the broader dimensions of Strauss's assessment of Hegel in works other than *On Tyranny*. Above all, Strauss flatly rejects the identification of Hegel's teaching with the UHS: for Hegel, history culminates in *Das Volk* and the modern nation-state. Strauss characterizes Hegel's dialectic as the synthesis of a Spinozist lifeworld with the conquest of nature advanced by the early moderns.[15] That synthesis doesn't prove that Hegel's philosophy successfully reconciled reason and revelation (as he explicitly claimed) any more than this could be proven about Spinoza, but it certainly demonstrates that Hegel was not—as Kojève claimed—an atheist in his own self-understanding. However, because Grant, believing that he is following Strauss, thinks that Hegel's teaching was the same as Hobbes's argument about the state of nature, he concludes that neither Hobbes nor Hegel is reconcilable with the classics or Biblical religion. You cannot synthesize Socrates and Hobbes. But, he insists—in my view plausibly—that the modern project of Machiavelli and Hobbes might still result "at least in part" from the Biblical orientation toward equality and compassion.

For Grant, it is "impossible to know" what Strauss thinks about this connection between the modern project and a Biblical orientation because of his "remarkable reticence" about Biblical revelation as a whole.[16] Who can tell, he asks, whether Strauss thinks the Bible has a claim of authority over the philosopher as much as over other men, and whether that assumption must be "inimical to the claims of philosophy"? To me, Strauss's decades-long meditations on Maimonides and Spinoza demonstrate that he is not an atheist in any straightforward or facile way, not a Voltaire. But he clearly does reject a "third way" between Jerusalem and Athens. The irresolvable tension between revelation and reason embodied by these two cities is the "spiritual nerve" of the West. By implication, Rome drops out. Further to his rejection of a third way, Strauss's Plato is in no way a mystic or a virtuous pagan pointing toward monotheism; Strauss does not recognize the claim that Augustine synthesized Plato with "the word . . . made flesh." Grant, by contrast, saw Platonic philosophy as reconcilable with Christian revelation, and believed that God had been immanentized in history through that revelation—the third way.

I have a rather different interpretation of Strauss's apparent silence about Christianity from that of Grant. I think it is perhaps best understood from the perspective of classical philosophy, whereby revelation corresponds to the realm of fate, chance, poetry, or an irrational enthusiasm. Viewed from this perspective, Strauss's fate was to be Jewish—that was his only avenue to the biblical orientation, a self-understanding at least indirectly confirmed by classical philosophy itself. If my argument is valid, we can assume that Strauss would neither care about nor presume to address the status of Christianity, not necessarily because he overlooked or denigrated it, but because it was not available to him as a direct experience.

Grant concludes that, for Strauss, the distinction between those capable of philosophy and those who are not is permanent and unalterable, and indicates the "proper ordering of society."[17] Therefore, he suggests, Strauss may be reticent about his view of revelation so as to protect the faith of the nonphilosophic from those contemporary intellectuals who take delight in puncturing it. For the nonphilosophic, the superficial materialistic rationality that debunks all forms of religious faith only undermines their moral decency without bringing them closer to the philosophic life. This is surely not unlikely as one explanation of Strauss's reticence. But in Grant's judgment, Strauss's reticent, perhaps esoteric view about the status of revelation puts him at a disadvantage with Kojève, who can account to some degree for its role in historical progress as the slave morality. Strauss, in Grant's judgment, may be able to refute Kojève's secular account of history culminating in the UHS, but does not provide his own account of the role of religion in promoting modern compassion for the suffering. Overall, then, Grant accepted Strauss's contention that the modern project constitutes a sharp break with the classics; but unlike Strauss, who saw this break mainly in terms of political theory beginning with Machiavelli, Grant increasingly saw it mainly in terms of a shift in the meaning of Christian revelation. This will become more evident in our discussion of his other writings.

Tyranny and Wisdom, in sum, sets forth the main contours of Grant's fruitful encounter with the thought of Leo Strauss, where he agreed with it, and where he departed from it. He is fully persuaded, I think, of the superiority of classical political philosophy to the modern project insofar as it defends excellence of soul as an eternal standard, as opposed to the modern project which, by claiming it can master nature, denies the possibility of the eternal truth and thereby of excellence of soul. But this agreement with Strauss is confined within the boundaries of political philosophy. When it comes to the role of Biblical revelation in the history of the West, Grant does not believe that Strauss makes his own view of it clear, and may overlook the very large extent to which the modern project for "the relief of man's estate" was grounded in Christian compassion even as the modern project attempted to replace the authority of Christian revelation with a purely secular standard. These differences are developed in Grant's later writings, even though Strauss's name is rarely mentioned.

The Protestant Primal

In his essay *In Defense of North America*, Grant acknowledges in the first footnote Strauss's influence on his reading of the history of political philosophy, but re-affirms that he differs with him over Christianity's relationship to modernity. Grant insists that while moderns like Machiavelli claimed to be reviving the practice of ancient political virtue as against Christianity, in actuality they critiqued the classical account of virtue from a source "hidden in the depths of Biblical religion" itself—the promotion of equality and compassion.[18] Grant argues that the foundation of modernity was the symbiotic interaction of Renaissance and Protestant individualism, of the Reformation and the new sciences for the mastery of nature—very different from Strauss, but in keeping with arguments made by Tocqueville and Tawney. As I would put it, Luther and Machiavelli wanted to free modern man from the Church of Rome for opposite reasons—Luther wanted to disentangle Christian faith from an involvement in worldly politics such as the Church undertook, and Machiavelli wanted to disentangle political power-seeking from curtailment by the authority of faith. The two interwoven strains exploded in the English civil wars and combined to increase the power of the secular state. I believe Grant is profoundly correct about this understanding of the origins of modernity and have tried to develop it in my own scholarship.[19]

The Protestant and especially Calvinist idea of God as a series of pure and unfathomable will-acts, with no intervening Thomistic natural teleology, drains the natural world of divine purpose, leaving man as a solitary individual in a world of random matter in motion.[20] Although Luther and Calvin stressed the avoidance of sin and the importance of conscience as central to a Christian's life just as they had always been, for Grant[21] the dynamic of modernity sprang from the fact that Protestant asceticism repressed sexual pleasure and sloth, whereas self-denying traits suitable for commerce such as deferred gratification and industriousness were released from traditional Christian restraints on money-making—a combination of self-denial and business acumen that Tawney referred to as "worldly asceticism." Moreover, when God's presence and the comfort of the liturgy were drained from the world by the Reformation's rejection of Thomism and the priestly hierarchy of the Church of Rome, the individual thrown back on himself came to identify the probity and thrift that led to success in commerce as likely indicators that one had been saved, since salvation could no longer be assured by traditional means such as the old Church promised in its sacraments or through good works. In this connection, one could adduce Hobbes's alleged theological nominalism. While some believe that Hobbes's nominalism drove him to his materialistic version of the state of nature, I believe it is at least equally likely that he invoked nominalism precisely in order to find a theological underpinning for that view of human nature as driven by self-preservation and acquisition. Whichever is right, it is a good illustration of the symbiotic relationship between Lutheran theology and secular appetitive individualism.

America was the tabula rasa for the expansion of Protestantism in its purest form.[22] As an apology for North America—the essay's title implies that North America both requires and deserves a "defense"—Grant pays a mixed tribute to "the hope, stringency and nobility" of the settlers, "the punishment they inflicted on themselves" through their "uncontemplative and unflinching wills." But whatever nobility that "primal" originally possessed, Grant maintains, today it is entirely at the service of the technological mastery of the world, eclipsing all political and social divisions: "The directors of General Motors and the followers of Professor Marcuse sail down the same river in different boats."[23] Here, in my view, one can detect Heidegger's influence on Grant—ideological differences within modern societies and the attempt to distinguish between better and worse contemporary regimes sink into insignificance, absorbed by the monolithic juggernaut of technology. The right, Grant says, likes technology because it increases individual prosperity, while the "new left" wants to enjoy the wealth created by technology, spread it around, and use the leisure facilitated by its affluence to dip into polymorphous sexuality: "Having first conquered nature, we can now enjoy her." Grant similarly equates the corporate right, government bureaucrats, and concerned citizens who all want to impose their "values" on the world and reshape it. The pursuit of values does not counteract technology, he argues, but pre-supposes it by supplying various agendas for imposing our mastery on existence. There is no need to discriminate among those agendas or their motivations. Again, Heidegger's influence is transparent here.

Downplaying the differences, as Grant does, between the left and the right in North America in the 1960s and 1970s arguably made some sense: one could argue that the New Left was from the outset tamed by the prosperity offered by liberal democracy and capitalism, sluicing its radical impulses off into hedonism, entertainment and the counterculture. Its co-optation by capitalism was perhaps not noble, but it was effective: getting stoned was vastly preferable to The Killing Fields. But when one ranges beyond North America, Grant appeared to overlook vastly the millenarian utopian and genocidal impulse in radical collectivism exemplified by the Bolsheviks, Nazis, Khmer Rouge, and Maoists; a reflection, in my view, of the fact that Heidegger would have said that, as variants of global technology, they were "metaphysically the same" as liberal democracy. Indeed, seen in this light, Grant's identification of the United States as the spearhead of global technology in its "crimes" against the Vietnamese people was, with the greatest respect, a rather disturbing instance of political myopia. The Heideggerian approach is explicit when Grant argues that, despite the contrast between America's individualism and the communist bloc's collectivism, "the rival empires agree . . . as to what is the goal of human striving."[24] There is no comparative assessment of the justice and injustice of different regimes such as Strauss identified as a central task of political philosophy. Yet when one considers the Soviet empire's millions of victims (through the terror famine in the Ukraine, the Hitler-Stalin pact, the Gulag), were they really merely "rival empires" with the same technological agenda? To pose this question is not to exculpate America from its not inconsiderable acts of injustice at home and abroad, only to restore a sense of our capacity to attempt a distinction between better and worse regimes. One must note in this connection what was, so far as I am aware, Grant's virtual indifference—always dismaying to me—toward the anti-communist dissident movements that began to sweep Europe in the 1970s and 1980s when he was writing, exemplified by Kundera, Milosz, Havel, and Solzhenitsyn. It is as if Grant lived in a world dominated exclusively by America.

It is still possible, Grant argues, for us to be touched by the redemptive possibilities of a "fuller Christianity" yet residing behind the North American Calvinist primal, a Christianity that still "held in itself the fruits of contemplation" and thereby enabled us to touch "Greekness."[25] We might still be touched by "something in Europe which stayed alive there from before the age of progress through all its acceptance of that age" as well as by a "surviving Judaism." This is where Grant, in my view, departs in important ways from Heidegger, who had no interest in premodern Christian theology or civilization; who favored Luther among Christian theologians because of Luther's inward-looking spiritual austerity and rejection of Thomism; and who never located technology in the rise of Protestantism, but instead identified incipient global technology with the very "Greekness" (in the form of Plato's metaphysics) to which Grant urges us to remain open. Grant agrees with Strauss as against Heidegger that there was a fundamental break between ancients and moderns, and like Strauss he prefers the ancients to the moderns philosophically. But he is unlike Strauss in stressing the character of Protestant faith as the seed-bed of the modern project and is unlike him as well in his openness to a "fuller" premodern Christianity as a route back to the ancients.

In what strikes me as a very distinctive insight Grant argues that until recently, North American Protestantism, due to "the very absence of a contemplative tradition," was innocent of the "public nihilism" that flowered in Europe with industrial society. I take this to mean that whereas in the New World appetitive individualism and the project of the conquest of nature was taken to be liberating, in Europe it was seen as a disaster of alienation and dehumanization (early examples include Rousseau and Schiller). Now however, Grant argues, the philosophy of Europe's "agony" is penetrating North America through the historicist and existentialist relativism of Nietzsche, Heidegger, and Sartre, summed up by the widespread cachet of the word "values." I am not certain what examples of Europe's "public nihilism" Grant had in mind, but I have my own interpretation. For Europeans, the concept of values was an agony because it laid bare the terrible truth that truth is relative, and that our choices and decisions are made in an ethical void—the agony that tormented Weber in his explication of the fact/value distinction. This agony drove Nietzsche and Heidegger, in my view, to embrace millenarian visions of apocalyptic destruction in which the reduction of existence to materialism and the corresponding emptiness and arbitrariness of our value choices, at bottom simply another way of mastering nature, would be swept away by a new epoch: the Overman and the National Socialist "community of destiny"[26]

But in North America, Grant observes, the relativity of values was cheerfully adopted by social scientists and filled with the "substantive morality of liberalism:" every value is subjective, so do your own thing.[27] At the same time, they took it for granted that liberalism, industrial democracy, social welfare, and egalitarianism were somehow immune to the "corrosive power" of the insight that liberal values, too, are but groundless projections into the void—the insight that, I would argue, gave rise in Europe to the catastrophes of Communism and Fascism as nihilistic rebellions against Enlightenment modernity. Now, however, in

Grant's prognosis for North American society, the old substantive morality of the Protestant bourgeois virtues—the work ethic and the moral code of delayed gratification—needed to prosper under capitalism were steadily being eaten away by a soft nihilism sustained by the affluence created by those very virtues, leaving only the right to enjoy whatever "idiosyncratic wants" seize us, like Marcuse's polymorphous sexuality and "the sperm-filled visions of Burroughs." Today, according to Grant, the young are increasingly cut off from even the very thin account of an objective good and justice contained in the original Calvinist primal. There may be similar implications in Strauss's depiction of the third wave of modernity, the radical historicism of Nietzsche and Heidegger, but Grant explores them much more robustly and sounds a louder tocsin. In the years since he wrote, given the rise of economic globalization, Grant in my view was undoubtedly prescient in foreseeing that the Protestant virtues of self-restraint and probity originally considered to be the characterological basis for economic success would be steadily hollowed out and replaced by rampant greed and hedonism.

The Call from That Darkness

In *English Speaking Justice*, Grant returns to the North American primal, but now with much more emphasis on Calvinism and less emphasis on its symbiotic interdependence with liberalism. His avenue is John Rawls's influential *A Theory of Justice*.[28] For Grant, the book's argument is both a major specimen of the fact/value distinction and a desperate attempt to keep at bay the nihilistic consequences of it that Grant detailed in *In Defense of North America*. Because Rawls operates within its assumptions, instead of deriving a theory of legitimacy from a description and analysis of the natural human condition like the philosophies of Hobbes and Locke, its aim is purely procedural—a set of rules to maximize equality by asking everyone to imagine how they would wish to be treated if stripped of all natural abilities, character traits and advantages. It is an "abstraction," as Grant terms it, whose only validity is self-referential because the analytical thought that guides it assumes that an ought cannot be derived from an is. To this we can add that Rawls explicitly excludes any account of intrinsic virtue or the good life from his theory.

Despite a superficial resemblance to Kant's categorical imperative, therefore, Kant's "central ontological affirmations" are "absent."[29] Rawls cannot say with Kant that the only unqualified good is a good will. For

Kant the categorical imperative is a "fact of reason," meaning that it possesses the structure of reason—universality and necessity—but has no empirical correlate. This opens the way for Kant's argument that by exercising the categorical imperative we strive to inject moral freedom into the very structure of nature otherwise studied by empirical science. This raises it from a mere human rule to a force for improving all of reality. Rawls, by contrast, cannot equate freedom with a "fact of reason" because, for him, there is no objective reason of any kind. His theory is therefore pure conventionalism. Rawls's premise of the original position cuts off all substantive discussions and disagreements about morality and the soul and their respective and differing accounts of the whole—the traditional subject matter of political philosophy—and reduces the meaning of justice to "American bourgeois common sense," or as Rawls himself admits, "our intuitive conviction."[30]

Grant next advances a bold and to my mind rather perplexing link between Rawls's theory of justice and "the savage imperial adventure" of the Vietnam War.[31] Let's take Grant's argument point by point: (a) the war's architects, Kennedy and Johnson, Grant argues, advocated domestically Rawls's own values of welfare equality and individualism; (b) the war was justified as defending liberal-democratic values around the world, and was planned by men at the liberal universities, especially Rawls's own Harvard; (c) Rawls's theory of justice abstracts from the real-world conditions of "war and imperialism" in his elaboration of the original position. But this evasion gave assistance to the American empire. By setting aside ordinary liberal moral and policy debates about internationalism and just relations between states of the kind that were conducted over the legitimacy of the war, Rawls, in Grant's view, silently laid bare the truth that America was a great empire and that this polite discourse about the proper conduct of international relations was mere window-dressing to soften or conceal its imperialistic agenda. After all, Grant claims, FDR, the great foe of war and imperialism, had also been "consolidating an empire" himself. All in all, Grant concludes, Rawls's theory was "enormously weakened" by its abstraction from the real conditions of American imperial aggression along with the depredations of "domestic corporate power."

While I agree that Rawls's theory is indeed weakened by its abstraction from these realities, by its abstraction from any account of intrinsic human virtue and the good life, and from any substantive account of merit whereby unequal status may be earned and not simply an accident of birth, I wonder if Grant's critique does not tax Rawls too much. Unquestionably the ahistorical emptiness of Rawls's social contract reminds us, by completely ignoring it, of a contradiction between democratic self-government at home and imperialism abroad stretching back to Thucydides and the Athenian empire. But Rawls's theory did not preclude others from exploring this contradiction in the case of the Vietnam War, nor was it entirely unreasonable to think that a wholly domestic account of justice could be given without a direct confrontation with it, however inadequate that account may ultimately have proven to be. And the mere physical presence of Rawls at Harvard, the university of some of the mandarin technocrats who planned the war, is not enough in itself to indict Rawls. As for Grant's remark that the war's architects advocated domestically Rawls's own values of welfare equality and individualism, a pacifist or a dove could have advocated those values too, so how were they intrinsically connected to the war? Finally, Grant's remark that FDR had been "consolidating an empire" while waging war against the Third Reich and Japan is redolent of Heidegger's view that all regimes, whether democratic, communist, or fascist, were "metaphysically the same," already encountered in Grant's earlier description of America and the Soviet bloc as "rival empires" whose joint aim was technological mastery.

Grant now turns again to the historical unfolding of liberalism that he discussed in *In Defense of North America*, adding a number of new dimensions. Because of England's "successes under bourgeois constitutional liberalism" after the Glorious Revolution, Grant writes, they were spared the great crisis of liberalism in Europe and the successively more extreme waves of attacks on it by Rousseau, Hegel, Marx, and Nietzsche. The English intellectual and political world had made up its mind—its internal distinctions between "whig" and "tory" were mere differences over the means and pace toward the jointly held end of "comfortable self-preservation." Burke's political theory did not differ essentially from that of Locke. But the price that the English paid for the comparative decency of their way of life was that they were "singularly unprepared" when the revolution against modernity exploded in "the extremities of communism and national socialism," especially because they had given up original thinking for a Burkean account of benign progress.[32] Not long after the towering figure of Locke, England's self-understanding became unphilosophic, identical with the Whig theory of history according to which its institutions had evolved largely peaceably since Magna Carta and had been in no need of radical ideas. For Grant, the silver lining in this intellectual philistinism was that the very disinterest of the English in great philosophy had saved them from the "lack of moderation inherent in modern political philosophy and technology"—inherent in (as I would term it) the original Machiavellian project of the conquest of nature on behalf of economic aggrandizement and the millenarian counter-reactions to it such as Marxist revolution, Nietzsche's will to power, and Heidegger's "community of destiny," populist existentialist rebellions against the liberal-contractarian conquest of nature that only intensified the revolutionary will-power to reshape nature and human nature so as to usher in a new world of communal virtue cleansed of the filth of modern bourgeois greed and baseness.

The contractual liberalism of Locke, Grant argues, flowered in its "purest form" in America because America lacked the residual premodern traditions of the English class system and an established Church. For a long time, he goes on, America preserved "decent legal justice" because of the "intimate and yet ambiguous co-penetration between contractual liberalism and Protestantism" spanning the generations.[33] Grant seems now to assign priority to Protestantism as providing for a time a seed-bed of moral decency and character to limit the tendency of contractual liberalism to unleash unbounded greed and plutocracy. In contrast with *In Defense of North America*, he no longer depicts the Protestant primal in an equal partnership with liberalism, a symbiotic interdependence between the Reformation and the Age of Reason, between Luther and Machiavelli. In this way, I believe, he sharpens his differences with Strauss, who appeared to believe that while modern social contract theories such as that of Locke were inferior to the account of the Good offered by the classics, they fostered a degree of moderation, respect for law, constitutional government, and rights of freedom of thought and worship that were higher than mere survival and material self-interest, all on their own, without supplementation by Protestant faith. I wonder, though, whether Grant isn't correct that the inherent relativism and *laissez-allez* greed unleashed by the early modern thinkers, perhaps through a misreading of them, were delayed in their effects for generations primarily by battening down an underlying Protestant ethic of character that modernity's worst tendencies have been increasingly wearing down.

Calvinists and other nonconformists fled to North America, Grant avers, because they feared any connection between church and state such as the Church of England had established, and also because they despised what they viewed as its residual Popish hierarchy and liturgy. The secularization of the state through its disentanglement from any particular religious creed, prevalent early on in the New World, was therefore a "means to their freedom," a dynamic originally going back, as we have observed, to Machiavelli and Luther. More fundamentally, Grant continues, the "fearful solitariness" of the Calvinist account of the individual's search for God in a world drained of the comfort of the liturgy and sacraments and guidance from teleological natural law found an obvious home in a politics defined in terms of the natural rights of the individual: "Calvinist individualism and the development of capitalism went hand in hand," and a regime based on the social contract served both entrepreneurialism and freedom of worship.[34] Again, differing from Strauss's exclusive emphasis on secular social contract theorists like Locke as sufficient for explaining liberalism, Grant gives Protestantism a larger role in this New World partnership: "Protestantism gave a firmer and more unyielding account of justice to its country's constitutionalism than would have been forthcoming from any simply contractarian account." Because American Calvinism was "less thoughtful" than its European original, which had had to develop the intellectual resources to contend with and justify itself against other creeds, it was for a time paradoxically "less vulnerable" to the extreme manifestations of modernity—Americans had never longed for a genuinely Marxist revolution or a Nietzschean Master Race. To my mind, the bland Hegelianism of St. Louis and its rapid supplanting by pragmatism; Emerson's blend of European worldliness with Protestant inwardness; or William Jennings Bryan's horrified gleaning of Nietzsche (in his view synonymous with Darwin's godless account of man as the survival of the fittest) resulting in his participation in the Scopes monkey trial, all speak to what Grant views as Protestant America's steady imperviousness to decades to European historicism and relativism.

In another new variation on his earlier theme of the symbiotic relationship between liberalism and Protestantism, Grant now stresses that this intertwining was not one in which Protestantism, as is often thought, was gradually secularized. On the contrary: Protestantism, Grant maintains, shaped liberalism at least as much as it was shaped by it.[35] Heidegger had argued that technology precedes the rise of the new empirical sciences and the actual modern machinery and industries that are its consequences—its origins are "as yet unknown." Grant's answer to this "most difficult" mystery is that technology originates in "the affirmation of human beings as 'will'" that broke forth in Calvinist theological voluntarism. That theology differed from the older Christian belief that God operated on nature through rational categories, through universal natural laws derived by Thomas Aquinas from Aristotle. As the Anglican Thomist Richard Hooker put it, the Calvinist error was that "there is no reason beside [God's] will." In locating the origin of technology in Calvinist voluntarism, Grant's position is distinct from that of Heidegger, who located incipient global technology in ancient metaphysics, and also from that of Strauss, who located it in Machiavelli's project of mastering Fortuna. I would only add that what became Calvinist theological voluntarism was deeply embedded as an alternative strain within Christianity from its earliest origins, before the triumph of Thomism. Luther saw himself as reviving the true Christian faith of Augustine as against Thomas's paganized "theology of the flesh," and Thomas had in his own era been fervently opposed by Augustinian fundamentalists like Bishop Étienne Tempier, who insisted that God's actions were utterly unfathomable and unconstrained by natural law. The Reformation was in large measure Augustine's delayed victory over Thomas.

Grant's main point is that Calvinism was not simply a temporary ally for an eventually triumphant secular liberalism, discarded when its religious window-dressing was no longer needed, but on the contrary infused liberalism with the idea of God's pure will and made will the basis of modern individualism. For Grant, Kant's identification of will as the "only good thing" in the world "that is good without limitation" and the guarantor of moral autonomy represented the philosophical refinement of a deeper Calvinist conviction that European secularists and Anglicans could find respectable. As Grant remarks, the secularization of the Calvinist God's will as boundless human autonomy was on one level the nemesis of Calvinist faith, but "in that very nemesis" it attached itself to the essence of modernity as pure will, and therefore provided the ground for technology. For Grant it is no coincidence that Rousseau and Sartre, who identify the essence of man as free will, were "impregnated with Calvinism." For my part, I remain divided in my mind as to whether I agree with Grant that Calvinist voluntarism was the senior partner in the unfolding of North American liberalism. At the same time, however, I definitely agree with him as against Strauss that its unfolding cannot be understood solely in terms of modern political philosophy. Finally, as between Grant's tracing of the technological project of the mastery of existence to a secularized divine will and Heidegger's tracing of it to Plato's metaphysics—whose theology did not even conceive of a Creator God who could shape and reshape nature—Grant's account seems far more plausible.

For several centuries, Grant continues, the "new co-penetration of 'logos' and 'techne'"—technology—has reduced nature to chance and necessity, converting it into fodder for our control and remaking. In order to reduce nature to matter in motion suitable for technological reshaping, the ancient teleological notion of the Good had to be eliminated from our understanding of the universe. But at the same time, our conception of justice remains rooted in "ancient science" and its notion that the cosmos is objectively structured according to the Good. In other words, we have tried to "hold together" the truth of the new science with a premodern account of justice, generating the great "civilizational contradiction" in whose net we are now trapped.[36]

The premodern view of philosophy and religion, Grant relates, was that justice is the order in which we find our place—it defines us, not we it. But the view of modern thought is that justice is how we choose freedom, and that we are responsible for how it works out. This is another way of evoking Kant's ethic of intentionality—by willing acts that are universalizable and devoid of natural content and inclination, including our own self-interest, love of honor and even love of others, we guarantee a morally autonomous outcome.[37] But Western Christianity introduced a third alternative between the ancients and moderns—the primacy of charity and our equality before God. (As we recall, the third way that, according to Grant, Strauss ignores.) So on one level Christianity restrains the materialistic excesses of secular liberalism, but on another level, liberal contractualism's "seedbed" is in Christianity's promotion of equality and the welfare of the common man. The link between them is that God's will to transform nature is transferred to human agency.

Kant was the "great delayer," as Nietzsche called him, in containing the forces of this civilizational contradiction—"accepting both the will to make one's own life and the old content of justice."[38] But what happens, Grant asks, when the will to autonomy breaks loose from this old content, when it wants to entirely remake nature and the world in pursuit of the abstract, empty, endless pursuit of freedom? This break-out, I would observe, may have already been present in the thought of Fichte, who, while believing himself to be carrying on Kant's project, in fact shattered the equipoise Kant had aimed to establish between nature as the limiting condition on freedom and freedom as the will to overcome nature by liberating the will from all such constraints, thereby reducing nature to "the material of our moral duty rendered sensuous." To my mind, in the open-ended voluntarism of his summons to action, Fichte was the true antecedent of Kojève, as opposed to Hegel.

Technology, says Grant, is the name we give to this breaking-out—freedom negates nature endlessly to produce more power with which to go on negating nature, including human nature and previous limitations on human autonomy such as procreation and pregnancy. Concerns about justice are swallowed up in an irresistibly more comprehensive global "destiny," an echo of Heidegger's view that traditional humanistic ethics are becoming ever more pointless in comparison with the "destining" of Being as technology. Again, we see how Grant in large measure shares Heidegger's identification of the West's destiny with technology, but like Strauss confines this project to modernity. At the same time, Grant does not embrace Heidegger's millenarian vision in which technology may yet turn in on itself to dissolve itself and yield the "Shepherd of Being." Grant's sobriety in this regard—along with his evident rejection of Heidegger's view that, far from containing, as Grant would have it, the only worthy philosophical account of justice that is, however battered, still available to us, "ancient science" itself generates technology—demonstrates Grant's common sense and refusal of easy ways out. He prefers thinking through modernity's perplexities and contradictions open to the possibility that they will not be resolved to either antiquarian nostalgia or apocalyptic dreams of a new world to come such as Heidegger's "Shepherd of Being."

As an illustration of the larger civilizational contradiction he is tracing out, Grant dwells on the contradiction between "the corporations" being "creative" in "carrying out the dynamic convenience of technology" and the liberal holdover of the values of liberty and equality. Why should other human beings and their rights "stand in the way" of technology's advances? The social contract, including its latest version, that of Rawls with which the essay began, may continue to try to limit the power of the corporations. But that attempt at limitation is undermined by the fact that the majority place their own hopes in technology for providing them with what Rawls terms "the primary goods" of a capitalist economy—the basic opportunities necessary for us to pursue our rights in "the original position"—and will often not defend more traditional accounts of justice when they conflict with economic maximization. For Grant, the deficiencies of Rawls's *A Theory of Justice*—its remoteness from the real-life crises of war and economic injustice, its empty, self-referential proceduralism, its psychological poverty, its avoidance of any account of virtue or the Good—are arguably prime examples of how the liberal contractarian dimension of modernity has been steadily drained of its original Calvinist account of justice to the point where only the most wan and spectral defense of liberal justice remains.

Because contractual liberalism thrives on the prosperity generated by technology, and by the reduction of human beings to isolated selves first launched by Protestantism, liberalism, Grant concludes, is not independent of technology and cannot transcend it.[39] As technology advances, the remnants within contractual liberalism of secularized Christianity and Judaism are bound to be exposed as "unthinkable" given their attempts, however feeble, to place restraints on technology's dynamic. Those remnants—let alone the original biblical revelations from which they derive—are rapidly fading from liberal justice. But that means our ability to explain why liberty, equality, and justice are our due as human beings, why they are our good, is slowly fading away, especially when those claims prove "inconvenient" for technology's advance. Again, for Grant in contrast with Strauss, liberalism is not able to sustain a compelling account of natural right or justice on its own. As its Protestant underpinnings dissolve, it will inevitably collapse.

English-Speaking Justice concludes with a twilight valedictory: Those of us "who for varying reasons cannot but trust the lineaments of liberal justice" cannot avoid asking how this justice, which we have been told is "somehow . . . due to all human beings," can be "thought together" with the truth of technology's increasingly insuperable sway.[40] This issues in "the call from that darkness" to think through how justice can survive together with the full coming to be of technology.[41] The "darkness that enshrouds justice"—the "civilizational contradiction" between modernity culminating in technology and our clinging to "ancient science"—means that it is "folly simply to return to the ancient account of justice" in Plato's *Republic* "as if the discoveries of the modern science of nature had not been made."[42] In other words, Grant is arguing, we cannot attempt to understand Plato as he understood himself if we seal that enterprise off from "the greatest theoretical enterprises of the modern world" that are premised on their disproof of Plato. In short, how can Plato have been right if modern natural science is right?

This reference to "the folly" of returning to the ancients in the absence of a confrontation with what is arguably the demonstrated truth of the modern understanding of nature is clearly to an unnamed Leo Strauss, his school, or both—it would be difficult to be more precise.

In other words, for Grant, like Heidegger, technology and the modern science that arose from it to recast nature in its image is historically true, is our destiny, or at least—for Grant—our modern destiny. That destiny cannot be evaded by going back behind it directly to Plato and the ancients, even on the level of principle. It appears for Grant that, while some substratum of human nature or the soul may have survived the passage from ancients to moderns and endures at least vestigially even now, open to the stirrings within us of ancient justice or revelation, human nature is sufficiently plastic that it has been altered in some very fundamental ways by the modern project of the conquest of nature and human nature. I do not find it possible to cull more specificity than this from Grant's writings. That may be because more specificity is not possible. I am certainly not equipped to provide it. But, Grant goes on, if the way directly back to Plato is inaccessible, it is equally "folly" to treat the ancient account of justice as being of merely "antiquarian interest," as a cultural bauble or interesting hobby, because without an attempt to persevere in thinking ancient justice through together with technological modernity, the justice of the future will be "terrifying in its potentialities for mad inhumanity."

Conclusion

In conclusion, Grant's ongoing encounter with the thought of Leo Strauss contributed to Grant's development of a deeply interesting contribution to contemporary political philosophy. Like Strauss, within the boundaries of political philosophy Grant preferred the classical approach over the modern approach. Unlike Heidegger and like Strauss, Grant accepted the notion that the modern project of the conquest of nature embodied a paradigm shift away from the classical search for the eternal order of the whole. He did not accept Heidegger's view that Plato's metaphysics were already incipiently "working themselves out as technology." Unlike Strauss and like Heidegger, however, Grant did accept the proposition that global technology summed up the essence of the modern project. Whereas Strauss, invoking classical political philosophy, held fast to the view that to distinguish between better and worse regimes is a possibility permanently open to thought, Grant tended, like Heidegger, to assimilate all such proximal distinctions to the sway of technology, implying that they were now of no more than secondary or nostalgic interest. But unlike Heidegger, who had located the origin of technology in the history of

Being launched by Plato, Grant traced it to the Calvinist assimilation of God to pure will beginning in the Reformation—agreeing, again, with Strauss that modernity was a new departure, but disagreeing with Strauss that it could be fully or best explained within the boundaries of a debate between classical and modern political philosophy without recourse to religion. And fundamentally, of course, Grant departed from Strauss in his central preoccupation with Christian revelation in both its positive and its baleful effects. This unique, ever-stimulating perspective on the crisis of modernity, born in large measure from a fruitful disagreement with Strauss, put Grant among a handful of truly important twentieth-century political thinkers.

Notes

1. For the background of Grant's interest in Christianity, consider Hugh Donald Forbes, *George Grant: A Guide to His Thought* (Toronto: University of Toronto Press, 2007) and Alexander Duff. "Response to the Strauss-Kojève Debate: Grant's Turn from Hegel to Christian Platonism." In Ian Angus ed. *Athens and Jerusalem: George Grant's Theology, Philosophy and Politics* (Toronto: University of Toronto Press, 2007).

2. Allan Bloom. "Justice: John Rawls Vs. The Tradition of Political Philosophy." *The American Political Science Review* 69, no. 2 (1975).

3. George Parkin Grant, *Technology and Empire* (Toronto: House of Anansi, 1968), 88–90. The text under consideration by Grant is Leo Strauss, *On Tyranny* (Chicago: University of Chicago Press, 2000).

4. Ibid., 91.

5. Ibid., 92.

6. Ibid., 102.

7. Ibid., 94. For my own interpretation of the Strauss-Kojève debate, see Waller R. Newell. "Kojève's Hegel, Hegel's Hegel, Strauss's Hegel: A Middle Range Approach to the Debate about Tyranny and Totalitarianism," in Timothy Burns and Bryan Paul Frost eds. *Philosophy, History and Tyranny: Reexamining the Debate between Leo Strauss and Alexandre Kojève* (Albany, NY: SUNY University Press, 2016).

8. Ibid., 95.

9. Ibid., 98–99.

10. Waller R. Newell, *Tyranny: A New Interpretation* (Cambridge: Cambridge University Press, 2013).

11. Grant, *Technology and Empire*, 102.

12. Ibid., 103.

13. Ibid., 104.

14. Leo Strauss, *What Is Political Philosophy?* (Westport, CT: Greenwood Press, 1959), 50–55, 78, 121, 221, 115–116. See also Newell, "Kojève's Hegel."

15. Leo Strauss. "Transcript of a Seminar in Political Theory: Hegel's Philosophy of History." The Leo Strauss Center, University of Chicago. Autumn Quarter, First Session, 1958.

16. Grant, *Technology and Empire*, 108.

17. Ibid., 109.

18. Ibid., 19.

19. Especially in Newell, *Tyranny* and Waller R. Newell, *Tyrants: A History of Power, Injustice and Terror* (Cambridge: Cambridge University Press, 2016).

20. Grant, *Technology and Empire*, 21. In the second footnote of the essay, Grant quotes three of Luther's theses that, as he rightly observes, sum up the Reformation with "brilliant directness." To me, the core of Luther's anti-Thomism is expressed in Thesis 19: "He is not worthy to be called a theologian who sees the invisible things of God as understood through the things that are made."

21. Ibid., 22–23.

22. Ibid., 24–25.

23. Ibid., 30.

24. Ibid., 33.

25. Ibid., 36–37.

26. Consider the discussion in Newell, ibid.

27. Grant, *Technology and Empire*, 38–39.

28. John Rawls, *A Theory of Justice* (Cambridge, MA: Harvard University Press, 1971).

29. George Parkin Grant, *English-Speaking Justice* (South Bend, IN: University of Notre Dame Press, 1985), 29.

30. Rawls, *A Theory of Justice*, 4.

31. Grant, *English-Speaking Justice*, 42.

32. Ibid., 51.

33. Ibid., 57–58.

34. Ibid., 59–61.

35. Ibid., 63.

36. Ibid., 73.

37. Ibid., 74–76.

38. Ibid., 79.

39. Ibid., 85–86.

40. Ibid., 86.

41. Ibid., 86.

42. Ibid., 88.

8

Strauss and Blumenberg on the Caves of the Moderns

Danilo Manca

In this chapter, I would like to compare Strauss's and Blumenberg's attempts to re-open the quarrel between the ancients and the moderns by considering their use of Plato's allegory of the cave. There is no proof of a direct influence of Strauss on Blumenberg. However, it seems to me that a comparison between these two thinkers offers the opportunity to illuminate some key aspects of their perspectives.

More specifically, in the first section I outline Strauss's idea of the cave of the moderns as a second, much deeper cave than the natural one Socrates deals with. After this I sketch the general view of Blumenberg's *Höhlenausgänge* (1989), wherein the caves of the moderns are many. In the second section, I focus on the meaning of Strauss's description of the cave of the ancients as natural, and try to illustrate the objections that Blumenberg raises against all those perspectives that envision an original horizon out of which history would have dangerously brought mankind. In the third section, I address the role that history could play in the practice by which modern philosophy seeks a way out of its caves. Finally, in the fourth section of the chapter I reflect on the obstruction by revelation-based tradition of the search for such a way out.

The Idea of a Second Cave

In 1931 Strauss wrote a review of Julius Ebbinghaus's *On the Progress of Metaphysics* for the Deutsche Literaturzeitung.[1] In a letter dated October

15, 1931, to his friend Gerhard Krüger, he announced his discovery of another man who agrees with them about the idea of the present as a "second cave." His review aims to point out the few excellent formulations of this idea that Ebbinghaus's writing contains.[2]

According to Strauss, the main merit of Ebbinghaus is that he questioned the belief in progress. The famous Hegelian image of the owl of Minerva beginning its flight only at dusk remains so pervasive in twentieth-century philosophy that even those thinkers who regard their present as a time of decline "usually still believe that there are more possibilities of knowledge in their present than ever before."[3] In contrast to this, Ebbinghaus abandons the typical modern prejudice that "*the* truth has not already been found in the past" and brings to light the destruction foretold by depiction of an alleged progress.

To Ebbinghaus, the present age appears to be "completely sold out of knowledge."[4] This generates philosophical chaos in his contemporary epoch, which is indeed characterized by the anarchy of systems; namely, by the conviction that each system should be relativized by considering the historical, psychological, sociological, and even the anthropological situation of its originator. Another view deriving from this idea is that "all treasures of the past do not suffice," and therefore "one must seek *new* answers that correspond to the need of the age."[5] In contrast to the widespread conviction that modern philosophy frees the mind from all prejudices, Ebbinghaus holds that "the freedom that is the result of the modern dissolution of all traditions is nothing but the freedom of ignorance (*Unwissenheit*)."[6] The only way to emancipate modern thinkers from this "freedom" is to nurture the disposition to learn through the reading of past writings. Such reading should be done "with the burning interest of one who wants to be *taught*."[7] A philosopher needs to learn from the past in order to avoid having his or her view invalidated by presupposition. To Strauss, this has to be seen as distant from the odd view of the philosopher: "The turn from avowed ignorance to learning through reading is not natural, as is shown by the position of the classical teacher of knowing about not-knowing with regard to learning through reading."[8] In his search for someone who holds the truth amongst the eminent figures of the *polis* representing the tradition, Socrates finds that nobody is able to recognize his or her natural ignorance. Yet this cannot be the starting point of the modern thinker, who lives in a world in which the notion of knowledge is abused. Everything seems to be a source of a new knowledge. Therefore, "a long detour and a great effort are first needed in order even to return to the state of natural ignorance."[9] In concluding his review, Strauss explains his position by referring to Plato's parable of the cave: "One may say that today we find ourselves in a second, much deeper cave than the lucky ignorant persons Socrates dealt with; we need history first of all in order to *ascend* to the cave from which Socrates can lead us to light; we need a propaedeutic, which the Greeks did not need, namely learning through reading. It is the merit of Ebbinghaus's writing that it has called attention . . . to this desideratum of all present-day philosophy."[10]

Strauss defines the cave of the moderns as "second" not only because chronologically it comes after the one Plato refers to in his allegory, but also because it appears to be built *within* the cave of the ancients, as if the first were a much deeper room of the latter. This explains why Strauss states that the first goal of the modern philosopher should consist in ascending to the cave from which Socrates started in his philosophical investigation.

This formulation of the idea of a second cave raises three issues at least. First, we should understand what Strauss means by natural ignorance. As is widely known, in Plato's allegory the cave stands for the *polis*, not for a primordial state of nature. Second, we should reflect on the function that Strauss ascribes to history. In his review of Ebbinghaus's essays, he seems to recognize that history plays a decisive role in philosophical investigation, whereas in other writings he sees the special position that history has acquired in the sphere of human knowledge as a danger for the development of philosophy. Third, the idea of ascending from the second to the first cave by means of "learning through reading" suggests that Strauss is assigning a role to tradition in the formation of a philosophical point of view.

Before addressing these issues, I would like to outline Blumenberg's idea of a second cave. In 1989, Blumenberg published a book entitled *Höhlenausgänge* (*Ways out of the Caves*). The use of the plural in the title suggests at once that, instead of a singular second cave, Blumenberg speaks of various caves. Also, in his view, Plato's cave is not the first, but the second one. Indeed, in prehistory "the human being had not been brought to light from the depths of the earth, as the Greeks thought."[11] Rather, at the beginning of human history, the caves represent "a shelter that man had learned to seek and inhabit, after that it comes out of the primordial forest, which was the original place where it feels to be protected."[12] Unlike Strauss, who focuses on the ways in which one can leave the two caves and conquer the light of the truth, Blumenberg is more interested in exploring the way in which the caves contribute to the acquisition of knowledge. Alluding to the prehistoric cave paintings, Blumenberg states that it was by passing through the cave that the human being became a "dreaming animal."[13]

However, as early as his first book, *Paradigms for Metaphorology*, Blumenberg gives credit to Plato for having transformed a myth into what he defines as an "absolute metaphor"; that is, one of the "foundational elements of philosophical language, translations that resist being converted back into authenticity and logicality."[14] Easier than a concept, a metaphor escapes being imprisoned within a particular epoch. It makes the historical development of philosophy possible, since it avoids the collapse of thought into a contingent form. A metaphor is better than a concept at letting philosophical perspectives intuitively emerge as alternatives.

In fact, Blumenberg distinguishes the reoccupations (*Umbesetzungen*) of Plato's metaphor of the cave from the counter-occupations (*Gegenbesetzungen*). Following *The Legitimacy of the Modern Age*, reoccupation means that different statements can be understood as answers to identical questions.[15] More specifically, reoccupation designates the case in which a philosopher recasts Plato's metaphor of the cave by yielding a re-contextualized answer to the same original question. In addition to this, in *Höhlenausgänge* Blumenberg introduces the notion of counter-occupation which by contrast designates any re-elaboration of an ancient metaphor as aiming to transform into a loss what originally appears as a new acquisition.[16]

Blumenberg finds in Aristotle's lost dialogue *On Philosophy*, reported by Cicero in his dialogue *On the Nature of Gods* XXXVII,[17] the basis for any following reoccupation of Plato's cave. In such a dialogue, Aristotle would have imagined human beings "who had always lived beneath the earth, in comfortable, well-lit dwellings . . . and who though they had never come forth above the ground had learnt by report and by hearsay of the existence of certain deities."[18] Aristotle replaces Plato's unreal depiction of the cave with a picture that more directly evokes the situation in which the Greeks ordinarily lived in their cities. If at some time the jaws of the earth opened and the dwellers of Aristotle's cave were able to escape from their hidden abode, when they saw the sky "surely they would think that the gods exist and that these mighty marvels are their handiwork."[19] With respect to Plato's metaphor, here

Aristotle extends the access to truth to all dwellers, and knowledge is described as a confirmation of what they learned in the cave.

The original model of any other counter-occupation of Plato's metaphor would be the parable of Arnobius the Elder, an early Christian apologist of Berber descent. In his treatise *Adversus Gentes* II 21,[20] Arnobius envisions a child raised in total isolation and on a simple diet by a nurse who, remaining naked and silent, cares for him. If this child emerged from his cave after twenty or more years, he most likely would remain "as baffled and mindless as an animal, a piece of wood or a stone."[21] Therefore, his impulse would be to come back into the cave where he feels to be at home. This is a counter-occupation of Plato's parable insofar as the transition from the cave to the light of the sun is experienced here as a deterioration of the human condition. This is why Blumenberg comments that Arnobius's tale is against any kind of Platonism.

Modern thinkers elaborate their point of view starting from the tension between these two different ways of recasting Plato's parable of the cave. They strive to resolve such a tension by developing a unique position that allows them to appear as alternative to the past. They reflect on the opportunity to make life outside of the cave possible, at least in an incidental and unconscious way. To explain this point, let me focus on the two most representative cases: that of Bacon's idols of the cave, and Descartes's fiction of a malicious demon.

Bacon adopts the expression "idola specus" to designate prejudices of the human understanding by which individuals inappropriately extend norms derived from their own culture. Blumenberg highlights a point in *The Advancement of Learning* (1605) where Bacon describes the idols of the cave as having their origin "from the nature, both of mind and body, in each person," and also "from education, custom, and the accidents of peculiar persons."[22] Here Bacon refers to the "beautiful emblem" that is "Plato's den," and adds that "to drop the exquisite subtlety of the parable, if any one should be educated from his infancy in a dark cave till he were of full age, and should then of a sudden be brought into broad daylight, and behold this apparatus of the heavens and of things, no doubt but many strange and absurd fancies would arise in his mind."[23] Blumenberg points out that here Bacon explicitly limits the "furniture" of the cave to the shadows; moreover, he rewrites Plato's allegory of the cave in a way whereby the influence of Arnobius's counter-occupation is evident.

However, there is an element of this writing that, to Blumenberg, contributes to laying the foundations for the constitution of the cave of the moderns: "Bacon's cave generates idols from within. It is the place of images, not that of the mere copies."[24] Nothing is more original than the images emerging from the inside of the cave. If the human being did not train its imaginative skills inside the cave, its imagination could not be activated when coming out of the cave into the light of the real sky. Although it is deceptive, imagination aids scientific intellect insofar as it prevents the light of the truth from dazzling the human mind. In the wake of these observations, in his book *The Genesis of Copernican World* Blumenberg strives to demonstrate that at the basis of the Copernican revolution there is a sort of optical cave that latently and involuntarily enhances humans' capacity to break through the ordinary way of representing the earth, the sun, and the heavens.[25]

To Blumenberg, Descartes recasts Plato's parable more radically than Bacon. Descartes suggests that the modern mind should learn how to rule the faculty of imagination in order to satisfy its impulse not only to contemplate, but also to dominate nature: "The attempt to doubt, which precedes the efforts for acquiring an absolute certainty, has assumed in Descartes the function that the parable of the cave played in Plato's work. The thought that man can be deceived in all respects by that *genius malignus* perfectly replaces the sophists who fiddle with shadows in Plato's myth."[26] In Descartes's fiction of the deceiving demon, the shadows are created by a singular individual whose aim is to challenge his or her own mind.[27] Through this experiment Descartes aims to understand to what extent human reason is able to attain truth in a difficult condition, which is comparable to life in a cave. Descartes's way of recasting the parable of the cave exemplifies the transition from the natural cave, in which the soul of the ancients finds itself imprisoned, to the cave of reason that facilitates the access to truth instead of hindering it.

The Naturalness of the Cave

Strauss's claim that the starting point of philosophical questioning should be natural ignorance could be quite misleading. The risk is to identify the cave with the mere state of nature, while Plato evidently uses this metaphor to designate the political affairs of the Greeks. Indeed, more than twenty years after his review of Ebbinghaus's essay, in his *Natural Right and History* (1953) Strauss identifies the cave with the opinions that have become "public dogma or *Weltanschauung*."[28]

Such a claim does not contradict Strauss's the review of Ebbinghaus's essay. The sphere of opinions (*Weltanschauung*) can be identified with the natural ignorance to which Strauss thinks that modern man should return insofar as the adherence to the system of norms occurs by nature; that is, by the spontaneous adoption of an attitude toward the world that is rooted in the essence of the human being. Moreover, the not-knowing from which philosophy starts its maieutic practice can be connected with the sphere of natural ignorance insofar as the latter represents a condition that, instead of hindering the awareness of man, leaves it as an open potentiality to be activated. In other words, Strauss speaks of naturalness insofar as the transition from the state of ignorance to the cognition of an eternal truth remains a real possibility for the citizens. Strauss ascribes two different, but closely connected, meanings to the term "natural": on the one hand, by natural he means that which is inherent to the eternal way in which the cosmos is; on the other hand, he means also that which concerns the spontaneous dimension of human life, that which is familiar to us. This evidently emerges from Strauss's appreciation of Husserl's lifeworld and Nietzsche's concept of the natural in his illuminating essay *The Living Issues of German Postwar Philosophy* (1940), which was published posthumously.

In this essay, Strauss aims to demonstrate that the return to reason, which makes the liberation from historicism possible, coincides with a genuine rediscovery of the original perspectives of Plato and Aristotle. A relevant implication of phenomenology had been the distinction between the scientific view of the world and the natural view of the world. The scientific view of the world is to be identified with the perspective elaborated by modern science, and the natural view with the subject of Plato's and Aristotle's analyses. Accordingly, a merit of phenomenology would be that of making the authentic rediscovery of Plato and Aristotle possible by suggesting that "that natural view is prior to, and the basis of, the scientific view."[29] In Strauss's eyes, Husserl's analysis of the assumptions of Galileo's physics surpasses in significance everything that was written in Germany in the previous fifty years.

Although Strauss does not explicitly employ the term "lifeworld" here, he is undoubtedly referring to Husserl's conviction that the task of philosophy should be that of conceiving a natural horizon in which the scientific view of the world is rooted.[30] In Strauss's view the other superior mind responsible for a great change in philosophy was Nietzsche, who identified the main concern of philosophy with "the sake of *natural* men, of men capable and willing to live 'under the sky,' of men who do not need the shelter of the cave, of any cave."[31] In referrring to the cave as an "artificial protection against the *elementary* problems,"[32] Nietzsche opposes the belief that history is the elementary subject of philosophy, and he strives to "drive home that the elementary, the natural subject of philosophy still is, and always will be, as it had been for the Greek: the cosmos, the world."[33]

In the two years before publishing *Höhlenausgänge*, Blumenberg exposes his criticism of Husserl's conception of the lifeworld in two interesting essays: "Lebensweltmisverständnis," which is the first chapter of the book entitled *Lebenszeit und Weltzeit* (1986), and the article entitled "Lebenswelt und Technisierung unter Aspekten der Phänomenologie" (1987).

Blumenberg sees Husserl's lifeworld only as an indirect phenomenon deduced from the needs of modern subjectivity. In *Lebensweltmisverständnis*, he finds in the Biblical paradise the model from which the concept of the lifeworld has been constructed. The lifeworld stands for the edenic state, that is, the original environment and condition in which the subject has taken shape and acquired the tools that helped it to satisfy its needs. The lifeworld coincides, at the same time, with the natural state located at the beginning of its human history and with the eschatological fiction of a final state. In this way, the origin of the concept of lifeworld is the modern will to transform time into an "a-phenomenal experience"[34] that can be lived only through a transcendental subjectivity, which differs from the way in which the human being straightforwardly lives every day.[35] In *Lebenswelt und Technisierung*, Blumenberg suggests that phenomenology could be seen as one of the outcomes of the modern process of "technization."[36] By making the sphere of the ordinary an object of reflection, phenomenology rises above the life that it aims to describe. Accordingly, the theoretical concept of the lifeworld bears witness to an attempt to evade the natural dimension of the philosophical investigation.

Blumenberg's objections to Husserl's concept of lifeworld can be addressed to Strauss's view. Indeed, Stanley Rosen reproached Strauss for having thought, in accordance with Husserl, that there was a time when such a thing as a natural consciousness existed. Rosen criticized the idea that the de-sedimentation of this pre-scientific lifeworld could purge modernity of its defects. Therefore, the idea of a lifeworld would be only a "theoretical artefact" derived from the modern contraposition to antiquity.[37]

In Strauss's view, the return to natural ignorance would consist of the transition from the second to the first cave, from the artificial cave of the moderns to the natural one of the Greeks. Following Blumenberg (and Rosen), we have to evaluate the possibility that such a return is actually an outcome of the modern way of thinking instead of a recovery of the authentic condition from which Plato and Aristotle moved on. From this perspective, Strauss's introduction of the notion of a second cave should be considered a manifestation of the modern strategy aimed at the self-legitimacy of legitimizing the status quo. However, Strauss's point of view should undoubtedly be taken to be a kind of counter-occupation of the modern depiction of the cave. In fact, Strauss reverses the situation by stressing that permanence in the cave brings no benefits, as Bacon and Descartes suggest. By introducing the difference between the first and the second cave Strauss carries out a reoccupation of Plato's cave that amounts to a counter-occupation not only of the modern depiction of the cave but also of the prehistoric myth and Arnobius's tale.

History as a Way Out of the Cave

In his review of Ebbinghaus's work, Strauss sees the act of "learning through reading" as the way to go out of the second cave, but he does not deal with the issue of how a person who lives within the cave could acquire self-awareness of his or her condition and read past thinkers without interpreting them on the basis of the paradigms of his or her time.

In his paper on *Political Philosophy and History* (1946), Strauss points out that even though political philosophy is not a historical discipline, in modern times it "is in need of the history of political philosophy or science as an integral part of its own efforts."[38] The history of philosophy contributes to the development of political philosophy, since it is after having realized that political forms are many that we ask about the best, or just, political order; besides, the history of philosophy prevents one from mistaking the specific features of the political life of one's time for the essential elements of political things.

By so arguing, Strauss realizes that the sole way to leave the second cave is to apply historicism to itself. Indeed, in a letter to Krüger dated December 27, 1932,[39] and then in *Natural Right and History*, Strauss identifies the second cave with the problem of historicism: "Whereas, according to the ancients, philosophizing means to leave the cave, according to our contemporaries all philosophizing essentially belongs to a 'historical world,' 'culture,' 'civilization,' 'Weltanschauung,' that is, to what Plato had called the cave. We shall call this view 'historicism.'"[40]

Yet, by taking history to be an integral part of political philosophy, Strauss evidently assigns a role to history in seeking a way out of the cave. This is a contradiction only in appearance, since in Strauss's view historicism is only one of the attitudes that the historian can adopt. It coincides with the moment in which "history . . . became the highest authority."[41] This occurred in the eighteenth century when the historical school emerged in reaction to the French Revolution. The thought of historical school discredits the universal principles and finds in history the field where the truth comes about in an empirically demonstrable way. But this is by no means the only way to use history in philosophy: "The unbiased historian had to confess his inability to derive any norms from history. . . . The historical school had obscured the fact that particular or historical standards can become authoritative only on the basis of a universal principle which imposes an obligation on the individual to accept, or to bow to, the standards suggested by the tradition or the situation which has molded him."[42] On the basis of this consideration, Strauss concludes the first section of his book by arguing that "we need, in the first place, a nonhistoricist understanding of nonhistoricist philosophy," but "we need no less urgently a nonhistoricist understanding of historicism that does not take for granted the soundness of historicism."[43]

In distinguishing the historiographical practice from the historicistic approach Strauss assigns to the history of philosophy the same propaedeutic function that, in his review of Ebbinghaus's work, is taken to be a prerogative of the reading of past writings. Admittedly, there is a close connection between the historical investigation of past culture and the reading of past writings. In his essay on *The Living Issues of German Postwar Philosophy*, Strauss explores this connection by emphasizing that the need to interpret past documents arises when historical studies become the most urgent necessity.[44] In particular, to Strauss, it is Heidegger's investigation that represents the turning point in this process since he does not only highlight the crisis of modern reason, but also questions the idea that modern philosophy has effectively understood Plato and Aristotle's philosophy: "Heidegger made it clear, not by assertions, but by concrete analyses . . . that Plato and Aristotle have *not* been understood by the modern philosophers; for they read their own opinions into the works of Plato and Aristotle." Accordingly, Strauss infers that "if Plato and Aristotle are not understood and consequently not refuted, return to Plato and Aristotle is an open possibility."[45]

Investigating the idea of a metaphorology, the impression emerges that Blumenberg's perspective can be described as presupposing a non-historicist understanding of historicism.

In the talk *Ernst Cassirer Gedenkend* (*In Remembrance of Ernst Cassirer*), presented in 1974 on the occasion of his acceptance of the Kuno Fischer prize, Blumenberg explicitly says he is honored that his approach can be considered a kind of historicism. However, he also reproaches Cassirer for being unable to embrace the inner tendency that he situated at the heart of his own conception, namely, the tendency "not to be of service to the self-confirmation of the present."[46]

Blumenberg describes his metaphorology as arising from within the branch of historical studies known as *Begriffsgeschichte* (conceptual history). After all, Blumenberg was a member of the committee for conceptual history at the University of Marburg, whose president was Gadamer. Generally speaking, the main thesis of conceptual history is that the history of philosophical issues cannot be separated from the history of terms. Conceptual history aims to delve deeply into the historical development of philosophical issues starting from the analysis of the ways in which terms are modified and re-elaborated over the centuries. In such a way, conceptual history demonstrates that philosophy cannot leave out the investigation of the rhetorical dimension of philosophical argumentations, since this activity is useful to bringing to light sedimented knowledge.

Blumenberg expands the approach of conceptual history by dealing with absolute metaphors rather than with concepts: "If it could be shown that such translations, which would have to be called 'absolute metaphors,' exist, then one of the essential tasks of conceptual history (in the thus expanded sense) would be to ascertain and analyse their conceptually irredeemable expressive function."[47] Blumenberg defines such metaphors as leftover elements that bear witness to the essential and transhistorical core of human history. These elements of philosophical language "have a history in a more radical sense than concepts, for the historical transformation of a metaphor brings to light the metakinetics of the historical horizons of meaning and ways of seeing within which concepts undergo their modifications."[48] In other words, studying absolute metaphors means delving deeper into the historical development of human thought. Blumenberg describes the relationship of his metaphorology to the history of concepts (understood in the narrower sense) as an ancillary one: "metaphorology seeks to burrow down to the substructure of thought, the underground, the nutrient solution of systematic crystallizations."[49]

On one hand, a metaphor becomes absolute when it crystallizes in an image a philosophical issue, that in the history of philosophy periodically emerges as an urgent question to be answered. On the other hand, the modifications that an absolute metaphor undergoes over the centuries bear witness to an unconscious attempt by philosophical thought to overcome the answers previously provided to the philosophical question underlying the emergence of such an absolute metaphor. This is why Blumenberg states that metaphorology "shows with what 'courage' the mind pre-empts itself in its images, and how its history is projected in the courage of its conjectures."[50] Human reason shows its courage more easily in the formulation of a metaphor than in the revision of a concept. Accordingly, looking at the history of absolute metaphors often means discovering the roots of a philosophical turn. As already said, in Blumenberg's view Descartes's fictional experiment the malicious demon is an exemplary re-elaboration of Plato's parable of the cave, but in a way that sanctions the self-constitution of the modern way of thinking in contraposition with the ancient one.

In exploring absolute metaphors, the historian of philosophy does not only focus on the philosophical terminology, but also on the paradigmatic way in which the use of metaphors lets a philosopher address some traditional issues. This leads the historian who investigates the absolute metaphors not only to connect him or herself with the entire philosophy of the past but also to bring to light the archetypes, that is, the original models of each philosophical question.

This account effectively seems to confirm the hypothesis that Blumenberg's metaphorology presupposes a nonhistoricist understanding of historicism. Blumenberg thinks that the study of the history of human culture could provide us answers to some key philosophical questions. He jointly acknowledges the presence of an eternal core of issues bringing themselves back up in the course of history. Nonetheless, Blumenberg's perspective cannot be identified with that of Strauss.

Strauss's main goal is the return to the investigation of the essence of things. Therefore, historiographical investigation can be taken to be only an auxiliary, albeit integral, part of philosophical inquiry. On the contrary, for Blumenberg, historiographical research embraces the entire field of philosophical investigation insofar as it is focused on the study of absolute metaphors. According to Strauss, when the philosopher realizes the limits of the historicist approach and re-opens the quarrel between the ancients and the moderns, the involvement of historiography is functional to the return to Plato and Aristotle. By contrast, Blumenberg does not present his metaphorology as leading back to Plato and Aristotle but rather as unmasking the presuppositions of ancient philosophy. For instance, Blumenberg likens the allegorical myth from book VII of the *Republic* to the reconstruction of human prehistory that Plato provides in Prometheus's myth of *Protagoras* 321C, where "the transition from earth to light is connected with the gift of 'wisdom in the arts together with fire,' hence an endowment that goes beyond the form of existence 'foreseen' for mankind."[51] In so doing, Blumenberg shows that Plato's metaphor "is grounded in the mythic tradition and authorized by that tradition."[52] No philosophy is independent of a tradition. The task of the metaphorologist is to examine the way in which each philosophy brings to light the latent thought underlying the tradition from which that philosophy emerges.

Secularization or Self-assertion

Up until now, I have considered the formulation of the idea of the second cave that Strauss provides in his review of Ebbinghaus's essay. Strauss, however, addresses the same issues in contemporaneous writings that remained unpublished until his death, such as *Religiöse Lage der Gegenwart* (1930) and *Die Geistige Lage der Gegenwart* (1932).[53] In both essays, Strauss quotes a passage taken from the *Guide of the Perplexed* I 31, where Maimonides comments on the three causes of disagreement that Alexander of Aphrodisias individuated in a treatise now preserved only in an Arabic translation and entitled "The Principles of the All According to the Opinion of Aristotle." The first cause is the love of domination; the second is the subtlety of the object of apprehension in itself; the third is the ignorance of he or she who apprehends. However, Maimonides holds that in his time there is a "fourth cause" that Alexander did not mention because it did not exist among the Greeks: "It is habit and upbringing, for man has in his nature a love of, and an inclination for, that to which he is habituated. . . . For this reason also man is blind to the apprehension of the true realities and inclines toward the things to which he is habituated."[54]

From Strauss's perspective, this entails that the difficulty of doing philosophy has fundamentally increased over the centuries, and the freedom of doing philosophy is fundamentally reduced, by the fact that "a tradition resting on revelation has entered the world of philosophy."[55] Revelation is the original source of the second cave, since it introduces historical prejudices into natural life: "the natural difficulties of philosophizing have their classical depiction in Plato's allegory of the cave. The historical difficulty may be illustrated by saying: there now exists another cave beneath the Platonic cave."[56] Once modern prejudices are removed, we ascend to the starting point of Plato's cave dwellers: "We know that we are deeply entangled in a tradition; we are yet much further down than Plato's cave dwellers. We must raise ourselves to the *origin* of tradition, to the level of *natural ignorance*."[57] This suggests that the strategy that modernity has usually adopted in order to ascend to the cave of the ancients substantially misses the point.

Early modern philosophy manifests the intention to restore Greek freedom insofar as it fights against prejudices. However, "it achieves the freedom of *answering*, but not the freedom of questioning, only the freedom of saying No instead of the traditional Yes."[58] For Strauss, the problem is that modern philosophy always defines its own attitude by conflicting with the revelation-based tradition. Therefore, the questioning of modern philosophy keeps a relationship of dependence with the tradition that has thrown philosophy itself into the second cave. It is as if the modern dwellers gradually went out of the second cave, but by walking backward. They keep their gaze pointed to the inside of the second cave. Hence, they cannot see the shadows of the first cave in their original form, but only as mirrored on the walls of the second cave. As long as modern philosophy fights against the Medieval tradition, it can acquire the courage to yield answers that are alternative to those of the previous age. Nonetheless, it remains unable to develop a free, independent view of the world. Different from that of the Greeks, the attitude of the moderns is rooted not only in the natural way of thinking of human beings, but also in its education, in the inherited tradition.[59]

In Blumenberg's words, here Strauss appears to claim that each counter-occupation of a previous view is in any case a peculiar kind of reoccupation. Strauss aims to awaken the spontaneous capacity of the modern man to question the horizon of his or her own opinions.

In his early writings Strauss approaches the idea of secularization in an ambiguous way. Let me explain this point by starting from Blumenberg's criticism of such a category.[60]

In the opening section of his *The Legitimacy of the Modern Age*, Blumenberg criticizes a specific use of the term "secularization" aimed at diminishing the depiction of modernity as a self-enclosed epoch. Blumenberg refers to Schmitt, who thinks that all relevant concepts of modern philosophy (and in particular those of the modern theory of the state) are secularized theological concepts "not only because of their historical development . . . but also because of their systematic structure."[61] The secularization thesis entails the idea of a loss. Modernity would have expropriated theological concepts from the original context in which they arose in order to transpose them into another context merely focused on human affairs. In such a way, modernity would have trivialized the meaning of the medieval theological view of the world. For instance, Löwith writes that "the philosophy of history of the Enlightenment, far from having enlarged the theological pattern, has narrowed it down by secularizing divine providence into human provision and progress."[62] Undoubtedly, Blumenberg would include Strauss's idea of a second cave much deeper than that of the Greeks in this perspective, such as he did with Husserl's conception of a crisis of the European sciences, which influenced Strauss's point of view, as has already been pointed out.

Blumenberg sets his conception of a series of reoccupations and counter-occupations against the secularization thesis: "what mainly occurred in the process that is interpreted as secularization, at least (so far) in all but a few recognizable and specific instances, should be described not as the *transpositions* of authentically theological contents into secularized alienation from their origin but rather as the *reoccupation* of answer positions that had become vacant whose corresponding questions could not be eliminated."[63] As I have explained, Blumenberg describes historical development as being based on a system of questions and answers, and he thinks that "questions do not always precede their answers."[64] In other words, the transition from one epoch to another is rooted in the possibility of answering a question yet to be formulated. Blumenberg scales down the idea of secularization to one of the various reoccupations that circumscribes epochs as wholes. Yet he does not underestimate either the fact that the early modern philosophers ascribe themselves self-sufficiency, or that they cannot cease to challenge the previous age.

That early modern philosophy tends to set its view against that of the Middle Ages can be interpreted as denoting a form by subordination of early modern philosophy of the scholastics or, alternatively, as a way in which modern man asserts his autonomy within the world. In accordance with the secularization thesis Strauss tends to endorse the first option whereas Blumenberg embraces the second point of view, which appears to him as rooted in the way in which early modern philosophy conceives itself. Nonetheless, Blumenberg does not fail to account for the emergence of the Modern from the Middle Ages. Indeed, in *The Legitimacy of the Modern Age*, Blumenberg interprets Descartes's malicious demon as the outcome of a long process beginning with early Christian Gnosticism, whose fundamental thought is that "a theology that declares its God to be the omnipotent creator of the world . . . cannot at the same time make the destruction of this world and the salvation of men from the world into the central activity of this God."[65] Gnosticism identifies the god who created man and the world with the evil demiurge and distinguishes from it the god who brings redemption to man, whom he did not create, and designates it as the "foreign god," seen as the essence of pure—because unreasoning—love. In this way Gnosticism did not destroy the ancient cosmos, but transformed it into a manifestation of evil and terror. The first attempt at warding off Gnostic dualism comes from Augustine, who formulates the dogma of man's universal guilt in order to unburden his God. To Blumenberg, in this way "the Gnostic dualism had been eliminated as far as the metaphysical world principle was concerned, but it lived on in the bosom of mankind and its history as the absolute separation of the elect from the rejected."[66] Therefore, the modern age arises only because the Middle Ages fail to neutralize the Gnostic general view.[67] Instead, "the Middle Ages came to end when within their spiritual system creation as 'providence' ceased to be credible to man and the burden of self-assertion was therefore laid upon him."[68] By self-assertion Blumenberg does not mean the biological and socioeconomic preservation of the human organism by means naturally available to it, but rather "an existential program, according to which man posits his existence in a historical situation and indicates to himself how he is going to deal with the reality surrounding him and what use he will make with the possibilities that are open to him."[69]

Descartes's experiment of the malicious demon wards off Gnostic view by means of a counter-occupation of theological absolutism. Descartes neutralizes the Gnostic dualism by describing the evil demiurge as a fiction of human reason. The problem of the late Middle Ages is that of justifying the bad aspects of the world. The solution that it finds is that of nominalism, according to which there is no reason for creation. God cannot be likened to the Platonic demiurge, since it is not the mere executor of a preexisting plan. Rather, creation is an expression of God's omnipotence, which makes God hidden and hardly understandable to the human mind except by means of its revelation. Through the idea of the malicious demon Descartes recasts the nominalistic God: "by transforming the theological absolutism of omnipotence into the philosophical hypothesis of the deceptive world spirit, Descartes denies the historical situation to which his initial undertaking is bound and turns it into the methodical freedom of arbitrarily chosen conditions."[70] In this way, "the exigency of self-assertion became the sovereignty of self-foundation."[71] To Blumenberg, this exposes Descartes and the entire modern philosophy to the risk of being unmasked by the discoveries of historicism: "the weak point of modern rationality is that the uncovering of the medieval 'background' of its protagonists can put in question the freedom from presuppositions of which it claimed to have availed itself as the essence of its freedom."[72]

Blumenberg expresses no kind for value judgment in relation to the concealment of the medieval background that modern philosophy pursues with the aim to satisfy its need of self-assertion. Instead, Strauss sees in what I may now call (in Blumenberg's terms) the modern strategy of self-assertion the limit that makes the way out of the second cave difficult.

Unlike the originators of the secularization thesis such as Schmitt and Löwith, whose main aim seems to be that of describing the concepts of the modern science of politics as borrowed from a theological context, Strauss's criticism of the modern attitude is aimed at leading back to the ancient way of addressing the issue of the political. In other words, for Strauss, to be committed to solving the theological-political problem means dealing with a preliminary investigation that should pave the way for retrieving another way of living and thinking. This brings Strauss very close to Blumenberg's way of formulating the quarrel between the ancients and the moderns. They share the idea that the radicalization of Descartes's rhetoric of a new beginning can in no way work. Indeed, Strauss stresses that modern philosophy could escape from the subordination to its sedimented history only by realizing its ignorance of ancient philosophy. Accordingly, his use of Plato's image of the cave to account for the situation of the modern philosopher is a way to escape from what

Blumenberg calls the rhetoric of secularization. Such an image refocuses the attention of the modern philosopher away from the cultural debt that he or she took on with the Middle Ages toward the debt he or she had contracted with ancient philosophy from the beginning of the history of philosophy.

Notes

1. L. Strauss, "Besprechung von Julius Ebbinghaus, *Über die Fortschritte der Metaphysik* (1931)." In Id., *Gesammelte Schriften*, Band 2: *Philosophie und Gesetz—Frühe Schriften*, ed. Heinrich Meier and Wiebke Meier (Stuttgart, Germany: J. B. Metzler, 1997), 437–439, Eng. trans. "Review of Julius Ebbinghaus, *On the Progress of Metaphysics* (1931)." In *The Early Writings (1921–1932)*, ed. by Michael Zank (Albany, NY: SUNY Press, 2002), 214–216.

2. L. Strauss, *Gesammelte Schriften*, Band 3: *Hobbes' Politische Wissenschaft und Zugehörige Schriften—Briefe* (Stuttgart, Germany: J. B. Metzler, 2008), 394. Here Strauss speaks of Ebbinghaus as the fourth man who endorses the idea of a cave being beneath Plato's cave. Scholars do not agree about the name of the third man: the most obvious candidates are Klein and Löwith; other options are Heidegger—because of the role that he had played in revealing the absence of an authentic understanding of Plato and Aristotle in modern times—or Schiller, who Strauss quotes in the letter to Krüger dated December 27, 1932, because of the idea that, differently from the naturalness of the ancients, "we moderns are necessarily 'sentimental'" (Id., *Gesammelte Schriften* 3, 422). Nonetheless, in my view, the third man is paradoxically Plato. Indeed, in the line just above the assertion on Ebbinghaus, Strauss had described Plato as the philosopher who has instructed him on the untenability of Hobbes's approach in the definition of natural right. For a general reconstruction of Strauss's conception of the second cave my main reference is D. Janssens, *Between Athens and Jerusalem. Philosophy, Prophecy, and Politics in Leo Strauss's Early Thought* (Albany, NY: SUNY Press, 2008), chapter 3.

3. L. Strauss, "Review of Julius Ebbinghaus," ibid., 214.

4. Ibid.

5. Ibid.

6. Ibid., 215.

7. Ibid.

8. Ibid.

9. Ibid.

10. Ibid.

11. H. Blumenberg, *Höhlenausgänge* (Frankfurt a.M.: Suhrkamp, 1989), 25; my translation.

12. Ibid.

13. Ibid. 29.

14. H. Blumenberg, *Paradigmen zu einer Metaphorologie*, in "Archive für Begriffsgeschichte," 6/1960, 5–142 (Frankfurt a.M.: Suhrkamp, 1997), esp. 11–12; Eng. trans. R. Savage: *Paradigms for a Metaphorology* (Ithaca, NY: Cornell University Press, 2010). ebook edition.

15. Id., *Die Legitimität der Neuzeit*, Frankfurt a. M.: Suhrkamp 1966, trans. R. M. Wallace: *The Legitimacy of the Modern Age* (Cambridge, MA: MIT Press, 1983), 65.

16. Id., *Höhlenausgänge*, ibid., 303.

17. See Cicero, *De Natura Deorum Academica*, trans. H. Rackham (London: Harvard University Press, 1968).

18. H. Blumenberg, *Höhlenausgänge*, 197.

19. Ibid., 198.

20. See Arnobius. *Adversus Gentes*, trans. H. Bryce and H. Campbell. In *The Ante-Nicene Fathers: The Writings of the Fathers down to A.D. 325*, ed. A. Roberts and J. Donaldson (Edinburgh: T. & T. Clark, 1885), vol. 19.

21. H. Blumenberg, *Höhlenausgänge*, ibid., 321–322.

22. F. Bacon, *The Advancement of Learning*, ed. J. Devey (New York: P. F. Collier 1901), 241.

23. Ibid.

24. H. Blumenberg, *Höhlenausgänge*, ibid., 288.

25. See *Die Genesis der kopernicanischen Welt* (Frankfurt a.M.: Suhrkamp, 1975), trans. R. M. Wallace: *The Genesis of the Copernican World* (Cambridge, MA: MIT Press 1987).

26. H. Blumenberg, *Höhlenausgänge*, ibid., 427.

27. See R. Descartes, *Meditations on First Philosophy. With Selections from the Objections and Replies*, ed. M. Moriarty (Oxford: Oxford University Press 2008), 16.

28. L. Strauss, *Natural Right and History* (Chicago: University of Chicago Press, 1965), 12.

29. Id., "The Living Issues of German Postwar Philosophy," *Philosophical Review* 49, no. 4 (1940); also published in H. Meier, ed., *Leo Strauss and the Theologico-Political Problem* (Cambridge: Cambridge University Press 2006), 115–140, esp. 137.

30. See E. Husserl. *The Crisis of European Sciences and Transcendental Phenomenology*, ed. D. Carr (Evanston, IL: Northwestern University Press 1970), para. 34.

31. L. Strauss, "The Living Issues of German Postwar Philosophy," ibid., 137.

32. Ibid.

33. Ibid., 138. In his seminars on Nietzsche, Strauss insists that Nietzsche incorporates the philosophical perspective of the contemporary age, the fourth and last wave of modernity; see L. Strauss, *On Nietzsche's Thus Spoke Zarathustra*, ed. R. Velkley (Cambridge: Cambridge University Press 2017), 6. In particular, in

the second of the four essays entitled *Untimely Meditations*—"On the advantages and disadvantage of history for life"—Strauss sees Nietzsche's attempt to return from history to nature. As is widely known, Nietzsche's starting point here is that, different from humans, animals "have a life neither bored nor painful" because "they live unhistorically," without the sense of time. F. Nietzsche, *Untimely Meditations*, ed. D. Breazeale, trans. R. J. Hollingdale (Cambridge: Cambridge University Press 2007), 60–61. In another of the *Untimely Meditations*, called "Schopenhauer as Educator," Nietzsche complains that "the inherited fear of the natural and, on the other hand, a renewed attraction for this naturalness . . . engenders a disorder in the modern soul which condemns it to a joyless unfruitfulness." Ibid., 133, trans. slightly modified. Nietzsche finds in Zarathustra the doctor that modern humanity needs because of his appeal to "remain faithful to the earth." F. Nietzsche, *Thus Spoke Zarathustra. A Book for All and None*, ed. A. Del Caro and R. Pippin (Cambridge: Cambridge University Press 2006), 6. Indeed, in Strauss's eyes, in Zarathustra's prologue we assist at the attempt to restore nature as an ethical principle for life. See L. Strauss, *On Nietzsche's Thus Spoke Zarathustra*, chapter 2, and R. Velkley, *Heidegger, Strauss, and the Premises of Philosophy: On Original Forgetting* (Chicago: University of Chicago Press 2011), chapter 3.

34. H. Blumenberg, *Lebenszeit und Weltzeit* (Frankfurt a.M.: Suhrkamp, 1986), 40; my translation.

35. See P. Stoellger, *Metapher und Lebenswelt. Hans Blumenbergs Metaphorologie als Lebenswelthermeneutik und ihr religionsphänomenologischer Horizont* (Tübingen: Mohr Siebeck, 2000).

36. See H. Blumenberg, "Lebenswelt und Technisierung unter Aspekten der Phänomenologie," In Id., *Wirklichkeiten, in denen wir leben. Aufsätze und eine Rede*, Stuttgart: Reclam 1981, 49.

37. See S. Rosen. *The Elusiveness of the Ordinary: Studies in the Possibility of Philosophy* (New Haven, CT & London: Yale University Press, 2002), esp. "Introduction," 1–13; "Husserl's Conception of the Life-World," 54–93; "Wittgenstein, Strauss, and the Possibility of Philosophy," 135–159. See also S. Rosen, *Leo Strauss and the Problem of the Modern*, in S. Smith, ed., *The Cambridge Companion to Leo Strauss* (New York: Cambridge University Press, 2009), 119–136.

38. L. Strauss, "Political Philosophy and History," *Journal of the History of Ideas* 10, no. 1 (January 1949); also published in H. Meier, ed., *Leo Strauss and the Theologico-Political Problem* (Cambridge: Cambridge University Press, 2006), 30–50, esp. 50.

39. L. Strauss, *Gesammelte Schriften* 3, 420. See T. L. Pangle, "The Light Shed on the Crucial Development of Strauss's Thought by His Correspondence with G. Krüger." In Martin D. Yaffe and Richard S. Ruderman, *Reorientation: Leo Strauss in the 1930s* (New York: Palgrave Macmillan 2014), 57–68.

40. L. Strauss, *Natural Right and History*, ibid., 12.

41. Ibid., 17.

42. Ibid.

43. Ibid., 33.

44. In his book entitled *Leo Strauss on the Borders of Judaism, Philosophy and History* (Albany, NY: SUNY Press, 2015), 72, J. Bernstein notices that "Strauss's concern is not over history as such, but rather over the grounding of philosophy in history."

45. L. Strauss, "The Living Issues of German Postwar Philosophy," ibid., 135. On the relationship between Strauss's criticism of historicism and his serious recovery of the ancient way of thinking I see Fussi, *La città nell'anima. Leo Strauss lettore di Platone e Senofonte* as decisive (Pisa: Edizioni ETS, 2011), part I. Let me also refer to my article "Naturalness and Historicity: Strauss and Klein on the Quarrel between the Ancients and the Moderns," *Philosophical Readings* 9, no. 1 (2017): 44–49. Here I discuss Strauss's treatment of historical activity as a way to rediscover the naturalness of ancient philosophy in comparison with Jacob Klein's conviction that doing history of philosophy is a way to lead modern man back to the roots of the philosophical investigation.

46. H. Blumenberg, *Wirklichkeiten, in denen wir leben. Aufsätze und eine Rede*, ibid., 168.

47. Id., *Paradigmen zu einer Metaphorologie*, ibid., 12.

48. Ibid., 15.

49. Ibid. Cf. also H. Blumenberg, "Beobachtungen an Metaphern," *Archiv für Begriffsgeschichte*, 15 (1971), 163: "metaphorology performs conceptual history the auxiliary service of guiding it to a genetic structure of concept formation." See J. C. Monod, "Postface: La patiente de l'image." In H. Blumenberg, *Paradigmes pour une métaphorologie*, trans. D. Gammelin (Paris: Vrin 2006), 178f.

50. Id., *Paradigmen zu einer Metaphorologie*, 15.

51. Ibid., 171.

52. Ibid.

53. L. Strauss, "Religiöse Lage der Gegenwart" (1930). In *Gesammelte Schriften* 2, 377–391, trans. "Religious Situation of the Present." In *Reorientation*, 225–235. Id., "Die Geistige Lage der Gegenwart" (1932). In *Gesammelte Schriften* 2, 441–464, Eng. trans. "The Intellectual Situation of the Present," *Gesammelte Schriften* 3, 441–464. In *Reorientation*, 237–253. In order to contextualize these essays, see T. W. Burns, "Strauss on the Religious and Intellectual Situation of the Present." In *Reorientation*, ibid., 80–113.

54. M. Maimonides, *The Guide of the Perplexed*, trans. S. Pines (Chicago & London: University of Chicago Press, 1963), vol. I, 66–67.

55. L. Strauss, "Religious Situation of the Present," ibid., 232.

56. Id., "The Intellectual Situation of the Present," ibid., 248.

57. Id., "Religious Situation of the Present," ibid., 235.

58. Ibid., 233.

59. Taking the various statements regarding the second cave together, in his book on *Heidegger, Strauss, and the Premises of Philosophy*, 51, R. Velkley points out a certain ambiguity in the meaning and the status of "second cave": "One side of the ambiguity is a very radical thesis. The second cave is not only the historical tradition created by Christianity and modern philosophy. . . . More

fundamentally the second cave is the ('nonsensical') Christian tradition of the fusion of revelation and philosophy, which prevented the founders of modern philosophy from attaining the natural philosophizing they sought."

60. For a deep examination of the link between secularization and modernity in both thinkers, Strauss and Blumenberg, see the essays collected in M. Foessel, J.-F. Kervégan, and M. Revault d'Allonnes, eds., *Modernité et sécularisation. Hans Blumenberg, Karl Löwith, Carl Schmitt, Leo Strauss* (Paris: CNRS Éditions, 2016). Consider in particular the following contributions: R. Brague attempts to demonstrate that the conditions making the secularization theorem possible derives from the Middle Ages (21–28); in her *Leo Strauss et le problem de la sécularisation* (81–91), C. Widmaier interprets Strauss's refutation of the secularization theorem as rooted in his aim to withdraw the legitimacy of modern age; in particular, she moves from *The Three Waves of Modernity*, where Strauss likens the idea that modernity is a secularized Biblical faith to "what Plato's claims to do in his *Republic*: to bring about the cessation of all evil on earth by purely human means"; in H. Gildin, ed., *An Introduction to Political Philosophy. Ten Essays by Leo Strauss* (Detroit: Wayne State University Press, 82); in his *Les ambiguïtés d'un théorème. La sécularisation, de Schmitt à Löwith et retour* (107–117), F. Kervégan questions Blumenberg's reduction of Schmitt's concept of secularization to that of Löwith; finally, consider Monod's quest for the end of the process of secularization in his *La sécularisation et ses limites: entre théologie politique et positivisme juridique* (155–168), while in his monograph *La querelle de la sécularisation, de Hegel à Blumenberg* (Paris: Vrin, 2002), he found in Hegel the beginning of such a process.

61. C. Schmitt, *Politische Theologie: Vier Kapitel zur Lehre von der Souveränität* (Berlin: Dunckler & Humblot, 1922), trans. G. Schwab, *Political Theology. Four Chapters on the Concepts of Sovereignty* (Cambridge, MA: MIT Press, 1985), 56. See H. Blumenberg, *The Legitimacy of the Modern Age*, ibid., 92f.

62. K. Löwith, *Meaning in History* (Chicago & London: University of Chicago Press, 1957), 103. See *The Legitimacy of the Modern Age*, ibid., 27f.

63. H. Blumenberg, *The Legitimacy of the Modern Age*, ibid., 65.

64. Ibid., 66.

65. Ibid., 129.

66. Ibid., 135.

67. See Lazier's discussion of Blumenberg's account of Gnosticism in his *God Interrupted. Heresy and the European Imagination between the World Wars* (Princeton, NJ & Oxford: Princeton University Press, 2008), chapter 1.

68. H. Blumenberg, *The Legitimacy of the Modern Age*, ibid., 138.

69. Ibid.

70. Ibid., 181.

71. Ibid.

72. Ibid.

9

Writing the *Querelle des Anciens et Modernes*

Leo Strauss and Ferdinand Tönnies on Hobbes and the Sociology of Philosophy

Peter Gostmann

Introduction

At the time when Leo Strauss took his first steps in the academic field of the first German republic, Ferdinand Tönnies was already an established figure. This different degree of establishment was reflected, for example, in Karl Löwith's suggestion (to Strauss) concerning asking "old Tönnies" for support in publishing his essay on Hobbes's *Criticism of religion*.[1] Tönnies himself, however, for a long time had been a relatively marginal man in Germany's academic establishment. He received his first professorship in 1913, at almost sixty years old. Since he had published his most famous writing with the subtitle "Treatise of Communism and Socialism as Empirical Forms of Culture,"[2] the state-supporting powers of the German Empire regarded him as politically untrustworthy. At the time when Löwith recommended to Strauss that he seek Tönnies's support, this early critic of National Socialism had already lost all academic offices by order of the new government.

Since the 1870s, Hobbes's writings were among the subjects of Tönnies's studies. He discovered the lost manuscript of *Behemoth*,[3] wrote a biography,[4] and published more than twenty writings dealing with Hobbes's work.[5] Thus, Löwith's recommendation was by no means original, but an expression of pragmatic consideration. In fact, Tönnies has no special relevance for the course of argumentation in *The Political Philosophy of Hobbes*, the book in which Strauss condensed his Hobbes studies shortly afterward. He repeats Tönnies's evaluation of Hobbes's judgment concerning the governmental quality of democracy, monarchy, and dictatorship respectively.[6] He concurs with his statement about the remarkably short description of the "state of nature" in *Leviathan*.[7] He refers to Tönnies's observation about the disappearance of the motif of "original democracy" from the *Elements* via *De Cive* to *Leviathan*,[8] as well as to his observation about the difference between *De Cive* and *Leviathan* with regard to treatment of the Bible.[9] He draws on Tönnies's book to underline that Hobbes in *Leviathan* has rejected all "criticism of political ideals, which is based on practice, i.e., on historical experience."[10] He consults Tönnies to confirm that Hobbes's "recognition of teleology here and there" was a "residue of tradition" contradicting the overall tendency of his work.[11] Apart from Tönnies's Hobbes biography, Strauss also mentions his introduction to the German edition of Hobbes's *Elements* as confirmation of his thought that Hobbes "identifies reason with fear."[12]

In Strauss's later writings, too, Tönnies has no particular significance for the course of his argumentation.[13] In *Natural Right and History*,[14] where Strauss clarifies Hobbes's position in the *querelle des ancients et des modernes*, he does not at all refer to Tönnies. The absence of Tönnies in this book is particularly interesting because one of its subjects is the criticism of modern social science: Tönnies, as a longstanding chairman of *Deutsche Gesellschaft für Soziologie*, had been one of social science's leading representatives.[15] We have every reason to assume that Strauss did not find anything in Tönnies's remarks about Hobbes's work that challenged his own interpretations, only here and there a confirmation or completion of his own findings.

Although Strauss mentions Tönnies's work rather marginally, there is an indication that Tönnies's thought had been a sort of departure point for one of the intellectual paths that Strauss pursued and connected over the years. According to a letter to Gerhard Krüger, Strauss's Hobbes studies were concerned with continuing Tönnies's "evolutionary historical research" with regard to the problem of "state and religion."[16] It is thus worth considering in more detail both what the teachings of Tönnies and Strauss have in common and what separates them from each other. The connection is supported not only by the evidence that Hobbes's writings had been a prominent subject for both of them for decades, but also by the observation that both were interested in Hobbes because of his remarkable importance for their evaluations of modernity.

It would be insufficient, in a text concerned with Strauss's teaching, to determine the intellectual connection between his teaching and that of Tönnies only from Strauss's side (and therefore to refer only to those writings to which Strauss himself referred). As is well known, Strauss emphasized the principle of understanding an author primarily in the same way as this author understood himself. If we want to understand Tönnies's interpretation of Hobbes as he himself understood it, we have to assume that he had said the most important things about Hobbes's thinking in a series of essays from 1879–1881, *Anmerkungen über die Philosophie des Hobbes* (and more precisely than on later occasions).[17] Strauss mentions the *Anmerkungen* only in an unpublished manuscript of the early 1930s. In a footnote, he refers to Tönnies to distinguish Hobbes from Descartes insofar as the former's "'phenomenalism' appears later than 'materialism.'"[18]

In 1964, in the preface to the first German edition of his Hobbes book of 1935, Strauss gives advice as to how we should orient ourselves in order to understand Tönnies's thoughts on Hobbes the way he understood them. Accordingly, our sources are two writings in which he "tacitly corrected" the book's "deficiencies": on the one hand, his extensive review of Raymond Polin's book *Politique et philosophie chez Thomas Hobbes* (1954), and on the other hand, "Chapter V A" of his book *Natural Right and History* (1953).[19] In *Natural Right and History*, Strauss deals with Hobbes as one important figure in the *querelle des anciens et de modernes*. For the purpose of our examination, we can refer to Tönnies's late work *Geist der Neuzeit*[20] as a counterpart to *Natural Right and History*. However, the fundamental difference between the two authors, as we shall see, is that for Tönnies there has not been a *querelle des anciens et des modernes*.

The fact that Tönnies's work lacks this topic that is of particular importance for Strauss is a very superficial observation. If we do not want to be content with superficialities, but to examine the intellectual connection between Tönnies and Strauss with a certain thoroughness, it is helpful if we orient ourselves toward Strauss himself, since an integral element of his teaching is careful reading. Interestingly, in his book dedicated to careful reading (one year before *Natural Right and History*) he once mentions the science to which Tönnies has made a significant contribution. In the introduction to *Persecution and the Art of Writing*, Strauss points out a deficiency of the conventional sociology of knowledge: the absence of discussion of "genuine knowledge," or more precisely, of a "sociology of philosophy." In addition, Strauss lets us know that the book provides "material useful for a future sociology of philosophy."[21]

Since Strauss was delicate in referring to a teaching as "philosophy," we must doubt whether Strauss himself would have understood a sociology of Hobbes's teaching as part of a sociology of *philosophy in a genuine sense* (as he obviously did with regard to the teachings of Maimonides, Halevi, or Spinoza in *Persecution*). Nevertheless, even if Hobbes's knowledge may not be genuine knowledge, we have a clear indication that, for Strauss, the examination of this somewhat philosophically deficient knowledge is of certain importance for the outlining of a sociology of philosophy. In the chapter on persecution Strauss mentions Hobbes, among others, as exemplars of the concern of modern authors "to enlighten an ever-increasing number of people who were not potential philosophers." Since Strauss explicitly refers here to Tönnies, who "clearly recognized" this tendency in Hobbes,[22] it seems reasonable to specify the intellectual connection between the teachings of Strauss and that of Tönnies by *interpreting them as two different variants of a sociology of philosophy*. Put differently, we will concentrate on the various social actors and groups that Tönnies and Strauss introduce and examine the qualities attributed to them, as well as the figures of argumentation and figures of speech that Tönnies and Strauss apply to explain the interrelations between them. We begin with the analysis of Tönnies's series of essays from 1879 to 1881. As a counterpart to this, we deal subsequently with Strauss's review of Polin's Hobbes book. We will stay with Strauss by supplementing our analysis of his remarks in the Polin review with an analysis of his remarks in the Hobbes chapter of *Natural Right and History* before returning in the chapter's penultimate section to Tönnies's late work *Geist der Neuzeit*, the counterpart to *Natural Right and History*. Finally, in our last section, we present the results of our analysis as a comparison of two distinct forms of a sociology of philosophy.

Tönnies on Hobbes, 1879–1981

According to the introduction to Tönnies's *Anmerkungen*, Hobbes represents a type of philosophy ("recent philosophy") hostile to another unit of philosophers ("ecclesiastical philosophy," or "scholasticism"). More precisely Hobbes, Tönnies suggests, is one of the "pioneers" of this group, while Thomas Aquinas is the other group's "master." Tönnies emphasizes Hobbes's "strong awareness" of the "depth" of this philosophical antagonism.[23] He places his protagonist in a "new era" distinguished from ancient days by the "growth of population"; the "advancement of production means"; and the "increase of commercial intercourse" demand "knowledge of the temporal things and earthly events." It is this demand, in contrast with the ancient "contemplative" mode of philosophizing, that Hobbes is so exceptionally aware of.[24]

The "strongest" exponents of recent philosophy are "positivist" scientists practicing "astronomy" and "mechanics." The career of mechanical science is interconnected with "economic development." The pioneer of the new mechanical "philosophy" is Galileo Galilei,[25] because he established a "science of bodies in motion" operating by means of "mathematics" (the "revolutionary" element in mechanical philosophy). Highlighting mathematics, the Galileans express a thought about which some ancient philosophers (Plato in particular) already knew. However, Galileo applied mathematics to physical bodies not for a "teleological" but for a "mechanical" reason; that is, not to "sort qualities," but to compare quantities—"to measure what is measurable, and make measurable what is not."[26]

In the second essay of *Anmerkungen* (partly published with the introduction,[27] and partly a year later),[28] Tönnies starts with the assumption that Hobbes's entire thought is "grounded" in the Galilean approach. He is, as Tönnies emphasizes, *not* a follower of Francis Bacon, whose glory is an effect of his political position as Lord Chancellor of England (confirmed by the Royal Society's exaggerated acclamations of his scientific curiosity), and of the "unhistoric" interpretation of modern science propounded by the French Encyclopédistes (another unit of recent philosophy).[29] Hobbes' pioneering act is the translation of Galilean mathematico-mechanical philosophy into a "moral and political" science,[30] based on the theory of a "dynamic" mechanism of optic perception[31] and completed in the (unpublished) treatise *The Elements of Law, Natural and Politic*.[32]

According to Tönnies, Hobbes's conception of "experience" demonstrates that he is an exponent of "rationalism" (as a "science"), opposing "empiricism" (whose exponents operate in a nonscientific mode).[33] This difference notwithstanding, both rationalism and empiricism are the names of two other units of modern thought—of which the former is the philosophically more adequate. The French Encyclopédistes, for Tönnies, practice in a more deficient mode than do pioneering actors such as Galileo or Hobbes. Compared with Hobbes, in particular, this is especially true with respect to morals and politics.

More precisely, Hobbes's pioneering act was to recognize that the objects of philosophy are not material "processes" or "facts," but "relations of concepts," and that the truth of a relation of concepts is dependent upon a person or group of affiliates willing it so.[34] However, as a consequence of adopting the *Galilean* concept of bodies in motion, Hobbes had to reconceptualize the "soul" that the older (Thomistic) philosophy had characterized as "substantial form of the subjective body" (*Leib*) as an "objective body" (*Körper*)[35]—which meant dislocation of the "will" (with the result that the moral-political scientist, in reference to any practical moral and political problem, would have to concede that in this situation will stands against will).[36] To solve this problem, according to Tönnies, Hobbes had to enthrone "pure reason" by proclaiming the "authentic rationalist dogma" that pure reason shapes adequate "factual knowledge."[37]

According to the system of a science based on this rationalist dogma, the science of "morality" is subordinated to "geometry," to the science of "abstract dynamics," to the science of "sensory perception" and "sensory qualities," and finally to "physics," whereas it is superior to "political philosophy." Tönnies points out that Hobbes's "universal scientific demonstration" remained incomplete, especially with regard to the question of transitions between "geometry" and "mechanics." With regard to "political philosophy," Tönnies assumes, the problem of universal science had no particular significance for Hobbes anyway, since he regarded political philosophy as a "*demonstrable*" science. It is, more precisely, demonstrable "because we create the community *ourself*," just as geometry is a demonstrable science because "the lines and figures from which we argue have been drawn and described by *ourselves*."[38]

According to Tönnies, Hobbes's initial problem is the resistance of individuals to reason due to their "interests"—interests that have found expression not least in all kinds of "voluminous works" of the representatives of older philosophy. From this observation of an orientation toward self-interest rather than reason, Hobbes concluded that there was a fundamental "equality" of all people. The *physical* component of this equality is that "everyone is strong enough to kill the other"; its *moral-political* dimension refers to a "natural right" according to which "a human being does what he can to protect his body and limbs from death and pain." Interests, and ultimately the interests that are reflected in the works of older philosophy, are an expression of this natural right. Some "natural law" corresponds to natural right, and it is derived not from interests but from "reason" (more precisely, from the rationalistic dogma). All reason-oriented works (and ultimately the works of the Galileans, including Hobbes) are expressions of natural law. The first (and most "fundamental") of the natural laws to which human life (and ultimately the Galilean moral-political scientist) is subject is to "seek peace." From this fundamental law the "main part" of Hobbes's moral-political demonstration is derived: "that contracts are to be kept"—which enables the emergence of moral-political bodies ("communities").[39]

Tönnies emphasizes Hobbes's anthropological conception of natural law as a response to existing political teachings. These include "Aristotelian ethics," the "Stoa," and the "Justinian Code," and culminate in the politico-juridical conceptions of "scholasticism" (especially Thomism, whose representatives want to lead the "secular or state community"—as "the recognized good"—back to "divine reason"). For Hobbes, on the other hand, according to Tönnies, the law of nature ("seek peace") is a matter of "*reasonable insight* gained through the experience of war."[40]

Due to Hobbes's conception of moral-political science as a division of Galileanism, he must assume that the communal "good" is identical with entities having at their disposal "active power"—insofar as they are able to set the individual bodies (human beings) in motion,[41]—as a result of "affect."[42] According to Tönnies, Hobbes identifies this affect as "fear" (especially in *De cive*), which, if recognized as a form of "reciprocity" (the *fundamental* rational insight), provides for the union of the participants.[43]

Tönnies points out that Hobbes was fully aware that the "state community" actually dissolves the state of war under natural right as little as human beings create the state of war without reasonable insight into mutual fear.[44] Therefore, it is not nature creating the state but a human act: the "conscious effort" of a science-oriented actor to name the "real names" of "objects," to establish "allegations" through connections between the names of objects, and to merge allegations into "syllogisms." For Tönnies it is particularly important that (according to Hobbes's conception) not every actor is suitable for this conscious effort, but on the contrary, "most people" do not even "know what science is." The political scientist for his part knows what science is, but he only knows the *concepts* of political science, but does not have the "power" to "demonstrate" this science himself. Only the "sovereign" has this demonstrative power. Against this backdrop, Tönnies concludes with Hobbes's laconic remark that his political philosophy is "as useless as Plato's Politeia," which is why the only "consolation" remaining for him is the hope that "some sovereign transforms this truth of speculation into the benefit of practice."[45]

Tönnies emphasizes that Hobbes is interested in the "rules" of "duties of the subordinates" and those of "powers and obligations of the sovereign," regardless of the question of their "origin" ("contract" or "submission"). The sovereign, as Tönnies notes, is the only one who has "committed himself to nothing." According to Hobbes, a person who could "judge" the sovereign's actions is unthinkable. Therefore, in any practical demonstration of political science, the political scientist is unable to distinguish between the political-philosophical community *more geometrico* and "mere power relations."[46] Thus, the problem of "will" returns, now under the horizon of rationalist dogma,[47] and in conjunction with it returns "interest," in whose place Hobbes wanted to establish reasonable insight. As a result, the separation of *natural law* and *natural right* cannot be maintained.[48] Nevertheless, Hobbes's work is not important for Tönnies because of these aspects, but because of the new rationalist moral philosophy[49] which he proposed against the older moral philosophies (of "scholastics" or "Jesuits"). The reason for this statement has to do with "tendencies' in *Leviathan* "to give a higher rank to certain affects," such as to "gentleness."[50]

In his conclusion, Tönnies sums up Hobbes's pioneering achievement ("model of the whole age of the Enlightenment"): He actually deserves the "fame" that Locke is usually awarded. According to Tönnies, he has replaced "awe of terms," which is the characteristic of "older philosophy," with "criticism of terms." Hobbes's conceptual critical approach had an impact, for one thing, on "physiological psychology," a "contemporary" form of modern "science." Also with regard to the problem of "rational ethics" Hobbes is a pioneer figure because his reflections enabled "Spinozism" to formulate a differentiated science of "affects." With regard to the political sciences, Hobbes has two groups of "successors": a science of "absolute sovereignty of the community will," and a politico-economic-oriented science of society which is anti-community oriented.[51]

Strauss on Hobbes, 1954

In the essay *On the Basis of Hobbes's Political Philosophy*, Strauss "begin[s]" with the question of the interrelation of "Hobbes's teaching" and the study habits of the "present generation."[52] From these study habits, he distinguishes those of older generations, namely, the scholars of the "seventeenth century"; that is, Locke or Spinoza, but also Hobbes himself. In contrast to the situation in the seventeenth century, the present situation is characterized by the fact that (in the meantime) these "decried" authors have become "rehabilitated."[53] Strauss notes that Hobbes has been rehabilitated relatively late. Hobbes was still suspect (especially for the scholars in times after the French Revolution) since his atheism was "dry," and because he was associated with the "soulless state-mechanism of eighteenth century enlightened despotism." According to Strauss, Hobbes's rehabilitation is not the result of the foundation of the "church" of modernity but, on the contrary, of its "decay." Hobbes's teaching, having been "offensive" to earlier generations, appears at a certain moment in modern history—at least for "serious people"—almost as an "incarnation of old-fashioned decency," in comparison with its successors (such as "Schopenhauer" and "Nietzsche"). Among the serious people, Strauss discriminates between those who only give a "first glance" at Hobbes's teaching and those who study them more thoroughly.[54] These two groups are linked by the fact that both take Hobbes seriously as the "originator of modernity." Strauss explains what it means to take this originality seriously in two sense. On the one hand, it means to understand that "our perspective is identical with Hobbes's perspective," as long as we understand this perspective as that of "modern philosophy." On the other hand, it means to understand Hobbes as an active participant in the "quarrel between the ancients and the moderns."[55]

Strauss mentions Alexandre Kojève's student "M. Raymond Polin" as an example of the study habits of serious people who give only a *first glance* at Hobbes's teachings. Characteristic of this Polinist unit of the present generation is that they accept Hobbes's "principle" (that Strauss names "the modern principle"), but interpret it differently than Hobbes himself. According to Strauss, this principle leads to a certain self-conception: that of a "radical innovator."[56] Polin characterizes Hobbes's reaction to "traditional doctrines" as artificial humanism. This basic position does not result in an orientation toward "interpretation of the past," but rather toward "construction of the present and the future."[57]

This constructivism is reflected, among other things, in Hobbes's strict limitation of the term "law" to "commands addressed to men," which distinguishes him from his contemporary "Grotius," who still believed that "human nature" was "given, not made." Human nature has given man the "power of speech" ("command") to "revolt against nature," that is, against a certain more-than-human nature. The "civil society," the "state," and generally the "social mechanism" are products of this revolt, that is, expressions of artificial humanism.[58]

Strauss attaches importance to the observation that, unlike what Polin suggests, Hobbes did not regard language as a "gift," just as he had actually defined the difference between "nature of man" and "nature of brutes" not in terms of essence, but merely as "difference of degree"[59]—from which it follows that Polin's designation of Hobbes as a humanist is inaccurate. According to Strauss, what Polin misses is Hobbes's "wavering" in determining the relationship between "men" and "brutes," just as he misses "the fundamental ambiguity of Hobbes's teaching" in general. Because Polin misses this fundamental ambiguity, he "reproduces" it by conceding "that there is both a discontinuity and an unbroken continuity between the natural mechanism and the social mechanism."[60]

By his criticism of Polin's Hobbesianism, Strauss demonstrates indirectly what it means to study Hobbes's teaching thoroughly, that is, he explains the study habit of the second group alongside the one exemplified by Polin. The representatives of this group of serious readers (including Strauss himself, and potentially his readers) study Hobbes's "political teaching . . . by itself, and not in the light of his natural science."[61] Any scholar who understands Hobbes's political teaching by itself will notice that, by rejecting all "vain opinions" about the "whole" presented by representatives of the traditional doctrines, Hobbes must represent the impossibility of determining the whole. A central element of Hobbes's political teaching is therefore a certain "mood" generated by this so-called "truth": "the fear experienced by a being exposed to a universe which does not care for it."[62]

According to Polin, fear corresponds to a specifically human "pride," which is based on the assumption that the depressingly undeterminable "whole" lacks specific human "intelligence." A scholar who not only approaches Hobbes's writings with *serious* intentions but who also reads them *thoroughly*, will notice that the Polinist "polarity" of cosmological fear, intelligence, and pride results in an upgrading of the scientific understanding of man in comparison to the common sense understanding.[63] This reader will also notice that Hobbes's wavering, if understood as *political* wavering, takes place between political common sense and political science. Moreover, this thorough reader will recognize in the Hobbesian decision "to replace . . . 'common-sense' understanding by a scientific understanding of man" the preparation of the 'value free' political science of our time."[64] He also will recognize, however, that Hobbes's "conception of understanding as making," in addition to monistic-positive Hobbesianism, provides the possibility of another form of Hobbesianism culminating in a "philosophy of freedom."[65] The thoroughness of the thorough readers is therefore not only characterized by the fact that they read a single author thoroughly. They have read *a large number* of authors thoroughly enough to be able to identify correspondence between them (e.g., between Hobbes and representatives of later "value free" political science or philosophy of freedom).

According to Strauss, the "most important" difference between a Polinist and a thorough reader is that the Polinist pays too little attention to the problem of Hobbes's political theology when he "states without any ambiguity that Hobbes was an atheist."[66] On the contrary, the thorough reader will discover a profound affinity between the atheistic surface of Hobbes's teaching and the teachings of the "Sadducees" in his defense against "superstition." The Sadducees, however, are not atheists but representatives of a priestly elite—even if they argue in a mode "very near to direct atheism" on this or that question, such as with regard to the problem of existence of spirits and angels.[67] Thus, the thorough reader of Hobbes's *Leviathan* will be able to identify a certain "Hobbesian God." However, this God is "indistinguishable from the ether which is a most fluid body, filling every place in the universe that is not filled by bodies of other kinds."[68]

Just as Strauss demonstrates that Hobbes's "natural theology" does not exclude the possibility of God, he also demonstrates that his observation of the "uncertainty of the revealed character of the Bible does not prove that the teaching of the Bible may not be true and above reason, and hence it does not prove that the teaching of the Bible cannot be believed."[69] For their part, the Sadducees differ from other "philosophy schools of the Jews" of their time in not accepting any other rules than "the [revealed] law," as we learn from Flavius Josephus.[70] That is, they begin with the assumption that the Bible's teachings are reasonable at their very core. Among the rules that the Sadducees accept, because "The Old Testament" specifies them, is not least "the rule of priests."

Thorough readers, whose thoroughness is obviously also due to a *political hermeneutics prepared by thorough reading*, will understand this "rule of priests" as a "form of government." Moreover, they will identify this form of government as "bound to issue in chaos"; that is, they will identify priests as activists of the establishment for the restoration of a *political* community. Since this thorough reader knows that Sadducees are priests, he will understand the Sadducean teaching as an *antichaotic* political teaching. In contrast, for Hobbes and the Hobbesians the establishment of the rule of priests poses a problem for the Leviathanic political order because its continued existence after the introduction of human kingship provides for a "dualism of power temporal and spiritual."[71]

As every thorough reader (but not a Polinist) notices, Hobbes's own (Leviathanic) antichaotic political doctrine does not rule out that "civil societies" also exist in a state of chaos, that is, in the "natural state."[72] Moreover, this state is characterized by the fact that "the root of justice" can be found in it: that is, "the right of nature" (i.e., the "right of every individual"), which "persists within civil society" and which (unlike the right of a sovereign) is "indefeasible."[73] The thorough reader will find out, more precisely, that Hobbes's political wavering is also reflected in his image of the state of nature. In it are rooted "justice" ("fear") *and* "injustice" ("glory")—that is, this image contains "the just man" *and* "the unjust man."[74]

One author who authenticates the thoroughness of the thorough reader is "the communist Plato." For this reason, and because of his mastery of political-hermeneutical comparison, the thorough reader (other than a Hobbesian like Polin) recognizes that Hobbes's understanding of natural right corresponds to that of Plato, at least in his own assumption of the "natural property" of the individual.[75] In addition, the thorough reader is able to understand Hobbes better than he understood himself. For example, he is able to recognize that Hobbes's theory of state is a variation of certain teachings of Socrates, that Hobbes himself called "anarchism."[76] Because of his thoroughness, it cannot happen that the thorough reader presents, as Polin does, an image of Hobbes that appears as "a synthesis" of two later authors such as "Hegel and Marx."[77]

The last example at Polin's first glance of Hobbes is his inadequate treatment of the problem of "aristocratic virtue." In contrast, a thorough reader will notice, for example, that Hobbes, as an aside, creates connections between "honor" and "honesty" or between "rank" and "nobility"; he even refers to the "origin of virtue" ("magnanimity") and repeatedly describes "justice" as consequence of a certain noble "passion" ("generosity").[78] It is remarkable, however, that, according to Strauss, "for the adequate interpretation" of texts such as "Hobbes's political philosophy" someone like Polin is just as much an option as "someone else."[79] In other words, there is nothing (e.g., no particular "nature") to prevent a reader with a serious claim from going through a development toward thoroughness and reaching the level of *perfect political hermeneutics*.

Strauss on Modern Natural Right (and Hobbes), 1953

In *Natural Right and History*, Hobbes's name is the heading of one of the two parts into which the chapter on "Modern Natural Right" is divided;[80] the second part is entitled "Locke."[81] According to its title, this chapter is connected with the following (and final) one that points out thast "Modern Natural Right" is in a state of "Crisis"; the protagonists here are "Rousseau" and "Burke."[82] In the first chapters, Strauss described the situation after the crisis. Here he thematizes natural right as a repressed idea. Strauss's focus deals with ways of thinking that work on this repression, first the "historical approach,"[83] and then the modern "social sciences" represented by Max Weber.[84] Between the chapters on modernity against natural right and those on modern natural right, Strauss places two chapters: on the first (Socratic) natural right, which implies the question of the first philosophy, and on its "classical" form.[85]

In his introduction, Strauss applies the category "modern" to indicate a particular affinity of protagonists who are usually understood as antipodes because of their conception of natural right: "liberals of various descriptions" are associated with "Catholic and non-Catholic disciples of Thomas Aquinas" because they "all are modern men." Strauss himself finds commonality with both groups ("we") insofar as he finds himself "in the grip of the same difficulty," which is derived from the "victory of modern natural science."[86] However, Strauss does *not* designate *himself* as a modern man. The victory of modern natural science has led to such divergent contemporary protagonists as liberals and Thomists being fundamentally connected (and distinct from all earlier scholars) despite all the superficial differences between them. Hobbes has special significance. He is the *first* modern man, in a sense: "the first to draw the consequences" of the "emergence of modern natural science." Before Strauss goes into Hobbes's teachings in more detail he characterizes him in a remarkable way, as an "imprudent, impish, and iconoclastic extremist," in summary the "first plebeian philosopher."[87]

Strauss attaches importance to the observation that Hobbes's political philosophy is explicitly *anti-Socratic*. However, Hobbes agrees with Socrates (and older philosophy in general) to the extent that he is convinced of the necessity of political philosophy (unlike many present-day scholars). According to Strauss, Hobbes's "rejection" of this tradition corresponds to a disinterest in the political philosophy of another unit of tradition that is "anti-idealistic" and represented, for example, by "Epicurus." Thus, Hobbes does not notice that his supposedly new political teaching is actually an element of "Epicurean tradition" because of his view "that man is by nature or originally an a-political and even an a-social animal."[88] Only the political conclusion Hobbes draws from this assumption is new: that is, "an artificial island . . . to be created by science."[89]

Although we may call Hobbes the first modern man because of the political conclusions he drew from natural science, and although he may appear as the herald of an artificial island, he is not the "discoverer" of the new "continent" of which this offshore island is to be created. This privilege (according to Strauss) goes to Machiavelli, who, like Hobbes, is an anti-idealist activist, but, unlike Hobbes, positioned "patriotism" and "power of chance" (instead of science) against the ideas of the old political philosophy ("moral virtue," "contemplative life"),[90] since he knew nothing about natural sciences. According to Machiavelli's teaching, the exemplary founding event of "civil society" is a kind of "fratricide." Mentioning this, Strauss obviously does not refer to the murder of the shepherd Abel by the farmer Cain, since this incident did not initiate the founding of "the most renowned of all commonwealths,"[91] but instead of a small town in the land of Nod, which after a while was destroyed by a flood. His reference is to the murder of Remus committed by Romulus—an incident institutionalizing an occupation of land (i.e., Machiavelli's measure is *Old Rome*). Be that as it may, Machiavelli examines politics from the point of view of the "extreme case." According to Strauss, Hobbes follows this orientation toward the extreme, even if he, in contradistinction to Machiavelli, wants to restore certain "moral principles of politics." For he builds his political ethics on the "most powerful of all passions" ("fear of death").[92]

"Liberalism" as one of the units of Hobbesian political teaching shares that passion with regard to the corresponding "desire for self-preservation." Liberals are interested in a "state" that translates this desire into a general natural right.[93] Because of this general dimension (with reference to "something that everyone actually desires anyway," rather than to different forms of life such as the contemplative life[94]), this is natural right without "natural judge," that is, without a someone who acquires the right to speak about law thanks to their "practical wisdom."[95] On the contrary, "consent takes precedence over wisdom," and the validity of the laws ultimately depends not on their "deliberation," but on the "authority" by which they are guaranteed.[96] Paradoxically, "liberality" (as well as "courage" or "wisdom") for modern (Hobbesian) liberalism is *not* a "virtue in the strict sense."[97] The virtue that this teaching suggests to people is "commodious living," that is, not a virtue in the proper meaning of the word, but a "reward for hard work."[98]

The second of the two units of modern (Hobbesian) political thought is "natural public law."[99] Like the liberals, the protagonists of natural public law do not care about the quest for wisdom or the nature of contemplative life. They are concerned (more than the liberals are) with "efficient government."[100] This kind of knowledge, which Strauss calls "doctrianism," is always "partisan."[101] It stands on the side of the "institutions" and "exists for the sake of power."[102]

Strauss concludes the Hobbes chapter by pointing out the close link between his protagonist and another group of authors, the representatives of popular enlightenment, whose field of activity is cultivation of public opinion; that is, a kind of higher journalism.[103] The phrase used by Strauss to express this journalistic Hobbesianism refers to Adam Smith: "The 'invisible hand' remains ineffectual if it is not supported by the *Leviathan* or, if you wish, by the *Wealth of Nations*."[104]

Tönnies on the Spirit of Modernity (and Hobbes), 1935

In Tönnies's late work *Geist der Neuzeit*, Hobbes is not an outstanding, but a recurrent, protagonist. Tönnies mentions him in three places: (1) in the second section (of six), entitled "The Modern Era as Evolution";[105] in the fourth chapter (of five), dealing with "political and moral individualism";[106] (2) in the third section ("The Modern Era as Revolution");[107] in the second chapter (of three), dedicated to "Revolution in the Political Domain";[108] and finally (3) in the fifth section ("Moving forces of social development")[109] in the context of the presentation of "Faith in the Middle Ages and Modern Times."[110]

Tönnies begins his discussion of modern times with the usual "threefold division," according to which the Modern Era is preceded by an "Ancient age" and the "Middle Ages." In contrast to "those who write 'world history,' "[111] he proposes a change of perspective. Tönnies assumes a multidimensional structure of "continuity." One continuity line represents the "significance of the Ancient World for the entire development of the Middle Ages and modern times." A second ("very different") line connects the Ancient World and the Middle Ages. A third line connects the Middle Ages and modern times, with the continuity being *purest* in this case: in the "hitherto" course of modern times (including Tönnies's lifetime) "nothing really new has occurred."[112] Tönnies explains the *far less pure* continuity between the Ancient World and the Middle Ages by the appearance of "predominantly new peoples," characteristically "wandering erratically," "fighting" and "conquering." In contrast, the relationship between modern times and the Middle Ages is characterized by only quantitative developments: "increase," "concentration," "accumulation," "intensified traffic," "improved technologies," etc.[113]

The fundamental process by which the differentiaton between modern times and the Middle Ages occurs becomes clear only through comprehensive overview of a continuous and evermore a comprehensive development over time: the "transition from community to society."[114] This transition, from the perspective of its anticipated conclusion (complete revision of the ties of old communities by means of society), represents a "revolution"[115] in comparison with its hypothetical point of departure (complete revision of the Ancient World by the Middle Ages by new peoples). Tönnies was concerned with it since the time he wrote his *Anmerkungen*. The representation of this transition in *Geist der Neuzeit* largely corresponds to that of fifty years before.[116]

According to Tönnies, the aforementioned process finds strongest expression "in the development of individuals and individualism as a whole."[117] For Tönnies, individualism is first and foremost a "general" orientation that is not limited to modern times but present at all times,[118] embodied in transhistorical social figures such as the "Master,"[119] the "Subordinate,"[120] or the "Stranger."[121] *Modern* individualism is an "economic" phenomenon, that is, of quantitative increase in the capacities of "banking," "production," "trade," and "organization of services."[122] This "generalisation of trade" (by means of money) means that "all values are successively mobilized," that is, "made the same."[123] With the increase of "monetary economy," the "basic concept" of "natural and therefore also rational private property" inherited from Roman law is generalized,[124] which results in "liberation of the isolated individuals" from their traditional "communal boundaries."[125]

Because of the continuing loss of importance of the old communities, Tönnies holds, the form of human association is also changing "in the political sphere." The "Middle Ages" had been characterized by a "relative state of nature," that is, by the coexistence of manifold "social bodies," which due to their willfulness were "easily at conflict," while their members were relatively cooperative on political issues.[126] In order to describe the specificity of modern (social) associations in which isolated individuals (free from earlier communal boundaries) should collaborate politically, Tönnies refers to Hobbes's "Theory of Contract" as exemplifying the transformation of the more or less organically grown, relatively natural political *manifoldness* into *one* state construct.[127]

Tönnies is remarkably disinterested in the details of contract theory. With regard to the relationship between Hobbes and Rousseau, he mentions only that the latter had "replicated" what the former had "set up."[128] Hobbes is an element of the "revolution" of the modern era as part of the "political sphere,"[129] as distinguished from the "economic"[130] and the "moral-intellectual" spheres.[131] Hobbes's part in this "long-term" revolution concerns neither events in "rural communities"[132] or "urban communities,"[133] nor art, scholarly culture,[134] or everyday life.[135] Hobbes has a share in this revolution in the way "Jean Bodin" has his part: in a revolution caused by the "concept" of state. Characteristic is his "clarity" and "clearness" in this respect.[136] This stylistic quality is reflected in his clearly formulated polemic against "Old Western Rome."[137] Hobbes's pioneering achievement, however, is *only* a pioneering achievement. It is outdated by developments that followed—that is, the elaboration of the "social question" and "state economic policy,"[138] and the construction of a system of "free trade"[139] and establishment of a "state monetary policy."[140]

According to Tönnies, Hobbes is one of the "moving forces of the modern era," because his attitude to religion ("near atheism") created a "trail" that which later authors, such as "Spinoza," could follow. As a result of this development, "today" (1935) the "advocates" of orthodox religion have diminished so far that their attitudes appear as "oddities."[141] Nevertheless, Hobbes's thought does not belong to the "essential" elements of the "spirit of modern times." In general, for Tönnies it is not so much the individuals that are of essential relevance, but rather the deeds and facts: "invention of machines" and "revolutionary wars," "empirical thinking" and journalism.[142]

Sociology of Philosophy

To begin our comparison of two variants of a sociology of philosophy with a simple statement, we can say that Strauss marks his own position within the structure of the authors and philosophical units he mentions much more clearly than Tönnies does.

Tönnies's views are clear: He distances himself from representatives of a *world historiography*. He has reservations about *empiricism* (and prefers *rationalism*), and is generally opposed to *flat thinking*, and thus positions himself against Bacon and the Encyclopédistes. Nevertheless, Tönnies does not attach any importance to the systematization of "flat thinking" (in contrast to *higher thinking)*, or to the definition of the *rank* he assigns to an author. Hobbes, for example, is generally characterized by a certain form of awareness and clarity that enables him to polemicize with lasting success against the *old* (*Roman*) teaching. However, Tönnies leaves no doubt that Hobbes *philosophically* failed completely. Apart from Hobbes's *success* (proof of his pioneering work by the presence of some sovereignty theorists, political economists and physical psychologists), his work is certainly no greater than that of Plato, Aristotle, the Stoics, Justinian, or Aquinas. These, like Tönnies himself, represent first of all *units in time*. In this respect, they are *equal*; they *differ* in the continuity of their success, their rhetorical skills, and their evolutionary standpoint.

Like Tönnies, Strauss is opposed to *flat thinking*. In contrast to Tönnies, he attaches great importance to the systematic determination of forms of flat thinking in contrast to forms of *higher thinking*. The fundamental distinction refers to modes of *studying*—that is, *careful readers* and *first glance readers*. In this way, Strauss's *own* position is clearly defined. He belongs to the group of thinkers who *teach* careful reading and know the criteria of carefulness. This group is, in principle, open to expansion, such as for Strauss readers. Practically speaking, this group is an exclusive circle. For example, it is impossible to belong to this group and at the same time be a *modern* person—which is part of Tönnies's self-description. For Strauss, a modern person is not the same as a *contemporary* one; one does not have to be a modern person in the twentieth century. Undoubtedly, Socrates and Plato belong to the group of careful readers. There is nothing to prevent us from assuming that one or the other of the *Sadducees* also might belong to this group. Machiavelli and Hobbes undoubtedly also has a certain (although not high-ranking) carefulness. In an even more vulgar form, this also applies to *historicism* or to Weber and the contemporary *social sciences*.

It can hardly be said that historicists or social scientists are careful readers in the narrow sense of the word, which is why they are rather *careless teachers*. Weber and the representatives of historicism are nevertheless *decent* scholars. The same applies, in other ways, to Rousseau or Burke, to this or that of the *liberal* theorists, and certainly many (Catholic and non-Catholic) *Thomists*. According to Strauss, careful readers belong to a broader and more diffuse group—the *decent*. There are decent people who simply do not (yet) read carefully enough, Polin for example. In this respect, someone like Polin is closer to someone like Strauss than any *non-decent* person is (an Epicurean, Schopenhauer, or Nietzsche). *Non-decent authors*, we note, are not a specifically modern phenomenon.

Hobbes is a particularly remarkable figure in this structure of the *thorough*, the *decent*, and the *non-decent*. For Strauss, as for Tönnies, Hobbes is an ambivalent figure. Just like Tönnies, Strauss recognizes in Hobbes's afterlife the phenomenon of success despite intellectual failure. But for Strauss, unlike Tönnies, Hobbes is not equal to the other authors he mentions precisely because of this combination. Hobbes's study habit is not the study habit of the Sadducees, Aquinas, or Plato; in contrast he is a *Galilean*. Nevertheless, his study habit is also not equal to the study habits of all those authors who elaborated their teachings under protection of the *Church of Modernity*.

The fact that Hobbes and the other authors are *units in time* is of no particular importance to Strauss's sociology of philosophy. Conversely, it is (in the literal sense) of vital importance for Tönnies's variant. For Strauss, Hobbes is primarily a unit with a certain position in a *transhistoric* environment. This position results from the (relatively deficient) care of his study and the (relatively low) level of care in presenting his teachings. Of course, in order to understand this position correctly, one must take into account the historical situation. However, the concept of evolutionary historical continuity is irrelevant for defining Hobbes's position. Accordingly, the category of *continuous success*—so fundamental to Tönnies's sociology of philosophy—does not matter to Strauss.

While Strauss (in displaying Hobbes's Galileanism) primarily refers to his deficient mode of thought, Tönnies (in displaying the same) refers to Hobbes's evolutionary-historical position.

The importance that Tönnies attaches to the concept of continuous success has a side effect. The group of those who are continuously successful includes a variety of persons who care about completely different things from Hobbes (or Plato, the Stoics, Aquinas, etc.). In fact, the success of these other successful persons is by far more resounding; for example, in the case of the *new people* who conquer their share of Old Rome by war, or in the case of *businesspersons* who enforce the quantitative growth of economy. The peculiarities that distinguish Tönnies's *philosophers* from their greater contemporaries are limited to their particular scientific awareness and an explicit orientation toward the principle of rational insight.

We have every reason to assume that Tönnies belongs to the group guided by the principles of rational insight and scientific awareness. One could speak of the continuous success of Tönnies's approach if, in the course of future social development (possibly through coming battles or in the course of further quantitative growth and continued generalization of the principle of deeds and facts) his intellectual preferences are preserved or prevail: Rationalism against Empiricism—an orientation toward awareness and clarity instead of flat glory, etcetera. However, Tönnies's continuous success would not necessarily correspond with the success or failure of other particular protagonists or groups. It may emerge in the form of a future science dedicated to a strong state as well as in a forthcoming higher journalism dedicated to liberal society. Strauss's reference to the problem of journalistic Hobbesianism in the form of which Leviathan and free trade are invisibly joining hands reminds us that, on closer examination, these are not primarily conflicting forces—and raises the question of what we can learn from that fact.

Tönnies's sociology of philosophy is, as his concept of a multidimensional structure of continuity demonstrates, a *historicist* teaching. Unlike genuine historicists or Weberian social scientists, Tönnies is not involved in the repression of natural right. On the contrary, Tönnies reads Hobbes carefully enough to discover in his writings, as Strauss did, the distinction between natural right and natural law. In addition, he is thoughtful enough to notice the inadequacy of Hobbes's solution to this problem. Tönnies also notes that Hobbes has not discussed the interrelation between political scientists and 'most people.' His knowledge of the canon is, after all, sufficiently broad to refer to Plato's solution in this context.

Nevertheless, Tönnies's sociology of philosophy remains a historicist teaching. By contrast, we can observe only *internal* historicism in Strauss. When he discusses modern authors, that is, those who consider themselves as historical protagonists, he applies historical categories, for example by establishing an historical order of rehabilitation of Locke, Spinoza, and Hobbes; by defining Hobbes as originator of modern thought; and by describing modern teaching in terms of a history of foundation and decay. Strauss's *internal* historicism corresponds *externally*—that is, in the broad (transhistoric) structure of his sociology of philosophy—to a fundamental contradiction that culminates in Hobbes's position: the aristocratic (philosophical) way of life versus the plebeian(scientific) way of life.

What Strauss means when he titles Hobbes as first plebeian philosopher we can infer from his description of the relationship between Hobbes and Epicurus, the Sadducees, and the older natural right teachings. Hobbes, like Epicurus, is a teacher of a fundamentally apolitical life style. Because he is not careful enough to understand this, he pursues this way of life on the path of politics—he is thus only a halfway Epicurian. He, like the Sadducees, turns against superstition and is, as the first Sadducee must have been, the pioneer of a new politico-theological elite cultivating a unique hermeneutic style. However, because he neither develops a careful understanding of Sadducean teaching nor has a clear idea of political hermeneutics, he constitutes his political theology in the form of atheism—so he is only a halfway Sadducee also. He is, like the old natural right teachers convinced of the need for political philosophy, but because he has no profound idea of political philosophy he writes a doctrine that does not defend the freedom of philosophizing, but enables either anti-liberal doctrinism or liberalism without liberality. He is thus only a *halfway natural right teacher*. The one aristocratic political philosopher who is really an inspiration for Hobbes's attempt to establish new moral principles, Machiavelli, is (if considered carefully) an oligarchic figure with no pronounced interest in moral principles.

Strauss's criticism of the plebeian philosophy of Hobbes, that originator of the quarrel of the ancients and the moderns, suggests that the quarrel is, if considered carefully, a plebeian movement against which Strauss, who does not want to be a modern man, positions himself and *all careful readers*. This does not necessarily mean that his sociology of philosophy is at the service of an aristocratic party or government, or that it would strive to make plebeians disappear. He uses it, we may presume, as a tool for a broader concern, in short: the problem of the best possible regime.

Unlike Strauss, Tönnies is convinced that there has never been a quarrel of the ancients and the moderns. There was, much earlier, a conflict between Old Rome and the new peoples of Europe: established groups versus wanderers, not aristocrats versus plebeians. The measure of the best possible regime Tönnies is concerned with, that is, the aim of his sociology of philosophy, is therefore a "natural" synthesis between institutions suitable for continuity and the mobile elements of society. Overall, this is the political consequence of the evolutionary historical approach that Strauss considered in need of supplementation already in his letter to Krüger in 1935. The aim of this chapter has been to demonstrate what Strauss proposed as a supplement.

Notes

1. Karl Löwith, "Postcard to Leo Strauss, December 6, 1933," in *Leo Strauss, Gesammelte Schriften, Band 3*, ed. Heinrich Meier (Stuttgart: Metzler, 2008), 640–641 (640). Cf. Leo Strauss, "Die Religionskritik des Hobbes: Ein Beitrag zum Verständnis der Aufklärung," in *Gesammelte Schriften, Band 3*, ed. Heinrich Meier (Stuttgart: Metzler, 2008), 263–369. Here, as in all following passages in which I quote from or paraphrase German-language texts, I have done the translation myself, unless I state otherwise.

2. Ferdinand Tönnies, *Gemeinschaft und Gesellschaft: Abhandlung des Communismus und des Socialismus als empirischer Kulturformen* (Leipzig: Fues, 1887).

3. Thomas Hobbes, *Behemoth or the Long Parliament* (London: Simpkin, Marshall, 1889).

4. Ferdinand Tönnies, *Thomas Hobbes: Leben und Lehre* (Stuttgart: Frommann, 2014).

5. Ferdinand Tönnies, *Schriften zu Thomas Hobbes* (München: Profil, 2015).

6. Leo Strauss, *The Political Philosophy of Hobbes: Its Basis and Its Genesis* (Chicago: University of Chicago Press, 1963), 60. Cf. Tönnies, *Thomas Hobbes*, 252–255.

7. Strauss, *The Political Philosophy of* Hobbes, 62. Cf. Tönnies, *Thomas Hobbes*, 255.

8. Strauss, *The Political Philosophy of* Hobbes, 63. Cf. Tönnies, *Thomas Hobbes*, 243.

9. Ibid., Hobbes, 71. Cf. Tönnies, *Thomas Hobbes*, 252.

10. Ibid., 97. Cf. Tönnies, *Thomas Hobbes*, 210, 244.

11. Ibid., 123. Cf. Tönnies, *Thomas Hobbes*, 182–184.

12. Ibid., 150. Cf. Tönnies, "The Editor's Preface." in *Schriften zu Thomas Hobbes*, ed. Arno Bammé (München: Profil, 2015), 88–96 (95).

13. Cf. Leo Strauss, *Persecution and the Art of Writing* (Chicago: University of Chicago Press, 1988), 28, 34. Cf. Leo Strauss, "On the Basis of Hobbes's Political Philosophy," in *What is Political Philosophy? And Other Studies* (Chicago: University of Chicago Press, 1988), 170–196 (178).

14. Leo Strauss, *Natural Right and History* (Chicago: University of Chicago Press, 1965).

15. Ferdinand Tönnies, "Ferdinand Tönnies," in *Die Philosophie der Gegenwart in Selbstdarstellungen*, ed. Raymund Schmidt (Leipzig: Meiner, 1924), 203–242 (231).

16. Leo Strauss, "Letter to Gerhard Krüger, Cambridge, May 12, 1935," in *Gesammelte Schriften, Band 3*, ed. Heinrich Meier (Stuttgart: Metzler, 2008), 443–447 (445).

17. Tönnies, "Ferdinand Tönnies," 12–13, 23. Cf. Ferdinand Tönnies, "Anmerkungen über die Philosophie des Hobbes," in *Schriften zu Thomas Hobbes*, ed. Arno Bammé (München: Profil, 2015), 7–82.

18. Strauss, "Die Religionskritik des Hobbes," 362.

19. Leo Strauss, "Hobbes' politische Wissenschaft in ihrer Genesis," in *Gesammelte Schriften, Band 3*, ed. Heinrich Meier (Stuttgart: Metzler, 2008), 3–192 (8).

20. Ferdinand Tönnies, *Geist der Neuzeit* (München: Profil, 2010).

21. Strauss, *Persecution and the Art of Writing*, 7. Cf. Peter Gostmann, "Humanism Is Not Enough: Leo Strauss und die Soziologie," in *Humanismus und Soziologie*, ed. Peter Gostmann und Peter-Ulrich Merz-Benz (Wiesbaden: Springer, 2018), 247–333.

22. Strauss, *Persecution and the Art of* Writing, 34. Cf. Tönnies, *Thomas Hobbes*, 195.

23. Tönnies, "Anmerkungen," 7.

24. Ibid., 8–9.

25. Ibid., 9.

26. Ibid., 11–12.

27. Ibid., 13–19.

28. Ibid., 20–39.

29. Ibid., 13–14.

30. Ibid., 15–17.

31. Ibid., 17–18.

32. Ibid., 19.

33. Ibid., 24–25.

34. Ibid., 22–23.

35. Ibid., 26–27.

36. Ibid., 25.
37. Ibid., 30–31.
38. Ibid., 32–34.
39. Ibid., 41–43.
40. Ibid., 43–46.
41. Ibid., 47.
42. Ibid., 52–54.
43. Ibid., 54–56.
44. Ibid., 57–58.
45. Ibid., 60–63.
46. Ibid., 64–66.
47. Ibid., 67.
48. Ibid., 72–73.
49. Ibid., 76–77.
50. Ibid., 75.
51. Ibid., 78–79, 81.
52. Strauss, "On the Basis of Hobbes's Political Philosophy," 170.
53. Ibid., 171.
54. Ibid., 171–172.
55. Ibid., 172.
56. Ibid., 173.
57. Ibid., 174.
58. Ibid., 175–176.
59. Ibid., 176.
60. Ibid., 177.
61. Ibid., 178–179.
62. Ibid., 180–181.
63. Ibid., 181.
64. Ibid., 181.
65. Ibid., 182.
66. Ibid., 182–183.
67. Ibid., 183.
68. Ibid., 184.
69. Ibid., 186.
70. Flavius Josephus, *Jüdische Altertümer* (Wiesbaden: marixverlag, 2015), 872–873.
71. Strauss, "On the Basis of Hobbes's Political Philosophy," 188.
72. Ibid., 190–191.
73. Ibid., 191–192.
74. Ibid., 192.
75. Ibid., 193.
76. Ibid., 194.

77. Ibid., 195.
78. Ibid., 196.
79. Ibid., 196.
80. Strauss, *Natural Right and History*, 166–202.
81. Ibid., 202–251.
82. Ibid., 252–323.
83. Ibid., 9–34.
84. Ibid., 35–80.
85. Ibid., 81–164.
86. Ibid., 7–8.
87. Ibid., 166.
88. Ibid., 168–169.
89. Ibid., 172.
90. Ibid., 177–178.
91. Ibid., 179.
92. Ibid., 179–180.
93. Ibid., 181–182.
94. Ibid., 182–183.
95. Ibid., 185.
96. Ibid., 186.
97. Ibid., 187.
98. Ibid., 189.
99. Ibid., 190.
100. Ibid., 191.
101. Ibid., 192.
102. Ibid., 193–194.
103. Ibid., 199–200.
104. Ibid., 200–201.
105. Tönnies, *Geist der Neuzeit*, 35–102.
106. Ibid., 80–96.
107. Ibid., 103–163.
108. Ibid., 126–150.
109. Ibid., 179–212.
110. Ibid., 206–209.
111. Ibid., 16–17.
112. Ibid., 21.
113. Ibid., 21–22.
114. Ibid., 32–33.
115. Ibid., 104.
116. Ibid. Cf. Tönnies, *Gemeinschaft und Gesellschaft*.
117. Tönnies, *Geist der Neuzeit*, 33.
118. Ibid., 39–40.

119. Ibid., 41–44.
120. Ibid., 44–46.
121. Ibid., 47–51.
122. Ibid., 59.
123. Ibid., 73.
124. Ibid., 77.
125. Ibid., 79.
126. Ibid., 84–85.
127. Ibid., 85.
128. Ibid., 85; cf. 88–89.
129. Ibid., 126–150.
130. Ibid., 111–125.
131. Ibid., 151–163.
132. Ibid., 113.
133. Ibid., 115.
134. Ibid., 154–159.
135. Ibid., 159–163.
136. Ibid., 129.
137. Ibid., 126.
138. Ibid., 135–141.
139. Ibid., 141–143.
140. Ibid., 143–145.
141. Ibid., 206–207.
142. Ibid., 210–212.

III. CULTURE AND CRITIQUE

10

Leo Strauss and Jürgen Habermas

The Quest for Reason in Twentieth-Century Lifeworlds

Rodrigo Chacón[1]

In 1964, Leo Strauss reported to Karl Löwith that he had received Jürgen Habermas's recent publications. He had been "impressed by [Habermas's] penetration and sagacity," Strauss wrote. "Since, however, he is not simply a Marxist, the basis of his own position remains wholly obscure to me."[2] Habermas—and perhaps most of Strauss's readers—could make the same claim about Strauss: the basis of *his* position has long remained obscure, for Strauss is not simply a Platonist or an Aristotelian or, say, a Nietzschean.

Strauss and Habermas worked at cross-purposes. Whereas Strauss sought to recover "classical political philosophy," Habermas has dedicated his life to defending modern rationality.[3] Whereas Strauss's ancients found "reason in reality," Habermas defends the Kantian view that the claim of reason is "never anything more than the agreement of free citizens."[4] Whereas Strauss defended philosophy as a way of life beyond hope or despair, Habermas's work draws heavily on such secularized Christian ideals as "universal egalitarianism" and "a collective life in solidarity."[5] Whereas Strauss affirmed the classical view that "man is generated by man and the sun," and "not by society,"[6] Habermas has done impressively wide-ranging work to defend a thoroughly "socialized" account of our cognitive capacities as dependent on social interactions.[7] These convictions resulted in starkly different political-philosophical quests. Whereas Strauss reserved the philosophical life and the quest for truth to the naturally gifted few, Habermas has tirelessly deflated the philosophic quest for knowledge of the whole and has defended a pragmatist conception of truth as the consensus toward which scientific inquiry moves.[8] Whereas Strauss affirmed the superiority of a "closed society," Habermas is today perhaps the foremost defender of a "world constitution."[9]

Yet there is at least one theme on which Strauss and Habermas come as close as few thinkers of their rank and influence do. This is their critique—and defense—of reason. Both thinkers dedicated enormous intellectual power to tracing the fate of reason in modernity as it descended from the highest self-confidence to defeatism and nihilism. Both also refused to capitulate. Against a growing clamor of voices proclaiming the inner connection between Enlightenment and barbarism, Strauss and Habermas remained steadfast in their defense of philosophy as the "guardian of reason."[10] They did so from an unusual standpoint. Following the young Hegelian critique of the Kantian philosophy of the subject, they began from the premise that philosophical problems are intimately linked to problems of human praxis. Yet in contrast to Marx and his followers, they did not believe that such problems could be practically or politically (dis)solved. They held on to the classical view that philosophy cannot betray the thought of the absolute and its connection to truth.[11] At the same time, neither philosophy nor science could ultimately supplant the prescientific understanding of the world that is the basis of any possible knowledge.[12]

Habermas and Strauss gave rise to highly influential schools of thought on opposite sides of the political spectrum. Strauss's retrieval of ancient political philosophy has been understood by the American Right as a return to immutable standards of right and wrong directed against the relativistic drift of twentieth-century thought. Habermas's defense of communicative rationality has experienced the opposite reception. It has been understood by the Left as a democratization of the old-European "imperialism of reason," which is meant to salvage the core of rationality in the practice of giving and asking for reasons.[13] Thus conceived, communicative rationality should allow for the inclusion of the Other into an increasingly democratized world—a world without authoritative standards and without domination, where the freedom of each is a condition for the freedom of all.[14]

Here I shall seek to question this reception of their thought. In their own self-understanding, Strauss and Habermas are critical thinkers.

"Critique" has meant many things in a long career from the Platonic conception Strauss defended to Habermas's movement between Kant and Hegel. Yet at its core, I shall argue, the work of critique consists in the dialectical overcoming of fixed oppositions into an expanded conception of reason. Strauss and Habermas defended radically different conceptions of the right or the good society. However, insofar as they were guided by problems which, in Strauss's words, are "coeval with human thought,"[15] they also advanced the work of reason in its movement toward self-consciousness. As classics of political and philosophic thought, their work participates in a rationality that transcends their political intentions.

In what follows, section I provides a sketch of the modern conception of critique and its limits, focusing on Kant. Section II turns to Strauss's critique of the Kantian Enlightenment as based on the public use of reason. Section III explores three conditions of freedom of thought in Habermas and Strauss: the use of immanent critique that begins from the world as we find it; the common quest for a radical epistemology that retrieves forgotten experiences of reflection; and the attempt to provide practical orientation, or the cautious intervention in contemporary crises. Finally, section IV seeks to bring to light the dialectical quests undertaken by Habermas and Strauss to overcome oppositions between skepticism and dogmatism, and secularism and religion.

I

The term "critique" can be defined rather simply by reference to current use, etymology, and philosophical provenance. Yet the essence of critique qua praxis remains elusive. Already Plato made philosophy "critical" in the original sense of discerning,[16] and philosophers since Kant have provided competing accounts of the meaning of critique.[17] Strauss and Habermas continued this tradition, while also moving beyond it by pointing to its problems.

Understood as a philosophical movement and problem, "critique" or "criticism" is, first of all, an "*age*" that in Kant's famous terms submits every authority to the "tribunal of reason," or to "the test of free and open examination."[18] More specifically, critique, in Kant's understanding, is a "perfectly new *science*" that examines the pure rational faculties as to their limits.[19] To do so, this science proposes a *method* that, in contrast to both skeptic and dogmatic approaches, suspends judgment on metaphysical questions, in order to first examine our rational capacities.[20] Finally, critique refers to the essential *function*—and even to the "proper use"—of reason in the modern age. Indeed, as Reinhardt Koselleck notes, in the eighteenth century the terms "critical" and "rational" begin to be used interchangeably.[21] And with Kant this equivalence becomes complete; or rather, it is raised to a higher plane as criticism becomes "the proper *use* of . . . theoretical reason."[22]

What modern critique does, in the most general terms, is provide enlightenment or knowledge that liberates us from unrecognized prejudices or dependencies. This is a radically new kind of knowledge that is neither philosophical theory nor practical worldview, yet intersects with both—when it is not a "science," as in Kant, it provides a "diagnosis" of the time, or it is an "attitude" or "virtue" that seeks to transform the way we think and act by resisting authority, which may be (inter alia) ecclesiastical, political, or epistemological.[23] Its concern is always the present for the sake of a different future. Critique puts into question values, practices, and institutions under the assumption that they must not be what they are.[24] In contrast to utopian thinking or contemporary "ideal theory," critique—at least in the Hegelian and Marxist conceptions—does not simply propose alternative institutions or practices, but rather seeks to develop the "immanent" potential of the old world into a new one. Critique means both dissociation (from the past) as well as association to what the past prefigures; in this respect, it is "progressive."[25]

The problems inherent in the practice of critique are manifold. Here I focus on three: First, critical thought is meant to be anti-dogmatic, yet it seems to discredit, once and for all, the traditionally *philosophic* use of reason. Critical thinking need not, in principle, exclude thinking about the whole, or about God, world, and man. Yet, insofar as it is elevated to the "proper use" of theoretical reason in Kant, critical reason subsumes, or extinguishes, philosophic reason—a process leading to what David Lachterman describes as "theoretical anorexia."[26] A second problem is the elevation of critique to supreme tribunal. There is no religion, no morality, no law that is not subject to critique: in Marx's terms, the essential means to progress is the "ruthless criticism of everything existing."[27] In Kant's terms, all politics—at least, all "true politics"—must be subject to critical reason in its public use.[28] Yet, again, this seems to dogmatically exclude the noncritical use of reason in public—the kind of reasoning, for example, that invokes comprehensive religious doctrines to uphold obligations to humanity or the world as a whole.[29] Finally, and most importantly perhaps, critical thought seems to constantly undermine itself, for it must apply the sword of criticism to itself. Though permanent (self-)critique may expand the realm of the thinkable and doable, it may also destroy the critical impetus by rendering the goal of critique empty.[30] Indeed, while critical reasoning may claim to be self-justifying on the grounds that it follows an interest in emancipation inherent in reason, the very meaning of "reason"—or related terms such as "freedom" and "humanity"—needs to be specified, or else critique may redound in cynicism, nihilism, or hypocrisy.[31]

II

Strauss may be read as deploying a point-for-point attack on the modern supremacy of critical reason. This is most evident in his early profession of sympathy for the "fascist, authoritarian, imperial" principles of the Right.[32] Strauss's political convictions in the 1930s, however, must be read in light of his primary *philosophic* interest in the thinkers he situates on the Left, namely Spinoza and Hobbes,[33] as well as of his lifelong critique of the principle of authority (as I shall argue in section V). Strauss's project in the 1930s involves an attempt to understand the available alternatives from Left and Right beyond the "*Karikatur*" that each side forms of the other.[34] In the complex movement of his thought, this is coupled with an attempt to move *beyond* the horizon of "progress/conservatism, Left/Right, Enlightenment/Romantic" by retrieving the ancient idea of *nomos* or "a *concrete* binding order of human life."[35] Whatever this may mean in practical-political terms, it certainly inverts the Enlightenment view that "everything is subject to the law" of critique:[36] if anything, human life is unthinkable without a "*given* law"—as, according to Strauss, "even psychoanalysis confirms."[37]

In his early American writings, published in *Social Research* in the early 1940s, Strauss also took aim at the idea of public reason. During a time when *Social Research* placed particular emphasis on free speech and the social responsibility of intellectuals, Strauss revived the Platonic "noble lie" as essential to "what we now call 'considering one's social responsibilities.'"[38] Subverting the law of critique, Strauss argues against the view that freedom of speech and thought presupposes the public use of reason. Rather to the contrary, Strauss suggests that "there [is] something about the *public* conditions of speech and thought that inherently limits [free] speech."[39] The basic reason for this is simple: there is only a "small minority of people who are public speakers or writers." Hence, according to Strauss:

> What is called freedom of thought in a large number of cases amounts to—and even for all practical purposes consists of—the ability to choose between two or more different views presented by the small minority of people who are public speakers or writers.[40]

Finally, Strauss's turn to "classical political philosophy" implies a break with the Kantian conception of reason that requires publicity. In radical opposition to the view that the claim of reason is "never anything more than the agreement of free citizens,"[41] Strauss suggests that reason is a faculty of perception that is aware of the "articulation of reality."[42] Though Strauss is careful to distinguish awareness from intellection—that is, from the Aristotelian (or Thomist) view that the mind "abstracts" the "intelligible species" of beings[43]—he holds that *if* philosophy conceived as knowledge of intelligible necessity is possible, *then* there must be an intelligible order, or the universe must be ruled by intelligence.[44] A crucial consequence of this premise is inequality rooted in different capacities to discern what (truly) *is*. The critical use of reason (in Kant's sense) excludes this possibility insofar as what truly is ("in itself") is forever screened from our perceptive faculties. Hence philosophic reason has no "objective" or "metaphysical" claim to superiority over common sense. For Strauss, on the contrary, we cannot assign limits to human knowledge, and it is also evident that humans, by nature, can "see" with the mind's eye: we can discern, distinguish, and take together—or be "critical" in the original meaning of the term.[45] Hence, Strauss suggests, there must be *some* kind of order or articulation, as well as minds more or less capable of discerning it.[46]

III

Strauss was opposed to the supremacy of critical rationalism as conceived by Kant, yet he was by no means opposed to critique in a wider sense. Indeed, the structure of "political philosophy" bears a striking resemblance to Habermas's early conception of critical theory.

Like Habermas's "critique," Strauss's "political philosophy" aims to provide a radically novel kind of knowledge that is as practical and evaluative as it is theoretical and "objective."[47] Both "political philosophy" and "critique" differ from modern science and philosophy by virtue of their reflection on their origins: whereas modern science and philosophy abstract from their "constitutive contexts" in the city or lifeworld, the new critical sciences make such contexts the "essential starting point" of inquiry.[48] Critical theory seeks to "decid[e] the process of crisis toward . . . the good" by providing "practical orientation" about "what is right and just in a given situation."[49] Similarly, Strauss's turn to classical political philosophy is motivated by "the crisis of the West," which calls for judgment and decision concerning right and wrong.[50] Once philosophy has become conscious of its dependence on political life and its imbrication in the process of crisis, it cannot but intervene to serve as a guide to action.[51] That philosophy is affected by the crisis further means that it must respond immanently. Insofar as the political philosopher, now conscious of being a "citizen philosopher,"[52] suffers from "historical sickness,"[53] or from the powerful grip of positivism as the "the myth of that which is the case,"[54] she must work through the symptoms rather than repress them.[55]

A closer look at both their diagnoses and responses to the crisis reveals further affinities—as well as important differences. The crisis both thinkers confront ultimately concerns forms of consciousness that limit what we consider to be possible and thinkable. Following Husserl, both thinkers zero in on positivism and historicism as the dominant ideologies of the twentieth century, that claim to provide a full account of both the object of knowledge and of knowledge itself.[56] To critique the dogmas of positivism and historicism, Habermas and Strauss engage in historical studies. Habermas proposes in the late 1960s to "reconstruct the prehistory of modern positivism" in order to retrieve "abandoned stages of reflection."[57] Similarly, Strauss proposes to recover the confrontation between ancient and modern rationalism to gain new insights into the conditions for the possibility of true freedom of thought. At stake is the recovery of forgotten or repressed conceptions of reason—in the case of Strauss, the perceptive and "dialectical" reason of ancient and medieval thought; in the case of Habermas, the "participating reason of mutual understanding."[58]

While the thinkers share a conception of the crisis in forms of consciousness, their responses to it differ sharply. According to Habermas (at least prior to his turn to religion), societies that have become conscious of their "historicity" must create their normativity out of themselves, "without recourse to exemplary pasts."[59] Modern societies must recognize, above all, that (whether they know it or not) their symbolically structured lifeworlds can be reproduced only through the medium of communicative action.[60] Thus the burden of any possible response to the crisis of modernity falls on the power of communication. The chief aim, which coincides with the aims of Hegelian critique, seems to be full reconciliation among citizens, as well as between citizens and their socioeconomic, political, legal, and religious institutions.[61] This requires, first of all, effective autonomy such that "at every stage mankind will ultimately recognize itself rationally in that which confronts it."[62] It also requires mutual recognition among citizens as free and equal beings—an ideal eloquently captured in the claim that "no one is free until we are all free."[63]

It is perhaps at this point, in his response to the crisis of modernity, that Strauss differs most sharply from Habermas and the tradition of the Left more generally. Strauss seems to deny the possibility that radical critique of ideologies such as positivism and historicism may only be possible, following Marx, as a critique of political economy; or, more generally, as a critique of social relations of material and symbolic reproduction. In the words of Karl Löwith, Strauss's working assumption seems to be that positivism and historicism can be "deactivated" through the sheer force of "historical *Destruktion*."[64] Thus, for Strauss there appears to be no need to revolutionize the way we *interact* in order to change the way we *think*. The study of history is certainly fundamental to the radical critique of knowledge that Strauss and Habermas develop, and so is the study of society, as Strauss's contributions to a "sociology of philosophy" suggest.[65] Yet the Habermasian, and ultimately Marxist, view that radical epistemology is only possible as social theory appears to lie beyond Strauss's horizon. "Political philosophy," it seems, cannot be understood as a *vérité à faire*, or a "truth" that will become actual only once it penetrates the consciousness of a certain class of citizens.[66]

IV

Or can it?[67] Let us first make the Habermasian objection to "political philosophy" more precise. "Political philosophy" (one could argue) does not consistently follow the principles of immanent critique. "Political philosophy" *is* immanently critical insofar as it knows that genuine refutation of a philosophical position (say, "historicism") requires that the refutation be "derived and developed from the principle itself."[68] The critic, that is, must "penetrate the opponent's stronghold and meet him on his own ground . . ."[69] Strauss does this in a masterful way with every important thinker he engages, perhaps most clearly with contemporaries such as Max Weber, Carl Schmitt, and Alexandre Kojève; but also, more subtly, with the great minds that shaped the Western tradition.[70] The standard of critique is already contained in the form of consciousness critiqued as an unacknowledged presupposition.

Yet "political philosophy" seems to break with the Hegelian tradition of critique on one key point. Genuine critique, according to Hegel, requires a criterion that is "independent of those who actually put forward the critique and those against which it is directed."[71] This criterion is the eternal "idea of philosophy," which "is only *one* and can only be *one*," and which in turn grows out of reason, also conceived as one.[72] If we consider Habermas's work as a whole, this seems to be the criterion: as tirelessly as he has worked to bring reason down to earth to distill its "post-metaphysical" core, he has held on to the Hegelian premise that "reason governs the world," or that there is an inner "relation of history to reason" (a *Vernunftbezug der Geschichte*).[73] Thus he has consistently held that the work of critical reflection is progressive, not indeed toward absolute knowledge as in Hegel, but toward an ever-sharper articulation of the reach—and the limits—of reason in the variety of its voices and domains, including science.[74] Strauss, by contrast, denies that philosophy (or science) can be progressive, for not only is philosophy primarily a way of life, but its subject matter—"nature" or "the whole"—exists for us only as a *problem* or a question. Strauss's critique of unacknowledged presuppositions, therefore, is not meant to discover the trace of communicative reason in the history of human thought in order to overcome fixed oppositions (say, between secularism and religion). Rather, it seeks to discover the most "fundamental problems," including the problem of "nature" as well as the problem of the right or the good life.

Is this not, however, *also* a form of overcoming fixed oppositions, as Habermas and Hegel seek to do? Does not Strauss *also* affirm that reason and philosophy are one and the only standard of critique? Can Strauss, after all, be read as a "critical" and "dialectical" thinker?

In Strauss's own self-understanding the answer seems to be yes. The basic opposition Strauss sought to overcome is that between skepticism and dogmatism—precisely an opposition that gave rise to Kantian critique. The "work" of a "truly critical philosophy," he writes, is not to find a "compromise" or a "synthesis" between opposing philosophic or scientific positions but to "uproot" and "suppress" both positions by "a prior, more profound question," "by raising a more fundamental problem."[75] The problems are "coeval with human thought":[76] they are grounded, as in Kant, in the structure of human cognition. In contrast to Kant, however, Strauss denies (with Hegel and Plato) that there are assignable limits to knowledge. More fundamentally, we cannot know the knowing "subject," for, as Strauss argues in reference to Marx, "the subject, far from being the origin from which everything can be understood is [in infinite ways dependent] on the objects," or "on the whole to which he belongs."[77] Thus, it seems that we *cannot* strictly know "perennial problems"—at least, we cannot know if they will not be supplanted by "a more fundamental problem." There may be, for Strauss, no internal "relation of history to reason" as there is for Habermas, and yet there is a movement toward greater self-consciousness of the problems, that is, of the truly fundamental and comprehensive problems.[78]

V

The most fundamental problem Strauss discovered, in his own account, is the "theological-political problem."[79] This problem is widely understood to be insoluble. That is, Strauss provides no final answer to the question of whether we can acquire knowledge of the good or must rely on divine revelation to guide our lives. The result is a kind of impasse, or a productive tension, where each side in the conflict between reason and revelation challenges its opponent to articulate its position with ever greater clarity. Perhaps the most important lesson Strauss draws from Biblical religion—a lesson he finds confirmed in ancient Greek thought—is the human need for coercive restraint as grounded in a propensity to evil.[80] This lesson is the basis of a conservative politics, which emphasizes the importance of obedience as essential to right living.[81] The contrast to Habermas is stark indeed. Yet again, a comparison will prove revealing. As concerns Strauss, in particular, I will seek to show that his ultimate quest, *at least as far as philosophy is concerned*, is to liberate us from authority, which is primarily religious authority.

Let us first consider Habermas's changing stance on the challenge of revealed religion. As noted earlier, one of his most important claims is that modern societies must "in the final analysis" be "integrated though communicative action."[82] Tradition no longer has this power in a disenchanted and rationalized world and neither does law, for even the strategic interactions regulated by law depend on shared meanings. The consequences of this premise for religion are expressed in Habermas's *Theory of Communicative Action*. There Habermas proposes the hypothesis that, through the process of occidental rationalization, "the authority of the holy [will be] replaced by the authority of an achieved consensus."[83] Thus sacred obligation will be replaced by—or sublimated into—secular obligation.

More recently, however, Habermas has retreated from this stance. Especially since 2001, he has suggested that the very emancipatory promise of critique depends on retrieving semantic contents from religious traditions. This is true insofar as religious traditions may respond to the "motivational weakness" of the secular state by waking us up to "what is missing," that is, to "the violations of solidarity throughout the world."[84] Religion may also help us to become moral by answering a question that philosophy cannot—why be moral at all?[85] It can do this, in part, by supplying us with "experiences of redemption, universal alliance, and irreplaceable individuality," which can be rationally retrieved and secularized into emancipatory projects or concepts.[86] Thus, in Habermas's late work critique becomes post-secular. It is now aware that modernity cannot, after all, generate normativity solely on its own—at least for the time being.[87]

Turning to Strauss, this appears to be a vindication of his view that politics and morality cannot be grounded "exclusively on rational foundations."[88] Yet to leave matters there would be to miss the larger movement of his thought. Throughout his work—and most clearly in *Spinoza's Critique of Religion* (1930) and *Thoughts on Machiavelli* (1958)—Strauss adopted the complex role of both defender and radical critic of Biblical morality.

Strauss's central question in his first book concerns "the condition of possibility of radical critique of religion."[89] This question situates him in the tradition he describes as "radical Enlightenment," or "radical atheism," as represented (among others) by Hobbes, Spinoza, Hume, Feuerbach, Marx, and Heidegger.[90] Strauss's basic argument in *Spinoza's*

Critique is that "radical critique" fails because it presupposes what it is meant to establish, namely, an unbelieving standpoint. Yet Strauss also argues that there has been *progress* in the critique of religion.[91] One key to progress is doing full justice to the position under critique; concretely, this means bringing to light the standpoint of belief "as it shows itself from itself."[92]

Thus, in his first book, Strauss stepped onto the plane of ambiguity that has determined the reception of his thought. On the one hand, Strauss's critique of modern rationalism as incapable of refuting the claims of revelation appears to vindicate obedience to divine law. On the other hand, Strauss's critique *is* an exercise of critical reason (a meta-critique of sorts) that builds on the work of Spinoza and Hobbes while silently introducing a new method of critique developed by Heidegger.[93] Through this method, Strauss suggested at the time, it should be possible to "overcome" religion by understanding it radically; that is, by providing a fully atheistic interpretation of belief.[94]

Now, this does not settle the issue of Strauss's intentions. After all, overcoming religion does not amount to overcoming revelation or the prescientific understanding of life articulated in the Bible. It is nevertheless clear that the young Strauss saw his work as a contribution to "radical critique" or "radical reflection," which seeks to expose the unacknowledged presuppositions, and thus the limits, of historical forms of consciousness. The result is an expanded conception of reason that includes experiences of being-in-the-world, like religious experiences, that had been previously explained away through the "hermeneutics of suspicion" of Marx, Nietzsche, and Freud.[95]

Recent scholarship suggests that Straus's radical critique of religion continued into his mature work. Here it must suffice to note the persistence of the critique of religious longings in *Thoughts on Machiavelli*, which is, at its core, a critique of the very principle of authority. According to Strauss, this principle is primarily expressed "in the equating of the good and the ancestral," which in turn implies a "theo-cosmological scheme" of "absolutely superior beginnings . . . or Paradise."[96] Strauss's complex argument includes two claims. First, the principle of authority is *necessary* on the Freudian grounds that, without it, "society would be in a state of perpetual unrest, or . . . ubiquitous repression."[97] Second, submission to Biblical morality is *also* "against nature," and may lead politically to the rule of evil men.[98] Thus, "political philosophy" as practiced by Strauss consists in a double movement of "radical critique" of religiosity, particularly as founded on Christian morality, *and* cautious defense of religion as essential to morality and political life.

VI

I have argued that Strauss and Habermas are critical thinkers whose work transcends the categories of Right and Left. Rather than defending worldviews or specific values, both thinkers must be read as philosophical voices in the "conversation of mankind" that extends from the ancients to the present. Indeed, what is most important in their work may be their extraordinary capacity to absorb and diagnose the long arc of Western thought as manifested in a plurality of fields—philosophy, politics, history, religion, law, science—without relinquishing the unity of reason and its guiding light.

Strauss and Habermas share the injunction to "say farewell to all that has been taken over as truth without critical examination."[99] Yet they also share a keen awareness of the grounds of reason, or of what cannot be explained without being explained away. It is this movement between critical subversion and critical awareness of limits—between radicalism and conservatism—that accounts for the fecundity of their work. Through their dialectical capacity to reconstruct opposing positions and move beyond them, they broke the hold of pictures that held twentieth-century thought captive—among them, positivism and historicism, as well as their naturalist and fundamentalist offshoots. This, I believe, is their common legacy as masters of critical thought.

Still, Habermas and Strauss were not brothers in arms, and the critical edge of their work must be brought to light—not least against each other. Though they expressed mutual respect, their conceptions of the uses and the limits of reason differed sharply. From Strauss's perspective, Habermas's abandonment of "the teaching of the good life" as "the true field of philosophy" amounts to a mutilation of reason.[100] Granted that teaching philosophic virtue may be impossible or dangerous, the *question* of the good life must always be kept in view, not least as the presupposition of any moral and political theory including Habermas's "discourse ethics." Indeed, Habermas's separation of ethics from moral theory on the grounds that moral reality is made by us or constructed,[101] while the good life is presumably disclosed to individuals or religious communities, appears to be dogmatic. In any case, Habermas would have to justify *why* the Judeo-Christian ethical teachings he has "translated" into discourse ethics are *good*, or how this can be consistent with his professed ethical agnosticism. Differently put, from Strauss's perspective there is an ontological blind spot in Habermas's thought: justice points back to the good life, and the good life points back to "nature"—for "modern man as little as pre-modern man can escape imitating nature as he understands nature."[102]

From Habermas's perspective, the claim that we can understand "nature," or natural "types"—such as the "moral person," or the "gentleman," or "the best men"—may be correct as a broad phenomenological generalization.[103] Yet the further claim that these human types point beyond themselves to the "self-subsisting truth" of human nature, or of what men can potentially *be*, would have to be rejected as dogmatic.[104] It may be a sound practice to teach the young exemplars of "the good life"—say, Socrates, or Xenophon, or Hypatia—and even to distill the essence of human excellence to the best of one's ability, drawing on decades of patient study.[105] But to suggest that education in excellence requires obedience to this tradition—or even a provisional acceptance of the tradition as simply true—is a morally unacceptable surrender of our critical intellect and humanity.[106] And it is also, as distorted or asymmetrical communication, the source of ideology. The Straussian scholar who does not participate in the conversation of mankind, who pays no heed to the technical-scientific and intersubjective reproduction of the social world, will inevitably become a sectarian—precisely what the edifice of Strauss's critical thought is meant to avoid.

Notes

1. Thanks are due to Hannes Kerber for very helpful comments and suggestions.

2. Letter of June 3, 1964, in Leo Strauss, *Gesammelte Schriften, Band 3: Hobbes' politische Wissenschaft und Zugehörige Schriften—Briefe*, ed. Heinrich Meier (Stuttgart: Metzler, 2001), 690. (Hereafter, GS3.)

3. Compare, e.g., Leo Strauss, "On Classical Political Philosophy," in *What Is Political Philosophy? And Other Studies* (Chicago: University of Chicago Press, 2008), 78–94, and Jürgen Habermas, *The Theory of Communicative Action*, vol. I. trans. Thomas McCarthy (Boston: Beacon Press, 1984), 74 (modernity has left us with a "procedural concept of communicative rationality").

4. Friedrich Nietzsche, *Twilight of the Idols*, X, 2 ("reason in reality"). Immanuel Kant, *Critique of Pure Reason*, translated/edited by P. Guyer and A.

Wood (Cambridge: Cambridge University Press, 1997), A738 f. /B766 f., 643. Cf. Jürgen Habermas, *Postmetaphysical Thinking: Philosophical Essays*, trans. W. M. Hohengarten (Cambridge, MA: MIT Press, 1992), 144–146. For Strauss, political philosophy ultimately transcends the perspective of the citizen, and thus the Kantian tribunal of reason. See Strauss, "On Classical Political Philosophy," 91, 94.

5. Cf. Leo Strauss, "On the *Euthyphron*," in Thomas L. Pangle (ed.), *The Rebirth of Classical Political Rationalism: An Introduction to the Thought of Leo Strauss: Essays and Lectures* (Chicago: University of Chicago Press, 1989), 206 (the spirit of philosophy "is not hope and fear and trembling, but serenity on the basis of resignation"), and Jürgen Habermas, *Religion and Rationality: Essays on Reason, God, and Modernity* (Cambridge: Polity, 2002), 149 ("Up to this day there is no alternative to [the Judaic and Christian legacy]," which also includes "human rights and democracy").

6. Leo Strauss, "Persecution and the Art of Writing," *Social Research* 8, no. 4 (November 1941): 503, n21. Cited in Meier, *Leo Strauss and the Theological-Political Problem* (New York: Cambridge University Press, 2006), 73, n21.

7. Jürgen Habermas *Between Naturalism and Religion*, trans. Ciaran Cronin (Cambridge: Polity Press, 2008), 14 (on the "intersubjective constitution of the human mind").

8. Leo Strauss, *Persecution and the Art of Writing* (Chicago: University of Chicago Press, 1952), 34, 36. Cf. Jürgen Habermas, *Truth and Justification*, trans. B. Fultner (Cambridge, MA: MIT Press, 2003), 8. On Habermas's shift from a pragmatist to a realist conception of truth, see Richard J. Bernstein, *The Pragmatic Turn* (Malden, MA: Polity, 2010), 168–199.

9. Cf. Leo Strauss, *Natural Right and History* (Chicago: University of Chicago Press, 1953), 130–132 and Jürgen Habermas, "A Political Constitution for the Pluralist World Society?," in *Between Naturalism and Religion*, 312–352 (317).

10. Cf. Richard J. Bernstein (ed.), *Habermas and Modernity* (Cambridge: Polity, 1985), 25. Jürgen Habermas, "The Unity of Reason in the Diversity of Its Voices," in *Postmetaphyiscal Thinking*, 115–148 (116) (for a concept of reason that is "skeptical and postmetaphysical, yet not defeatist"). Leo Strauss, "German Nihilism," *Interpretation: A Journal of Political Philosophy* 26, no. 3 (Spring 1999): 353–378 (365) (for civilization as "the conscious culture of reason").

11. Cf. Jürgen Habermas, *Philosophical-political Profiles*, trans. Frederick G. Lawrence (Cambridge, MA: MIT Press, 1985), 1; *Postmetaphysical Thinking*, 37–38, 144. Strauss, *Natural Right and History*, 124.

12. Cf. Leo Strauss, *Liberalism Ancient and Modern* (Chicago: University of Chicago Press, 1995), 213; *Natural Right and History*, 78–80; *The Rebirth of Classical Political Rationalism*, 28–29, 253–254; Jürgen Habermas, *On the Pragmatics of Social Interaction*, trans. Barbara Fultner (Cambridge, MA: MIT Press, 2001), 25.

13. Cf. Hauke Brunkhorst, "Rationalität und Rationalisierung," in H. Brunkhorst, et als. (eds.), *Habermas-Handbuch* (Stuttgart: Metzler, 2009), 368.

For Habermas's critique of the imperialistic universalism of "supposedly rational standards," see the interview "Critique and Communication," *Eurozine*, October 16, 2015 (online).

14. On the exclusion of philosophical or epistemic authorities in the discursive formation of legitimate norms, see Christina Lafont, "World-Disclosure and Critique: Did Habermas Succeed in Thinking with Heidegger and against Heidegger?" *Telos* 145 (Winter 2008), 174–175.

15. Strauss, *Natural Right and History*, 35.

16. Strauss, *Liberalism Ancient and Modern*, 213. In ancient Greek the term refers to the art of judging or deciding (*techne kritike*), and more generally of distinguishing the true from the false. Cf., e.g., Plato, *Theaetetus*, 150 b 2f. Helmut Holzhey (et al.), "Kritik," in J. Ritter, K. Gründer, and G. Gabriel (eds.), *Historisches Wörterbuch der Philosophie* (Basel: Schwabe, 1971–2007), vol. 4, 1249–1282.

17. Karin de Boer and Ruth Sonderegger (eds.), *Conceptions of Critique in Modern and Contemporary Philosophy* (New York: Palgrave, 2012). Rahel Jaeggi and Tilo Wesche (eds.), *Was ist Kritik?* (Frankfurt am Main: Suhrkamp, 2009).

18. Kant, *Critique of Pure Reason*, A5, cited in Reinhart Koselleck, *Critique and Crisis: Enlightenment and the Pathogenesis of Modern Society* (Cambridge, MA: MIT Press, 2015), 121.

19. Immanuel Kant, *Prolegomena to Any Future Metaphysics* (1950), 9–10, cited in Richard L. Velkley, *Being after Rousseau: Philosophy and Culture in Question* (Chicago: University of Chicago Press, 2002), 67.

20. Kant, *Critique of Pure Reason*, B35.

21. Koselleck, *Critique and Crisis*, 108, n29.

22. Immanuel Kant, KGS XVII, Reflection 4457, 558; cited in Velkley, *Being after Rousseau*, 78.

23. See Michel Foucault, "What Is Critique?" in *The Politics of Truth* (Los Angeles: Semiotexte, 2007), 41–82.

24. Cf. Rahel Jaeggi and Tilo Wesche, "Einführung," in R. Jaeggi and T. Wesche (eds.), *Was ist Kritik?* (Frankfurt am Main: Suhrkamp, 2009), 9.

25. Ibid., 10. This brief sketch abstracts from phenomenological critique, which is "deconstructive" (rather than progressive) insofar as it seeks to retrieve the forgotten practices and institutions that gave rise to current regimes of meaning and intelligibility. According to Foucault, how meaning is constituted "out of nonsense" by "signifying machinieries" (such as states or mental institutions) is the key question that ushers in his own critical quest for the relation between knowledge (or "*ratio*") and power. Cf. Foucault, "What Is Critique?," 53–54. Habermas and Strauss may be read as attempting similar archeologies of forgotten meanings and practices, notably of "natural right" and philosophy as a way of life (in Strauss) and communicative rationality (in Habermas).

26. Cf. Velkley, *Being after Rousseau*, 77–78; David Lachterman, "Kant: The Faculty of Desire," *Graduate Faculty Philosophy Journal* 13, no. 2 (1990): 201–202.

27. Karl Marx, "For a Ruthless Criticism of Everything Existing," in Robert C. Tucker (ed.), *The Marx-Engels Reader*, 2nd. ed (London: Norton, 1978), 12–15.

28. Koselleck, *Critique and Crisis*, 116.

29. See Giorgi Areshidze, "Taking Religion Seriously? Habermas on Religious Translation and Cooperative Learning in Post-Secular Society," *American Political Science Review* 111, no. 4 (November 2017): 724–737.

30. See Bruno Latour, "Why Has Critique Run Out of Steam? From Matters of Fact to Matters of Concern," *Critical Inquiry* 30 (Winter 2004): 225–248.

31. See ibid.; Kosseleck, *Critique and Crisis*, 98–123; Jürgen Habermas, *Knowledge and Human Interests*, trans. Jeremy J. Shapiro (Boston: Beacon Press, 1971), 292.

32. See Strauss's letter to Karl Löwith of May 19, 1933, in GS3, 625.

33. Strauss to Löwith (February 2, 1933), in ibid., 620–621.

34. The Left includes Spinoza, Hobbes, and Marx; the Right includes Nietzsche, Dostoevsky, Carl Schmitt, and Charles Maurras. See ibid. and Strauss's letters to Carl Schmitt in Heinrich Meier, *Carl Schmitt & Leo Strauss: The Hidden Dialogue* (Chicago: The University of Chicago Press, 1995), 123–128.

35. Strauss, "Cohen und Maimuni" (1931), in Leo Strauss, *Gesammelte Schriften*, Bd. 2: *Philosophie und Gesetz; frühe Schriften*, Heinrich Meier (ed.) (Stuttgart: Metzler, 1997), 428 f. (Hereafter GS2.)

36. In the words of Denis Diderot, "tout est soumis à sa loi" (1765), cited in Kosseleck, *Critique and Crisis*, 116.

37. Strauss's letter to Gerhard Krüger (27 December 1932), in GS3, 417. See also Leo Strauss, *The City and Man* (Chicago: University of Chicago Press, 1964), 5.

38. Benjamin A. Wurgaft, *Thinking in Public: Strauss, Levinas, Arendt* (Philadelphia: University of Pennsylvania Press, 2015), 49. Strauss, *Persecution and the Art of Writing*, 36.

39. Wurgaft, *Thinking in Public*, 54.

40. Strauss, *Persecution and the Art of Writing*, 23.

41. Kant, *Critique of Pure Reason*, A738f/B766 f.

42. Strauss, *Natural Right and History*, 77. See also Strauss's 1957 course on Plato's *Republic*, https://leostrausscenter.uchicago.edu/course/republic, 71.

43. Thomas Aquinas, *Summa theologiae* I, 12,13, as cited in Thomas Sheehan, *Making Sense of Heidegger: A Paradigm Shift* (London: Rowman, 2015), 94.

44. Cf. Leo Strauss, "On a New Interpretation of Plato's Political Philosophy," *Social Research* 13, no. 3 (September 1946): 338.

45. Strauss, Course on Plato's *Republic* (1957), 172.

46. Ibid.: "A certain awareness is coeval with the human mind. To have a mind means to be able to number . . . to discern, to distinguish . . . this is a leg; this is another leg . . ."

47. On "evaluative," see Leo Strauss, *What Is Political Philosophy?*, 12; *An Introduction to Political Philosophy: Ten Essays by Leo Strauss* (Detroit: Wayne

State University Press, 2005), 130. On the necessity of understanding society both in its own terms as well as in itself or "objectively"—and the enormous difficulties involved—see José A. Colen and Svetozar Minkov, "Leo Strauss on Social and Natural Science: Two Previously Unpublished Papers," *The Review of Politics* 76 (2014), 619–633, esp. 630–631. Habermas, like Strauss, rejects "objectivism" or the view that there exists a "self-subsistent world of facts" that is independent of its linguistic and historical constitution. Cf. Habermas, *Knowledge and Human Interests*, 69; Strauss, *Natural Right and History*, 79. With Strauss, he also rejects both linguistic idealism and historicism (or "radical contextualism"), which deny the possibility of access to mind-independent reality. See Habermas, *Postmetaphysical Thinking*, 135–139. By the "objective world," Habermas means "the totality of things about which we may state facts," or "everything that subjects capable of speech and action do not 'make themselves,'" . . . or the "truth that exceeds all justification." Habermas, *Truth and Justification*, 254, 33–34. Strauss avoids the Kantian language of worlds and refers instead to the "articulated whole" that makes knowledge possible by "soliciting" *contradictory* (and not merely different) opinions that point beyond themselves to "self-subsistent truth." *Natural Right and History*, 124–125. The key difference seems to be that Habermas remains a Kantian in his separation of theoretical from practical (moral) reason. "Moral validity claims lack reference to the objective world that is characteristic of claims to truth . . . The reference to the world is replaced by an oriention toward extending the borders of the social community and its consensus about values" (*Truth and Justification*, 256–257). And yet, Habermas places *above or beyond* the "objective" and "moral" worlds the "trans-subjective *logos* of language" as "the new authority." The Platonic (and Hegelian) view that reason, or a principle of intelligibility, *somehow* rules the world seems to unite both thinkers. See Jürgen Habermas, *Postmetaphysical Thinking II*, trans. Ciaran Cronin (Malden, MA: Polity, 2017), 55.

48. Strauss, *What Is Political Philosophy?*, 92; Habermas, *Theory and Practice*, trans. John Viertel (Boston: Beacon Press, 1974), 2.

49. Habermas, *Theory and Practice*, 214, 44.

50. Strauss, *The City and Man*, 1; *What Is Political Philosophy?*, 12.

51. In Strauss's conception, philosophy must become political (and practical), first of all, to guarantee its own possibility, and indirectly to restore freedom of thought as essential to humanity. See Leo Strauss, *Persecution and the Art of Writing*, 56: "Freedom of thought being menaced in our time more than for several centuries, we have not only the right but even the duty to explain the teaching of Maimonides . . ." This was already Strauss's position in 1932: that we have become incapable of asking radical questions concerning *the* right and *the* good, Strauss argues, is "the clear symptom that we are threatened in our humanity in a way that humans have never been threatened." "Die geistige Lage der Gegenwart," in GS2, 451.

52. Leo Strauss, *On Tyranny*, ed. Victor Gourevitch and Michael S. Roth (Chicago: University of Chicago Press, 2000), 77.

53. Friedrich Nietzsche, *Untimely Meditations*, trans. R. J. Hollingdale (Cambridge: Cambridge University Press, 1997), 11.

54. Max Horkheimer and Theodor W. Adorno, *Dialectic of Enlightenment: Philosophical Fragments*, trans. Noerr G. Schmid (Stanford, CA: Stanford University Press, 2009), xii.

55. Cf. Leo Strauss, "Historicism," in Emmanuel Patard (ed.), *Leo Strauss at the New School for Social Research (1938–1948): Essays, Lectures, and Courses on Ancient and Modern Political Philosophy*. Unpublished English translation of a doctoral dissertation completed at the Université Paris I (Panthéon-Sorbonne), 2013, 210: "To-day, we all are historicists to begin with."

56. Cf. Edmund Husserl, *The Crisis of the European Sciences and Transcendental Phenomenology: An Introduction to Phenomenological Philosophy*, trans. David Carr (Evanston, IL: Northwestern University Press,1970), 6–7.

57. Habermas, *Knowledge and Human Interests*, vii.

58. Brunkhorst, "Rationalität und Rationalisierung," 367. On Strauss, see note 44 above.

59. Jürgen Habermas, *The Philosophical Discourse of Modernity: Twelve Lectures*, trans. Frederick G. Lawrence (Cambridge: Polity Press, 1987), 30.

60. Jürgen Habermas, *On the Pragmatics of Communication*, trans. Maeve Cooke (Cambridge: Polity Press, 2014), 215–256 (248). Jürgen Habermas, *Between Facts and Norms: Contributions to a Discourse Theory of Law and Democracy*, trans. William Rehg (Cambridge, MA: MIT Press,1998), 26.

61. Habermas, *Religion and Rationality*, 161. Cf. Robert B. Pippin, "The Modern World of Leo Strauss," *Political Theory* 20, no. 3 (August 1992): 448–472; Karin de Boer, "Hegel's Conception of Immanent Critique: Its Sources, Extent and Limit," de Boer and Sonderegger (eds.), *Conceptions of Critique in Modern and Contemporary Philosophy*, 83–100.

62. Habermas, *Theory and Practice*, 218.

63. Habermas, *Religion and Rationality*, 161.

64. See Karl Löwith's letter to Leo Strauss (April 15, 1935) in GS3, 645–646.

65. See Strauss, *Persecution and the Art of Writing*, 7, cf. 21.

66. Cf. Habermas, *Theory and Practice*, 214.

67. Consider Strauss's references to philosophers as a "class" with its own interests. As Rob McDaniel notes, Strauss sometimes "hints that he is waging a class war" against the modern conditions that suppress genuine freedom of thought. Robb A. McDaniel, "The Nature of Inequality: Uncovering the Modern in Leo Strauss's Idealist Ethics," *Political Theory* 26, no. 3 (June 1998): 317–345 (334). See Strauss, *Natural Right and History*, 143; *Persecution*, 7 ff.; *On Tyranny*, 211.

68. G. F. W. Hegel, *Phenomenology of Spirit*, trans. A. V. Miller (Oxford: Oxford University Press, 1977), 13.

69. G. F. W. Hegel, *Science of Logic*, trans. A. V. Miller (London: G. Allen & Unwin, 1969), 580–581.

70. For a brilliant reading of Strauss's *Natural Right and History* as a "dialectical" work that immanently critiques (and supersedes) the insights of Heidegger and Weber by returning to "Socrates," see McDaniel, "The Nature of Inequality."

71. Karin De Boer, "Hegel's Conception of Immanent Critique," 86.

72. Georg W. F. Hegel, *Jenaer Schriften 1801–1807, Werke*, vol. 2 (Frankfurt am Main: Suhrkamp, 1986), 172.

73. Habermas, *The Philosophical Discourse of Modernity*, 392, n4.

74. See, e.g., *Reason and Religion*, 154, 158; *Truth and Justification*, 27–28; *Postmetaphysical Thinking II*, 40f. Jürgen Habermas, *An Awareness of What Is Missing: Faith and Reason in a Post-Secular Age* (Cambridge: Polity Press, 2010), 16.

75. Leo Strauss, "Some Remarks on the Political Science of Maimonides and Farabi," trans. Robert Bartlett, *Interpretation* 18, no. 1 (Fall 1990): 6. See also GS3, 440 (on "Plato's critical philosophy").

76. Strauss, *Natural Right and History*, 35.

77. Strauss's 1957 course on Plato's *Republic*, https://leostrausscenter.uchicago.edu/course/republic, 170.

78. See, especially, *The City and Man*, 10–11, and "Some Remarks on the Political Science of Maimonides and Farabi," 6. In the same way that Strauss dismantles the opposition "naturalism" v. "supernaturalism," he also suggests that the fact-value opposition is "part of a larger issue," namely, the relation between the prescientific and the scientific understanding of political life. The prescientific understanding of "common sense," in turn, is *also* part of a larger issue, insofar as it presupposes "science." Strauss's thought moves dialectically *back* to more fundamental problems—in a way that also constitutes "progress" in awareness of presuppositions. This is the procedure of Hegel, who conceives science as a "logic of presuppositions" (*Logik des Voraussetzens*) and who seeks to expose such presuppositions as what they are. Yet, according to Strauss, it is not logic (or Hegelian science) that is "the pursuit concerned with the presuppositions of social science," but rather "history of political philosophy." Strauss, *The City and Man*, 10. On Hegel's science as "logic of presuppositions," see Helmut Hühn, "Voraussetzungslosigkeit," in Ritter (et al.) (eds.), *Historisches Wörterbuch der Philosophie*, vol. 11, 1166–1180 (1169).

79. Leo Strauss, "Preface to *Hobbes' Politische Wissenschaft*," in Kenneth H. Green (ed.), *Jewish Philosophy and the Crisis of Modernity: Essays and Lectures in Modern Jewish Thought by Leo Strauss* (Albany, NY: SUNY Press, 1997), 453.

80. Cf. Strauss, *The City and Man*, 5, 23, 96–97, 153. *Jewish Philosophy*, 118, 153, 162, 371, 389. *Persecution*, 17, 140.

81. Cf. Strauss, *The Political Philosophy of Hobbes. Its Basis and Its Genesis*, trans. Elsa M. Sinclair (Chicago: University of Chicago Press, 1963), 128; *Das Erkenntnisproblem in der philosophischen Lehre Fr. H. Jacobis*, in GS2, 281–282.

82. Habermas, *Between Facts and Norms*, 26.

83. Jürgen Habermas, *The Theory of Communicative Action, vol. 2: Lifeworld and System: A Critique of Functionalist Reason*, trans. Thomas McCarthy (Boston: Beacon Press, 1987), 77.

84. Habermas, *An Awareness of What is Missing*, 74, 19.

85. Habermas, *Religion and Rationality*, 108; *The Future of Human Nature*, trans. William Rehg (Cambridge: Polity Press, 2003), 4.

86. Habermas, *Religion and Rationality*, 74.

87. Peter E. Gordon, "Critical Theory between the Sacred and the Profane," *Constellations* 23, no. 4 (2016): 466–481, esp. 470. Habermas's reliance on religion as a source of normativity amounts, in Gordon's reading, to an abandonment of "the thought of a non-heteronomous life that has guided critical theory from its inception" (476). From a Straussian perspective, by contrast, Habermas has not gone far enough in acknowledging the human need for divine guidance, especially in political life. Indeed, Habermas suggests that "secular (scientific) reason" retains the upper hand. See Areshidze, "Taking Religion Seriously?," 724–737.

88. As Areshidze puts it in ibid., 4.

89. Strauss, *Spinoza's Critique of Religion*, 108; see also 165.

90. Cf. Strauss, *Spinoza's Critique of Religion*, 45, 37, 165. For Strauss's silent inclusion of Heidegger, see Leo Strauss, *Philosophy and Law: Contributions to the Understanding of Maimonides and his Predecessors*, trans. Eve Adler (Albany, NY: SUNY Press, 1995), 26; see also 23, 33, esp. 37f (on "radical atheism"); letter to Gerhard Krüger of January 7, 1930, in GS3, 378–381.

91. Ibid., 380 (on progress thanks to Heidegger).

92. Leo Strauss, *Die Religionskritik Spinozas als Grundlage seiner Bibelwissenschaft*, in *Gesammelte Schriften, Bd. 1. Die Religionskritik Spinozas und zugehörige Schriften*, 2nd ed., Heinrich Meier (ed.) (Stuttgart: J. B. Metzler), 2001, 196; cf. also 152, 195. Strauss's terms, which are lost in the English translation—"so wie diese von sich selbst her zeigt"—repeat almost exactly Heidegger's definition of phenomenology in *Being and Time*. Cf. Martin Heidegger, *Sein und Zeit* (Tübingen: Max Niemeyer Verlag, 2001), 34.

93. Letter to Gerhard Krüger of January 7, 1930, in GS3, 380. Heidegger's method of hermeneutic phenomenology is eloquently described as a "postcritical faith" or "second naivete" by Paul Ricoeur in *Freud and Philosophy*, trans. Denis Savage (New Haven, CT: Yale University Press, 1970), 28.

94. See Strauss's letter to Krüger of January 7, 1930 in GS3, 380.

95. Cf. Ibid., 35.

96. Leo Strauss, *Thoughts on Machiavelli* (Chicago: University of Chicago Press, 1958), 165. Cf. Heinrich Meier, *Politische Philosophie und die Herausforderung der Offenbarungsreligion* (Munich: C. H. Beck, 2013), 100 f.

97. Strauss, *Thoughts on Machiavelli*, 230.

98. Ibid., 180: "Non-resistance to evil would secure for ever the undisturbed rule of evil men."

99. Strauss, *Spinoza's Critique*, 130.

100. Cf. Habermas, *The Future of Human Nature*, 1.

101. Habermas, *Truth and Justification*, 268.

102. *Thoughts on Machiavelli*, 298, cf. 193.

103. Cf. Strauss, *Natural Right and History*, 140.

104. Cf. Ibid., 124. For Habermas, if not the human "essence," at least the human *mind* is "intersubjective[ly] constitut[ed]" through our interactions as soon a we are born; our capacities as *homo sapiens* are also evolving. Hence human nature can hardly be said to be immutable. Habermas, *Between Naturalism and Religion*, 14; *Postmetaphysical Thinking II*, 52 f. On the risks of genetic intervention into "the natural essence" of a human being, see *The Future of Human Nature*, 115.

105. Cf. Strauss, *Thoughts on Machiavelli*, 192–193.

106. From Strauss's standpoint the response could be that without assuming the possibility that a teaching may be simply true one cannot even begin to understand. Habermas would agree that truth must be presupposed. See, e.g., *Between Naturalism and Religion*, 44.

11

Heidegger's Challenge to the Renaissance of Socratic Political Rationalism

Alexander S. Duff

Leo Strauss counsels that the appropriate response in our time to the challenges posed by the thought of Martin Heidegger is to reconsider the "problem of Socrates"[1] or to return to "philosophy in its original, Socratic sense."[2] As Strauss and others have noted, however, Heidegger has little directly to say about Socrates in all of his vast corpus.[3] To be sure, there is an important remark in *Was Heisst Denken?*, where Heidegger remarks that Socrates is the "purest" of all thinkers, as evidenced by his not have written.[4] Strauss is said to have sometimes remarked that to understand Heidegger it is crucial to see that he was, in a way, formed by both Nietzsche and Kierkegaard and that Socrates was very important for each of them, whereas Socrates is virtually absent from Heidegger's thought.[5] Yet it would be absurd to suggest that Heidegger's thought proceeds in ignorance of Socrates or what he represented.[6]

In very brief compass, and in the meanest terms, let me sketch what is at stake in "the problem of Socrates," as it may have been understood by Heidegger. Socratic philosophy, the core of which is the Socratic question *What is it?*, has constructed an essentially nihilistic edifice, namely, Western Civilization. The history of the West is metaphysics, according to Heidegger. Metaphysics is the answer to the question *What is being?*, and metaphysics as such is nihilism. This may be expanded in terms slightly alien to Heidegger. Socratic philosophy has two guiding questions: What is the *archē*, and what is the best way of life? Related intimately to the second of these is the question: What is the best political order? The characteristic "method" of Socrates, or the means of pursuing this investigation, is to ask about the beings: "What is it?" This question, in itself, appears to constitute the turn to speeches or opinion; when one asks "What is it?" one begins with opinions. Responses to such questions are set against one another, and to the extent that they contradict each other they point the way toward the truth. This approach is so much characteristic of Socrates that the *What is it?* question, *ti esti*, is known as "the Socratic question." The result, one could say, is "self-knowledge" or human wisdom, where the examined life is the "foundation," so to speak, of a civilizational conglomerate that equates virtue with happiness and knowledge.

Heidegger rejects or, more properly speaking, attempts to overcome the Socratic way of being. In this sense, his thought—from its earliest mature expressions to its fullest adumbration—is *counter-Socratic*. To take the elements of the Socratic edifice one by one:

1. The claims to self-knowledge are dubious when the question *Who is Dasein?* remains unclarified.

2. The *archē* are missed when Nothing and Being (as such) are passed over.

3. The most appropriate way of life is misconstrued, as Heidegger implies in his account of what he calls the "*existentiell* ideal" of "anticipatory resoluteness," which accepts the widest possible variety of purposes provided they are true to one's most particular character; that is, *Who* one is.

4. Similarly the "method," if that term is not too grotesque, is mistaken, as Heidegger suggests in his early phenomenological forays and then the analytic of Dasein and the *Seinsgeschichte*, expressly in contradistinction to proceeding by asking the Socratic question "What is this?"

The basis of the problem, here is the question, or the *aptness* of the question "What is it?" for providing guidance to human living or existence. One inviting approach to the difference between Heidegger and the Socratism of Leo Strauss appears by looking at the following question: How does human openness relate to the fact of the articulation of the world or the whole? For Heidegger, the mistaken priority of the *What is it?* question obscures the deeper ways that humans are involved with articles in the world—practically, pragmatically, caring about them as they relate to ourselves—by implying (questions imply in advance their acceptable answers) that the "theoretical" response to such a question will explain things; in particular, the being of things. These deeper ways that we are involved are announced by the mood that Heidegger refers to variously as *Bekumerung* (distress) or, most famously, *Angst* (anxiety).

In what follows I trace out Heidegger's consideration of the *What is it* question at three different points in his career: in his early work, in *Being and Time*, and in some of the Nietzsche lectures. I will then turn to Strauss with the following question in mind: given that Heidegger is counter-Socratic, may we simply "return" to Socrates? Or does Strauss return to dimensions of a certain Socrates that Heidegger misses? If so, does his return to these dimensions of Socrates constitute an adequate response to Heidegger? I will suggest that Strauss points to a shortcoming of Heidegger's construal of the Socratic question. In particular, I will tease out what Strauss means when he criticizes Heidegger for overlooking the comic and the laughable and how this connects to the Socratic turn to opinion to understand the articulation of the whole.

Before turning to Heidegger, let me state with maximum brevity what is at stake in the discussion. Politically, the full consequences of Heideggerian politics have yet to be fully appreciated; this perhaps owes to their nearly unthinkable indifference to the titanic political struggles of our age. To wit, Nazism is just the first essential step in Heideggerian politics. The next is a denial of any important difference between free government and totalitarianism of the left and right. Strauss suggests that Heidegger's indifference in fact derives from a blindness to the character of these struggles, which led to his enslavement by the most vulgar, the lowest, of political movements.[7] To the extent that we can follow Strauss, then, there is some prospect of us seeing politics for what it is and then possibly attaining some measure of freedom from its basest elements.

Early Heidegger: from Theory to *Existenz*

A tension in Heidegger's work runs through all periods of his thought, between his sense that the key to human openness to the world is expressed in anxiety, distress, trouble (*Sorge*); and the difficulty of representing any apprehended articulation of the world with sufficient clarity not to obscure the priority of distress.

In his earliest mature thought, these tensions are expressed in Heidegger's sense of the character and limitations of theoretical philosophy.[8] He develops the view that theory, as he refers to it in this period, "stills the stream;" in trying to account for the vital motion of life, it replaces what's in motion with a static "picture." It therefore cannot understand the "motives" of the investigating subject because these are, as the term implies, in motion. Theoretical generalizations are bound by the "material domain (*Sachgebiet*)" of the (as he strikingly puts it) "what" being asked about. Asking "what is it?" produces theoretical answers that are limited by the "content" of "what" is being asked after. (And, again, this "material domain" appears *in abstraction from* our interest or motives in looking at it—the investigator is missing from the picture.) What is needed, therefore, is a way of thinking that allows one to include the "subject" in the disclosure along with the "object." The "motivation" that discloses the inadequacy of theory—that is, that discovers its limitations—needs to be grasped and understood by a new method of philosophy that Heidegger himself proposes to develop. Because he understands the promise of phenomenology precisely in terms of its "fundamental demand to bracket all standpoints," he thinks it is a candidate for a method of philosophy sufficiently attentive to issues of motivation. Such a program of "radical suspicion" understands any foundational concepts as merely the dross of a desire for comfort. The only "foundation" is that which is discerned by profound anxiety; that is, one that is *not* foundational. As he puts this in the "Comment on Karl Jaspers," "an incessant enactment of our concern for achieving primordiality is what constitutes primordiality."[9]

The refusal of all standpoints in service to primordial disquiet shows the motive of theory—the *What is it* question and answer—to be the preference for stability, clarity, and regularity; in other words, the desire for comfort. We cannot understand ourselves when we take our bearings from the *what is it* question because, while the beings about which we are asking come into existence and pass out of existence as we do, we are aware of and concerned with our own perishing from, as it were, a "first-person" perspective. There is no "translation," then, from those "whats" to us. Genuine thinking, thus, needs to begin by accounting for us, the beings with "*Existenz*." *Existenz*, though, is understood without any comforting, stabilizing "concepts": *Existenz* means *bare* existence; it means "I am because I am not *not*."

Articulation in *Being and Time*

Being and Time is a working-out of such an approach—"radical suspicion"—in a broader way, taking an analysis of the being with *Existenz* as a path to greater understanding of the question of the meaning of Being. We could rephrase the question of *Being and Time* as follows: Why is it that the meaning of Being—that is, our sense of what it means To Be—has become so thoroughly identified with the copula (namely, *is* statements of the sort that respond to the question, *What is this? What is it?*), when this still leaves the question of the meaning of Being so little clarified, leaves us so perplexed, so disturbingly, embarrassingly, confused?

In *Being and Time*, Heidegger provides an account of "radical suspicion" that shows theoretical rationality—what he glosses in this text as the present-at-hand (*vorhanden*)—as deriving from our situatedness among and involvement with other beings of the world, that is, the beings as they are articulated one from another. Our involvement with beings shows itself as chiefly "practical" (*zuhanden*, ready-to-hand), which is to say governed by pragmatic purposes and therefore their character primarily determined by the goals and uses we freely set for them. To see them as items or "things" in their own right is to interrupt their involvement with us in our busy doings. This interruption can assume two main forms: (1) a kind of restful, idle tarrying where we relax from our work and look at the beings, considering—in Heidegger's terminology—their *eidos*, look; or (2) they can break down. In such moments of disruption we (a) become aware of the perishing, temporary character of the beings, our purposes for them, and ourselves—a kind of flare-up of the anxiety from within which *Being and Time* is written and to which it tries to provoke us—and then (b) we summon to mind a picture of the items of concern, that is, we flee from the disturbing anxiety and breakdown to an attitude toward the beings and the world that is more reliable and stable.

Being and Time provides what might be called, with some cheek, a description of how this happens, but the description never really attains to the level of answering *why*. Indeed, Heidegger concludes *Being and Time* with the admission that he has not yet accounted for why the present-at-hand, theoretical vision of the world has come to predominate over a more immersed, practical involvement with the things of the world, especially given that we are closer to this latter way of being involved with things.[10]

Human existence is originally situated in a web of relationships to other people, and involved with articles of use. Our encounter with such items is hermeneutical, in the broadest sense of the term. As Heidegger accounts for it, all of everyday life—one's comings and goings, handling of affairs, and involvement with other people—are interpretive, hermeneutical dealings, mainly with *pragmata* whose purposes (wherefores, for-the-sake-of-whiches, and such) are determined or accepted in an unreflective fashion. To say that we interpret such articles is to refer to our freedom in using them, a finite freedom bounded by possibilities (in the future tense) set by the situation into which we find ourselves somehow thrown (from the past). The freedom in question is, precisely for all practical purposes, quite limited.

Thus, human existence is situated within a world whose articulation, while apparently quite fixed and thus inclined in its everydayness toward objectification, at the deepest levels is resistant to theoretical clarification. The beings show themselves initially as items for use, *pragmata*; the world is articulated in what might be called pragmatic heterogeneity. The class character of the beings reveals itself especially with regard to their purposes, which can be understood only with reference to the choices and decisions of the existing human. This articulation is expressed in what Heidegger calls the "as-structure" of interpretation. This means to refer simply to our use, for example, of this-thing-here as a hammer, or that-thing-there as a table, without making the more theoretically determinative claim that this *is* a hammer, or that *is* a table. The difference between these claims is as that between deciding to use something as a corkscrew and stating determinately that this, this-thing-here, in its Being *is* a corkscrew. Claims of the latter sort are only indirectly clarifying, if at all, in the more pressing matters of opening bottles.

Heidegger's counter-Socratism here emerges in his claim that reflection on what we are handling and doing does not clarify it. In "everydayness" (*Alltäglichkeit*), how we are "proximally and for the most part," we tend toward understanding ourselves and the world in their most stable and secure dimension and hence privilege the theoretical aspect of the beings with which we are involved. This is a fine, but important, point: because it is comfortable or easy, we attribute the Being of something to what we use it "as," thus obscuring that part of its Being—that is, part of what it truly "is"—is that we employ it, that it is employable or "handy." When we pause from our use and ask *What is it?* of the *pragmata* with which we are engaged, we narrow our apprehension of them. In Heidegger's formulation, our understanding of them is "dimmed down." He discusses this in his treatment of what he calls "statement" (*Aussage*—assertion). A statement is made in response to the question, *What is it?*, or implicitly premised on such a response. It is a particular sort of interpretation where the as-structure that characterizes the world in which we find ourselves is transformed or, as he puts it, "switched over," from pragmatic to theoretical: "When a statement has given a definite character to something present-at-hand, it says something about it as a 'what;' and this 'what' is drawn from that which is present (*vorhanden*) as such. The as-structure of interpretation has undergone a modification."[11] In stating, the *interpretive-as* is replaced with an *apophatical-as*; the *as* shifts toward expressing the mere *is* of the copula.[12] It is in this sense that Heidegger connects the term statement to the post-Socratic meaning of *logos*, the uniquely privileged site for the disclosure of the truth of being.[13]

The Socratic question and stated response focus on only one way in which the articles of the world are in their Being and confounds any further consideration. Stating what something is points it out, removes it from the context within which it would be understood by being used purposively. This renders the rich, temporal network of possible futures—each reckoned only with reference to the human's own finitude—which in their turn summon up relevant pasts into a mere backdrop for the presence of the being in question.[14] Heidegger supplies a definition of statement—"a pointing-out which gives something a definite character and which communicates"[15]—giving three discrete significations of the term. First of all, statement signifies "pointing out," *Aufzeigen*, from the "primordial meaning" of logos as apophasis, namely, "letting a being be seen from itself." Pointing out thus seems to refer to setting out a being from the context in which it would otherwise be enmeshed or embedded. It is seen "from itself," not from its surroundings. The second signification of statement is "predication." This sense of the term depends on the first, that the being has already been set out or indicated separately from its meaning. Hence, "we 'state' a 'predicate' of a 'subject' and the 'subject' is determined [*bestimmt*] by the 'predicate.'"[16] The third signification of statement is "communication [*Mitteilung*]." What may be shared with another is our own Being toward the being that has been pointed out; this is what is expressed in the communication, and does not depend on being close enough to have likewise grasped the being: "But at the same time, what has been pointed out may become veiled again in this further retelling."[17] Communication in the spoken word inherently obscures a broad and deep connection between the human and its involvement with its surroundings, both human and nonhuman.

Each of the significations of "statement" represents a further narrowing or "dimming down" of the original interpretive discovery of that which shows itself. Thus, far from each signification of the character of the statement representing a further clarification and refinement of what is captured in the initial interpretation, each step marks a further remove from the meaningful situatedness in which Dasein initially discovers the world. The shift at work in the first signification of statement—the *Aufzeigen*, pointing out—is slight but nonetheless crucial. In pointing out the being, Heidegger seems to suggest, it is being indicated separately from its sense; that is, pointed-out as being distinct from the ordered, meaningful context and patterns of use within which it recently had been fitted. How is it that the statement becomes the predominant interpretation of an otherwise rich, variegated, meaningful, pragmatically articulated world? If Dasein is nestled among articles of use whose Being it discloses in its use of them, in its dwelling among them, then why does a narrowed, deracinated, dimmer account of their meaning come to the fore?

In *Being and Time*, Heidegger supplies a number of descriptions of how this happens but does not fully elucidate the matter. He describes a shift, a "change over" in the structure of interpretation from the initial pragmatic orientation to the theoretical orientation of the statement. The being remains the same, but it shifts from being related to as *something handy with which* to *something "about which."* The interpretation focuses on "something present [*vorhanden*] in what is handy [*zuhanden*]." In this way of looking, the ready-to-hand [*zuhanden*] is "veiled as ready-to-hand."[18] The as-structure of the interpretation also undergoes a modification. The statement speaks to properties visible in the discovery of the present-at-hand that accompanies the veiling of the ready-to-hand. In "giving" the present-at-hand being a "definite character," a statement thus speaks to the being "as a '*what.*'"[19] In speaking of a being as a what, Heidegger says, the "as" "no longer reaches out into a totality of involvements"; that is, into the dense and meaningful context in which the thing must have been discovered.[20] The future collapses into the present as the being is no longer determined by possibilities: "As regards its possibilities for articulating reference-relations, it has been cut off from that significance which, as such, constitutes environmentality. The 'as' gets pushed back into the uniform plane of that which is merely present-at-hand."[21] The "primordial 'as' of an interpretation (*hermeneia*) which understands circumspectively" is thus leveled to the "apophatical 'as' of the statement," which gives a "definite character" to the present-at-hand.

As I have been suggesting, this characterization of the "apophatical-as" implies that the Socratic question itself—"What is it?"—contributes to the dimming down, leveling, deracinating, and narrowing of a statement, which rips articles from their meaningful totality of involvements, an environment constituted by a dense, rich, temporal network of reference-relations pointing backward and forward in time, and flattens their "meaning" into a simple, present *whatness*. Further, the *What is it?* question does not point by way of the *eidos* to the *telos* of a being, according to Heidegger. For Heidegger, the *telos*, such as it is, is resistant to theoretical clarification and refinement. It only emerges as a future point with reference, always with reference, to each Dasein, but remains within the realm of Dasein's purposes and its for-the-sakes-of-which; it remains possible, not actual. The counter-Socratism of *Being and Time*, then, here consists in indicating the pragmatic heterogeneity that exists beneath the screen of Socratic *logoi*-statements. Heidegger diagnoses statements as responses to the question "What?" and locates that question and answer as part of a broader phenomenon, "everydayness," where the finite involvement of human life in projects slips into understanding itself in terms of a seductive, misleadingly stable clarity, abstracted from deeper currents of temporality and care. The indication of this pragmatic heterogeneity, however, would be misconstrued if it were taken as somehow constituting practical advice or direction.

What Is Nihilism?

In his earliest mature thought, Heidegger lays out an anxiety-laden approach to thinking that discerns the happenstantial, accidental, and therefore distorting character of the *What is it?* question. In *Being and Time*, he provides a rather detailed description of how the present-at-hand statement emerges in response to the *What is it?* question from our more pragmatic-interpretive immersion in the network of articles of use, itself only ever appearing within the temporal structure of human caring or troubling. The very orderliness and functionality of this array of beings, this "web" as I have called it, privileges and brings out its dimensions of stability and reliability. The compatibility of human ends—our whys and wherefores, "for the sakes of which," and so forth—and the means we have at our disposal to achieve our ends encourages a certain relaxation, and comfort and, as such, privileges theory. To the extent that the world is amenable to our chosen ends, those ends indeed seem amenable to theoretical clarification.

But as Heidegger himself acknowledges, we might still ask the following: if distress, anxiety, and apprehension of our finitude is more disclosive, then what explains the ascension of the theoretical, indeed metaphysical, accounts of the meaning of Being? Why has the copula *is* replaced the interpretive *as* in our understanding of the articulation of the world? To express this question differently, saying that the Socratic "What is it?" question contributes to the dimming down obscures the crucial point, Where did the question come from? In his *Nietzsche* volumes, and in particular in a long essay included within them, "Nihilism as Determined by the History of Being," Heidegger supplies something of an answer to this question.

In his discussion there, he looks to the "History of Being"; that is to, the changes in the meaning and even the truth of *Sein* throughout history. He describes this history as a "withdrawal" of Being from the "site" of Dasein, meaning not just us humans, but us and the world in which we exist and with which we are concerned. In this withdrawal, Being *leaves* the "beings," *ta onta*, "in the light" *as* beings. That is, it gives itself to us in or through the beings. The ensuing thinking—what we might call Socratic thinking—is "metaphysics." It takes the *What is it?* question as the guiding question, and construes a series of responses that Heidegger calls "ontotheology." This happens, according to Heidegger, not because of any wickedness of one thinker or another because but "Being as such" has concealed itself as though it were the same as "the Being of the beings."

Heidegger lays out two ways the concealing of Being may be understood. First, the presence of the beings may be understood to conceal or cover over what he calls Being "as such." But what is more, the "as such" is concealed in the beings. To ask *What is it?* is to ask, Heidegger claims, what are the beings as such, without pondering "the 'as such' itself."[22] The "as such," however, is what designates the unconcealment of the being itself being what it is: "The *hei* in on hei on, the *qua* in ens qua ens, the 'as' in 'the being as a being,' name unconcealment, which is unthought in its essence."[23] In order to account for the cause of metaphysics, or the cause of the priority of the Socratic question and its development into nihilism, Heidegger suggests that both the "as such" and "Being," each of them passed over, are "selfsame": "Then the unthought unconcealment of the being would be unthought Being itself."[24]

In such a possibility, Being is not just unconcealment, but concealed unconcealment. Each part is important to the emergence of the Socratic question. Concealment: as Being withdraws, the being is put forward to be inquired of. Concealed: the very presence of the being disguises that this has happened. Metaphysics, on such an account, has not neglected Being; rather, in its character it has been determined by the departure of Being.

> Metaphysics asserts and knows itself as a thinking that always and everywhere thinks "Being," although only in the sense of the being as such. Of course, metaphysics does not recognize this "although only." And it does not recognize it, not because it repudiates Being itself as to-be-thought, but because Being itself stays away. But if that is so, then the "unthought" does not stem from a thinking that neglects something.[25]

By staying away itself, Being leaves beings in the light to be inquired of.

Heidegger gestures, thus, to something like the redemption of nihilism. As nihilism emerges into the open now as never before, in the culminating maturation of metaphysics, it points beyond the beings to Being. In both the destructive phenomena of the twentieth century and their anticipation in the thought of Nietzsche, nihilism shows that Being, in its withdrawal and concealment, "is" nothing:

> In the meantime, it has become clearer that Being itself happens (occurs essentially) as the unconcealment in which the being comes to presence. Unconcealment itself, however, remains concealed as such. With reference to itself, unconcealment keeps away, keeps to itself. The matter stands with the concealment of the essence of unconcealment. It stands with the concealment of Being as such. Being itself stays away.[26]

In nihilism it is revealed that Being should not even be called "Being" for it is so radically other than itself. Nihilism reveals that Being "even 'is' not."[27]

The eventuation of nihilism is captured, therefore, in a deep but cautious hopefulness: "the essence of nihilism in the history of Being still does not reveal those features that usually describe what one means by the familiar term "nihilism": something that disparages and destroys, a decline and downfall. The essence of nihilism contains nothing negative in the form of a destructive element that has its seat in human sentiments and circulates abroad in human activities."[28] This is not to advocate overlooking the destruction characteristic of the phenomena of nihilism. But still its essence—as distinct from its phenomena—facilitates a passage "into the free region."[29]

The anxiety provoked by the Heideggerian account is meant to be the accompaniment to the release from the Socratic question, bound as it is to the "what-content" of the investigation. It is also, however, entirely appropriate to our time as the newly given sense of the "errancy" of the Socratic question for understanding Being, and metaphysics as the series of worked-out responses to that question. Whatever merit there was in the original formulation of the Socratic question, determined as it was by the history of Being, there can be no possible defense of a return to it now, in our present condition of being given an apprehension of the essence of nihilism. The resuscitation of the Socratic question would only, thus, ensnare us in the grisly phenomena of nihilism, obscuring what purchase we have been granted on its essence.

Strauss on the Comic Dimension of Philosophic Speech and Inquiry

Thus, Heidegger's challenge to Socratic philosophy goes like this: (1) The guidance we take from what the beings are is really motivated by our search for comfort and tranquility in this stable, reliable, visible, calculable aspect of them. The metaphysical systems we have expounded and the civilizational edifice we have erected on this basis are profoundly mistaken, not to say fraudulent. (2) The true character of our relationship to Being is revealed in our profound anxiety, discomfort, and disquiet about our own finite *Existenz*, which remains profoundly unfathomable to us. Living as though (1) were true alienates us from the truth, which contributes on one hand to a numbing, dissipating, confusing sterility in our lives; and, on the other hand, to perpetual warfare and destructive, technological manufacturing. (3) That all this is so is uniquely available for us to grasp now, as in our age the deep meaninglessness of the

Socratic approach to the nothing has become manifest as never before. Thus, in the deepest dark of the present moment of nihilism, there is cause for serious hope for the future in a new dispensation of Being that will make possible new ways of living.

The political consequences of Heideggerian thought are, in a word, horrible. As Strauss appreciates, however, mere revulsion is not an adequate response. We should like to try and think through the problem. Strauss points the way, I suggest. In particular, I want to take up an underappreciated element of his response to Heidegger; namely, his criticism of Heidegger for being inattentive to the comic or the laughable in human experience. And giving unwarranted emphasis to the dour, the serious, the anxiety inducing, the disquieting, the tragic. By following Strauss's Socratism, the impulse informing the renaissance of Socratic rationalism in his work, we will find a different and possibly more satisfying approach to understanding both the human openness to the world or whole and to the articulation of that whole.

Beginning with some of Strauss's general claims, first, a logical point: Strauss suggests that existential anxiety or disquiet must not be taken to be as disclosive a passion as Heidegger claims.[30] The logic of his critique of intellectual probity in his autobiographical preface to *Spinoza's Critique of Religion* applies to anxiety as well: "Just as an assertion does not become true because it is shown to be comforting, it does not become true because it is shown to be terrifying."[31] Theoretical insight is not less true because it is comforting—tranquil or serene, let us say—nor is disquiet as such a necessary marker of the truth.

Second, in contrast to Heidegger, Strauss presents the heterogeneity of being as given to noetic—that is, intellectual or theoretical—classification. In Heidegger's account, the articulation (*Rede*) of the world comes primarily in the tools and articles among which we find ourselves. The beings are handy. To "look" at this articulation is already to contribute to its corrosion; its theoretical inspection diminishes its clarity, which was apprehended unreflectively. Strauss, by contrast, understands the Socratic position to be that the articulation of the beings comes to light in opinion, especially opinions that disagree with one another about contestable matters such as justice, and is inherently susceptible to the question "What is it?" The dispute between Heidegger and Strauss thus turns, in part, on which one of them is right about this: do the beings as beings come to sight first in our opinions about them, or is opinion principally to be understood with regard to its inclination toward privileging stability and clarity, thus obscuring the primary manifestation of the beings in their handiness?

These elements of Strauss's Socratic riposte to Heidegger may be brought into clearer focus if we consider Strauss's suggestion that a sense for comedy is lacking in Heidegger, and that in order to understand the presentation of Socrates in Xenophon and Plato one must first remind oneself of the Aristophanic depiction of Socrates. Strauss writes to Gadamer that "Heidegger is silent about comedy."[32] In the conclusion to his eulogy for the gentleman-statesman Kurt Riezler, he praises Riezler by way of indicating a deficiency in Heidegger: "His [Riezler's] analyses of the passions are also meant as a critique of the 'narrow humanity' that informs Heidegger's analysis of *Existenz*; they point to the riddle posed by Heidegger's obstinate silence about love or charity on the one hand, and about laughter and the things which deserved to be laughed at on the other."[33]

What does Strauss think might be revealed by comedy, or in laughter, that is absent from Heidegger's thought? Strauss suggests two things that comedy reveals that do not, we may say, appear in Heidegger. The first of these is that comedy communicates—indirectly, but appropriately—the order of rank within human things, or among human beings. Shortly before the remark about Heidegger, Strauss says this in defense of Riezler's broader insights into the human: "To understand the fact of laughter means to realize the variety of levels of laughter with the silly laughter of silly people about things which are not ridiculous at the bottom and divine laughter at the top."[34] Laughter reveals something of the noble and the base in distorted or ridiculous form, but it reveals nonetheless. That silly people laugh at things that are not ridiculous communicates, backhandedly, that they are silly and that other things are higher. This should be considered alongside related remarks Strauss makes in his 1958 series of lectures entitled "The Problem of Socrates." Comedy expresses both the serious and the ridiculous—that is, the high and the low—but does so in such a manner that both are presented in the guise of the ridiculous. The high is permitted to laugh at the low for its vulgarity and crudeness; the low laughs at the high in its exposure to frank impropriety.[35]

Strauss praises comedy for its attention to and preservation of the surface, opinion and convention. Opinions about the highest things conflict with one another, and so are exposed to ridicule in the disproportion between their claims and their being. Comedy punctures convention by lampooning it, but also shows the need for its preservation. Comedy forswears tragic depths not out of ignorance, but for the sake of presenting a more complete picture of the whole. Comedy is thus superior to tragedy; it transcends and presupposes tragedy.

These qualities of comedy apply to irony in Strauss's reading of the Socratics Plato and especially Xenophon. "The ironical," Strauss writes, "is a kind of the ridiculous."[36] In the Plato chapter in the *City and Man*, Strauss gives a picture of irony that makes it seem, in relation to comedy, like polite humor, "noble dissimulation."[37] The implication of irony is that there is "a natural order of rank among men." In comedy, rank ordering appears as the mutual ridicule of high and low. Comedy and irony reflect the natural articulation of kinds of men, or "nature in its practically most important respect: the natural differences among men."[38] Irony and comedy defer, in a manner, to their audience and so respond to the opinions held by the audience.[39]

By looking first at the comic dimension of Strauss's reconsideration of Socrates—where a ridiculous reflection of rank and the surface are preserved—we are in a position to understand how Strauss reads the Socratic "what is it?" question and the Socratic discovery of what Strauss refers to as noetic heterogeneity. Strauss repeatedly distinguishes the Xenophontic Socrates for having two modes in which he speaks to others: one includes asking the "What is it?" question, and leads to a consideration of "hypotheses"; the other leads his interlocutors to agreement rather than truth about whatever is being discussed.[40] When he spoke to interlocutors who contradicted him, Socrates led the conversation back to its underlying hypotheses by asking "what is it?" and answering "step by step." In this way "the truth became manifest."[41] The other kind of conversation, when Socrates spoke with more placid interlocutors—"i.e., when he talked to people who merely listened"—Socrates produced agreement based on the accepted opinions. The first mode of discussion is the "higher form of dialectics."[42] The second mode "is the most important part of the political art;" it is the art that Homer ascribes to Odysseus. Socrates had the first kind of conversation with intelligent, good-natured interlocutors; the second kind of conversation typified his interactions with the vast run of people. Socrates's mode of speaking reflected the fact that there is a natural order of rank among men.

Socrates's ironic approach to different kinds of men is reflected in Xenophon's humorous depiction of Socrates, for Xenophon only shows Socrates engaged in the higher form of dialectics with evidently inferior minds. Xenophon hides the delicate peaks of the Socratic life from vulgar scrutiny by portraying Socrates as something of a genius surrounded by fools, a kind of Attic Jeeves. "Xenophon's Socratic writings, one might dare to say, constitute a reply to Aristophanes' *Clouds* on the level of the *Clouds*, and with a most subtle use of the means of Aristophanes."[43] Xenophon presents Socrates "in the guise of the ridiculous."[44] As Strauss repeatedly avers, to understand the heights of Socrates as understood by Xenophon, we need to follow Xenophon's indications and look where he is pointing, reconstructing or imagining what a Socratic conversation with a worthwhile interlocutor would be like.

Strauss's suggestive presentation of Xenophon's depiction of Socrates's higher form of dialectics thus refers to the discovery of noetic heterogeneity from within opinion.

Noetic heterogeneity refers to the articulation of the whole into parts, each of which is open to being asked "what is it?" These questions in turn point to "'essential' differences."[45] This distinguishes the Socratic approach from that of the pre-Socratics, for whom the whole was understood either as noetically homogeneous (Parmenides) or as sensibly heterogeneous (as constituted by, e.g., the four elements). Noetic heterogeneity intended to express the insight that "while there are infinitely many things, there is only a finite number of kinds or classes of things . . . Those kinds or classes, as distinguished from the individual things, are unchangeable and do not come into being or perish."[46] To understand the whole, therefore, means to understand how each of these kinds and classes relates to one another. This requires that they not simply be reduced to one another, as one causing another: "the class, or the class character, is the cause par excellence."[47] Among the distinctions between the classes of beings, the most important for the purposes of philosophy is the distinction between the human things and the nonhuman things, or the discernment of the political as a class of things distinct from the rest of the whole; indeed, as the part of the whole that is most open to the whole.[48]

Being first manifests in opinion; "the core of the whole, or of nature" is "in a manner, but necessarily" revealed in opinion.[49] Strauss repeatedly characterizes Socratic philosophy as a return to sobriety or moderation from the madness of the pre-Socratics. This consists dually in the former's respect for political authority and so for opinion as such. Such respect includes a sense of the danger of "persecution," to be sure. Strauss, however, claims that there is more to it than, let us call it defensive exotericism.[50] The "what is it?" questions characteristic of Socratic philosophy look first to opinion as the source for their answers; they arise from obscurity within opinions, and begin to seek clarity there. So even the investigations conducted by Socrates and his best interlocutors—the dialectical considerations of hypotheses—depend on opinions about what is in order to get started. That the high, the highest, should be so dependent on the low is ridiculous, or comical. The very dependence of the discovery of the truth on the fact of ignorance is likewise, it could be said, ridiculous.

Opinion as Strauss presents it, though, is not simply a cognitive half-way house between ignorance and knowledge. It contains, as we have seen, an element of ranking, ranking enforced by authority: "The highest opinions, the authoritative opinions, are the pronouncements of the law."[51] In the law the human things, justice and nobility, are "manifest;" the law "speaks authoritatively," however, "about the highest beings, the gods."[52] The law manifests or shows, shows as what they are the just and noble things, but may only speak authoritatively—that is, with the support of compulsion—of the utmost beings. Opinion, certainly in its highest form, contains an element of authority that depends on compulsion or necessity (*anangke*). Opinion is the shadowy world where necessity appears as authority: necessity first comes to light as conventional compulsion; rank first manifests in conventional hierarchies. In each case, however, opinion preserves—in however convoluted a form—rank as such, necessity as such. In beginning with and finally deferring to opinion, this natural necessity and natural rank is what is preserved to be investigated in Socratic philosophy.

Strauss's account of comedy illuminates two different sorts of articulation, or sets of distinctions. There is first the different ranks, or different kinds of men: the superficial difference between the noble and the base, revealed to have its grounding in the difference between the philosophers and the many. Then there is the different kinds of beings: the heterogeneity of beings as this comes to sight in opinion means initially the class character of the beings, but perhaps more fundamentally the class character of the political or human things as distinct from the nonhuman (divine and subhuman) things; that is, the appearance of the political as a class of things distinct unto itself. How ought these distinctions to be understood together, the different kinds of men or souls and the different kinds of beings?

Conclusion

How should we understand these considerations as illuminating the position of Heidegger? In his 1970 lecture on "The Problem of Socrates," Strauss makes this almost offhand remark about Heidegger's characterization of Socrates as the "purest" thinker: "Is he [Heidegger] insufficiently aware of the Odysseus in Socrates? Perhaps."[53] What to make of a perhaps from Strauss without looking silly? Heidegger takes Socrates as the purest thinker, and this to be shown by his refusal to write: "All through his life and right into his death, Socrates did nothing else than place himself into this draft, this current, and maintain himself in it."[54] Serious stuff. But what of the Odysseus in Socrates, of Socrates's practice of speaking to the common run of men by getting them to seek agreement? Heidegger's Socrates takes no account of Socratic irony, his noble dissimulation. He misses the status that opinion has in Socratic philosophy, where opinion is the matrix of thought because it contains a distortion of the truth—a ridiculous distortion?—a reflection of the truth which, though a distortion, does not simply have the character of Heideggerian "everydayness," where stability, clarity, and permanence are privileged because they are less discomforting. Could it be that Strauss is more reasonable about politics, sounder, because he takes its medium, opinion, less "seriously" than Heidegger? As Strauss says of Xenophon: "the apparent frivolity of Xenophon's account of things political . . . [is] the reflection of Socratic serenity."[55] That Strauss, following Socrates, returns to opinion, or preserves it in its ignorance, ought not then to be understood as "philosophic conservatism" but as an orientation by the good of moderation.[56] Moderation of this sort, however, may emerge only by observing (pace Heidegger) an ineliminable distinction between practice and theory; or between the active movement of the human amidst the things of the world, and the questions, riddles, and problems generated and reflections thereupon entertained by the human mind.

Notes

1. Leo Strauss, "The Problem of Socrates," *Interpretation* vol. 22, n3 (1995), 321–338.

2. Leo Strauss, *Natural Right and History* (Chicago: University of Chicago Press, 1965), 32.

3. Leo Strauss, "The Problem of Socrates," 324. Cf. Graeme Nicholson, "The Constitution of our Being," *Heidegger's Being and Time: Critical Essays*, ed. Richard Polt (Lanham: Rowman & Littlefield Publishers, 2010), 47–74.

4. Martin Heidegger, *What Is Called Thinking?* (New York: Perennial, 2004), 17.

5. "The Problem of Socrates," 324.

6. As the remark from *Was Heisst Denken* suggests, Heidegger is not without regard for Socrates. Another striking passage may be found in his lecture course entitled "On the Essence of Human Freedom," in a comment on the Platonic dialogue *Theaitetos*. Here, Heidegger praises the Socratic investigation, "What is knowledge," for in this question, man "places himself in question. Such questioning brings man himself before new possibilities. The apparently innocuous what-question is revealed as an attack by man on his own self, on his proximal persistence in the usual and common, on his forgetting of first principles. It is an attack by man on what he proximally believes himself to know, and at the same time it is a determining intervention in what he himself can be, in what he wants to be or wants not to be" (Martin Heidegger, *The Essence of Truth: On Plato's Cave Allegory and Theaetetus* [London: Bloomsbury Academic, 2014], 114).

7. This is captured in Richard Velkley's trenchant and elegant formulation in his superb study of Heidegger and Strauss: "Heidegger has a profound grasp of the radicality of philosophical questioning comparable with that of the greatest figures in the tradition. But his divorce of questioning from any natural-teleological basis, for which the German Idealist concepts of freedom helped set the stage, has a paradoxical consequence. Such questioning is unable to see clearly the political-moral phenomena that must nourish it; a questioning that cannot see these phenomena cannot gain true distance on them, and so risks becoming their slave. The paradox is not mitigated if the servitude is not unwitting but voluntary, as in the case of Heidegger" (Richard Velkley, *Heidegger, Strauss, and the Premises of Philosophy: On Original Forgetting* [Chicago: University of Chicago Press, 2011], 95).

8. One may consult the 1919 KNS course, the 1920 "Comment Karl Jaspers' Psychology of Worldviews," and the 1920–21 course on "Phenomenology of Religious Life." For more extensive discussion, see my *Heidegger and Politics: The Ontology of Radical Discontent* (Cambridge: Cambridge University Press, 2015), chapters 1 and 2.

9. Heidegger, *Pathmarks* (Cambridge: Cambridge University Press, 2010), 4.

10. "It has long been known that ancient ontology works with 'Thing-concepts' and that there is a danger of 'reifying consciousness.' But what does this 'reifying' signify? Where does it arise? Why does Being get 'conceived' 'proximally' in terms of the present-at-hand and not in terms of the ready-to-hand, which indeed lies closer to us? Why does this reifying always keep coming

back to exercise its dominion? What positive structure does the Being of 'consciousness' have, if reification remains inappropriate to it?" Martin Heidegger, *Being and Time* (New York: Harper & Row, 1962), trans. John Macquarrie and Edward Robinson, 437.

11. Ibid., 158; emphasis in original.

12. "Like understanding and interpretation in general, the 'as' is grounded in the ecstatico-horizonal unity of temporality. In our fundamental analysis of Being, and of course in connection with the interpretation of the 'is' (which, as a copula, gives 'expression' to the addressing of something as something), we must again make the phenomenon of the 'as' a theme and delimit the conception of this 'schema' existentially." Ibid., 360.

13. Ibid., 159–160.

14. ". . . the analysis of the temporal Constitution of discourse and the explication of the temporal characteristics of language-patterns can be tackled only if the problem of how Being and truth are connected in principle, is broached in the light of the problematic of temporality. We can then define even the ontological meaning of the 'is,' which a superficial theory of propositions and judgments has deformed to a mere 'copula.' Only in terms of the temporality of discourse—that is, of Dasein in general—can we clarify how 'signification' 'arises' and make the possibility of concept-formation ontologically intelligible" Ibid., 349.

15. Ibid., 156.

16. Ibid., 155.

17. Ibid.

18. Ibid., 158. This part of Heidegger's discussion relates to the fore-structure of understanding; I have abbreviated it for reasons of space.

19. Ibid.; emphasis in original.

20. Ibid.

21. Ibid.

22. Martin Heidegger, *Nietzsche vol. 4* (New York: HarperCollins, 1991), 212.

23. Ibid.

24. Ibid.

25. Ibid., 213.

26. Ibid., 213–214.

27. Ibid., 215.

28. Ibid., 221.

29. Ibid., 250. For a more extended discussion of the promise of nihilism, see Duff 2015, chapter 5.

30. Leo Strauss, *What is Political Philosophy? And Other Essays* (Chicago: University of Chicago Press, 1959), 260.

31. Leo Strauss, *Liberalism: Ancient and Modern* (Chicago: University of Chicago Press, 1968), 235.

32. Leo Strauss and Hans-Georg Gadamer, "Correspondence Concerning *Warheit und Methode*," *Independent Journal of Philosophy* 2 (1978), 7.

33. Leo Strauss, *What is Political Philosophy?*, 260. The present study is limited to a consideration of what Strauss is implying about the comic and laughable in Heidegger's shortcomings. A fuller treatment of Strauss's indication here would explore his suggestion about charity and love, too.

34. Ibid., 259.

35. Leo Strauss, *Rebirth of Classical Political Rationalism* (Chicago: University of Chicago Press, 1989), 107–111.

36. Ibid., 129.

37. "The magnanimous man—the man who regards himself as worthy of great things while in fact being worthy of them—is truthful and frank because he is in the habit of looking down and yet he is ironical in his intercourse with the many. Irony is then the noble dissimulation of one's worth, of one's superiority. We may say, it is the humanity peculiar to the superior man: he spares the feelings of his inferiors by not displaying his superiority. The highest form of superiority is the superiority in wisdom. Irony in the highest sense will then be the dissimulation of one's wisdom, i.e., the dissimulation of one's wise thoughts. This can take two forms: either expressing on a 'wise' subject such thoughts (e.g., generally accepted thoughts) as are less wise than one's own thoughts or refraining from expressing any thoughts regarding a 'wise' subject on the ground that one does not have knowledge regarding it and therefore can only raise questions but cannot give any answers. If irony is essentially related to the fact that there is a natural order of rank among men, it follows that irony consists in speaking differently to different kinds of people." Leo Strauss, *City and Man* (Chicago: University of Chicago Press, 1964), 51.

38. Leo Strauss, *Socrates and Aristophanes* (New York: Basic Books, 1966), 49.

39. "Aristophanes makes us see this audience at its freest and gayest, from its crude and vulgar periphery to its center of sublime delicacy; we do not see it equally well, although we sense it strongly, in its bonds and bounds. We see only half of it, apparently its lower half, in fact its higher. We see only one half of humanity, apparently its lower half, in fact its higher" (Strauss, *Rebirth*, 107).

40. Leo Strauss, "The Problem of Socrates," 333; *Rebirth of Classical Political Rationalism*, 139; *City and Man*, 53.

41. *City and Man*, 53.

42. *Rebirth*, 139.

43. Ibid., 130.

44. Ibid., 109.

45. *City and Man*, 19. For valuable elucidation of this theme in Strauss, see Jeremy Mhire, "What is Really Different about *What is Political Philosophy?*," *Perspectives on Political Science* 40.1 (2011), 54–57.

46. *Rebirth*, 142.

47. *City and Man*, 19.

48. Richard Velkley's singular study locates this aspect of the city, that it is the part of the whole that is open to the whole, when in turn the human is open dually to the whole and to the city, as the source of the distinct unity of Strauss's manifold investigations. *Heidegger, Strauss and Original Forgetting: On the Premises of Philosophy*.

49. *Rebirth*, 142.

50. Cf. Arthur Melzer, *Philosophy Between the Lines* (Chicago: University of Chicago Press, 2017).

51. *City*, 19–20.

52. Ibid., 20.

53. Leo Strauss, "The Problem of Socrates," 325.

54. Heidegger, *Was Heisst Denken?*, 17.

55. Strauss, *Rebirth*, 102.

56. Cf. Stanley Rosen, *Nihilism: A Philosophic Essay* (New Haven: Yale University Press, 1969).

12

The Wheel of History

Nihilism as Moral Protest and Destruction of the Present in Leo Strauss and Albert Camus

Ingrid L. Anderson

> Jacques, dizzy with the rapidity of a victory he had not even hoped would be so complete, could hardly hear the congratulations around him and the already embellished accounts of the fight. He wanted to be glad, and somewhere in the vanity of his ego he was glad, and yet, when he looked back at Munoz as he was leaving the green field, a bleak sadness suddenly seized his heart at the sight of the crestfallen face of the boy he had struck. And then he knew that war was no good, because vanquishing a man is as bitter as being vanquished.
>
> —Albert Camus[1]

> Moderation will protect us from the twin dangers of visionary expectations from politics and unmanly contempt for politics.
>
> —Leo Strauss[2]

Leo Strauss's and Albert Camus' respective methodologies and unique formulations are often so formative for scholars and students that they give rise to special "schools" of thought. "Camusians" and "Straussians" are likely to assume that the philosophies of Strauss and Camus are different in ways that do not promote, or even merit, putting these two thinkers in conversation with one another. We might justifiably argue that Strauss and Camus are not even the same *kind* of thinkers. After all, Camus primarily wrote French works of fiction championed by existentialists and is considered an important twentieth-century moralist. Strauss developed his own brand of philosophical history—written in German and English—and was preoccupied with themes such as esotericism and the ongoing modern project to separate theology from politics. Yet Strauss's 1941 lecture on German nihilism (which remained unpublished until 1999) and Camus' 1951 treatise, *The Rebel*, offer unmistakably similar understandings of the iteration of nihilism that dominated twentieth-century Western thought and politics. Both formulate this nihilism as a resounding "No!" directed toward a justifiably disappointing liberal democracy; it was precisely because interwar German nihilism's "No" was not followed by a succinct, practical, or substantive "Yes" that its effects were so devastating. Perhaps most revealing is their shared assertion that resistance to German nihilism and its successors requires a rediscovery of and renewed adherence to some semblance of absolute universal values, that are not created by the forces of history but identified *in* history as enduring and therefore fundamental.

Strauss's and Camus' analyses of modern political nihilism are profoundly instructive, and illustrate substantively similar understandings of history. In much of his work Strauss sounds the alarm about the prevalence of moral relativism in contemporary Western politics and thought, a phenomenon he identifies as a kind of "positivism" or a worldview that sees "all human thoughts or beliefs [as exclusively] historical."[3] Strauss argues implicitly in "German Nihilism"—and explicitly elsewhere—that human beings surely accept some semblance of universal or absolute moral standards to which we adhere when we are at our best. Belief in an enduring universal moral code that transcends politics and dogma and sustains us as a species during periods of intense factionalism is among Camus' definitive concerns, as well. Among his better-known works on this matter is *The Plague*, in which the Algerian town of Oran is beset with a bubonic plague epidemic of medieval proportions. For Camus, ethical absolutes are what enable an atheist scientist and a deuteronomistic priest to work together to stave off the ravenous annihilation caused by the resurgent plague for the survival of their town. As Doctor Rieux and Father Paneloux struggle against the toxic allure of the pointless destruction wrought by the plague it is only by working together, and by deriving shared meaning from their partnerships with others, that the plague is vanquished. Camus makes it clear that the plague in Oran (and elsewhere) is only in remission, and will come again in the future.

Mid-twentieth-century nihilism, a unique and virulent but recognizable strain of its earlier iterations, was even an important focus of Camus' 1957 Nobel Prize acceptance speech:

> Nobody, I think, can ask them[4] to be optimists. And I even think that we should understand—without ceasing to fight it—the error of those who in an excess of despair have asserted their right to dishonour and have rushed into the nihilism of the era.[5] But the fact remains that most of us, in my country[6] and in Europe, have refused this nihilism and have engaged upon a quest for legitimacy. They have had to forge for themselves an art of living in times of catastrophe in order to be born a second time and to fight openly against the instinct of death at work in our history.[7]

It is worth noting that for Camus it is not enough to fight against that form of nihilism that shouts "No!" without offering a "Yes." We also need to understand it. For Camus, the impulse toward nihilism is as intrinsic to humanity as any primal instinct; better we should understand it than fail to address it, to recognize that it is a kind of hunger that must be sated rather than allow its appetite to destroy us all.

It is likely that Strauss and Camus each adapted their formulations of nihilism from the work of Friedrich Nietzsche, which both men admired, bemoaned, and engaged with deeply. They both mourned what they considered a lack of foresight and a disturbing absence of concern on Nietzsche's part regarding the ease with which his project could be misused. As Strauss asserted in "German Nihilism," no other thinker "was more responsible for the emergence of German nihilism, than was Nietzsche . . . [and] by interpreting Nietzsche in the light of the German revolution, one is very unjust to Nietzsche, but one is not *absolutely* unjust."[8] In 1951, Camus similarly insists:

> If Nietzsche and Hegel serve as alibis to the masters of Dachau and Karaganda, that does not condemn their entire philosophy. But it does lead to the suspicion that one aspect of their thought, or of their logic, can lead to these appalling conclusions.[9]

As many scholars and biographers have pointed out, the rift between Camus and other well-known left-wing philosophers of the time, such as Jean-Paul Sartre and Simone de Beauvoir, was primarily political. While Sartre and de Beauvoir became increasingly committed to communism in the years following World War II, Camus expressed a growing disgust with political dogma in general and an intensified suspicion of communism in particular. The primary source of his objection was the increasingly common justification of violence in revolutionary movements whose stated end goal was the achievement of collective human freedom. For Camus, the problems inherent in this formulation manifested themselves most poignantly in the Algerian revolution. His statements about Arab Algerian nationalist movements and subsequent French attempts to destroy them are well known. Many left-wingers could never forgive Camus for claiming that "At this moment, bombs are being planted in the trams in Algiers. My mother could be on one of those trams. If that is justice, I prefer my mother."[10] Iconic postcolonial theorist Edward Said, for example, considered Camus a "colonialist sympathizer" in part due to statements such as these. Camus' exasperated statement about the ease with which humans often pervert justice both in theory and in practice for the sake of political dogma is not the only evidence of his thinking on the Algerian revolution specifically and revolution more broadly to which we have access. But even if it were, it would still be reductive to label Camus a "sympathizer" with French colonialism.

Yet responses to Camus' work are frequently reductive. After all, he was a white Algerian, a *pied noir* who spent many of his adult years living in provincial France, and during the Algerian uprising Camus refused to align himself with communist sympathizers who supported Algerian nationalism. It would be easy to ignore the nuances and singularities in his thinking and simply miscast him as a well-camouflaged colonialist. But he also insisted that French colonialism was an evil system that corrupted colonized and colonizer alike. He insisted that native Algerians deserved equal rights, and *pied noirs* like his mother and that millions of others were *also* native Algerians. How could displacing either population as a means of correcting the wrongs of French colonialism truly address the problems at hand in Algeria? Neither of the existing approaches to such conflicts were "just" because they ignored the undeniable reality of the existence of the *pied noir*, many of whom were (like Camus' deaf and nearly mute mother) members of the working poor. Camus' concerns about the Algerian revolution expose the complex nature of his identity *and* his thought; he was both an establishment figure and an undisputed outsider. Perhaps he said it best himself when he wrote of his fictionalized *doppelgänger* in *The First Man*, "What they did not like in him was the Algerian."[11]

As Jennifer Renee Stanford points out, interpretations and applications of Strauss's thought are also frequently reductive. According to Stanford this is partly because his work did not have a "concrete political plan" like that of Marx or Engels, but the term "Straussian" is nonetheless politically and intellectually charged. Leora Batnitzky asserts that many unjustifiably consider Strauss the "intellectual godfather of the neoconservative political movement," and that adherents of this idea primarily arrive at this claim about Strauss's personal political beliefs from his work on esotericism, which is admittedly easy to vulgarize. No other aspect of Strauss's thinking has been as "hotly contested as his claims about esotericism." Batnitzky notes:

> Interpretations of Strauss's view of esotericism include: that Strauss advocates clandestine cabals with secrets imparted from teacher to disciple; that Strauss's writings are themselves esoteric documents; that Strauss thinks that all thinkers write esoterically; that Strauss claims to know a secret; that Strauss promoted mass deception and perpetual war; and that, in one particularly crude rendering, Strauss used his esoteric methods to hide his fascist sympathies, if not his secret Nazism.[12]

Batnitzky is right when she calls these interpretations of Strauss's work "fundamentally problematic"; they are quite frankly a waste of time, since they at the very least willfully miss—by many miles—the complexity of Strauss's work.

As Steven B. Smith argues, "Strauss bequeathed not a single legacy, but a number of competing legacies. It is a gross distortion to retrofit Strauss' teachings to conform to the political Right."[13] For Smith, the claim that Strauss exempted philosophers from moral principles "applicable to the rest of humanity" is likewise unfounded. Smith, who studied under self-avowed Straussians, admits that some of Strauss's students have indeed been "hardcore Right." Yet he contends that "Strauss's politics, such as they were, had more in common with cold-war liberals of his generation . . . than with any of the major conservatives of the same period . . . [and for Strauss] the freedom of an educated mind [is the] best antidote to the pathologies of modern mass politics."[14] Strauss's work on German nihilism indicates that his greatest worry was the advent of National Socialism. But he also wanted to expose what he felt were the "shaky foundations" of the goals of liberalism, including its steadfast belief in the inevitability of linear progress. These concerns are not incompatible, although, admittedly, it is a rare philosopher who expresses both concerns with marked fervor. That Strauss continued to address both these problems as potential dangers to society made his work easy to misappropriate; and, for some, his intentions somewhat mysterious. Yet, as Smith points out, Strauss fretted openly about the steady erosion of democracy "into a form of mass culture . . . a culture manipulated by marketing techniques and other forms of commercial propaganda." Our best approach to preventing this steady decline, in Strauss's opinion, was the "counterpoison" of liberal education.[15] It is not surprising that some clues to what Strauss meant by "liberal education" can be found in his analysis of German nihilism, as we shall soon see.

Strauss's work on German nihilism continues to be relevant to us today, and deserves more than the kind of reductionist approach many use to understand Strauss. Like Camus, Strauss eventually became an establishment thinker. After all, he was a celebrated tenured professor at the University of Chicago whose teaching appears to have permanently impacted many of the people who studied with him. Yet as a German Jew who had misgivings about the feasibility of Enlightenment claims about history and the nature of man, he was also undeniably an outsider. After all, what kind of German Jew takes issue with the very political movement that permitted him to attend a secular university, live wherever he pleased, and take a position as a philosopher in a Western university? Clearly, Strauss challenges more than just our unexamined assumptions about the nature of philosophy.

Strauss's misgivings about the ultimate success of Enlightenment-inspired secular government were multifarious, and were likely derived from personal experience as well as from serious study. Among the claims made by proponents of the Enlightenment to which Strauss objected was that the movement was secular in nature; and that, under its banner, Jews and other religious minorities could find emancipation and an end to legal discrimination. Strauss contended that whether or not Enlightenment ideals were perceived as informed by Christianity they most undoubtedly were; and that while Jews were offered access to full citizenship (in exchange for traditional Jewish practice and culture), anti-Semitism would not and did not abate, but rather changed its form. Regarding the Jews of Europe, the Enlightenment's laudable reverence for science was misused to racialize what was once theological: the hatred of Jewishness and the criminalization of Jews. For Strauss, Europe's failure to understand itself as primarily *culturally* Christian led to as many problems as the Enlightenment's failure to provide an account of its value that was not simply a character assassination of "traditional" values and ways of knowing. This aspect of Strauss's misgivings about the Enlightenment—less well known than his related objections to "historicism" and "positivism," for example—is critical to understanding the depth and breadth of his insights into European political and philosophical history. Sadly, as it turns out, Strauss was right to mistrust Enlightenment promises about the end of anti-Semitism in Europe.

Like Camus, Strauss begins from the premise that nihilism must first be understood as a response to real problems that nihilists feel extant political systems fail to address. Despite his penchant for universal absolutes, Strauss undeniably understood that human beings—including philosophers—are in some way limited by their social realities, and that the "objectivity" so prized by the Enlightenment was not in fact objective. He nonetheless attempted to identify characteristics that might be definitive of the human condition, and not merely products of historical time and place.

In 1938, Strauss was one of 180 refugees sponsored by the University in Exile at the New School—later called the Graduate Faculty of Political and Social Science. The program was created as a response to the threat posed to European scholarship by National Socialism, and Strauss stood out among his fellow émigrés because of his more conservative views.[16] Strauss taught and published while employed in this program until 1949, and gave his public lectures on German historicism and German nihilism in 1941. In them he insists repeatedly that German nihilism began as a *moral* movement, and should not be considered a mental disease or a form of "absolute nihilism" (that is, per Strauss, a nihilism that wishes to also destroy itself):

> That moral meaning of modern civilization to which the German nihilists object, is expressed in formulations such as these: to relieve man's estate; or: to safeguard the rights of man; or: the greatest possible happiness of the greatest possible number. What is the motive underlying the protest against modern civilisation, against the spirit of the West, and in

> particular of the Anglo-Saxon West? The answer must be: it is a moral protest. That protest proceeds from the conviction that the internationalism inherent in modern civilisation, or, more precisely, that the establishment of a perfectly open society which is as it were the goal of modem civilisation, and therefore all aspirations directed toward that goal, are irreconcilable with the basic demands of moral life. That protest proceeds from the conviction that the root of all moral life is essentially and therefore eternally the closed society; from the conviction that the open society is bound to be, if not immoral, at least amoral: the meeting ground of seekers of pleasure, of gain, of irresponsible power, indeed of any kind of irresponsibility and lack of seriousness.[17]

It follows, according to Strauss, that for the German nihilist Western societies that aspire to openness are really closed societies in decline. Strauss asserts that the passionate desire to rescue a perceived "endangered morality" is not *in itself* nihilistic, and post–World War I German nihilism is not dangerous or unique because of its zealous fixation on morality. Rather, it is dangerous because it is unable to succinctly identify what it wants to build in place of the present world that it aims to destroy. This is not the kind of nihilism Strauss associates with Nietzsche directly; he sees it as the result of a misreading of Nietzsche, or an understanding of morality and power that departs from Nietzsche's precisely because it cannot see *past* the abhorrent flaws of society and *toward* anything more than sibylline prediction.

According to Camus, Nietzsche made nihilism "sound prophetic," like a beginning and an end in itself. Per Camus, Nietzsche always saw the apocalypse just over the horizon, and did not "extol" it but rather hoped to "transform it into a renaissance."[18] According to this line of thinking, birth must be preceded by destruction; transformation requires the loss of *something*. "To raise a new sanctuary," Camus writes, "a sanctuary must be destroyed, that is the law."[19] This state of affairs—the destruction of the old sanctuary—is of course the result of Nietzsche's claim that God is dead, and with Him all sources of morality external to human kind. In Camus' own words, Nietzsche argued that "this rebellion on the part of men [in declaring God dead] could not lead to a renaissance unless it was controlled and directed."[20] The very idea of imposing a direction implies that law or at least judgment is necessary: not *this*, but *that*. For

Camus, it follows that "Nietzsche enlists values in the cause of nihilism which, traditionally, have been considered as restraints on nihilism—principally morality."[21] After all, Camus contends, "a nihilist is not one who believes in nothing, but one who does not believe in what exists."[22] And is this not a judgment, based in some way on a set of values presented as superior to those offered by the old sanctuary? "If chance is king," Camus muses, "then there is nothing but the step in the dark and the appalling freedom of the blind."[23]

Camus remarks that it is toward this very impasse that Nietzsche drives his nihilism, "where it is no longer possible to say what is black and what is white." In fact Nietzsche "rushes [to this point] . . . with a kind of frightful joy."[24] As Camus understands it, Nietzsche's "only hope seems to be to arrive at the extremity of contradiction. Then if man does not wish to perish in the coils that strangle him, he will have to cut them at a single blow and create his own values."[25] But what if man does not create what amounts to values? What if a clear "Yes!" does not follow the resounding, sanctuary-razing "No"?

For Camus, this metaphysical need, which animates the rejection of "the now"—in Strauss's terms, the passionate desire to protect an endangered morality—*is* universal. Camus admits to an underlying sympathy to the very movements he opposes, including communism and fascism because, as Ronald Aronson suggests, "he [Camus] and they share the same starting points, outlook, stresses, and pitfalls." Ultimately, "those he disagrees with are no less and no more than fellow creatures who give into the same fundamental drive to escape absurdity that we all share."[26] In Camus' own words:

> metaphysical rebellion and nihilism have witnessed the persistent reappearance, under different guises, of the same ravaged countenance: the face of human protest. All of them, decrying the human condition and its creator, have affirmed the solitude of man and the nonexistence of any kind of morality. But at the same time, they have all tried to construct a purely terrestrial kingdom where their chosen principles will hold sway.[27]

In other words, the rebellion that succeeds in annihilating what *is* will always be confronted by the need for new institutionalized principles. Again, "to destroy an old sanctuary, a sanctuary is required."

Camus certainly embraces the impulses and the observations of the metaphysical rebel. But for him, the force that wills the destruction of the conditions that impose subjugation must categorically understand itself as finite. Such violence cannot go on without end—or one ends up with no sanctuary at all, only rubble. Just as Camus does, Strauss sees National Socialism (what he felt was the most base expression of German nihilism) and communism as fundamentally in disagreement about the nature of history. For young people drawn to National Socialism—or rather, as Strauss might formulate it, young people opposed to communism—the primary objection to communism was not its claim that the state of things was deplorable. They objected to the historical argument communism embraced—that human progress was inevitable, and that history should be seen as marching toward an ultimate, ideal end.

Interestingly, Strauss notes that most young nihilists before World War I were leftists. Conversely, the young people coming of age in Germany after the Great War were not leftists but hard-right German nationalists. The education received by these young people, Strauss contends, did not offer what they most needed: "teachers who could explain to them in articulate language the positive, and not merely destructive meaning of their aspirations."[28] Perhaps even more importantly, the old guard, the "great authorities of modern civilization . . . did not even *try* to understand the [young nihilist's] ardent passion underlying the negation of the present world and its potentialities."[29] For both Strauss and Camus, this unwillingness to understand the "ardent passion" of the rebel is often the establishment's first and greatest mistake. In the 1941 lecture, Strauss interestingly suggests that these young nihilists needed what he called "old fashioned teachers, such old fashioned teachers of course as would be undogmatic enough to understand the aspirations of their pupils."[30] For Strauss, such aspirations—the destruction of "the now" in order to make way for a more just system—are eternal, but we must be taught how to channel, temper, and guide this passion so that it is not merely a tool of demolition.

So what *content* might Strauss have taught these ardent German youth—his peers, really—if given the chance? We likely would hesitate to venture a guess. But insight into how Strauss himself might have understood the relation between history and universality might offer some clues. Strauss sought, in his own words, a "universal structure common to all historical worlds." In his 1957 lecture, "On the Interpretation of Genesis," Strauss states:

> We might say, what we truly know are not any answers to comprehensive questions but only . . . [to] questions imposed upon us as human beings by our situation as human beings. This presupposes that there is a fundamental situation of man as man which is not affected by any change, any so-called historical change in particular. It is man's fundamental situation within the whole—within a whole that is so little subject to historical change that it is a condition of every possible historical change.[31]

And what does Camus say about history and the human condition? In his concluding chapter of *The Rebel*, Camus proposes:

> There does exist for man . . . a way of acting and of thinking which is possible on the level of moderation to which he belongs. Every undertaking that is more ambitious than this proves to be contradictory. The absolute is not attained nor, above all, created through history. Politics is not religion, or if it is, then it is nothing but the Inquisition. How would society define an absolute? Perhaps everyone is looking for this absolute on behalf of all. But society and politics only have the responsibility of arranging everyone's affairs so that each will have the leisure and the freedom to pursue this common search. History can then no longer be presented as an object of worship. It is only an opportunity that must be rendered fruitful by a vigilant rebellion.[32]

Both Strauss and Camus reject teleological understandings of history that posit a final cause or destination for human societies. Camus' objection to making history an "object of worship" is also a refusal of any dogma that requires or encourages the rote processing of philosophical and political phenomena: history does not unfold without us, or carry us along to our destined end. In fact, "the absolute," the philosophical or political ideals toward which impassioned rebels often gallop, do not manifest themselves whole cloth unless moderation is abandoned; without moderation, rebellion—sometimes in spite of itself—becomes totalitarianism, the end of human freedom. Moderation is the tool with which we can actualize the fundamentally human desire to destroy one sanctuary and raise another.

Strauss, too, sees moral protest expressed in rebellion as innate to the human condition, an impulse that if tempered by education can bear real fruit. History comes out of our largely unchanging human "condition" or nature. In other words, history is what we make it and is contingent on ourselves as ourselves. What remains constant—or eternal, if you will—are the questions we ask. Improvements in society, politics, and the like occur only to be reversed once more by the limitations of our species. In a very real sense, history is not so much a wheel as it is a gear that turns in its reliable but redundant way. Perhaps it is, as Strauss's Greeks claimed, that "the contemplation of heaven . . . is the ground by which we are led in the right conduct. True knowledge . . . is knowledge of what is always."[33] Strauss's philosopher gazes ever upward, even as the gears beneath him turn. We can recall here Camus' Sisyphus, whose repetitive labors are as certain as the sunrise; Sisyphus is eternally bound to watch his work undo itself at the end of each day. His life is bound to the endless rotation of a single gear turning in a vast expanse filled with other endlessly turning gears. And yet, for Camus, "the struggle toward the heights is enough to fill a man's heart."[34] We cannot forget Sisyphus's smile.

Notes

1. Albert Camus, *The First Man*. Trans. David Hopgood (New York: Vintage Books, 1995), 155.

2. Leo Strauss, *Liberalism Ancient and Modern* (New York: Basic Books, 1968), 24.

3. Leo Strauss, *Natural Right and History*, 25.

4. Here Camus refers to the men and women of his generation who were young adults at the onset of World War II.

5. Camus is likely referring to the demands of France's postwar political left to prosecute and hang all known French fascists and Nazi collaborators for treason.

6. Camus is from Algeria, which was still a colony of France in 1957.

7. Albert Camus, "Banquet Speech at the City Hall in Stockholm," December 10, 1957. www.nobelprize.org

8. Leo Strauss, "German Nihilism," eds. David Janssens and Daniel Tanguay. *Interpretation: A Journal of Political Philosophy* 26, no. 3: 372.

9. Albert Camus, *The Rebel: An Essay On Man in Revolt*. Trans. Anthony Bower (New York: Alfred A. Knopf, 1984), 145–146.

10. Peter Beaumont, "Albert Camus, the outsider, is still dividing opinion in Algeria 50 years after his death," *The Guardian*, February 20, 2010.

11. Camus, *The First Man*, 326.

12. Leora Batnitzky, "Leo Strauss: Controversies," *Stanford Encyclopedia of Philosophy*, 2016.

13. Steven B. Smith, *Reading Leo Strauss: Politics, Philosophy, Judaism* (Chicago: Chicago University Press, 2006), 4.

14. Ibid., 15.

15. Ibid., 14.

16. Notable fellows from the 1938–1939 academic year are pacifist Jewish Viennese filmmaker Carl Mayer, Catholic anti-Nazi activist Ernst Karl Winter, and Jewish Austro-Hungarian Max Wertheimer, one of the three founders of Gestalt psychology. For a more complete list of fellows as well as a partial list of course offerings for this year, see the *New School for Social Research*, "The Graduate Faculty of Political Social Science Supplementary Bulletin, 1938–1939," New School for Social Research: New York, 66 West Twelfth Street.

17. Strauss, "German Nihilism," 357–358.

18. Albert Camus, *The Rebel: An Essay on Man in Revolt*. Trans. Anthony Bower (New York: Alfred A. Knopf, 1984), 74–75.

19. Ibid.

20. Ibid., 77–78.

21. Ibid., 75–76.

22. Ibid., 78.

23. Ibid., 80.

24. Ibid., 80.

25. Ibid., 80.

26. Ronald Aronson, "Albert Camus: Philosopher of the Present," *Stanford Encyclopedia of Philosophy*, 2017.

27. Camus, 109.

28. Strauss, "German Nihilism," 52.

29. Ibid.

30. Ibid., 51.

31. Leo Strauss, "On the Interpretation of Genesis," in *Leo Strauss, Jewish Philosophy and the Crisis of Modernity*, ed. Kenneth Hart Green (Albany, NY: SUNY Press, 1997), 361.

32. Camus, *The Rebel*, 311.

33. Strauss, Leo. "On the Interpretation of Genesis," 91.

34. Camus, Albert. "The Myth of Sisyphus," *The Myth of Sisyphus and Other Essays*. Trans. Justin O'Brien (New York: Vintage International, 1991), 135.

13

Who's Laughing?

Leo Strauss on Comedy and Mockery

Menachem Feuer

> The same thing can be said of the Thracian maidservant who exercised her wit at the expense of Thales, when he was looking up to study the stars and tumbled down a well. She scoffed at him for being so eager to know what was happening in the sky that he could not see what lay at his feet. Anyone who gives his life to philosophy is open to mockery. . . . His terrible clumsiness makes him seem so stupid. . . . So in his helplessness he looks like a fool.
>
> —*Theatetus* 174b–d

> I divine, he said, that you are considering whether we shall admit tragedy and comedy into our city or not. Perhaps, said I, and perhaps even more than that.
>
> —*Republic* III 393d

> No, if we convalescents still need art, it is another kind of art—a mocking, light, fleeting, divinely untroubled art that, like a pure flame, licks into unclouded skies. Above all, an art for artists, for artists only!
>
> —*Gay Science*, 37

Leo Strauss is not known for his views on comedy or humor. When scholars think of Strauss, they think only of his most serious works and ideas: his celebrated exploration of the Jerusalem/Athens distinction, his esoteric "literary" reading of Maimonides, and his influential writings on political philosophy. None of the above-mentioned accounts appears to include any mention of comedy or humor. But amidst all of the serious philosophizing and reflection, one will in fact find a series of important and perhaps foundational reflections on comedy and humor. Attention to Strauss's observations on the differing uses and divergent meanings of humor and comedy may prompt us to think differently about the meaning and place of comedy in his work. To initiate this reflection, I will explore three important moments in Strauss's reflections on comedy and humor: (1) his discussion of Aristophanes and Socrates; (2) his investigation of Enlightenment mockery and the arguments of the ancients; (3) his analysis of Nietzsche's notion of greatness (and its relationship to mockery) and the Jewish tradition of extreme humility (and its relationship to comedy).

Strauss shows us (via these three readings) that comedy has an ambiguous meaning that can be drawn on by or against a community. It has been the weapon of both community and tradition on the one hand, and modernity and Enlightenment on the other. As Strauss suggests, the city and its opponents need comedy and mockery to justify themselves; they don't need reasoning. Strauss shows us how humor and comedy can disclose both the bonds of the community and the hopes of those who, like Enlightenment thinkers or like Nietzsche, want to leave it behind for new, unknown and uncharted horizons. Strauss's most important claim about comedy and mockery is that new thinking in general, and Jewish philiosophy in particular, can begin (again, and today) only once they expose the meaning and limits of mockery for the ancients, the Enlightenment thinkers, and for ourselves. After founding the new beginning for Jewish philosophy—based on an exposure to the relationship between mockery and greatness on the one hand, and mockery and humility on the other—Strauss suggests we *can* understand comedy and humor in terms of two ways of being (or as Strauss would say, ways of life) in the modern era that pass between two cities: Jerusalem and Athens.

The problem for us, then, is to figure out the place of mockery, humor, and comical humility in or between these two cities. Strauss suggests that Spinoza's, and more generally the Enlightenment's notion of mockery needs to be unmasked as covering up the problem of Athens and Jerusalem. But does comedy—in contrast to the via fides, the via contemplativa and the mockery that conceals the problem of Athens and Jerusalem—offer a third way of life that draws on both cities, either through Nietzsche's overman; through a kind of comical, secular knowledge (rather than Nietzsche's Greek-inspired reading of "tragic knowledge") that challenges modern optimism (which Strauss argues has its roots in Socrates); or a kind of humble comical faith? Each of these possible "third ways"—for lack of a better term—suggests that our discussion of Jerusalem and Athens in Strauss's work is nourished by and can be understood in terms of a kind of humility that is comical, not tragic.

Two Versions of Socrates: Strauss on Aristophanes and Humor

Strauss agreed with Nietzsche that the focal point of modernity is the "problem of Socrates." Everything turns around it. To demonstrate the central ancient Greek argument that gave birth to this problem, Strauss looks at two versions of Socrates. In his introduction to *Socrates and Aristophanes*, Strauss discusses two versions of Socrates: the young and the old—the former offered by Aristophanes and the latter by Plato. The subject that concerns both Plato and Aristophanes, albeit for different reasons, is the meaning of comedy and of tragedy. Their common concern, as Strauss demonstrates, pits the poet against the philosopher. Strauss looks at this difference in terms of the poet and his relationship with the community (or city) and Socrates's indifference to it:

> One may say that the Socrates presented by Plato . . . agreed entirely with Aristophanes' judgment on the Socrates presented by the comic poet. Aristophanes and Socrates meet before our eyes in Plato's Banquet (Symposium) about seven years after the performance of the *Clouds*. The occasion was a banquet at the end of which only three men were still awake and sober, two of them being Aristophanes and Socrates. At the time the three were engaged in a friendly conversation that ended in an agreement about a subject of the greatest importance to Aristophanes, the subject of comedy and tragedy; Aristophanes agreed to a view propounded by Socrates. In the only Platonic presentation of Aristophanes, the poet appears to be very close to Socrates. From this fact we may understand the Platonic Socrates' analysis of the state of the soul at comedies. In that analysis we discern this strand. The state of the soul at comedies is a mixture of being pleased by our friends' innocuous overestimation of their wisdom and

> being pained by envy; that state of the soul is never free from injustice . . . Far from being the enemy of Socrates, Aristophanes was his friend, but somewhat envious of his wisdom—even the wisdom of the young Socrates. Or, as one might also say, the primary object of the comic poet's envy was not Socrates' wisdom but his sovereign contempt for that popular applause on which the dramatic poet necessarily depends, or Socrates' perfect freedom.[1]

Strauss elaborates this difference: "The philosopher is necessarily ridiculous in the eyes of the multitude and therefore a natural subject for comedy."[2] Even though Aristophanes depicts Socrates as the subject of laughter, Strauss argues that he has deeper concerns that touch on the meaning of justice:

> He is as much concerned with saying serious things as he is with saying laughable ones. Being a poet, he is concerned with making men in cities good and noble; being a comic poet, he is concerned with concealing vice, i.e., with depriving vice of its attraction by ridiculing it. Acting in accordance with justice he teaches things that are good for the city, or he takes the risk of saying among the Athenians what is justice; but being a comic poet he cannot do this except by treating the just things themselves comically. Goodness and justice fight on his side. He is indeed as much concerned with the approval of the laughers as with that of the wise. But does this not imply that those who love or admire him because he makes them laugh are a class distinct from his wise lovers and admirers? We are surely entitled to assume that his presentation of Socrates also serves, and perhaps above all, the teaching of justice—perhaps of defending justice against Socrates' attack on it by presenting Socrates as ridiculous.[3]

Comedy, in this sense, has the purpose of "teaching" and "defending" justice. Philosophy, embodied in the figure of Socrates, apparently poses a threat to the city and justice. After making this point in the introduction to his book on Aristophanes and Socrates, Strauss brings in Nietzsche who, as Strauss well knew, took tragedy, comedy, and mockery seriously and—more often than not—sided with the pre-Socratics against Plato. Strauss argues that Plato's sketch of Socrates—vis-à-vis Aristophanes—is "preparatory" for understanding what Nietzsche called the "problem of Socrates."[4] The questions that beset the poet (who came first) at the onset of philosophy's incursion into the "great tradition" are about Socrates (the first "thinker," as Aristotle would say, of the West, since he asked the question "ti esti?"—"what is it?").[5] Is philosophy the right or wrong way of life for one who dwells in the city and amidst the gods? Does the comic poet or the philosopher have the right reading of Socrates? Does the life guided by phronesis matter more than the life guided by theoria? We need to ask these questions again because of Nietzsche.

Strauss clarifies when he argues that the "return to the origins of the Great Tradition" have become "necessary" in response to "a questioning that may be said to culminate in Nietzsche's attack on Socrates or Plato."[6] Socrates was the "single turning point and vortex of so-called world history" and this happened "within the context" of Nietzsche's concern with the "science of aesthetics."[7] Strauss's reading of comedy—he seems to suggest—should be read within this "science of aesthetics": "According to the suggestions of *Beyond Good and Evil*, it belongs to the context of a historical physiopsychology."[8] But while Nietzsche often writes about laughter (see below), Strauss notes that the main aesthetic of concern to Nietzsche—in which we find the "peak of man"—"found its expression" not in comedy but "in Greek tragedy."[9] This "tragic understanding of the world"—the poetic understanding, if you will—was "rejected or destroyed by Socrates."[10] This effacement of the "tragic understanding" is what makes Socrates—in Nietzsche's eyes—"questionable."

Strauss, miming Nietzsche, argues that Socrates is the "first theoretical man, the incarnation of the spirit of science, radically unartistic or a-music."[11] Strauss calls Socrates "the prototype of the rationalist and therefore the optimist, for optimism is not merely the belief that the world is the best possible world, but also the belief that the world can become the best of all imaginable worlds, or that the evils that belong to the best possible world can be rendered harmless by knowledge: thinking can not only fully understand being, but can even correct it."[12] The tragic, pessimistic understanding of the human condition is displaced not by a comic understanding but a theoretical understanding. And this creates another problem: the problem of universalism.

Strauss, like Nietzsche, sees the "contemporary West" as the "full and ultimate consequence of the change effected or represented by Socrates: in the belief in universal enlightenment and therewith in the early happiness of all within a universal state, in utilitarianism, liberalism, democracy, pacifism, and socialism."[13] However, Nietzsche's insight is that in modernity the "time of Socratic man has gone," and now there is a "hope for a future beyond the peak of pre-Socratic culture, for a philosophy of the future that is no longer merely theoretical, but knowingly based on acts of the will or on decisions, and for a new kind of politics" that is merciless.[14] In other words, Nietzsche doesn't want to go back to a tragic understanding so much as to a "philosophy of the future . . . based on acts of the will," not theory. If the tragic understanding is behind us, does comedy correlate with these "acts of the will"?

While Strauss agrees with Nietzsche that we are now in a period in which we are passing from theoretical man to a new kind of philosophy that is "knowingly based on acts of will" rather than on reason, he slights Nietzsche's classic work on tragedy (*The Birth of Tragedy*) for being "almost silent about comedy."[15] Nietzsche "uses Aristophanes's critique of the young Socrates as if it had been meant as a critique of the Platonic Socrates."[16] What hasn't been properly assessed in Nietzsche—as Strauss suggests in his observation of the content of The Birth of Tragedy—is the relationship of comedy to justice and the city. What *hasn't* been addressed by Strauss in these readings—that which underlies most of Nietzsche's discourse—is Nietzsche's use of mockery. This omission is odd since, as most readers of Nietzsche knows, mockery is Nietzsche's hallmark.[17]

Most of Nietzsche's aphorisms are dedicated—through "acts of the will"—to defeating his opponents through mockery, not argument. Strauss's reading of Aristophanes must be, as he himself suggests above, coupled with his reading of Nietzsche. Let's take a closer look at his reading of Aristophanes and the relationship of the poet to the community and justice, as this may help us to understand the place of comedy in his work. We must do this before we can see what is at stake in Nietzsche's overthrow of the Socratic "theoretical man." In this reading, we can find another way of interpreting comedy that is more in tune with the community (city) and tradition than in disharmony with them. This is what Strauss called the "problem of Socrates."

Reading Aristophanes—Reading Socrates

At the outset of the first essay in his book on Aristophanes and Socrates, Strauss focuses on how Aristophanes, in *The Clouds*, presents Socrates as the subject of comedy:

> Aristophanes presents Socrates as saying and doing many laughable things; he makes him a laughingstock. Yet he surely does the same with all his characters, at least to all of his important characters, regardless of whether they stand for the new ways or the old. The old-fashioned is no less laughable, no less unreasonable, than the newfangled. Following this thought to its conclusion, one might say that Aristophanes celebrates everywhere the triumph of unreason and madness. Yet he surely does nothing of this kind in the *Clouds*. While his laughable Lysistrate, for instance, is victorious, is laughable, Socrates is defeated: A former disciple burns down Socrates' schoolhouse, and it is only lucky or by a laughable accident that Socrates and his disciples do not perish in the flames. Socrates has been responsible for the victory of Unjust Speech over Just Speech, and he has asserted that "Zeus is not." Surely making that assertion was a capital crime; what happens to him is too little for someone who has committed a capital crime, but it is the utmost that could befall him in a comedy.[18]

Strauss gives a very close reading of the play and makes several observations regarding the "Just and Unjust Speeches" made for and against Socrates:

> Like the Unjust Speech, he is characterized by daring and cleverness (wisdom); continence and endurance, as distinguished from moderation, are required for the study of the things aloft. Above all, Socrates' way of life differs from the ways recommended by the two Speeches because the latter are based on the premise, vouched for by the poets, that the gods lead a life of bliss, whereas Socrates holds that the gods do not even exist; even if they did exist, he would not have taken them as his model because of their childishness as shown by their indifference to learning. In the Socratic scheme the debate between the Speeches is only a stage in the ascent toward the right life: The Unjust Speech is, as it were, the self-destruction of justice as supported by the gods. The Socratic way of life is supported neither by the gods, nor by the orators and tragic poets, nor by the majority. . . . Therefore it is indefensible from the point of view of Aristophanes.[19]

Socrates is not interested in the city. He does not have any "awareness of his dependence on the city."[20] He doesn't show the "slightest sense of civic responsibility."

> He has the defect of the pure theoretician; he lacks phronesis; he has not reflected on the context of his own being . . . Owing to his lack of phronesis he cannot imitate life properly . . . Thanks to his mastery of the art of speaking, he is indeed beyond the reach of the law, or the law qua speech is at his mercy. Nothing is sacred for him because nothing can withstand his logos; but he forgets the power of that alogon which is the basis of the family and hence the city; he forgets the fact that he is at the mercy of force, of superior force, or that force that is the ultima ratio, the ultimate logos of the city.[21]

Given all of these negative—from the view of the city—traits, what is so comic about Socrates? Strauss answers and swings the discussion around to Socrates as a "comical subject":

> What makes Socrates a comical subject is, on the lowest level, the fact that his looks, his deportment, and his way of life he differs strikingly from everyone else without these differences being manifest i.e., generally recognized, superiorities on his part; more specifically, Socrates is a comic subject because of his lack of prudence. . . . There is a story of Hegel's preferring the company of a particularly stupid man to that of others; this preference was wittily explained as due to Hegel's not understanding that man. Surely Socrates does not understand Strepisades (the main character of the *Clouds* who is corrupt, according to the city) or see him as he is.[22]

In other words, Socrates can't see or act as other people in the community—with phronesis—can. And that is, in the eyes of the community, laughable. This reading is echoed in Plato's reading of the Thracian maidservant in the *Theatetus*:

> The same thing can be said of the Thracian maidservant who exercised her wit at the expense of Thales, when he was

> looking up to study the stars and tumbled down a well. She scoffed at him for being so eager to know what was happening in the sky that he could not see what lay at his feet. Anyone who gives his life to philosophy is open to mockery. . . . His terrible clumsiness makes him seem so stupid. . . . So in his helplessness he looks like a fool.[23]

Be that as it may, Strauss is not satisfied with the reading of Socrates in *The Clouds*. While it does give the outlines of Socrates as a comic character, it doesn't fully answer Strauss's main question: "Is he (Socrates) a comic equivalent of Aristophanes who, perhaps also charmed or instructed by Socrates, also accepts only a part of the Socratic teaching?"[24] Strauss avers that "The answer to our question depends decisively on whether Aristophanes can be presumed to have agreed with Socrates regarding the gods."[25] Based on this observation, Strauss turns to Aristophanes's other comedies that include, each in its own way, reflections on "the gods, viz, family and city, pleasure and justice, nature and convention, the ancient and the novel, the Muses, and father-beating."[26]

After going through several plays, Strauss concludes that he is astonished at how much "the poet's judgment of Socrates would be identical with his judgment of sophists and philosophers in general."[27] Stated bluntly, "*Aristophanes' presentation of Socrates is the most important document available to us on the ancient disagreement and opposition between poetry and philosophy as such—between the two forms of wisdom, each of which claims supremacy—as this feud appears from the side of poetry*."[28] It is to be read, in other words, in contrast to Plato, who gives the most important document on this opposition but (for Plato) on the side of philosophy. Strauss, in his conclusion, wants to revisit this tension because it shows what is, in the origins of the West, at stake with philosophy and poetry. As in his Jerusalem/Athens distinction, which is superior and why? Will they always be at odds? And is the poet, in this sense, more a comic than a tragic poet?

> The other comedies confirmed the view that Aristophanes regards himself as superior to his greatest antagonist on account of his self-knowledge and prudence (phronesis): Whereas Socrates is wholly indifferent to the city that feeds him, Aristophanes is greatly concerned with the city; whereas Socrates does not respect, or comply with, the fundamental

> requirements of the city, Aristophanes does. The kind of wisdom that exhausts itself in the self-forgotten study of the things aloft and in its corollaries is unable to protect itself against its enemies because it is unable to act on the city or to humanize it counteracting the waspishness of the city, and it is unable to do this because it doesn't recognize the necessity of that waspishness; the poet however, whether comic or tragic, can protect himself against persecution.[29]

Strauss deftly moves from this tension to that between comedy and tragedy. What is the relationship between comedy and justice? How wide is the scope of comedy?

> The just things and the laughable things do not occur in his plays side by side, but they are inextricably interwoven. By presenting as laughable not only the unjust but the just as well, he brings it about that comedy is total: There is no Aristophanean character of any consequence who does not act laughably, let alone who is good sense incarnate. This does not mean that in his view life as a whole is a comedy; if it were, there would be no need for comic equivalents of non-comical things. The Aristophanean comedy is only a partial mirror of life. Therefore, it points to what escapes it or transcends it.[30]

In a note to this, Strauss points out that Sophocles (the playwright most identified with Greek tragedy) appears in only one play, *The Frogs*, and is absent from all the others. Strauss builds on this to offer a very important reflection on the relationship of comedy to tragedy and its meaning. Strauss tells us that *since comedy builds on tragedy, it is higher*. Yet, at the same time, it points to what our world lacks—an awareness of evil:

> The Aristophanean comedy certainly presupposes tragedy; it builds on tragedy; in this sense, at any rate, it is higher than tragedy. It conjures up for us, within the limits of that possibility which it must respect, a simply pleasant falsehood: a life without war, law courts, terrors caused by gods and death, poverty, and coercion or restraint or nomos. The falsehood points to the truth; the truth is the inevitable suffering, coeval with man, that is caused by both physis and nomos.[31]

While in tragedy hubris marks the transgression against the gods, in Aristophanes' plays boasting (alazoneia) is the main topic of concern.[32] There is "vulgar" and "non-vulgar" boasting.[33] Boasting, suggested here as a comic flaw, is the first Socratic trait that distinguishes him from the poets. He boasts—*he is not humble*. But here is Strauss's esoteric twist: The real "boaster par excellence" isn't Socrates. "The boaster in a non-vulgar sense, is the comic poet himself, who after all is responsible especially for those successful transgressions of sacred laws that he celebrates in his plays."[34]

Socrates's second trait (distinguishing him from poets), according to Strauss's reading of Aristophanes, is "his ineptitude in judging human beings and in handling them"; or as we noted above, phronesis.[35] The final trait is that, for Aristophanes, the philosopher is "anerotic" rather than erotic.[36] He would prefer the company of other men or friends to a sexual other and the family. He is also—as a result of being anerotic—a-music: he "does not love the beautiful in any form; including the beautiful use of the ugly . . . For the same reason, he lacks the spiritedness or waspishness that is an indispensable ingredient of the comic poet: Socrates' arrogance and impatience with stupidity can not be mistaken for anger and indignation."[37]

In direct contrast, notes Strauss, the Platonic version of Socrates sees the wisdom of the philosopher as superior to that of the poet.[38] There appears to be no balance between the two versions. Strauss, in response, suggests the Islamic philosopher Razi as having found a way to bring the two into harmony.[39] That aside, what we find in Strauss's account of comedy, vis-à-vis the tension between the poet and the philosopher, is fascinating. It suggests that while the philosopher, for Plato, is ironic, he really isn't comic. Irony is for the elite. Comedy, as per Aristophanes's reading, is more in line with the community and phronesis. Irony is tied to theoria. Irony, in fact, may be read as a kind of mockery of the community (and phronesis) because it turns to things beyond the purview or understanding of the community—irony has an esoteric aspect. Yet at the same time, and as Strauss—playing on Aristophanes—suggests, philosophy may be out of touch with the nature of evil. Only comedy, he suggests, and the comic poet can allude to evil.

Philosophy, it seems, cannot comprehend evil because evil is more grounded in the community and everyday life. Comedy, as Strauss notes, builds on tragedy. It is, as Walter Benjamin notes in the *Trauerspiel*, the inner meaning of tragedy. Mockery, as Strauss understands it, is used by poets on behalf of the community. It isn't the philosopher's domain. The two shouldn't cross genres. But they do, as Strauss argues, with Spinoza and other Enlightenment thinkers, and this opens up a wholly new era that makes comedy into the maidservant of philosophy. The novelty is that when it does, it leaves the debate with the ancients—over Jerusalem and Athens—intact and overlooks the relationship of comedy to justice and the community.

Modernity and Mockery: Strauss on the Enlightenment, Spinoza, and Modern Jewish Philosophy

The tension between Jerusalem and Athens—which for Strauss begins in the wake of monotheism and is, in many ways, metahistorical (and paradigmatic)—isn't as apparent in Strauss's writings on Plato, Aristotle, and Aristophanes as it is in his writings on Maimonides, Islamic philosophy, Spinoza, the Enlightenment, Modern Jewish philosophy, Nietzsche, and Heidegger. What needs to be considered, with respect to comedy, is (1) if and how the contrast between the poet and the philosopher (and their differing relationships to the city) is carried over, rejected, or altered in Strauss's readings of Maimonides, Spinoza, Nietzsche, and modernity; (2) if and how comedy is carried over, rejected, or altered in these readings; and (3) how comedy functions in the distinction between Athens and Jerusalem.

In *Philosophy and Law: Contributions to the Understanding of Maimonides and his Predecessors*, Strauss prefaces his criticism of the historicist reading of Maimonides—which reads him in terms of itself rather than in terms of what he believed to be true—with a reading of the Enlightenment and its false claim to have won the argument with the ancients regarding the validity of revelation. The false claim of triumph is based on the fact that, for Strauss, the argument was thought to have been won by virtue of mockery. Before laying this out, Strauss takes one of modern Jewish philosophy's most important readers of Maimonides, Hermann Cohen, to task for reading Maimonides as a rationalist who had no interest in miracles, etc. Cohen reads Maimonides and a kind of imperfect rationalist.

Strauss, in contrast, suggests that instead of reading Maimonides in our terms, it is our terms that should be put into question: "Maimonides' rationalism is the true natural model, the standard to be carefully protected from any distortion, and thus the stumbling block on which modern rationalism falls. To awaken prejudice in favor of this view of Maimonides and, even more, to arouse suspicion against the powerful opposing prejudice, is the aim of the present work."[40] In other words, Strauss's first major book sought to challenge modern prejudice against a work that may be deemed inferior from the perspective of the modern (enlightened) present. Strauss homes in on the present age's sense of progressive superiority over the past—from which, it believes, it has nothing to learn—as the biggest stumbling block:

> Even if one is free of all natural inclination towards the past, even if one believes that the present, as the age in which man has attained the highest rung yet of his self-consciousness, can really learn nothing from the past, one still encounters Maimonides' teaching as soon as one seriously attempts to make up one's mind about the present so assessed. For such an attempt can succeed only if one continually confronts modern rationalism, as the source of the present, with medieval rationalism.[41]

Strauss sees his project—in this book—as a "critique of modern rationalism as a critique of modern sophistry."[42] It is, as he says, a "necessary beginning, the constant companion, and unerring sign of that search for truth which is possible in our time."[43] In other words, all true criticism in our time, should begin by exposing the false pretenses of historicism and progressivism that deem all things from the past to be diminutive and of lesser greatness than the present. This requires a careful analysis of the sophistic—the use of rhetoric to claim superiority over the past—because, as Strauss explains, the argument between the moderns and the ancients, as claimed (rhetorically) by the Enlightenment thinkers, was not won. As we shall see, that claim was not supported by reason so much as by mockery and laughter.

For Strauss, as a Jewish thinker one must address the lens through which medieval Jewish thinkers like Maimonides are seen. It is the lens of the Enlightenment rationalism that is, as noted above, tainted:

> The present situation of Judaism—leaving aside, therefore, the fundamental constitution of Judaism, which is not affected in or by this situation—is determined by the Enlightenment. For all phenomenon peculiar to the present . . . refer back to the

> Enlightenment, that is, to the movement of the seventeenth and eighteenth centuries initiated by Descartes' *Meditations* and Hobbes' *Leviathan* as their source. This fact is hard to contest; only its bearing and significance are, certainly, contestable. The premises about which the present is at one with the Age of Enlightenment have now become so self-evident that it is only or chiefly the opposition between the Enlightenment and the present that tends to be remarked and taken seriously: the Enlightenment appears long since to have been "overcome."[44]

The Enlightenment—for argument's sake—has cast itself as the heir of Athens. Jerusalem, in contrast, has been thought to have been "overcome" and any concern with it is "shallow" and "trivial":

> How remote from our age is the quarrel about the verbal inspiration vs. the merely human origin of Scripture; about the reality vs. the impossibility of the Biblical miracles; about the eternity and thus the immutability vs. the historical variability of the Law; about the creation of the world vs. the eternity of the world: all discussions are now conducted on a level on which the great controversial questions debated by the Enlightenment and orthodoxy no longer even need to be posed, and must ultimately be rejected as "falsely posed."[45]

The problem, then, is that modern Jewish philosophy—because it is influenced by the Enlightenment—is more in line with Athens than with Jerusalem. It has betrayed one for the other and this, as Strauss suggests, is a kind of sophistry that must be exposed. Such criticism is the "necessary beginning" that can bring Jewish philosophy closer to the truth. He takes "radical Enlightenment's" (as opposed to the "moderate Enlightenment" as found in Moses Mendelssohn) displacement of Jewish philosophy's source in revelation as his initial target:

> If, however, the foundation of the Jewish tradition is belief in the creation of the world, in the reality of the Biblical miracles, in the absolutely binding character and essential immutability of the Law, resting on the revelation at Sinai, then one must say that the Enlightenment has undermined the foundation of the Jewish tradition. Indeed from the very beginning it was with

> complete consciousness and complete purposefulness that the radical Enlightenment—think of Spinoza—did this.[46]

Strauss argues that—in the 1920s, in Germany—the "Enlightenment is far more radical today than it was in the seventeenth and eighteenth centuries."[47] Even the returns to tradition by Jewish thinkers like Herman Cohen and Franz Rosenzweig (and the "new thinking") are tainted by this radicalism.[48] The "new thinking's" overcoming of Hegelianism has led, in fact, to a "rehabilitation of the Enlightenment."[49] (We will return to this below in our analysis of Strauss's reading of Spinoza.) This prompts Strauss to call for a recovery of the "quarrel between the Enlightenment and Orthodoxy."[50]

However, he takes note that since the Enlightenment thinkers realized that "orthodoxy's ultimate premise"—that miracles and revelations are possible—is "irrefutable" (by any form or argument since it remains a possibility) and that "all assertions based on this premise are unshakable," they had "decided" the "victory of Enlightenment over orthodoxy."[51] This act of the will—this decision (which Strauss discusses more in depth in his Spinoza essay and in relation to Nietzsche)—is demonstrated through the turn to mockery:

> For all these tenets rest on the irrefutable premise that God is omnipotent and that His will is unfathomable. If God is omnipotent, then miracles and revelations in general, and in particular the Biblical miracles and revelations are possible. Of course for orthodoxy, and therefore also for the Enlightenment, it is a question not so much of the possibility or impossibility as of the reality or unreality of the Biblical miracles and revelations; but in fact almost all the Enlightenment's attempts to demonstrate the unreality of the Biblical miracles and revelations depend on the express or tacit premise that the impossibility of miracles and revelations in general is established or demonstrable. Yet in carrying out their critique, precisely the most radical Enlighteners learned—if not as something clearly known, then at least as something vividly felt—that as a consequence of the irrefutability of orthodoxy's ultimate premise, all individual assertions resting on this premise are unshakable. Nothing shows more clearly that this is the case than the main weapon which they employed, and which

> they handled so aptly, so masterfully, that it—it alone, one might say—decided the victory of the Enlightenment over orthodoxy. This weapon is mockery. As Lessing, who was in a position to know, put it, they attempted by means of mockery to "laugh" orthodoxy out of a position from which it could not be dislodged by any proofs supplied by Scripture or even by reason . . . Thus the importance of mockery for the Enlightenment's critique of religion is an indirect proof of the irrefutability of orthodoxy. As a result, orthodoxy was able to survive the attack of the Enlightenment, and all later attacks and retreats, unchanged in its essence.[52]

Mockery is not isolated to this time period. It is connected, argues Strauss, to a kind of post-Epicurean existentialism that is in vogue with the current era (for the intellectual elite).

At the end of his preface to *Spinoza's Critique of Religion*, Strauss repeats the argument he made in *Philosophy and Law* with a few minor modifications:

> For all assertions of orthodoxy rest on the irrefutable premise that the omnipotent God, Whose will is unfathomable, Whose ways are not our ways, Who has decided to dwell in the thick darkness, may exist. Given this premise, miracles and revelations in general, and hence all biblical miracles and revelations in particular, are possible. Spinoza has not succeeded in showing that this premise is contradicted by anything we know. For what we are said to know, for example, regarding the age of the solar system, has been established on the assumption that the solar system has come into being naturally; miraculously it could have come into being in the way described by the Bible. It is only naturally or humanly impossible that the "first" Isaiah should have known the name of the founder of the Persian empire; it was not impossible for the omnipotent God to reveal to him that name. The orthodox premise cannot be refuted by experience nor by recourse to the principle of contradiction. And indirect proof of this is the fact that Spinoza and his like owed such success as they had in their fight against orthodoxy to laughter and mockery. By means of mockery they attempted to laugh orthodoxy out

> of its position from which it could not be dislodged by any proofs supplied by Scripture or by reason. One is tempted to say that mockery does not succeed the refutation of the orthodox tenets, but is itself that refutation. The genuine refutation of orthodoxy would require the proof that the world and human life are perfectly intelligible without the assumption of a mysterious God; it would require at least the success of the philosophic system: man has to show himself theoretically and the practically as the master of the world and master of his life; the merely given world must be replaced by the world created by man theoretically and practically.[53]

Strauss tells us that this has failed. Neither Spinoza—with his *Ethics*—nor Hegel have *not* accomplished such a feat, nor has the world.[54] The "clear and distinct account of everything" remains a "hypothesis," not a proven theory. It has, therefore, the same "cognitive status" as the "orthodox account."[55] This difference, argues Strauss, is moral: "the quest for evident and necessary knowledge, rests itself on an unevident decision, on an act of the will, just as faith. Hence, the antagonism between Spinoza and Judaism, between unbelief and belief, is ultimately not theoretical, but moral."[56] In other words, the mockery used by Spinoza ("and those like him") obscures this moral difference by acting "as if" the argument is won by the laugh itself. This is, for Strauss, a fallacy that needs to (or, as he says in his introduction to *Philosophy and Law*, must) be unmasked if Jewish philosophy in particular and philosophy in general is to begin again. The clarification of this very omission would be the new foundation or starting point for Strauss's revised version of the "new thinking" or Jewish philosophy.

Nietzsche and the Problem of Jewish Philosophy's "New Thinking"

Spinoza is not the only Jewish thinker who needs to be addressed in terms of these questions. Strauss suggests that the "new thinking" presented by Rosenzweig (and Heidegger) has avoided orthodoxy but has, nonetheless, harbored the Judeo-Christian in its emphasis on conscience, guilt, anxiety, etc.[57] The Jewish people, for Spinoza and Rosenzweig, are thought of as a people—not as a people *with* a scripture. This, for Strauss, misses the mark. It also overlooks the possibility of miracles, etc., which, he argues, are situated in the text (since revelation and the Torah go hand in hand). Without the acknowledgment of this possibility, it remains a lingering question. To not address it is to not see its presence working behind the scenes.

Strangely enough, it is Nietzsche—not Spinoza, Rosenzweig, or Cohen—who exposes this missing link. He also discloses, unlike any thinker before him, the connection of will to mockery. Strauss is a close reader of Nietzsche and sees him as providing the clearest diagnosis of the influence of Jerusalem on modern thought (the "new thinking"): "We will be helped in that reconsideration [of the Jerusalem/Athens distinction and the topic of assimilation] by this statement of a non-Jew, of a German . . . and that man is Friedrich Nietzsche."[58]

Strauss focuses on the issue of assimilation in his discussion of Nietzsche, Jerusalem, and Athens: "Assimilation is an intermediate stage in which it means distinguishing oneself in pursuits which are not as such Jewish but, as Nietzsche would say, European, or as we would say, Western."[59] In an aphorism entitled "What Europe owes the Jews" (aphorism 250 of *Beyond Good and Evil*), Nietzsche sees the Jewish appeal to morality as a "grand style." What makes it important and unique are its "infinite demands" and "infinite significances":

> Many things, good and bad, and above all one thing that is both of the best and of the worst: the grand style in morality, the terribleness and majesty of infinite demands, infinite meanings, the whole romanticism and sublimity of moral questionabilities—and hence precisely the most attractive, captious, and choicest part of those plays of color andseductions to life in whose afterglow the sky of our European culture, its evening sky, is burning now—perhaps burning itself out. We artists among the spectators and philosophers are—grateful for this to the Jews.[60]

This passage makes Jews distinct—something that he does throughout *The Genealogy of Morals*—and associates them with moral seriousness and depth, not lightness and humor. But why must Jews remain distinct? Why does Strauss see this as ironic (for Nietzsche)? Did Nietzsche want—as Strauss argues in his essay "Why We Remain Jews?"—to have Jews assimilate or become singular, different?

Here, Strauss argues that Nietzsche does in fact see assimilation as an imperative. Strauss points out how the tension between the particular and the universal was something that Nietzsche wanted to change. The Jews, according to Strauss's reading of one of Nietzsche's aphorism, were the litmus test for a "cleansing" process happening throughout Europe in the modern period.

On the other hand, Strauss notes in his essay on "Jerusalem and Athens" that Nietzsche wanted to have the overman bring together Jerusalem and Athens: "Nietzsche sought therefore for a culture that would no longer be particular and hence in the last analysis arbitrary. The single goal of mankind is conceived by him as in a sense superhuman: he speaks of the superman of the future. *The superman is meant to unite in himself Jerusalem and Athens on the highest level.*"[61] This higher vision starts with a sense of one's unique particularity. The mockery of this—the laughter at oneself—may be the key to transcending this particular (albeit not completely) to attain a higher vision of the superman who sees—united in himself—Jerusalem and Athens. In other words, Nietzsche's vision of the *Uebermensch* has much in common with Heinrich Heine's vision (Nietzsche deeply admired Heine), which looks at Jewishness in a self-mocking way while going beyond it to something more universal.

The irony of this, however, is that for Heine the greatest figure of self-mockery and the greatest figure of critiquing (and living through) Jewish assimilation was the Jewish comic character otherwise known as the schlemiel. This, at least, is Hannah Arendt's claim in her essay "The Jew as Pariah." The schlemiel marked the limit between the pariah and the parvenu, and did so through mockery and humor. According to Arendt, we see this especially in the work of Heine.[62] This is something that Strauss overlooks, but—because the schlemiel is a figure of Jewishness that draws on mockery—it gives us a keener sense of the role humor plays in the Jerusalem/Athens distinction and the relationship (harkening back to Aristophanes) between humor, the community, and justice.

The Hidden Distinction: On Nietzsche and Laughter

While Strauss discusses the meaning of mockery and explains that Nietzsche understood how Spinoza's work—like his own—was motivated by a religious consciousness and a "spirit of revenge,"[63] he doesn't explain

Nietzsche's view of mockery. We can only infer, by way of Nietzsche, that Spinoza's mockery was motivated by a "spirit of revenge" against Judaism itself. In contrast, Nietzsche's view of laughter and mockery is not discussed in much of Strauss's work, and I would suggest—in the spirit of Strauss's literary reading of Maimonides and the esoteric—that we make a distinction between two kinds of mockery: one concealing a problematic and the other disclosing it. While we know one—the kind of mockery that disguises the problematic (as we see with Spinoza and "those like him")—what is the other kind of mockery, and how does it relate to Nietzsche's view of Jewishness, the Greeks, etc? What kind of mockery discloses the problematic rather than effaces it?

The *only* place that Strauss discusses Nietzsche and laughter or comedy can be found in a 1967 Nietzsche lecture.[64] It is obvious what Strauss thinks about Thomas Hobbes, Nietzsche, and the relationship of comedy to philosophy. According to Strauss there is a natural fit between comedy and philosophy. This comes up after one of Strauss's students reads aphorism 294 from *Beyond Good and Evil*: "*The Olympian vice* . . . they cannot suppress laughter even during holy rites."[65] Strauss notes that Nietzsche associated this passage with Hobbes, but he observes: "I have never found this passage in Hobbes, and I don't think Nietzsche was ever a close student of Hobbes. It may just be an error, for all I know; or do you know the passage?"[66] The student says that Kaufmann—the editor of the Nietzsche volume he is reading—said the same thing. The source in Hobbes is not to be found. Strauss replies:

> Yes, that is easy: he discusses it in the chapters on the passions in the *Leviathan*; in *De Homine*, and in *The Elements*, there is nothing said about it of this nature. He regards [inaudible] his explanation of laughter is very simple: When you suddenly see someone fall, as he puts it, then you laugh; and when you yourself suddenly fall, then you weep. That is the gist of Hobbes' definition. At any rate, the main point which Nietzsche makes here, and which hadn't been made explicitly for some time before Nietzsche, is that philosophy is more akin to laughter than to compassion, and surely than to weeping. This is an old story.[67]

In other words, Strauss sees this relationship between philosophy and comedy as a *given*. Philosophy and comedy *are* linked and that is because philosophy has less to do with "weeping" and "compassion," which are more akin to revelation and faith, and more to do with comedy and thought (which can laugh at fallen-ness by way of a philosophical transcendence). In the same lecture, Strauss takes note of a passage from *Thus Spake Zarathustra* (1.7 "Reading and Writing") about laughter: "The atmosphere rare and pure . . . It wants us to laugh." Commenting on this, Strauss says that "the knowledge which is worthwhile (for Nietzsche) requires daring, courage, laughter."[68] This kind of laughter and knowledge is in contrast to the knowledge and the "spirit of heaviness" that comes with religion.[69]

Near the end of his lecture, Strauss discusses a passage from the third part of the *Genealogy of Morals* and makes a key distinction between revelation and Nietzsche's comical, post-Enlightenment reading of comedy. Wisdom is equated, by Nietzsche, with mockery: "Careless, mocking, forceful—so does wisdom wish us: she is a woman, and never loves anyone but a warrior." Is the philosopher, then, wise?

Strauss remarks that the philosopher, for Nietzsche, is an ascetic: "The philosopher is poor, he is chaste . . . and he is humble in the sense defined by Nietzsche. He avoids all loud things. But why is he not obedient?"[70] His student responds about the philosopher that "he can be humble because he realizes his ignorance, but he may not be obedient because there is no other human being, or as a matter of fact anything."[71] Humility and obedience, for Nietzsche, are defining features of slave morality. If the philosopher is not obedient but is humble, then he is transvaluing the meaning of humility. Strauss separates the philosopher/ascetic—unlike Nietzsche, apparently—from the priest/ascetic:

> He could not possibly obey. . . . It's traditionally said he would have to have reasons for why he should do this and that. But if he does this for these reasons known to him, even if he has learned them from somebody else, he does not obey. Is this not clear? Obedience presupposes a recognition of authority, but the philosopher doesn't recognize this. So that is [inaudible]. You see, one has to be very careful; there are all kinds of traps there. This, incidentally, would explain the motto of treatise 3, which was understood also by some of the papers as the aphorism introducing the third treatise, contrary to what I think is the true [inaudible]. . . . Whether that is compatible with humility is another matter, but it is

> surely not compatible with obedience. *It is compatible with humility as defined by Nietzsche, which has very little to do with humility in the traditional sense.* There is one more point I would like to make. Nietzsche begins his discussion of the ascetic priest with the assertion that the ascetic ideal originates in a fundamental need of the very life which that ideal denies. The ascetic ideal denies this life by the mere fact that it asserts another life. That alone is sufficient. Whether there is a relative recognition of this life is ultimately unimportant, because in the light of the other life this life loses its ultimate importance. That is, I believe, Nietzsche's point.[72]

In other words, there can be a humility that is *not* based on authority—since, for Nietzsche, the thinker does not recognize any authority. Humility, just as much as mockery, in other words, need not be beholden to the authority of revelation or authority in general.

In *The Gay Science*, Nietzsche spells out the transcendence of laughter in relation to art. It deals with suffering in ways that are different from the ascetic. Laughter at oneself can grant one transcendence. Laughter is the basis of "Gay Science" and a challenge to the seriousness of philosophy, nationalism, and politics. It is beyond morality and, as I noted above, authority. Laughing and crying—comedy and tragedy—can happen only when we reflect on our sad or ridiculous suffering:

> We do not always keep our eyes from rounding off something and, as it were, finishing the poem; and then it is no longer eternal imperfection that we carry across the river of becoming—then we have the sense of carrying a *goddess*, and feel proud and childlike as we perform this service. As an aesthetic phenomenon existence is still *bearable* for us, and art furnishes us with eyes and hands and above all the good conscience to be *able* to turn ourselves into such a phenomenon. At times we need a rest from ourselves by looking upon, by looking *down* upon, ourselves, and from an artistic distance laughing *over* ourselves or weeping *over* ourselves. We must discover the *hero* no less than the *fool* in our passion for knowledge; we must occasionally find pleasure in our folly, or we cannot continue to find pleasure in our wisdom.[73]

This suggests that, for Nietzsche, one must laugh at oneself and not simply others. Humor is necessary to modern thought, and brings on a certain kind of secular humility. Moreover, although philosophy's relationship to comedy is, as Strauss says, an "old story," it initiates a new beginning for philosophy. If you couple this insight with Strauss's call to recover the debate between Jerusalem and Athens, it becomes necessary to think about the meaning of the schlemiel, comedy, and humility.

Conclusion: Maimonides, Extreme Humility, and Comical Stupidity

Strauss's work on Maimonides is well known in the academy. It launched a resurgence of Maimonides studies in the United States. While he pays great attention to the tension between the esoteric and the exoteric in Maimonides' work (highlighting the tension between Athens and Jerusalem as it relates to the tension between the philosopher and the prophet), he doesn't spend as much time on the tension between Athens and Jerusalem as it pertains to ethics. This difference, I aver, would give us access to the problematic that is at the heart of the discussion about the meaning and place of humor in Strauss's work.

David Shatz, in an essay on Maimonides and ethics, argues that there is a fundamental difference between Maimonides and Aristotle in terms of their readings of "pride" and "anger" vis-à-vis character. While for Aristotle extreme humility is a vice, for Maimonides it is a virtue; and while for Aristotle anger and pride have a place, for Maimonides they don't.[74]

As Nietzsche notes—with respect to "slave morality"—humility is one of the primary character traits of the Jewish people. Nietzsche associates it with stupidity because, citing Pascal, he sees it in terms of negating what he calls "intelligence" in the name of via fides (faith). Self-deprecation and self-mockery may be said—in light of Maimonides—to be Jewish expressions of extreme humility. Although Nietzsche seems to divest himself of the humility that comes with via fides, Strauss suggests—as we saw above—that there is a space for humility in Nietzsche's secular reading of the overman. The difference, however, is that Nietzsche would not (like Aristotle), make room for extreme humility. There is humility, but it is not extreme. This marks a limit.

In his aphorism in the *Gay Science* about laughter, cited above, Nietzsche sees it as a way of transcending existence and finding meaning in becoming an "aesthetic phenomenon." In contrast, as we see above with Maimonides, extreme humility finds a figuration in being abject (the figure used in Maimonides's work—borrowed, Shatz argues, from the Sufis—is a man being urinated on in a boat). It is grounded in the body and in existence (physiopsychology, as Nietzsche would say)—not in aesthetics. Moreover, self-deprecation, as we see in Heine's Jewish humor, is more grounded in the body than in pride. There is in Jewish humor a kind of grounding with the schlemiel who is—as Daniel Boyarin[75] or Paul Breins[76] might argue—a figure characterized by un-heroic conduct.

More to the point, Nietzsche (as per his aphorism in the *Gay Science*) characterizes the artist as a *hero* who can—through comedy, or even tragedy—gain transcendence and give meaning to the meaninglessness of abject suffering. He is a hero in the sense that he can fight back against the suffering that comes with one's fate and existence. What we find in the schlemiel, in contrast, is not so much a heroic figure as an ethical figure—as Paul Breins argues—of gentleness and humility. The schlemiel—in this light—may not be seen as a figure of mockery (in Spinoza's or Nietzsche's sense) because it isn't taking orthodoxy as a target and elevating Athens over Jerusalem. In truth, the schlemiel puts the two into tension because the issue of character deals with a way of life that exists between the two cities. As Strauss notes, the key question for Athens and Jerusalem is that of the right way of life. If the overman fuses the two then it would be—as Breins says of the post-67 Jewish Jew—a combination of a schlemiel and a "tough Jew" (who can defend himself and take up arms if necessary). He is tough on the outside and soft on the inside, like Superman/Clark Kent.

What kind of life does this suggest? In his lectures on Nietzsche Strauss discloses something that he doesn't address in his writings on Maimonides, Spinoza, or the new thinking—namely, that comedy and philosophy go hand in hand and that humility can, in fact, pass over from the religious sphere into the philosophical sphere. Taking this to heart, one can read Socrates as a humble comic figure who—between Aristophanes and Plato—can figure the tension between the city (community)/poet and the philosopher. This tension, I would argue, can also be generalized and applied to the Jewish community, but in terms of prophecy and comedy.

While neither Strauss nor Maimonides discusses the meaning of *Jewish* comedy, we should because it suggests the biggest challenge to the contrast that Nietzsche makes between the serious moral aspect of Judaism and the comical style of the Greeks. In his essay on Jonah, Gershom Scholem suggests that Jonah is a comic figure and that he, in fact, discloses the essence of prophecy.[77] It isn't moral seriousness so much as the inversion of fate and the surprise that comes with the realization that—to the chagrin of Spinoza—God can change his mind and have mercy. Perhaps this inversion of fate—in contrast to Nietzsche's embrace of fate (amor fati)—is the Jewish contribution to the West. Strangely enough, Walter Benjamin and Strauss see this inversion with respect to Socrates who leaves tragedy behind for comedy and reason. Strauss makes this explicit in *The City and Man* when he writes of the *Republic* that "Socrates left us no example of weeping, but on the other side, he left us an example of laughing. The relation of weeping to laughing is similar to that of tragedy and comedy. We may therefore say that the Socratic conversation and hence the Platonic dialogue is slightly more akin to comedy than tragedy."[78] The main thing for both the Socratic/Platonic approach to philosophy and the Jewish approach to prophecy is that chance and comedy displace fate and tragedy.

Comedy—in the spirt of self-deprecation—suggests a way of life, a character, and an attitude toward existence that are unique to Judaism. Instead of suspending or negating the tension between the ancients and the moderns by way of mockery, Jewish comedy can maintain it. In Jewish humor revelation is still possible, although deferred. Here's a joke to illustrate how reason—narrating this joke—meets with faith in a form of self-deprecation; it maintains the tension, points toward deferral, and purports a (comical) way of life of such a deferral (that characterizes, for Scholem, the prophetic—which displaces fate and the apocalyptic). This joke demonstrates an attitude which sees both reason and faith as possible and complimentary, albeit in a way that is self-deprecating and humbling:

> In the middle of the forest is a small town. It was built far from the main roads and the Jews living there were afraid that when the Messiah came, he would not know they were there and would pass them by. So they built a tower on the edge of town and appointed the town beggar as a watchman. If the Messiah should come, the watchman would give him directions to the town.
>
> One day a stranger visits the tower, and as instructed the watchman comes down to greet him. "What are you doing in the middle of nowhere?" asks the stranger.

"My job is to sit on top of this tower and wait for the Messiah," answers the watchman.

"So, how do you like your job?" the stranger asks. "It can't pay much."

"I know," replies the watchman, "but at least it's steady work."

Notes

1. Leo Strauss, *Socrates and Aristophanes* (Chicago: University of Chicago Press, 1980), 5.

2. Ibid.

3. Ibid., 7.

4. Ibid., 6.

5. Aristotle, *Metaphysics* I.6.987a29–b14; cf. b22–24, b27–33; see XIII.4.1078b12–34).

6. *Socrates and Aristophanes*, 6.

7. Ibid., 7.

8. Ibid., 6.

9. Ibid.

10. Ibid.

11. Ibid., 7.

12. Ibid.

13. Ibid.

14. Ibid.

15. Ibid., 8.

16. Ibid.

17. Nietzsche's mockery is not simply aimed at the opponent, however. In *Allegories of Reading*, Paul de Man sees mockery as quintessential to Nietzsche's project. De Man takes it on himself as the bearer of Nietzsche's tradition to also espouse mockery as a hallmark of his version of deconstruction. Contrary to Strauss's reading of *The Birth of Tragedy*, de Man argues that Nietzsche is in full comic mode since he mocks the "deadly power of 'Dionysian music' [as a] myth that cannot stand the ridicule of literal description." De Man's description of Nietzsche's mockery is different from what Strauss finds in Spinoza and the Enlightenment thinkers. For de Man, Nietzsche's mockery is marked by a kind of self-destructive or self-deprecating (and even horrific) "process." It is called, by "Nietzsche, 'an artistic game that the will, in the eternal plentitude of its pleasure, plays with itself,' a formulation in which every word is ambivalent and enigmatic, since the will has been discredited as a self, the pleasure shown to be a lie, the fullness to be the absence of meaning, and the play and the endless

tension of a nonidentity, a pattern of dissonance that contaminates the very source of the will, the will as source." In other words, Nietzsche's mockery, for de Man, leaves nothing untouched and is nihilistic. When compared to Strauss's reading of Nietzsche, this one opens up another discussion about the meaning and place of mockery in Nietzsche and in modernity. See Paul de Man, *Allegories of Reading: Figural Language in Rousseau, Nietzsche, Rilke, and Proust* (New Haven, CT: Yale University Press, 1982), 97–99.

18. *Socrates and Aristophanes*, 11.
19. Ibid., 33.
20. Ibid., 49.
21. Ibid.
22. Ibid., 51.
23. Plato, *Theatetus* 174b–d, *Plato: Collected Dialogues* (Princeton, NJ: Princeton University Press, 879.
24. *Socrates and Aristophanes*, 52.
25. Ibid.
26. Ibid., 53.
27. Ibid., 311.
28. Ibid; my emphasis.
29. Ibid.
30. Ibid., 312.
31. Ibid.
32. Ibid.
33. Ibid., 313.
34. Ibid.
35. Ibid.
36. Ibid.
37. Ibid.
38. Ibid., 314.
39. Ibid.
40. Strauss, Leo. *Philosophy and Law: Contributions to the Understanding of Maimonides and His Predecessors*, trans. Eve Adler (Albany, NY: SUNY Press, 1994), 21.
41. Ibid.
42. Ibid., 22.
43. Ibid.
44. Ibid.
45. Ibid., 23.
46. Ibid.
47. Ibid., 26.
48. Ibid., 27.
49. Ibid., 28.
50. Ibid., 29.

51. Ibid.

52. Ibid., 29–30.

53. Strauss, Leo. *Jewish Philosophy and the Crisis of Modernity* (Albany, NY: State University of New York Press, 1997), 170.

54. Ibid., 170–171.

55. Ibid., 170.

56. Ibid., 171.

57. Ibid., 151.

58. Ibid., 323.

59. Ibid., 325.

60. Nietzsche, Friedrich. *Beyond Good and Evil*, Aphorism 250, in *Basic Writings of Nietzsche*, trans. and ed., Walter Kaufmann (New York, NY: Random House, 2000), 375.

61. Ibid., 379; my emphasis.

62. Arendt, Hannah. *The Jewish Writings*, ed. Jerome Kohn and Ron H. Feldman (New York: Schocken, 2007), 278.

63. Leo Strauss, *Jewish Philosophy and the Crisis of Modernity*, 166.

64. Strauss, Leo. 1967 Lecture on Nietzsche, http://leostrausstranscripts.uchicago.edu/navigate/15/table-of-contents/.

65. Ibid.

66. Ibid.

67. Ibid.

68. Ibid.

69. Ibid.

70. Ibid.

71. Ibid.

72. Ibid; my emphasis.

73. Nietzsche, Friedrich. *The Gay Science*, trans. Walter Kaufman (New York: Vintage, 1974), Aphorism 107, 163.

74. David Shatz, "Maimonides' Moral Theory," in *The Cambridge Companion to Maimonides*, ed., Kenneth Seeskin (Cambridge, UK: Cambridge University Press, 2005), 175–176.

75. Boyarin, Daniel. *Unheroic Conduct: The Rise of Heterosexuality and the Invention of Jewish Man* (Berkeley, CA: University of California Press, 1997).

76. Breins, Paul. *Tough Jews, Political Fantasies, and the Dilemma of American Jewry* (New York, NY: Basic Books, 1990).

77. Gershom Scholem, "On Jonah and the Concept of Justice," *Critical Inquiry* 25, no. 2 (Winter 1999): 353–361.

78. Strauss, Leo. *The City and Man*, 61.

14

Leo Strauss and Walter Benjamin

Thinking "in a Moment of Danger"

Philipp von Wussow

Introduction

It may seem odd that the relationship between Leo Strauss and Walter Benjamin has been almost entirely disregarded. Upon a closer look, however, this is little surprising because the two figures do not even have a common readership. Benjamin, an icon of critical theory and proponent of a playful political radicalism, and Strauss, the vanguard of an untimely return to the classics of political philosophy, appeal to very different groups of academic readers. The shared intellectual provenance in the German-Jewish world of the interwar period seems to create as little connection as the common fate of expulsion and exile.

This image changes to some extent once we add two figures who at least temporarily were significant for both Strauss and Benjamin: Gershom Scholem and Carl Schmitt. It was Scholem who introduced them to one another. There are a number of instances in their respective correspondences with Scholem in which the two mentioned each another, often prompted by Scholem himself, who had a complicated friendship with both of them. Contextualizing and interpreting instances helps to create a common language in which the two philosophical projects illuminate each other. Any comparison between these projects should focus on the writings of the late 1920s and 1930s to retain the simultaneity of their pursuits. This methodological precaution helps to understand what it means to think "in a moment of danger," to use Benjamin's famous phrase—a moment when all previous intellectual certainties vanish and philosophical thinking is compelled to rebuild itself in new ways. Strauss and Benjamin show how differently the same "moment of danger" can shape in the foundations and transformations of philosophical projects.

The name Carl Schmitt also evokes a certain theoretical interest. References to Schmitt in Benjamin and Strauss not only help us to understand the political dimension of their projects; the triangle of Schmitt, Strauss, and Benjamin also helps to clarify how the concept of "the political" relates to culture and religion in modernity. Contemporary usages often place the political in opposition to politics so that the former provides the event of "true" politics as opposed to politics in its vested domain of political institutions. German-Jewish philosophy in the interwar period offers a different understanding of the political and its basis. Following the Schmittian distinction between politics and the political, the latter refers to political phenomena not in the framework of political institutions but rather in the sphere of culture. This conception offers a new perspective on a certain political preoccupation in the cultural sciences, with their inclination toward "radical" politics. It limits the *political* pretensions of "the political" and its contemporary uses and abuses—after all, despite those pretensions, "the political" is in a sense merely a cultural discourse.

However, there is another concept of the political that is determined by its opposition to theology and religion. This chapter addresses the distinction between a polemical notion of the political and a nonpolemical notion that is derived from the relationship between theology and politics. Both notions of the political can be found in Benjamin as well as in Strauss.

Benjamin and Strauss: Contours of a Nondialogue

Walter Benjamin and Leo Strauss crossed paths in the Prussian State Library in Berlin, where both worked in the late 1920s. As Benjamin wrote to Scholem in 1929, he occasionally "intercepted" Strauss there to hand him some clandestine writings of Scholem for dissemination. Strauss had been working at the Akademie für die Wissenschaft des

Judentums since 1925 and was deeply immersed in Jewish and Islamic medieval philosophy. He had reluctantly begun this work in 1928 as a commentary on Gersonides's *Milkhamot ha-Shem* (Wars of the Lord), but soon he became excited by the subject matter and shifted his attention to Maimonides and his Islamic predecessors.[1] In 1929, he reportedly made the discovery in the State Library that would become the center of his master work *Philosophy and Law* (1935) and a lifelong preoocupation. In Avicenna's treatise *On the Division of the Sciences*, Strauss found the proposition that the treatment of prophecy and divine law is contained in Plato's *Nomoi*. This observation provided a new approach to Plato's political philosophy, through the lens of the medieval Islamic and Jewish Enlightenment (Farabi, Avicenna, Averroes, and Maimonides). Strauss's discovery marked the birth of *Philosophy and Law*, and he still believed in 1970 that he had understood the entire *Guide of the Perplexed* (Maimonides) from here.[2]

Benjamin had been living in Berlin again since October 1928, interrupted by occasional travels to Königstein (Taunus) and Tuscany.[3] For the most part he was working on his *Pariser Passagen* (the *Arcades Project*), which he first presented in two legendary conversations with his friends and acquaintances in Königstein in 1929. Following Benjamin's letter to Adorno from May 1935, these conversations ended the "epoch" of his "carefree, archaic philosophizing," "especially the 'historical' conversation in the little Swiss house [the Schweizer Haus in Königstein] and, after that, the definitely historical one held around the table with you, Asja [Lacis], Felizitas [Gretel Adorno], and Horkheimer. It was the end of rhapsodic naïveté."[4] Adorno later recalled in a letter to Scholem that these days were "unforgettable, inasmuch as Benjamin back then in Königstein read us for the first time from the Arcades work, namely, things that were never again accomplished with the same conceptual freshness and brilliance."[5] As Howard Eiland and Michael Jennings sum up, "these 'Königstein conversations' left an imprint on the thinking of all the participants and helped shape what came to be known as the Frankfurt School of cultural theory."[6] The *Arcades Project*, the unfinished master work that occupied Benjamin for the rest of his all-too-short life, was meant to decipher the nineteenth century through the architectural forms of the Paris arcades.[7] The stark contrast to Strauss's project on medieval philosophy and his larger attempt to "return" to premodern thought points to some of the theoretical differences between the two. The fact that both were in the earliest stages of their respective master works in 1929—and that both these master works would hardly be recognized as such (Strauss), or even remain unfinished (Benjamin)—provides the necessary background for their occasional meetings at the time.

On February 14, 1929, Benjamin reported to Scholem regarding his letter on Oskar Goldberg: "I passed it on to someone you are sure to know, Dr. Strauss of the Jewish Academy, to be copied and further distributed *in partibus infidelium*. I won't deny that he awakens my trust and I find him sympathetic. I will soon intercept him once again at the state library, at which time I hope to get his reports from the theater of war."[8] On March 15, he wrote: "Strauss, whom I mentioned previously, has disappeared from sight. But I will send out a warrant for his arrest since he took with him an extensive bibliography on the nature of the fairy tale."[9] It has been suspected that Strauss had "disappeared from sight" because he was at Davos to attend the disputation between Heidegger and Cassirer. But despite his late claims to be a witness,[10] it is far from clear that he was even there. Another reference to Strauss in a Benjamin letter to Scholem, written a week later—and therefore a week before the Davos disputation—states that the Goldberg letter had been duplicated by Strauss in the meantime.[11] It suggests that Strauss had already returned to Berlin a week before the Davos disputation, which took place on March 29.

The last piece of evidence of a direct, albeit brief encounter between Benjamin and Strauss comes from an October 1931 letter to Scholem, when Benjamin was working on his *Deutsche Menschen* and Strauss had first outlined his ideas about how to "return" to the ancients.[12] Benjamin wrote: "I also made available to Leo Strauss something you mailed earlier, a piece in which you discuss a mystical examination of the Kabbalah by a later—I believe, English—scholar."[13] Perhaps they had already met in Zionist circles in the early 1920s, as has occasionally been suggested; and they also could have met in 1933 in the Bibliothèque Nationale in Paris, where Strauss had been working with the help of a Rockefeller fellowship before moving to England in January 1934. However, no documents support these suspicions. The marginal comments in their correspondences provide a number of hints of how their personal relationship and the theoretical affinities can be interpreted. They knew or understood almost nothing of each other's writings, but they had a mutual fascination and recognized each other for their intellectual independence—after all, neither could be absorbed by any master narrative or "school." It is not far-fetched to assume that this is what Benjamin had in mind when he wrote in 1932 that he found Strauss trustworthy and sympathetic.[14] In December of that year, he wrote to Scholem that Strauss had "always made an excellent impression on me,"[15] and in May 1935 he emphasized "the pleasant image of him I have always made for myself."[16]

Strauss first mentioned Benjamin three decades later. In 1965 he borrowed Scholem's article on Benjamin, which had appeared that year in the journal *Neue Rundschau*, and reported to Scholem: "I read it at once with the greatest interest but with very imperfect understanding. I hardly knew more of him than that he was a man of extraordinary seriousness and perfect integrity."[17] The "substance" of Benjamin's philosophical doctrine remained wholly inaccessible to him, and he wondered what Scholem meant when he described this substance as "metaphysics." One might wonder if Strauss noticed the ambiguity in Scholem's stance on Benjamin here. After all, Scholem's characterization of Benjamin as a "metaphysician" combines the traits of the philosopher (exoteric) and the theologian (esoteric).[18] But Strauss was far more interested in the personal dimension. As he concluded: "Perhaps it would help me if I knew how Benjamin saw me."[19]

To sum up these scattered references, neither Benjamin nor Strauss could translate the other's views into their own. There is no dialogue to begin with, and no starting point to stage such a dialogue retroactively. However, there are a number of theoretical similarities and differences. We may distinguish a few common themes: (1) the stance toward tradition and modernity and the critique of history as progress; (2) the reading of Carl Schmitt; the relationship between aesthetics and politics, and the notion of the political; (3) the stance toward theological and political concepts; namely, the concepts of messianism and redemption (to which Strauss was, unlike virtually all other German-Jewish thinkers, wholly indifferent), law (which was important for both), and revelation (which is central for Strauss, while it gradually vanishes in Benjamin's writings); (4) a rare methodological emphasis on reading, and a strong sense for esoteric meanings hidden beneath the surface of a text that was fueled by a deep suspicion of the grand schemes of "theory"; and (5) their relationships to the two major schools of German academic philosophy. Both had a complicated relationship to neo-Kantianism and phenomenology: whereas Benjamin's thought is closer to neo-Kantianism, Strauss is closer to phenomenology.

These thematic and methodological differences *almost* conceal the obvious political difference between the anarchist-communist radical and the heterodox conservative (and later Cold War liberal). The differences between their concepts of the political are not due only to these political leanings, however, more importantly, perhaps, there is also a fundamental difference in their theoretical frameworks, in which Carl Schmitt' thought figured differently. Strauss and Benjamin were influenced by Schmitt, and both interpreted his teachings in rather idiosyncratic ways. To recall the basic facts in the case of Benjamin: he had already referred to Schmitt's *Political Theology* in his *Trauerspielbuch*, and in a 1930 letter to Scholem he wrote that his ideas about the philosophy of art had been "confirmed" by Schmitt's philosophy of the state. The Schmittian influence reappeared in the eighth thesis of "On the Concept of History," in the notion that the state of emergency "is not the exception but the norm." Claiming that the "task" was "to bring about a real state of emergency," Benjamin sought to appropriate Schmitt for "the struggle against fascism."[20]

Strauss had reviewed the book version of Schmitt's *The Concept of the Political* in 1932 and published the piece—with the support of Schmitt himself—in the *Archiv für Sozialwissenschaft und Sozialpolitik*. In the highly politicized scholarly debate about this essay, Strauss's central question—and perhaps his lasting contribution—has been strangely overlooked. There is a surprisingly systematic line of argument in the text, which refers back to his early acquaintance with the Marburg School of neo-Kantianism (Hermann Cohen, Paul Natorp, Ernst Cassirer). The inconspicuous but central question is how the political relates to other "spheres" or "domains" of society and culture such as morals, economics, law, art, etc.: is the political equivalent to the other "spheres" of culture (*Kulturgebiete*), or is it located *beyond* them? Strauss continued his hidden argument with neo-Kantianism here—which had asked the same question with regard to religion—but also showed that Schmitt himself was trapped in the systematic presuppositions of the "prevailing concept of culture,"[21] against which the concept of the political was directed. Accordingly Schmitt could not attain a "pure and whole knowledge" but remained caught in a "polemical" knowledge. Strauss also noticed the ambivalent position of "the aesthetic" in Schmitt's argument, which both thwarts the recognition of the political and reflects the aesthetic sensibility that shapes his thought.

Aesthetics and Politics or Philosophy and Law?

The relation of art to politics recalls Benjamin's afterword to his article "The Work of Art in the Age of Its Technological Reproducibility" (1935–1936). According to Benjamin, the aestheticization of politics under fascism gives the masses a means of expression while preserving "property relations," and hence culminates in war. As he wrote, fascism expects from war "the artistic gratification of a sense perception altered by technology. This is evidently the consummation of *l'art pour l'art*."[22] Benjamin had first encountered these ideas in Ernst Jünger's *Krieg und Krieger* (1930), in which he found a "reckless transposition of the theses of l'art pour l'art on war,"[23] and in Marinetti's "Manifesto on the Ethiopian Colonial War" (1934). His plan was to transpose these aesthetico-political ideas into a revolutionary (communist) conception of political art. As he wrote, the self-alienation of mankind "has reached the point where it can experience its own annihilation as a supreme aesthetic pleasure. *Such is the aestheticizing of politics, as practiced by fascism. Communism replies by politicizing art*."[24]

This blunt juxtaposition is clearly motivated by the political struggle in which Benjamin situated his work in the mid-1930s. It belongs to the task of thinking "in a moment of danger,"[25] as Benjamin famously described the situation shortly before his death. But the afterlife of the juxtaposition reaches far beyond its immediate political context and into the language of critical theory, including its asymmetric coupling with communism and fascism. We are today no longer as certain as Benjamin was that the communist politicization of art is in principle superior to the fascist aestheticization of politics. This is not only because we are dealing with two similarly murderous and indefensible political ideologies. At the very least, we may doubt whether aesthetics is the proper location for the political quarrels of the cultural sciences. As another, more principled, philosophical consideration we may ask whether the relation of aesthetics to politics really poses such a central problem, and hence whether it provides a useful starting point of reflection. Despite the common origin of *aisthesis*, aesthetics and politics involve with two different modes of judgment. Political judgment operates primarily with a binary semantics. Aesthetic judgment—or the type of judgment shaped and nurtured in the cultural sphere—is primarily *plural* and oriented toward the idea of the peaceful coexistence of a multitude. The widespread confusion of culture and politics is often due to the fact that aesthetic judgment is turned into—or misunderstood as—a model for political judgment.[26]

This is the starting point for Strauss, who had a clear grasp of the aesthetic dimension of Schmitt's "affirmation of the political."[27] As he claimed at the end of his review essay, this affirmation showed that Schmitt was caught in the very liberalism he opposed. For Strauss, an integral, nonpolemical knowledge of political things could be found only beyond modern oppositions. Ever since his Avicenna discovery in the Prussian State Library, he envisioned a return to Platonic political philosophy mediated by Maimonides and the Islamic medieval Enlightenment. As he wrote in 1931:

> We will not be able to understand Plato, and thereby also not Rambam, until we have acquired a horizon beyond the opposition progress/conservatism, Left/Right, Enlightenment/Romanticism, or however one wants to designate this opposition; not until we again understand the idea of the *eternal* good, the *eternal* order, free from all regard for progress or regress.[28]

These claims attest to Strauss's search for a nonpolemical concept of the political, which he came to explicate in *Philosophy and Law.* This concept appears to be strangely antiquated if approached from Benjamin's point of view, but Strauss showed—although not as openly as Benjamin did—that it belonged to the same "moment of danger." His strategies of addressing that danger, however, were altogether different.

Strauss staged an argument between modern rationalism and medieval rationalism as if it were a contest among equals: he juxtaposed two rationalisms and asked "which of the two opposed rationalisms is the true rationalism?" The surprising answer is that modern rationalism is a "sham rationalism" that leads to the self-destruction of reason, whereas Maimonidean rationalism is the "natural model," the "standard" of rationalism.[29] What Strauss found in Maimonides was an ideal foundation for philosophy in its opposition to revealed law. By recognizing and presupposing the authority of revelation at least in a formal sense, Maimonides and his Islamic predecessors made sure that philosophizing is subject to an order that is "not laid as a foundation by human thought, but . . . imposed beforehand upon human thought."[30] This is a model of human reason that refers to a horizon beyond itself—beyond the world of culture—and thus does not turn to irrationalism. Strauss thereby presented a solution to the problem that bothered all serious proponents and opponents of cultural philosophy in the twentieth century: the problem of how to see culture from outside without evading it altogether. The task was always to identify those phenomena that presumably preceded culture and hence provided an outside perspective on culture ("the political" in Carl Schmitt, "Being" in Heidegger, and "society" in the Frankfurt School). Strauss found the antidote to culture in Jewish law.[31] He traced a theologico-political order that was imposed on human reflection and thus provided a point of ethical and political orientation within the world of man.

The point of this "legal foundation of philosophy" is that it paradoxically secures the freedom of philosophizing: "philosophizing as authorized by the law enjoys full freedom, is wholly or nearly as free as if it stood under no law."[32] Thus philosophizing is commanded and authorized by the law. At the same time it recognizes by way of its commitment to revelation that it is ultimately insufficient, inasmuch as it cannot discover the truth from its own presuppositions.

Strauss demonstrated this freedom in the introductory chapter, *Of Philosophy and Law* where he gave a bold reinterpretation of the *modern* quarrel between reason and revelation. As he suggested, the eighteenth-century argument about reason and revelation needed to be radicalized and rephrased as an ongoing quarrel between atheism and orthodoxy. Strauss had a unique perspective on the topic: he argued from the standpoint of a sincere atheist who rejected Jewish belief and thereby remains true to it. At the same time he acknowledged that, from these presuppositions, a return to orthodoxy would also be possible—a return, however, that Strauss as a philosopher believed he could not accomplish himself. The lesson of this quarrel is that the legal foundation of philosophy, in its opposition to revealed law, allows for two different conclusions: a resolute atheistic position or a return to orthodox Judaism. Strauss could restore the notion of premodern law only from modern presuppositions; that is, through a Nietzschean act of the will. This notion of law has no particular authority. It merely provides a formal framework in which the fundamental alternative between the philosophical life and the religious life could be posed again.

Benjamin and Strauss on Theology, Politics, and Culture

The publication of *Philosophy and Law* provided Gershom Scholem with a new opportunity to alert Benjamin to Strauss's work. In March 1935 he wrote from Jerusalem:

> Any day now, Schocken will bring out a book by Leo Strauss (I devoted great energy to obtaining an appointment for Strauss in Jerusalem), marking the occasion of the Maimonides anniversary. The book begins with an unfeigned and copiously argued (if completely ludicrous) affirmation of atheism as the most important Jewish watchword. Such admirable boldness for a book that will be read by everyone as having been written by a candidate for Jerusalem! It even outdoes the first 40 pages of your postdoctoral dissertation! I admire this ethical stance and regret the—obviously conscious and deliberately provoked—suicide of such a capable mind. As is to be expected here, only three people at the very most will make use of the freedom to vote for the appointment of an atheist to a teaching position that serves to endorse the philosophy of religion. I hope I will be able to furnish you with a copy of the book once it comes out.[33]

It appears that these words aroused Benjamin's deeper interest in Strauss. In May 1935, he wrote back: "I am also very interested in Leo Strauss's book. What you tell me about him fits in with the pleasant image of him I have always made for myself."[34] By May 1936 he had formed the plan to write an article on Strauss: "Is Leo Strauss in Palestine? I would not be averse to addressing his works in the journal *Orient und Okzident*—for which I'm writing the Leskov piece. Perhaps you'll be seeing the author; if so, you can prevail upon him to send me the books."[35] As Scholem briefly replied, Strauss was not in Palestine but in England. He had moved in January 1934 from Paris (his first place of exile) to the United Kingdom, from where he eventually moved to New York in 1937–1938. Benjamin most likely never received any of Strauss's writings.

The counterfactual notion of a Benjamin essay on Strauss sparks the imagination of later-borns. Most scholars believe that Benjamin was to address medieval Jewish political philosophy proper. Friedrich Niewöhner contended that Benjamin had sought "to review Strauss's book under the aspect of a political philosophy of Judaism."[36] Benjamin biographer Jean-Michel Palmier proposed that Benjamin had spoken with Scholem, "starting" from Strauss's book, "about the status of Maimonides in Judaism."[37] These claims are highly disputable. Their only source is a rather dubious reference in Scholem's *Walter Benjamin—The Story of a Friendship*. Scholem wrote:

> Benjamin even considered writing a review of this book, which was a searching though problematical analysis of the central role of political philosophy for Maimonides' view of Judaism. In such a review he could have put at opposite ends the two poles of a 'political philosophy' of Judaism, both of which aroused his interest and were bound to strike related chords in his own thinking: the liquidation of that magical element in a rational esotericism and on the other side the nurturing of a strictly magical, mythical view.[38]

All speculation about the possible content of Benjamin's planned review article is based on this passage, which is carefully marked as speculation (*could have*, *were bound to*) and, reveals more about Scholem's own interests than about Benjamin and Strauss. Its authority in the scholarly literature attests to Scholem's crucial role in the post–World War II canonization of interwar German-Jewish thought. But Benjamin's way of reading was far too eccentric to allow for thematic outline of his unwritten Strauss essay. Like Strauss himself, he would start from some inconspicuous details of a text; and, only casually touching upon its most obvious aspects, transform them with the stroke of a pen. More likely, then, Benjamin would have highlighted entirely different themes in *Philosophy and Law*.

The principal argument between Strauss and Benjamin would be about the notion of law. An important question about their theoretical affinities concerns how *Philosophy and Law* relates to Benjamin's discussion of law and justice; and conversely how Strauss's concept of law would be transformed before Benjamin's melancholic gaze. There are a number of obvious differences, but in general both sought to confront the human order with the idea of the divine order. In this sense, the term "political" designates the relation of philosophy and revelation, or the manner of mediating between the divine to the profane order. Benjamin leaves the matter open: profane politics draws its energy from a theological source, but this source itself is not explicated and explicitly related to politics. This is the thrust of Benjamin's position on the relationship between law and justice: manmade law is to be confronted with the notion of divine justice, thus revealing itself to be unjust. In Strauss's terms, the order of human culture is to be brought back into a tension by rethinking the alternative between Athens and Jerusalem (reason and revelation *viz.* philosophy and law), thereby revealing its own estrangement from what really matters. Hence the non-argument between Strauss and Benjamin pertains to the way in which theology and politics relate to each other in modernity—a question both regarded as unresolved and highly topical.

But here we are in grave danger of entering into the morass of political theology. We need to take into account a third element alongside theology and politics that profoundly affects the discourse of political theology: Namely, the decisive difference between Strauss and Benjamin stems from their respective stances toward culture. This difference has its roots in their early writings and their respective position in the matrix of German-Jewish thought. Benjamin had allied himself with cultural Zionism early on,[39] whereas Strauss had altogether dismissed cultural Zionism in his early works.[40] Benjamin followed the model of the "intellectual Jew of letters [*Literaten-Jude*],"[41] whereas Strauss understood his philosophical work as an antidote to the intellectual "hairdressing industry"—a term that applied to professors, journalists, demagogues (i.e., politicians), business leaders, and poets alike.[42] This difference extended deep into the foundations of their philosophical works. Both Benjamin and Strauss changed their stances on "culture" to some extent. Most notably, Benjamin addressed the dialectic of culture and barbarism. As he quipped, "there is no document of culture which is not at the same time a document of barbarism."[43] Like Benjamin, Strauss later moved slightly away from his early occupation with the neo-Kantian systematics of "culture" and came to address a new form of culturalism; namely, the notion of cultures (or, *a* culture as opposed to culture as such).[44]

But especially in Strauss's later remarks, the fault lines between him and Benjamin widened. An important hint can be found in his last remark about Benjamin. In March 1970, after he had read Benjamin's letters (namely, the collection of Benjamin's correspondences edited by Scholem and Adorno),[45] he reported to Scholem that he understood Benjamin (and Scholem as well) much better now. His idiosyncratic conclusion is as follows: "What Benjamin seriously intended, it seems to me, has been done in a much more radical and clear fashion—and thus maybe reduced ad absurdum—by Heidegger."[46] Strauss did not elaborate on what he thought Benjamin had intended. To make sense of this enigmatic statement, we must start from what *Heidegger* did according to Strauss. Despite some famous statements he made, Strauss did not primarily see Heidegger in terms of the problematic entanglement of

German philosophy and politics. He had first encountered Heidegger in the early 1920s as a meticulous interpreter of Aristotle. Strauss had attended Heidegger's Aristotle lectures as a young post-doc and mentioned him ever since for his careful and radical interpretations of philosophical texts.[47]

The point where Benjamin was comparable to Heidegger is marked by his relationship to tradition; namely, to the project of uprooting the tradition—re-reading it after the break with it and hence dislocating the tradition in order to examine it even though it is no longer valid and authoritative. Tradition could no longer be understood in a traditional way; in this respect Strauss and Benjamin were in perfect agreement. The difference between them concerned with how to arrive at a post-traditional understanding of the tradition. Strauss's primary task was to overcome the prejudices of the modern interpretations of the tradition. It is in this respect that he appreciated Heidegger as a radical thinker who suspended the presuppositions of modern thought. As Strauss explained, "by uprooting and not simply rejecting the tradition of philosophy, he made it possible for the first time after many centuries . . . to see the roots of the tradition as they are." Against his own intention Heidegger had opened up the possibility of returning to classical Greek philosophy—"a return with open eyes and in full clarity about the infinite difficulties which it entails."[48]

Benjamin had his own view of philosophical radicalism, which did not quite match the Heidegger/Strauss view. As he quipped in a different context, "my stance would be to behave always radically and never logically when it came to the most important things."[49] Benjamin was neither Platonic nor Aristotelian. He did not seek to challenge for presuppositions of modernity by returning to the foundational texts of Western philosophy. He had a completely different view of the dialectics of modernity and premodernity. The "primal history of the nineteenth century" (namely, the *Arcades Project*, which occupied Benjamin throughout the 1930s) shows how archaic residues present themselves *in* modern forms. As he explained, the point was not that "forms of primal history are to be recovered among the inventory of the nineteenth century." The task was to present the nineteenth century "as an originary form of primal history—in a form, that is to say, in which the whole primal history groups itself anew in images appropriate to that century."[50] In other words, Benjamin played out the dialectics of modernity and premodernity entirely within the nineteenth century.

Benjamin always took his bearings from the forms of an already-constituted culture in order to show their cracks, break up their historical continuum, and re-translate them into figures of natural history. In Benjamin, the past became visible as a brief flash in a dialectical image: "what has been comes together in a flash with the now to form a constellation."[51] The task was always to show that a "document of culture" is "at the same time a document of barbarism."[52] From Benjamin's perspective, the return from the theoretical premises of modern thought to the classical understanding of the political is itself a *modern* endeavor which possibly leads only deeper into the dialectics of modernity and premodernity. We may seek to understand his idiosyncratic perception of Socrates from here, whose figure he once described as an "erection of knowledge."[53] Strauss took his bearings from Socrates to avoid the political battleground of culture. Seen from Strauss's persepctive, Benjamin's fixation on the "documents of culture"—modern literature, art, and everyday culture—ensures that he remains caught in a polemical understanding of the political: his preoccupation with the nineteenth century marks the limit of Benjamin's approach.

Strauss did not fully spell out this argument with regard to Benjamin, but he had a somewhat similar discussion of the nineteenth century with Karl Löwith in 1935. The occasion of the brief exchange was the publication of Strauss's *Philosophie und Gesetz* and Löwith's *Nietzsches Philosophie der ewigen Wiederkehr*, and the correspondence shows how each project reflected the influence of the other. Löwith ostensibly admired how Strauss proceeded by "the virtuous use of polemical alternatives" up to the point when the problem would turn out to be resolvable only by transforming the systematic question into historical analysis." Löwith cast doubt on the assumption that the modern presuppositions could be invalidated; but most of all he voiced his discontent with modern eccentricity: "I consider all radical turnovers to be principally wrong and un-philosophic."[54] In June 1935 he came out as an avid reader of Jacob Burckhardt. To avoid the radicalism and eccentricity of nineteenth-century philosophy—especially Nietzsche—he sought to return to Burckhardt's rediscovery of the Greek ideal of medium and proportion (*Mitte und Maß*). For Löwith, Burckhardt was the great teacher of the century because he re-understood and repeated the ancient virtue of moderation in an age of decline.[55]

Strauss had initially ignored these ideas, but on Löwith's insistence he wrote a few remarks that channeled his discontent. As he explained, the repetition of ancient moderation was possible only on the grounds of modern immoderacy. And unlike Burckhardt, the Greek philosophers were not historians. "No, dear Löwith: Burckhardt, that really won't do."[56] As it often did, Strauss's criticism remained brief and somewhat superficial, but it shows that he understood Löwith's inclination better than Löwith had understood it himself: he was an anti-Nietzschean Nietzschean who appealed to Burckhardt for help against his own Nietzschean preoccupation. He was the epitome of an anti-nineteenth-century philosopher entirely in the grip of the nineteenth century. Löwith was rattling the cage of "history" and "progress," but he did not find a way out.

The two cases of Benjamin and Löwith are not fully comparable. Unlike Löwith, Benjamin did not conceptualize the nineteenth century as a period of decline. He knew well that the notion of "decline" was merely the flipside of belief in the progress of mankind.[57] And he did not appeal to the nineteenth century for moderation. The two cases are comparable as far as we are willing to follow Strauss in his typical overgeneralizations, with their characteristic combination of blindness and insight. According to Strauss, both Löwith and Benjamin were caught in their polemical stance toward the nineteenth century. To some extent, then, the matter is a case of different historical tastes, but there is also a difference in the philosophical lineage involved. Strauss himself alluded to the difference when he quipped in his letter to Löwith: "I do not think as unfavorably as you do about nineteenth-century academic philosophy—after all, phenomenology emerged from it."[58]

If we retranslate the constellation of Strauss and Benjamin into the situation of German academic philosophy—from which the two idiosyncratic conceptions derived—Strauss was the phenomenologist and Benjamin the neo-Kantian. This attribution must be taken with a grain of salt. Benjamin referred to himself in a letter to Adorno as a "pupil of Rickert." Despite the irony, the remark indeed refers to a neo-Kantian streak in his thought. Benjamin had not only studied with Rickert, the head of the Southwestern school of neo-Kantianism; he also retained the orientation, even in its collapse, toward the systematics of cultural philosophy that Strauss exposed and critiqued in the first chapter of *Philosophie und Gesetz*.[59] As Scholem recalled Benjamin's stance: "For about ten years he upheld the concept of the philosophic system as the form proper to philosophy, after which he himself was groping. . . . But this ideal of the system, reflecting the traditional canons of philosophy, was corroded and eventually destroyed in his mind by a skepticism that stemmed in equal proportions from his study of neo-Kantian systems and from his own specific experience."[60]

According to Scholem, the systematic streak in Benjamin's philosophy had retreated but not altogether vanished in his later thought: "For all his renunciation of system, his thought, presented as that of a fragmentarian, yet retains a systematic tendency."[61] As should be noted, there are also references to phenomenology in Benjamin, and to neo-Kantianism in Strauss (despite his predominant lineage from phenomenology and its restoration of the natural view of reality prior to its constitution by science). The asymmetric attribution of the two major schools of German academic philosophy to the great German-Jewish figures of interwar philosophical thought is replete with historical fallacies. But it should not be dismissed entirely. It provides the necessary foundation for some otherwise inexplicable differences, which alltoo often can only be explained with regard to minor differences in taste and style. Strauss and Benjamin had a fascination for each another from afar, but the philosophical templates of their thought were too different to allow for any significant point of convergence between their projects. The two figures of interwar German-Jewish thought represent two different ways of conceptualizing the dialectics of modernity and premodernity; two models of viewing society and culture from outside; and two different foundations for the understanding of the political in its relation to culture.

Notes

1. Cf. Strauss's letter to Gerhard Krüger, June 26, 1930, *Gesammelte Schriften*, vol. 3, *Hobbes' politische Wissenschaft und zugehörige Schriften—Briefe*, ed. Heinrich and Wiebke Meier, 2nd ed. (Stuttgart/Weimar: Metzler, 2008), 382.

2. Strauss, "A Giving of Accounts," *Jewish Philosophy and the Crisis of Modernity*, ed. K. H. Green (Albany, NY: SUNY Press, 1997), 463; cf. *Philosophy and Law: Contributions to the Understanding of Maimonides and his Predecessors*, trans. Eve Adler (Albany, NY: SUNY Press, 1995). As Georges Tamer has shown, the "discovery" presented by Strauss is rather his construction out of several versions of the Avicenna quote. See Georges Tamer, *Islamische Philosophie und die Krise der Moderne. Das Verhältnis von Leo Strauss zu Alfarabi, Avicenna und Averroes* (Leiden: Brill, 2001), esp. 64–65.

3. On the chronology of Benjamin's travels, see Willem van Reijen and Herman van Doorn (eds.), *Aufenthalte und Passagen. Leben und Werk Walter Benjamins. Eine Chronik* (Frankfurt am Main: Suhrkamp, 2001), 111–114.

4. *The Correspondence of Walter Benjamin, 1910–1940*, ed. Gershom Scholem and Theodor W. Adorno (Chicago & London: University of Chicago Press, 1994), 488–489.

5. Theodor W. Adorno/Gershom Scholem, *Briefwechsel. "Der liebe Gott wohnt im Detail," 1939–1969*, ed. Asaf Angermann (Berlin: Suhrkamp 2015), 350–351.

6. Howard Eiland and Michael W. Jennings, *Walter Benjamin: A Critical Life* (Cambridge & London: Belknap, 2014), 333.

7. See especially the two drafts, "Paris, the Capital of the Nineteenth Century" (1935) and "Paris, Capital of the Nineteenth Century" (1939), *The Arcades Project* (Cambridge & London: Belknap, 1999), vol. 1, 3–26.

8. *The Correspondence of Walter Benjamin, 1910–1940*, ed. Gershom Scholem and Theodor W. Adorno (Chicago & London: University of Chicago Press, 1994), 347. Scholem explained: "After [Goldberg's] *Die Wirklichkeit der Hebräer* had appeared, I wrote a long, critical letter about the book; Benjamin and Leo Strauss disseminated copies of it in Berlin, and it won me no friends among Goldberg's adherents." Gershom Scholem, *Walter Benjamin: The Story of a Friendship* (Philadelphia: Jewish Publication Society of America, 1981), 98.

9. Ibid., 349.

10. Leo Strauss, "An Introduction to Heideggerian Existentialism," *The Rebirth of Classical Political Rationalism: An Introduction to the Thought of Leo Strauss*, ed. Thomas L. Pangle (Chicago & London: University of Chicago Press, 1989), 28.

11. Walter Benjamin, *Gesammelte Briefe*, ed. C. Gödde and H. Lonitz (Frankfurt am Main: Suhrkamp 1997), vol. III, 460.

12. Cf. Walter Benjamin, *Deutsche Menschen: Eine Folge von Briefen* (published in 1936 under the pseudonym Detlev Holz in Lucerne); Leo Strauss, "Religious Situation of the Present," *Reorientation: Leo Strauss in the 1930s*, ed. Martin D. Yaffe and Richard S. Ruderman (New York: Palgrave Macmillan, 2014), 225–235; "Cohen and Maimonides," *Leo Strauss on Maimonides: The Complete Writings*, ed. Kenneth Hart Green (Chicago & London: University of Chicago Press, 2013), 173–222.

13. *The Correspondence of Walter Benjamin, 1910–1940*, 382.

14. Ibid., 340.

15. *The Correspondence of Walter Benjamin and Gershom Scholem, 1932–1940*, ed. Gershom Scholem (Cambridge, MA: Harvard University Press, 1992), 24.

16. Ibid., 160.

17. Strauss, *Gesammelte Schriften*, vol. 3: *Hobbes' politische Wissenschaft und zugehörige Schriften—Briefe*, ed. Heinrich and Wiebke Meier (Stuttgart/Weimar: Metzler, 2001), 753.

18. The characterization as a "metaphysician" was already prevalent in Scholem's dedication to Benjamin in his *Major Trends in Jewish Mysticism* (1941), along with the "critic" and the "scholar."

19. Strauss, *Gesammelte Schriften*, vol. 3, 754.

20. Walter Benjamin, *Gesammelte Schriften*, vol. I.3, 887; *The Origin of German Tragic Drama* (London & New York: Verso, 1998), 65–66; "On the Concept of History," *Selected Writings*, ed. Howard Eiland and Michael W. Jennings (Cambridge, MA & London: Belknap Press, 2003), vol. 4: 1938–1940, 392.

21. Leo Strauss, "Notes on Carl Schmitt, *The Concept of the Political*," Heinrich Meier, *Carl Schmitt & Leo Strauss: The Hidden Dialogue* (Chicago & London: University of Chicago Press, 1995), 95.

22. Walter Benjamin, "The Work of Art in the Age of Its Technological Reproducibility," *Selected Writings*, vol. 3: 1935–1938, 121–122.

23. Walter Benjamin, "Theorien des deutschen Faschismus," *Gesammelte Schriften* (Frankfurt am Main: Suhrkamp, 1997), vol. III, 240.

24. Walter Benjamin, "The Work of Art in the Age of Its Technological Reproducibility," 122.

25. Cf. Walter Benjamin, "On the Concept of History," *Selected Writings*, vol. 4: 1938–1940, 391.

26. The point to dissolve this alliance of aesthetics and politics would be Hannah Arendt's derivation of political judgment from Kant's *Critique of Judgment.*

27. Strauss, "Notes on Carl Schmitt," 113, 117.

28. Strauss, "Cohen and Maimonides," 222.

29. Strauss, *Philosophy and Law*, 22 (translation altered).

30. Ibid., 59.

31. It is beyond the scope of this chapter to show how the notion of law is a composite of Jewish *halakha* and Greek *nomos*.

32. Strauss, *Philosophy and Law*, 60, cf. 88, 92.

33. *The Correspondence of Walter Benjamin and Gershom Scholem, 1932–1940*, 156–157.

34. Ibid., 160.

35. Ibid., 179.

36. Friedrich Niewöhner, "Platons Höhle wurde unterkellert. Leo Strauss wollte raus," *Frankfurter Allgemeine Zeitung*, November 4, 1997.

37. Jean-Michel Palmier, *Walter Benjamin. Lumpensammler, Engel und bucklicht Männlein. Ästhetik und Politik bei Walter Benjamin* (Frankfurt am Main: Suhrkamp, 2009), 215n67. Palmier also counts Strauss among Benjamin's "friends" (ibid., 626).

38. Gershom Scholem, *Walter Benjamin—The Story of a Friendship*, 201.

39. See his letter to Ludwig Strauss, October 10, 1912, *Gesammelte Briefe*, vol. I, ed. C. Gödde and H. Lonitz (Frankfurt am Main: Suhrkamp, 1995), 72.

40. Strauss, *The Early Writings*, ed. Michael Zank (Albany, NY: SUNY Press, 2002), passim.

41. Benjamin to Ludwig Strauss, January 7, 1913, *Gesammelte Briefe*, vol. I, 83.

42. Strauss to Gerhard Krüger, *Gesammelte Schriften*, vol. 3, 404.

43. Walter Benjamin, *The Arcades Project*, vol. 2, 462.

44. The most pertinent reference is to be found in his *Liberalism Ancient and Modern* (Chicago & London: University of Chicago Press, 1995), 5; cf. also "Jerusalem and Athens," *Jewish Philosophy and the Crisis of Modernity: Essays and Lectures in Modern Jewish Thought*, ed. Kenneth Hart Green (Albany, NY: SUNY Press, 1997), 377–379.

45. Walter Benjamin, *Briefe*, 2 vols. (Frankfurt am Main: Suhrkamp, 1966).

46. Strauss to Scholem, 8 March 1970, *Gesammelte Schriften*, vol. 3, 757. Strauss did not know that Benjamin stood in a complicated relationship to Heidegger. Upon reading *Being and Time*, Benjamin had written to Scholem in April 1930: "We were planning to annihilate Heidegger here in the summer in the context of a very close-knit critical circle of readers led by Brecht and me." *The Correspondence of Walter Benjamin*, 1910–1940, 365. Benjamin's negative view dates back to Heidegger's early book on Duns Scotus; cf. ibid., 82, 168, 172.

47. Leo Strauss, "The Living Issues of German Postwar Philosophy," Heinrich Meier, *Leo Strauss and the Theologico-Political Problem* (New York: Cambridge University Press, 2006), 134–135; cf. "A Giving of Accounts," *Jewish Philosophy and the Crisis of Modernity*, ed. Kenneth Hart Green (Albany, NY: SUNY Press, 1997), 461; see however "An Introduction to Heideggerian Existentialism," *The Rebirth of Classical Political Rationalism* (Chicago: University of Chicago Press, 1989), 29.

48. Leo Strauss, "An Unspoken Prologue," *Jewish Philosophy and the Crisis of Modernity*, 450.

49. Benjamin to Scholem, May 29, 1926, *The Correspondence of Walter Benjamin, 1910–1940*, 300.

50. Walter Benjamin, *The Arcades Project*, vol. 2, 463.

51. Ibid., 462.

52. Walter Benjamin, *Selected Writings*, vol. 4, 392.

53. Walter Benjamin, "Sokrates," *Gesammelte Schriften*, vol. II.1, 131.

54. Leo Strauss, *Gesammelte Schriften*, vol. 3, 646.

55. Ibid., 654.

56. Ibid., 657.

57. Cf. Walter Benjamin, *The Arcades Project*, vol. 2, 460: "Overcoming the concept of 'progress' and overcoming the concept of 'period of decline' are two sides of one and the same thing." See ibid., 458: "The pathos of this work: there are no periods of decline. Attempt to see the nineteenth century just as positively as I tried to see the seventeenth, in the work on *Trauerspiel*. No belief in periods of decline."

58. Leo Strauss, *Gesammelte Schriften*, vol. 3, 656.

59. Leo Strauss, *Philosophy and Law*, 41–42. For a brief discussion of Strauss's argument, see my article "Leo Strauss and Julius Guttmann: Some Remarks on the Understanding of *Philosophy and Law*," *Idealistic Studies* 44 (2015): 2–3, 297–312.

60. Gershom Scholem, "Walter Benjamin," *On Jews and Judaism in Crisis*, ed. Werner J. Dannhauser (Philadelphia: Paul Dry Books, 2012), 180.

61. Ibid., 182.

About the Contributors

Ingrid L. Anderson is associate director of the Elie Wiesel Center for Jewish Studies at Boston University and a full-time instructor in the College of Arts and Sciences Writing Program. Her current research focuses on the influence of French existentialism on modern and contemporary Jewish thought, and modern Anglo-Jewish thought and experience.

Jeffrey A. Bernstein is professor of philosophy at the College of the Holy Cross. He works in the areas of Spinoza, German Philosophy, and Jewish Thought. His book *Leo Strauss on the Borders of Judaism, Philosophy, and History* was published with SUNY Press in 2015.

Rodrigo Chacón is assistant professor of international studies at ITAM in Mexico City. His research on Leo Strauss has been published in *The Review of Politics*, *European Journal of Political Theory*, *Idealistic Studies*, and *Interpretation*. He is currently writing a book titled *Recovering Political Philosophy: Leo Strauss and Martin Heidegger in Weimar, 1922–1933*.

Alexander S. Duff, assistant professor of political science at University of North Texas, holds a B. Hum. from Carleton University and a PhD from the University of Notre Dame. He is the author of *Heidegger and Politics: The Ontology of Radical Discontent*.

Menachem Feuer has taught in the Center for Jewish Studies at York University in Toronto. He has published over twenty-five essays and book reviews on philosophy, literature, and Jewish studies in several book collections and peer-reviewed journals, including *Modern Fiction Studies*, *Shofar*, *MELUS*, *German Studies Review*, *International Studies in Philosophy*, *Comparative Literature and Culture*, *Ctheory*, *The Journal of French and*

Francophone Philosophy, and *Cinemaction*. Feuer's current scholarly focus is on Jewish philosophy and comedy.

Peter Gostmann is senior lecturer in the Department of Social Sciences, Goethe University, Frankfurt. He has published widely in the areas of intellectual history, philosophy of the social sciences, and sociology of culture. His books include *Beyond the Pale: Albert Salomon und das intellektuelle Feld im 20. Jahrhundert* (2014); *Emil Lederer: Schriften zur Wissenschaftslehre und Kultursoziologie* (2014, co-edited with A. Ivanova); *Einführung in die soziologische Konstellationsanalyse* (2016); and *Humanismus und Soziologie* (2018, co-edited with P. U. Merz-Benz).

Danilo Manca is a post-doc Fellow at the University of Pisa. His main interests are classical German philosophy, phenomenology, philosophy of literature, and the theory of modernity. He wrote a book in Italian on the concept of experience in Hegel and Husserl and another book on Paul Valéry. He is currently working on a study examining the reopening of the quarrel between the ancients and the moderns focusing on the perspectives of Jacob Klein, Leo Strauss, and Hans Blumenberg.

Waller R. Newell is professor of political science and philosophy and professor of the College of the Humanities at Carleton University. His books include *Ruling Passion: The Erotics of Statecraft in Platonic Political Philosophy*; *Tyranny: A New Interpretation*; and *Tyrants: A History of Power, Injustice and Terror*. He is currently working on a new book, *The Recollection of Freedom: The Dangerous Search for Political Wholeness from Rousseau to Heidegger*.

Jessica L. Radin is assistant professor of comparative liberal studies at Habib University in Karachi, Pakistan. She is currently working on an English-language critical edition of Maimonides's *Introduction to the Commentary on the Mishna*.

Isabel Rollandi is a doctoral student at the University of Buenos Aires. Her work focuses on the writings of Claude Lefort, Hannah Arendt, and Leo Strauss.

Jade Larissa Schiff is assistant professor of politics at Oberlin College. She works mainly at the intersections of political theory, phenomenology, and literary criticism. She is the author of *Burdens of Political Responsibility: Narrative and the Cultivation of Responsiveness*, as well as several articles on Leo Strauss.

Matthew J. Sharpe teaches philosophy at Deakin University, Australia. He is the author of *Camus, Philosophe: To Return to Our Beginnings*, as well as articles and chapters on Leo Strauss and Jacques Lacan.

Miguel Vatter is professor of politics at Flinders University, Australia. His main areas of research are republicanism, biopolitics, and political theology. He is author of *The Republic of the Living: Biopolitics and the Critique of Civil Society* (2014) and *Machiavelli's* The Prince: *A Reader's Guide* (2013). His most recent books are: *Divine Democracy: Political Theology after Carl Schmitt* (2020) and *Living Law: Jewish Political Theology from Hermann Cohen to Hannah Arendt* (2021).

Philipp von Wussow obtained his PhD in philosophy from Düsseldorf University in 2006. He was a Research Fellow at the Hebrew University of Jerusalem, at the Simon Dubnow Institute in Leipzig, and the Martin Buber Chair for Jewish Thought and Philosophy at Goethe University in Frankfurt am Main. After a Visiting Research Fellowship at the Herbert D. Katz Center in Philadelphia, he obtained his *Habilitation* at Goethe University in 2017. He specializes in twentieth-century Jewish philosophy and political thought. His book *Leo Strauss and the Politics of Culture* was published by SUNY Press in 2020.

Index

Adorno, Theodor, 255, 325, 334, 337, 339
Agamben, Giorgio, 69, 137, 138, 155–157
Alexander of Aphrodesias, 199
Aquinas, Thomas, 106, 180, 213, 221, 226–228, 253
Arendt, Hannah, 253, 313, 322, 340, 344–345
Aristophanes, 1, 6, 44, 106, 168, 274, 279, 296–298, 300–301, 303–306, 313, 318, 320–321
Aristotle, 34, 37, 52, 59, 61, 67, 100, 106, 123, 130–131, 133, 152, 156, 166, 180, 190–191, 193, 195–197, 199, 204, 226, 299, 306, 317, 320, 335
Averroes, 1, 34, 67, 325, 338
Avicenna, 34, 325, 330, 338

Bacon, Francis, 167, 191–192, 195, 205, 213, 226
Berlin, Isaiah, 11, 129
Benjamin, Walter, 6, 70, 305, 319, 323–342
Blumenberg, Hans, 2, 4, 187–208
Buber, Martin, 52
Burckhardt, Jacob, 336–337
Burke, Edmund, 177, 221, 227
Burroughs, William S., 175

Calvin, John, 171, 173, 175, 178–180, 183, 185
Camus, Albert, 5, 281–292
Cassirer, Ernst, 52, 197, 326, 328
Cicero, 46, 190, 205
Cohen, Hermann, 52, 55, 70–73, 253, 306, 309, 312, 328, 339, 340

Darwin, Charles, 39, 179
de Man, Paul, 320–321
Derrida, Jacques, 2–3, 11–28, 137, 156
Descartes, René, 4, 191–192, 195, 198, 202–203, 205, 211, 308

Ebbinghaus, Julius, 182, 188–189, 192, 195–196, 199, 204
Emerson, Ralph Waldo, 179
Engels, Friedrich, 253, 285
Epicurus, 222, 229

Farabi, 1, 15–16, 31, 34, 36–37, 48, 52, 67, 90, 93, 102, 104, 106, 117, 130, 132, 256, 325, 338
Feuerbach, Ludwig, 247
Foucault, Michel, 2, 4, 27, 135–159, 252
Freud, Sigmund, 3, 17, 26, 30–35, 39–47, 49–50, 248, 257

Gadamer, Hans-Georg, 24, 197, 272, 279
Galileo Galilei, 193, 213–214
Goldberg, Oskar, 326, 339
Grant, George P., 4, 161–186

Halevi, Judah, 31, 34, 212
Habermas, Jürgen, 5, 237–258
Hegel, George Wilhelm Friedrich, 33, 154, 161, 163–169, 177, 179, 182, 185–186, 188, 208, 220, 238–240, 244–246, 254–256, 283, 302, 309, 311
Heidegger, Martin, 4–5, 24–25, 27, 32, 46, 53, 161–162, 164, 166–167, 172–175, 177–180, 182, 184, 196, 204, 206, 207, 247–248, 252–253, 256–257, 259–280, 306, 311, 326, 331, 334–335, 339, 341
Heine, Heinrich, 313, 318
Hesiod, 1, 34
Hobbes, Thomas, 2, 5, 30, 34, 39, 44, 49, 105–106, 163, 167–169, 172, 175, 204, 209–223, 225–232, 241, 247–248, 250, 253, 256, 308, 314, 338–339
Homer, 1, 273
Hooker, Richard, 180
Horkheimer, Max, 255, 325
Hume, David, 247
Husserl, Edmund, 3, 53–55, 57, 59, 63, 70–72, 193–194, 201, 205–206, 243, 255

Jaspers, Karl, 262, 277
Josephus, Flavius, 219, 232
Jünger, Ernst, 329

Kant, Immanuel, 42, 50, 52, 66, 70, 162, 165–166, 175–176, 180–181, 237–240, 242, 246, 250–254, 328, 334, 337–338, 340
Kepler, Johannes, 40
Kierkegaard, Søren, 52, 259
Klein, Jacob, 1, 71, 202, 207, 344
Kojève, Alexandre, 29, 33, 44, 46–47, 147, 149, 151, 159, 163–170, 182, 186, 217, 245
Krüger, Gerhard, 70, 188, 195, 204, 206, 210, 230–231, 253, 257, 338, 341

Lacan, Jacques, 2, 3, 29–50, 345
Lefort, Claude, 2, 3, 75–107
Leskov, Nicolai, 332
Lessing, Gotthold Ephraim, 34, 37, 52, 310
Lévi-Strauss, Claude, 30
Livy, 77, 78
Locke, John, 175, 177–179, 216–217, 221, 229
Löwith, Karl, 201, 203–204, 208–210, 230, 237, 244, 253, 255, 336–337
Luther, Martin, 171–173, 178–180, 186

Machiavelli, Niccolò, 1, 3, 30, 37–39, 41, 45, 47–49, 75–107, 156, 158, 166–171, 178–180, 222, 227, 229, 247, 251–258
Maimonides, Moses, 1, 6, 16, 19–21, 27, 31, 34, 36–37, 46, 49, 52, 58, 62, 67–68, 70, 117, 130, 132, 169, 199, 207, 212, 254, 256–257, 296, 306–307, 314, 317–318, 321–322, 325, 330, 332–333, 338–340
Marcuse, Herbert, 172, 175
Marinetti, Filippo Tommaso Emilio, 329
Marx, Karl, 17–18, 27, 97, 124, 177–179, 220, 237–238, 240, 244, 246–248, 253, 285
Mendelssohn, Moses, 60, 308

Merleau-Ponty, Maurice, 97, 101
Montaigne, Michel de, 39

Nancy, Jean-Luc, 69
Natorp, Paul, 71, 328
Nietzsche, Friedrich, 6, 24, 38, 42, 48–50, 70–71, 112, 115, 118, 124, 131, 162, 174–175, 177–179, 181, 193–194, 205–206, 217, 227, 237, 248, 250, 253, 255, 261, 268, 278, 283, 288–289, 296–300, 306, 309

Plato, 1–2, 4, 6, 13–16, 18–19, 21–22, 24–28, 32–38, 43–48, 50–52, 59–62, 66–72, 83, 102, 106, 130–132, 135–157, 159, 161, 163, 165–166, 169, 174, 180, 183–185, 187, 189–193, 195–200, 202–204, 207–208, 213, 216, 220, 226–229, 237, 239, 241, 246, 252–254, 272–273, 277, 297–300, 302, 305–306, 318–319, 321, 325, 330, 335, 340
Poe, Edgar Allan, 29–30
Polin, Raymond, 211–212, 217–221, 227

Rawls, John, 140, 157, 162, 175–177, 182, 185–186
Rickert, Heinrich, 337
Riezler, Kurt, 272
Rosenzweig, Franz, 309, 311–312
Rousseau, Jean-Jacques, 155, 174, 177, 180, 221, 225, 252, 321

Schmitt, Carl, 22, 47, 107, 138, 155–157, 201, 203, 208, 245, 253, 323–324, 327–328, 330–331, 340
Scholem, Gershom, 70, 319, 323–327, 331–334, 337–342
Schopenhauer, Arthur, 206, 217, 227
Smith, Adam, 223
Socrates, 5–6, 25, 33, 36, 43–44, 52, 81, 106, 139–142, 146, 149–150, 154, 158, 169, 187–189, 220, 222, 227, 250, 256, 259–261, 272–277, 279–280, 296–303, 305, 318–321, 336
Soloveitchik, Joseph, 3, 51–72
Spinoza, Baruch, 1, 6, 25, 32, 34, 37–38, 45–46, 48, 50, 163, 169, 212, 217, 225, 229, 241, 247–248, 253, 257–258, 296, 306, 309–314, 318–320

Taylor, Charles, 4, 111–133
Tempier, Étienne, 180
Thucydides, 34, 52, 177
Tönnies, Ferdinand, 2, 4–5, 7, 209–234

Voltaire, 169

Walzer, Michael, 113, 119–120, 124, 129, 131, 133
Weber, Max, 174, 221, 227, 245, 256

Xenophon, 1–2, 36–37, 48, 52, 102, 106, 137, 147, 158–159, 250, 272–274, 276

www.ingramcontent.com/pod-product-compliance
Lightning Source LLC
LaVergne TN
LVHW040201080826
844660LV00001B/62

* 9 7 8 1 4 3 8 4 8 3 9 5 5 *